Maqāṣid al-Sharīʿah as Philosophy of Islamic Law A Systems Approach

MAQASID AL-SHARIAH AS PHILOSOPHY OF ISLAMIC LAW

•

A SYSTEMS APPROACH

JASSER AUDA

THE INTERNATIONAL INSTITUTE OF ISLAMIC THOUGHT
LONDON • WASHINGTON

THE INTERNATIONAL INSTITUTE OF ISLAMIC THOUGHT
P.O. BOX 669, HERNDON, VA 20172, USA
WWW.IIIT.ORG

LONDON OFFICE
P.O. BOX 126, RICHMOND, SURREY TW9 2UD, UK
WWW.IIITUK.COM

ISBN 978–1–56564–424–3 paperback
ISBN 978–1–56564–425–0 hardback

Typesetting by Shiraz Khan
Cover Design and Chart illustrations by Sideek Ali
Printed in the United Kingdom by the MPG Books Group

CONTENTS

List of Charts xi
Acknowledgements xvii
Foreword xix

INTRODUCTION xxi

In the Name of the 'Islamic Law'? xxi
Where is the 'Islamic Law'? xxii
Is There a Problem with the 'Islamic Law'? xxiii
Scope of Disciplines xxv
Abstract xxvii

1 MAQĀṢID AL-SHARĪʿAH A CONTEMPORARY PERSPECTIVE 1

Overview
1.1. *Maqāṣid al-Sharīʿah*: Early History of the Idea 1
What is *Maqāṣid*? 2
Dimensions of *Maqāṣid* 3
Al-Maqāṣid in the Companions' Ijtihad 9
Early Theories of *Maqāṣid* 13
1.2. *Al-Maqāsid* as a Developed Theory: 5–8 Centuries 16
The Emergence of a Philosophy for Islamic Law 16
Abū al-Maʿālī al-Juwaynī 17
Abū Ḥāmid al-Ghazālī 18
Al-ʿIzz ibn ʿAbd al-Salām 18
Shihāb al-Dīn al-Qarāfī 19
Shams al-Dīn ibn al-Qayyim 20
Abū Isḥāq al-Shāṭibī 20

1.3. Contemporary Conceptions of *Maqāṣid* 21
From 'Protection' and 'Preservation' to 'Development' & 'Rights' 21
'Human Development' as a *Maqāṣid* in its Own Right 24

2 SYSTEMS AS PHILOSOPHY & METHODOLOGY FOR ANALYSIS 26

Overview
2.1. Systems and Systems Philosophy 27
Teleology, Causality, and Irrationality 27
Towards an 'Islamic' Systems Philosophy 28
Are Systems 'Real' or Mental Creations? 30
2.2. A Systems Approach to Analysis 31
Traditions of 'Decompositional' Analysis 31
Systems Analysis 33
Theories of System Features 34
Theories of System Hierarchies 42
Proposed System Features 45
Cognitive Nature of the System of Islamic Law 45
Wholeness of the System of Islamic Law 46
Openness of the System of Islamic Law 47
Interrelated Hierarchy of the System of Islamic Law 48
Multi-Dimensionality of the System of Islamic Law 49
Purposefulness of the System of Islamic Law 51

3 ISLAMIC LAW, IMAMS, & SCHOOLS: A HISTORICAL SURVEY 56

Overview
3.1. What is 'Islamic Law'? 56
Fiqh and Shariʿah 56
Qānūn and *ʿUrf* 57
The Importance of Differentiating between Fiqh and Shariʿah 99
3.2. Schools of Islamic Law: A Brief History 60
Overview
Post-Prophetic Era 60

The Imams' Era 65
A Formal Critique of *Madhāhib* Categorisation 69
Chains of Studentship and Narration 71
The 'Era of Declination' 75

4 CLASSICAL THEORIES OF ISLAMIC LAW 76

Overview
4.1. Fundamental Sources/Scripts 76
Qur'an 77
Sunnah 79
4.2. Script-Based Linguistic Evidences 88
Overview
Clarity 89
Implication 93
The Ḥanafī Classification of Implications 94
The Shāfiʿī Classification of Implications 95
Contrary Implication 98
Scope 100
Generality 101
Qualification 102
Linguistic Evidence: The Impact of Greek Philosophy 105
4.3. Script-Based Rational Evidences 107
Overview
Consensus 109
Analogy 112
Interest 120
Juridical Preference 122
Blocking the Means 125
Previous Jurisprudence 127
A Companion's Opinion 128
Tradition of People of Madinah 129
Custom 130
Presumption of Continuity 131
Prioritisation of Evidences 132
4.4. Rulings 135

Overview
Levels of Approval 136
Obligations and Prohibitions 136
Optional Levels 137
Declaratory Rulings 139
Legal Capacity 140

5 CONTEMPORARY THEORIES IN ISLAMIC LAW 143

Overview
5.1. Contemporary Classifications and Labels 144
Background 144
Islamic 'Ideologies' 145
RAND's Classification 147
'Script-Based' Classifications 150
5.2. A Proposed Classification 153
Levels of Authority 153
Current 'Sources' in Islamic Law 156
Current 'Tendencies' in Islamic Law 160
5.3. Traditionalism 162
Scholastic Traditionalism 162
Scholastic Neo-Traditionalism 164
Neo-Literalism 166
Ideology-Oriented Theories 168
5.4. Islamic Modernism 168
Reformist Re-interpretation 171
Apologetic Re-interpretation 174
Maṣlaḥah-Based Theories 176
Uṣūl Revisionism 177
'Science'-Oriented Re-interpretation 179
5.5. Postmodernist Approaches 180
Post-Structuralism 182
Historicity of Means and/or Ends 184
Neo-Rationalism 188
Critical Legal Studies 189
Post-Colonialism 190

6 A SYSTEMS APPROACH TO ISLAMIC JURIDICAL THEORIES 192

Overview

6.1. Towards Validating All 'Cognitions' 193

'Revealed' Ijtihad 193

Separating the Revealed from its 'Cognition' 194

6.2. Towards 'Holism' 197

The 'Uncertainty' of Individual Evidence 197

Limitation of 'Causation' in Traditionalist and Modernist Theories 198

Towards a 'Holistic' *ʿIlm al-Kalām* 200

6.3. Towards Openness and Self-Renewal 201

Change of Rulings with 'Cognitive Culture' 201

Self-Renewal via Philosophical Openness 206

6.4. Towards Multi-Dimensionality 211

Spectrum of Certainty 211

Resolving 'Opposition' through Multi-Dimensionality 218

Multi-dimensionality and Postmodernism 226

6.5. Towards 'Purposefulness' 227

The 'Implication of the Purpose' 228

Purposeful Interpretations of Primary Sources 232

Prophetic Purposes and Intents 233

Analogy via Purposes 236

Interests Coherent with Purposes 238

Juridical Preference Based on Purposes 239

'Opening the Means' to Achieve Good Ends and *Maqāṣid* 241

Customs and the Purpose of 'Universality' 241

Presumption of Continuity 243

'Purposefulness' as Common Grounds for Schools of Law 243

'Purposefulness' as the Fundamental Criteria for Ijtihad 244

7 CONCLUSIONS 246

Classic Conceptions and Classifications of *Maqāṣid* 246

Contemporary Conceptions of *Maqāṣid* and Their Significance 248

Multi-Disciplinarity 249

Systems Analysis 249

Classifying Theological Schools Regarding 'Causation' 250
What is 'Islamic law'? 250
The Evolution of Traditional Schools of Islamic Law 251
Fundamental Sources/Scripts 251
Linguistic Evidences 252
Rational Evidences 252
Contemporary Theories in Islamic Law 253
A Proposed Classification for Theories of Islamic Law 253
A Systems Approach to Theories of Islamic Law 255

Notes 259
Bibliography 305
Glossary of Islamic Terms 329
General Index 332
Notes on Sources of Information, Transliteration and Translation 348

List of Charts

page

3 **Chart 1.1.** Hierarchy of the purposes of the Islamic law (dimension of levels of necessity).

7 **Chart 1.2.** Based on the 'cognitive nature' of the Islamic law, all of the above structures of the law's purposes are valid.

15 **Chart 1.3.** The first page of Egyptian Dār al-Kutub's manuscript of al-Qaffāl al-Kabīr's *Maḥāsin al-Sharā'iʿ* (The Beauties of the Laws).

44 **Chart 2.1.** (a) Laszlo's parallel hierarchies. (b) Salk's hierarchy of the 'categories of nature.'

50 **Chart 2.2.** A gray-scale picture distorts the variety of detail of a colored picture. Its two-color 'distortion,' however, filters out a great deal of information. In this example, viewing the two-color picture alone creates an interesting puzzle.

58 **Chart 3.1.** A diagram illustrating the (traditional) relations between the concepts of shariʿah, fiqh, *ʿurf*, and *qānūn*. Notice the inclusion of fiqh with the Qur'an and the prophetic tradition in 'the revealed.'

63 **Chart 3.2.** This map illustrates the seventh-century paths that battles, and immigrants, took. Scanned from: R. Roolvink et al., *Historical Atlas of the Muslim Peoples* (Amsterdam, 1957). Available in soft form on: http://www.princeton.edu/thumcomp/dimensions.html (visited: April 13, 2006).

69 **Chart 3.3.** A summary of the 'sources of legislation' that are used as 'classifying features' between the schools of Islamic law. This classification approach has a number of limitations, including single-dimensionality and overgeneralisations.

72 **Chart 3.4.** Chains of students who eventually formed the schools of Islamic law, starting with (a selected group of) the companions and ending with (a selected group of) the *uṣūlīs*.

77 **Chart 4.1.** A list of 'evidences' and a classification according to their endorsement (in principle) within the schools of Islamic law.

79 **Chart 4.2.** A classification of the Qur'anic narrations according to their 'level of authenticity.'

80 **Chart 4.3.** A classification of the possible relationships between the traditions of the Sunnah and the Qur'anic verses.

81 **Chart 4.4.** Types of Prophetic actions according to their implications on 'legislation.'

83 **Chart 4.5.** Types of Prophetic narrations in terms of their number of narrators.

85 **Chart 4.6.** Conditions for validating single-chains narrations in traditional Sciences of Hadith.

87 **Chart 4.7.** Positions of some schools of law regarding the *mursal* hadith.

88 **Chart 4.8.** Classification of terms/expressions in terms of clarity, implication, and scope.

89 **Chart 4.9.** Classification of 'clear' and 'unclear' terms.

90 **Chart 4.10.** Classification of clear terms according to the possibility of their specification, re-interpretation, and abrogation.

91 **Chart 4.11.** Classification of types of unclear expressions, based on the reason behind their non-clarity.

94 **Chart 4.12.** Implications of expressions according to the Ḥanafīs.

96 **Chart 4.13.** Implications of expressions according to the Shāfiʿīs.

98 **Chart 4.14.** Types of contrary implication.

100 **Chart 4.15.** Classification of expressions in terms of their scope.

101 **Chart 4.16.** Difference of opinion over the relationship between an *āḥād* narration and a 'general' verse.

102 **Chart 4.17.** Difference of opinion over qualified versus unqualified terms/expressions.

105 **Chart 4.18.** Classification of knowledge in Islamic philosophy.

106 **Chart 4.19.** Classification of terms in Islamic philosophy.

108 **Chart 4.20.** Some of the many differences of opinion over the definition of *ijmāʿ*.

110 **Chart 4.21.** A comparison of some of the views of the requirements of a *mujtahid* who could take part in consensus.
112 **Chart 4.22.** Difference of opinion over the legitimacy of *qiyās*.
113 **Chart 4.23.** (a) The four components/units of analogy and (b) how the components interact in the analogy process.
117 **Chart 4.24.** The four categories of appropriate attributes.
119 **Chart 4.25.** Formal procedure of *qiyās*.
120 **Chart 4.26.** Classification of interests based on their (literal) mention in the script.
121 **Chart 4.27.** Difference of opinion over *al-maṣlaḥah al-mursalah*.
123 **Chart 4.28.** Difference of opinion over *istiḥsān*.
123 **Chart 4.29.** Judging a certain situation based on a basis that is different from the principle upon which similar situations are judged.
124 **Chart 4.30.** Classification of the bases of *istiḥsān*.
126 **Chart 4.31.** Difference of opinion over *sadd al-dharā'iᶜ*.
126 **Chart 4.32.** Four 'categories' of probability, according to jurists who endorsed blocking the means, namely, certain, most probable, probable, and rare.
128 **Chart 4.33.** Difference of opinion over *sharᶜu man qablanā*.
129 **Chart 4.34.** Difference of opinion over *ra'ī al-ṣaḥābī*.
130 **Chart 4.35.** Difference of opinion over *ᶜamal ahl al-madīnah*.
131 **Chart 4.36.** Difference of opinion over *al-ᶜurf*.
133 **Chart 4.37.** An overview of the prioritisation of evidences in various schools of Islamic law.
136 **Chart 4.38.** Classification of rulings into accountability and declaratory rulings.
137 **Chart 4.39.** Difference of opinion over 'levels of approval' in the Islamic rulings.
138 **Chart 4.40.** Classifications of obligations.
139 **Chart 4.41.** The Ḥanafī classification of levels of obligation and prohibition based on the evidence's 'certainty.'
140 **Chart 4.42.** The jurists' classification of legal capacities in terms of human life stages (from Hasaballah's *Uṣūl al-Tashrīᶜ*).
146 **Chart 5.1.** A summary of the expressions used in typologies of 'Islamic ideologies.'

153 **Chart 5.2.** Traditionally, evidences/arguments are always divided between two categories, sound (*ḥujjah*) and unsound (*bāṭil*).

154 **Chart 5.3.** Supporting evidence (*isti'nās*) is an intermediate level of *ḥujjiyyah* that appears in a few rulings.

154 **Chart 5.4.** *Ta'wīl* is a level of *ḥujjiyyah* between *ḥujjah* and *isti'nās*.

155 **Chart 5.5.** *Fīhi shai'* is a minor criticism between *isti'nās* and *buṭlān*.

156 **Chart 5.6.** This book suggests five additional levels of 'authority' between 'proof' and 'void.'

156 **Chart 5.7.** A multi-valued spectrum of *ḥujjiyyah*, from 'proof' to 'void.'

160 **Chart 5.8.** A multi-valued spectrum of sources according to a dimension of 'human-experience' versus 'revelation.'

161 **Chart 5.9.** A two-dimensional illustration of where the proposed tendencies stand in terms of sources of the Islamic law versus 'levels of authority.'

163 **Chart 5.10.** Traditionalism tendency in terms of its contributing streams.

172 **Chart 5.11.** Modernism tendency in terms of its contributing streams.

183 **Chart 5.12.** Postmodernism tendency in terms of its contributing streams.

196 **Chart 6.1.** Fiqh and a section of the prophetic tradition are shifted from being expressions of the 'revealed' to being expressions of 'human cognition of the revealed.'

204 **Chart 6.2.** The jurist's 'worldview' is a prime factor in shaping fiqh.

212 **Chart 6.3.** Traditionally, juridical evidences are divided between 'certain', and 'uncertain' categories.

216 **Chart 6.4.** An evidence that is historically 'authentic' and linguistically 'implied' entails being an 'integral part of the religion.'

217 **Chart 6.5.** Certainty/Probability increases (non-linearly) with the number of available evidences.

223 **Chart 6.6.** Seemingly contradicting 'attributes' in one dimension could be positively contributing to a different dimension related to purposes.

230 **Chart 6.7.** Adding the implications of the purpose (*dilālah al-maqṣid*) to valid implications/meanings. Its priority should depend on the importance of the implied purpose.

238 **Chart 6.8.** Classification of interests based on their coherence with the scripts or their purposes.

240 **Chart 6.9.** Levels of ends and alternative levels of means, according to al-Qarāfī.

240 **Chart 6.10.** A spectrum of levels between good ends/required means and repugnant ends/prohibited means.

ACKNOWLEDGEMENTS

God has given me an abundance of blessings that are far beyond my comprehension! I hope that He accepts this modest addition to knowledge, with all of its shortcomings, as some form of worship, in gratitude for His many bounties. I would also like to pay a special tribute to a number of scholars and mentors, who have greatly contributed to my scholarly development. Appreciation is due to the late Shaykh Mohammad al-Ghazaly, late Shaykh Ismail Sadiq al-Adawi, and Shaykh Mahmoud Faraj, for what I have learned from them about the Islamic law and the Qur'an in my early years, to Professors Mohamed Kamel and Hazem Rafat for the ideas I developed based on my Ph.D. studies in Systems Analysis at the University of Waterloo, Canada, to Professors Ahmad al-Assaal and Salah Soltan for encouraging me to pursue research on *maqāṣid al-sharīʿah* during my Masters of Jurisprudence studies at the Islamic American University, Michigan, to Dr. Gary Bunt for the research I developed under his supervision during my Ph.D. studies in Religious and Islamic Studies, at the University of Wales, Lampeter, U.K., and last but not least, to H.E. Ahmad Zaki Yamani, the Founder and Chairman of Al-Maqasid Research Centre in the Philosophy of Islamic Law, London, U.K., for entrusting me with the position of the Founding Director, and for his great and continuous support. I would also like to mention a few scholars, who have contributed significantly, although in various ways, to the scholarly contents of this book. May God reward and bless the following scholars: Abdallah Bin Bayyah, Mohamed S. El-Awa, Yusuf al-Qaradawi, Taha al-Alwani, al-Habib ibn al-Khoujah, Faisal Mawlawi, Hasan Jabir, Mohammad K. Imam, Ibrahim Ghanim, Saif Abdul-Fattah, and Ahmad al-Raysuni. I am also grateful to the International Institute of Islamic Thought (IIIT) especially to Dr. Jamal Barzinji and Dr. Anas al-Shaikh-Ali, for their high level of professionalism and support, as well as Shiraz Khan, Maryam Mahmood, and Maida Malik, for their hard work and valuable comments, and to Sideek Ali for the chart illustrations. Thanks also go to Suhaib Elamin for the initial setup of the charts and references that appear in this book. Finally, I shall always remain deeply indebted to my family, especially my mother, Layla al-Tahery, my wife, Wanda, and Radwa, Omar, Ahmed, and Sarah!

JASSER AUDA

FOREWORD

بسم الله الرحمن الرحيم

Of knowledge, we have none, save what
You have taught us. (The Qur'an 2:32)

The International Institute of Islamic Thought (IIIT) has great pleasure in presenting this scholarly work on the topic of *maqāṣid al-Sharīʿah* (the higher objectives and intents of Islamic Law). The author, Dr. Jasser Auda, is a well-known multi-disciplinary scholar, who has developed a specialization in this field. This novel work of serious and careful scholarship, presents a new approach to the methodology and philosophy of Islamic law that is based on *maqāṣid al-Sharīʿah*. We hope that the important analysis and ideas contained in this study, will not only make an important contribution to the field of *maqāṣid al-Sharīʿah*, but also attract wider attention and generate greater interest among readers.

Since few works, if any, are available in the English language on this subject, *al-maqāṣid,* the IIIT decided to fill the vaccum by initiating the translation and publication of a series of books on *maqāṣid al-Sharīʿah* to introduce this important area of thought to English readers. In addition to this particular work the series so far includes: *Ibn Ashur Treatise on Maqāṣid al-Sharīʿah* by Muhammad al-Tahir ibn Ashur, *Imam al-Shāṭibī's Theory of the Higher Objectives and Intents of Islamic Law* by Ahmad al Raysuni, and *Towards Realization of the Higher Intents of Islamic Law: Maqāṣid al-Sharīʿah a Functional Approach* by Gamal Eldine Attia. Although the topic is a complex and an intellectually challenging one, it needs to be emphasized that these books are not only for specialists, scholars and intellectuals alone, but additionally provide very interesting and useful reading for the general reader.

In this pathbreaking study, Dr. Jasser Auda presents a systems approach to the philosophy and juridical theory (*uṣūl*) of Islamic law based on its purposes, principles, higher objectives, and ends (*maqāṣid al-sharī^cah*). For Islamic rulings to fulfil their purposes of justice, equality, human rights, development, and civility in today's context, the author places *maqāṣid*, as the group of divine intents and moral concepts, at the heart and basis of Islamic law. He introduces a novel method of analysis, classification, and critique that utilises relevant features from systems theory such as wholeness, multidimensionality, openness, cognitive nature, and especially 'purposefulness' of systems. More broadly, this systematic methodological approach has implications for the reconstruction of the law, human rights institutions, civil society, and governance anchored in Islamic principles and juridical thought.

The IIIT, established in 1981, has served as a major center to facilitate sincere and serious scholarly efforts based on Islamic vision, values and principles. Its programs of research, seminars and conferences during the last twenty four years have resulted in the publication of more than two hundred and fifty titles in English and Arabic, many of which have been translated into several other languages.

We would like to express our thanks and gratitude to the author, who throughout the various stages of the book's production, co-operated closely with the editorial group at the IIIT's London Office. We would also like to thank the editorial and production team at the London Office and those who were directly or indirectly involved in the completion of this book: Maida Malik, Dr. Wanda Krause, Shiraz Khan, and Sideek Ali. May God reward them and the author for all their efforts.

Ramadan 1428
September 2007

ANAS S. AL-SHAIKH-ALI
Academic Advisor, IIIT London Office, UK

INTRODUCTION

IN THE NAME OF 'ISLAMIC LAW'?

I am writing these lines after I drove this morning through London, UK, to my office. It was supposed to be a pleasent experience, given the great July weather and the (unusual!) clear skies today. However, unfortunately, this morning's drive to work was not a pleasant experience, because the city, and the whole country, is on the 'highest level of alert.' Security people told us yesterday that this means that another 'terrorist' attack is 'eminent'! So, like all Londoners, I was nervous about travelling through the city, and was constantly looking around for any 'suspicious behavior,' whatever that means.

Nevertheless, I was additionally annoyed with all that is happening in this city these days, because what I simply call 'crimes' (rather than 'acts of terrorism') are done 'in the name of the Islamic law,' so declared some of the people who were responsible for them. I was angrily exclaiming: 'Islamic law'? What 'Islamic law'? Does 'Islamic law' sanction indiscriminate killing of people in peaceful cities?! Where is 'wisdom and people's welfare,' which every Muslim knows is the basis of the 'Islamic law'?

I remembered Ibn al-Qayyim's (d. 748 AH/1347 CE) words about the 'Islamic law,' which I am quoting below and will be referring to more than once throughout this book. Note that in Arabic, Ibn al-Qayyim used the word 'shariᶜah,' which I shall explain in detail later.

> Shariᶜah is based on wisdom and achieving people's welfare in this life and the afterlife. Shariᶜah is all about justice, mercy, wisdom, and good. Thus, any ruling that replaces justice with injustice, mercy with its

> opposite, common good with mischief, or wisdom with nonsense, is a ruling that does not belong to the Shariʿah, even if it is claimed to be so according to some interpretation.[1]

This is what this book is about, despite its specialised language that I am aware a non-specialised reader would find difficult to digest.

WHERE IS THE 'ISLAMIC LAW'?

Islam is the religion of roughly one-quarter of the world's population.[2] Most Muslims live in the region that extends from North Africa to South East Asia, and Muslim minorities across Europe and the Americas are the second or third largest religious communities.[3] Islam comprises people from almost every ethnicity, including Arabs (currently 19%), Turks (4%), Indians/Pakistanis (24%), Africans (17%), and South-East Asians (15%). Muslims grew from a small group in Makkah at the beginning of the seventh century CE to an established 'Islamic State' that overpowered both the Roman and Persian empires by the end of the same century. Islam, then, became the religion of a variety of cultures and a civilization that spanned over the medieval centuries.

Today, however, the most recent United Nation Development Programme (UNDP) Annual Reports show a Human Development Index (HDI) on the lower side for most countries with majority of Muslims.[4] The HDI is calculated based on a number of factors, which include literacy, education, political and economic participation, women empowerment, in addition to standard of living. Some wealthy Arab states, which rank exceptionally high in terms of average income per capita, rank much lower in terms of justice, women empowerment, political participation, and equal opportunity. Related UN reports also point to various forms of human right violations and corruption in most countries with majority of Muslims, as well as dilemmas with co-existence and citizenship of Muslim minorities in their societies. In summary, Muslims everywhere are currently facing major development challenges, which are posing a large number of serious questions.

I understand the 'Islamic law' to be a drive for a just, productive, developed, humane, spiritual, clean, cohesive, friendly, and highly democratic society. However, throughout my travels in various countries, I see little evidence for these values, on the ground, in Muslim societies and communities everywhere. So, the big question that I have is: Where is the 'Islamic law'? How could it play a role in this crisis?

This book attempts to provide an answer to the second question, which, I believe, will eventually bring about an answer for the first question. In other words, when the 'Islamic law' proves to have the capacity of making a real change in average-Muslims' lives, they will embrace it and it will eventually make a difference.

IS THERE A PROBLEM WITH THE 'ISLAMIC LAW'?

So far, I have put the 'Islamic law' between quotes, because I have to define what I mean by 'Islamic law' before I could claim that it brings justice, mercy, development, and so on. This definition is in addition important in order to answer the question of whether there is something wrong with 'Islamic law,' and hence the critique that this book presents.

A detailed analysis of the terms fiqh, sharīʿah, fatwa, *madhāhib*, ijtihad, *qānūn*, and *ʿurf*, and the intricate relationships between these terms, will be explained in this book. However, for now, I would like to differentiate between three different meanings of the general term 'Islamic law,' in order to answer the above question at this point.

1. Shariʿah: The revelation that Muhammad (*ṢAAS*)[5] had received and made practicing it the message and mission of his life, i.e., the Qur'an and the Prophetic tradition.
2. Fiqh: The huge collection of juridical opinions that were given by various jurists from various schools of thought, in regards to the application of the shariʿah (above) to their various real life situations throughout the past fourteen centuries.
3. Fatwa: The application of shariʿah or fiqh (above) to Muslims' real life today.

Detailed analysis of these issues and related issues is the mission of this book. However, my answer to the above question (Is there a problem with the 'Islamic law'?), in plain English, is the following:

• If you mean by the 'Islamic law' the shariʿah, i.e., the revelation that was given to Muhammad, which he internalised, practiced in his own life, and went through a long educational process to educate his companions and the world about it – then the answer is: No. There is no problem with the 'Islamic law.' It is a way of life that is all about justice, mercy, wisdom, and good, as Ibn al-Qayyim had mentioned.

• If you mean by the 'Islamic law' the fiqh, i.e., the Islamic schools of law's wealth of heritage, then the answer is, also: No. There is nothing wrong, generally speaking, with juridical reasoning carried by scholars for their own environemnets and times. It is true that some individual scholars had made mistakes and/or had taken controversial positions on issues. However, this is the nature of juridical research. The role of scholars, at all times, is to correct each others and participate in the ongoing debates.

• However, if you mean by the 'Islamic law' fatwa, then the answer is: It depends on how the fatwa is issued! Some *fatāwā* are manifestations of Islam and its moral values, and some others are simply wrong and un-Islamic. If the fatwa is copied verbatim from some classic book in the Islamic law, then it is quite possibly flawed because it is quite probably addressing a different world with different circumstances. If the fatwa is based on some sort of twisted interpretation of a script, with an aim to serve the political interests of some powerful people, then it is wrong and un-Islamic. If the fatwa is allowing people to commit an act of injustice, discrimination, harm, or immorality, even if it were to be based on some sort of 'interpretation,' then it is also wrong and un-Islamic. If the fatwa is issued based on the Islamic authentic sources, on one hand, while keeping people's welfare and the principle values/purposes of the Islamic law (Arabic: *maqāṣid al-sharīʿah*) in mind, on the other hand, then it is a correct and valid fatwa.

You can see from what I mentioned above the scope of this book, and the issues that it will be dealing with. However, the issues related to the above concepts that this book is discussing are complex and require a detailed treatment. That is why I prefer at this point to provide below, a general scope of the disciplines involved in this book, and finally, an abstract summary of what this research is trying to achieve. Thence, I shall leave the reader with the material in the chapters themselves.

SCOPE OF DISCIPLINES

Classifying human knowledge into 'disciplines' reduces the complexity of concepts by grouping them under identifiable fields, rather than dealing with each concept individually.[6] These identifiable fields allow seekers of knowledge to develop expertise in specific disciplines. Non-expert enquirers are then able to identify a field of knowledge to which their enquiry belongs and refer to specialists in that field to answer their questions. However, 'disciplinisation' should not be an obstacle in the way of using relevant concepts from 'different' fields in research endeavors. Nor should it be a way of monopolising sources of reference in any discipline in order to restrain creativity and control new ideas. This book takes a multidisciplinary approach that integrates relevant knowledge from a variety of fields within the general 'disciplines' of Islamic law, philosophy, and systems. The following is a brief outline on how knowledge from these fields will be integrated. More details will be provided throughout the book.

Within the discipline of Islamic law, this book is concerned with the 'fundamentals of Islamic law' (*uṣūl al-fiqh*). However, topics related to Islamic law (fiqh) itself, the science of narration (*ᶜilm al-ḥadīth*), and the science of exegesis (*ᶜilm al-tafsīr*) are also discussed. For example, rulings from fiqh are mentioned to illustrate the practical impact of fundamental theories. Moreover, basic rules (*qawāᶜid*) from the sciences of hadith and *tafsīr* are discussed in the context of their relation with the fundamentals of law. The purposes (*maqāṣid*) of the Islamic law are proposed by some twentieth century reformers as a standalone discipline.[7] However, traditionally, *al-maqāṣid* were studied as a secondary topic within *uṣūl al-fiqh*, usually under the category of 'unrestricted interests' (*al-maṣāliḥ al-mursalah*) or the appropriate attribute for analogy (*munāsabah al-qiyās*).[8] This work, however, will endorse *maqāṣid* as 'fundamental methodology' for *uṣūl al-fiqh*, regardless of the debate over whether or not it should be considered a standalone discipline.[9]

Within the discipline of philosophy, the fields of logic, philosophy of law, and postmodern theory are directly related to this book. Logic is at the heart of reasoning about law, Islamic law included. Of specific significance to this book is philosophers/jurists within the fifth to eighth Islamic centuries who endorsed, developed, or criticised Greek logic, and how their own logic influenced their methodology of reasoning. Modern logic is also of special significance here, since its points of departure from traditional logic will be our drive for criticising the logic of *uṣūl al-fiqh* itself. Philosophy of law, in a modern sense, will be addressed in this book in terms of how philosophy of Islamic law could benefit from its concepts and structure, especially its recent systems-based developments. Postmodern theory is an 'anti-modernism' branch of philosophy that has inspired some powerful contemporary critiques of law in general and Islamic law in particular. This book will analyze these critiques and 'criticise' them in turn.

'Systems' is a new independent discipline that encompasses a number of sub-disciplines, amongst which systems theory and systematic analysis are specifically relevant to this work. Systems theory is another 'anti-modernism' philosophical approach which criticises modernism in a way that is different from postmodern theories. In this book, concepts from systems theory, such as wholeness, multidimensionality, openness, and purposefulness, will be utilised in developing our analysis methodology itself, which will, then, be utilised throughout. Related to systems is the new discipline of cognitive science. Concepts from cognitive science will be used to develop fundamental concepts of the theory of Islamic law, such as the concepts of classification/categorization and the 'cognitive nature' of the law. The concept of 'cognitive culture' will also be used to develop the concept of custom (*al-ʿurf*) in the theory of Islamic law.

Without incorporating relevant ideas from other disciplines, research in the fundamental theory of Islamic law will remain within the limits of traditional literature and its manuscripts, and Islamic law will continue to be largely 'outdated' in its theoretical basis and practical outcomes. The relevance and need for a multidisciplinary approach to the fundamentals of Islamic law is one of the arguments of this book.

ABSTRACT

This book presents a multi-disciplinary research that aims to develop the fundamental juridical theory of Islamic law via a systems approach. Current applications (or rather, mis-applications) of Islamic law are reductionist rather than holistic, literal rather than moral, one-dimensional rather than multidimensional, binary rather than multi-valued, deconstructionist rather than reconstructionist, and causal rather than teleological. There is lack of consideration and functionality of the overall purposes and underlying principles of the Islamic law as a whole. Moreover, exaggerated claims of 'rational certainty' (or else, 'irrationality') and 'consensus of the infallible' (or else, 'historicity of the scripts') add to lack of spirituality, intolerance, violent ideologies, suppressed freedoms, and authoritarian regimes. Dominant methodology generally resists learning from other philosophies that did not originate from the Islamic tradition, or else, totally adopts other philosophies that contradict with basic Islamic beliefs.

This research is divided into three themes, (1) methodology, (2) analysis, and (3) theoretical developments.

(1) Methodology in this endeavor is based on two theories: (a) theory of the purposes of Islamic law or *maqāṣid al-sharīʿah* (Chapter 1) and (b) systems theory (Chapter 2). Recent theories of *maqāṣid* (a) which introduce new notions related to reform and development, are surveyed. *Maqāṣid* is proposed as a philosophy, and fundamental methodology for assessing classic and current juridical theories of Islamic law. Systems theory (b) is utilised to define a new method for analysis that relies on the systems features of cognition, wholeness, openness, hierarchy, multi-dimensionality, and purposefulness. Purposefulness is the core feature of systems.

(2) This research will define 'Islamic law' (Chapter 3), carry out a critical analysis of various classic and contemporary theories and schools of Islamic law (Chapters 4 and 5, respectively), and introduce new classifications of classic methods and contemporary tendencies (Chapters 4 and 5, respectively). In order to develop the analysed theories of Islamic law, the above two approaches to methodology (a and b) will merge into one approach (in Chapter 6); Islamic law is defined as a

'system,' whose feature of purposefulness is realised through the realisation of *maqāṣid al-sharīʿah*.

(3) Therefore, a number of theoretical developments are proposed (Chapters 6 and 7), such as, legitimising the juridical implication (*dilālah*) of the purpose of scriptural evidence, resolving opposing evidences by considering their multiple dimensions, and contextualising hadith narrations by considering prophetic intents in various forms.

The theoretical outcome of this book is that the validity of any method of ijtihad is determined based on its degree of realisation of *maqāṣid al-sharīʿah*. The practical outcome is Islamic rulings which are conducive to the values of justice, moral behavior, magnanimity, co-existence, and human development, which are '*maqāṣid*' in their own right.

JASSER AUDA
London, UK
July 2007, Jumada II, 1428

I

Maqāṣid al-Sharīʿah A Contemporary Perspective

Overview

Why is giving charity (zakah) one of Islam's principle 'pillars'? What are the physical and the spiritual benefits of fasting the month of Ramadan? Why is drinking any amount of alcohol a major sin in Islam? What is the link between today's notions of human rights and Islamic law? How can the Islamic law contribute to 'development' and 'civility'?

'*Maqāṣid al-sharīʿah*' are principles that provide answers to the above questions and similar questions about the Islamic law. *Maqāṣid* include the wisdoms behind rulings, such as 'enhancing social welfare,' which is one of the wisdoms behind charity, and 'developing consciousness of God,' which is one of the wisdoms behind fasting. *Maqāṣid* are also good ends that the laws aim to achieve by blocking, or opening, certain means. Thus, the *maqāṣid* of 'preserving people's minds and souls' explain the total and strict Islamic ban on alcohol and intoxicants. *Maqāṣid* are also the group of divine intents and moral concepts upon which the Islamic law is based, such as, justice, human dignity, free will, magnanimity, facilitation, and social cooperation. Thus, they represent the link between the Islamic law and today's notions of human rights, development, and civility. This chapter explains what '*maqāṣid al-sharīʿah*' is and how it could play a fundamental role in the much-needed 'contemporarisation' of the Islamic law. It will introduce traditional and current definitions and classifications of *maqāṣid*, and elaborate on three historical stages that the idea of *al-maqāṣid* went through, namely, the Companions' era, the schools of law foundational era, and the era between the fifth and eighth Islamic centuries. Finally, recent developments of *al-maqāṣid* terminology will be surveyed, and the relevance and significance of some of the terms will be explained. '*Maqāṣid al-sharīʿah*' is given a fundamental status in this book. Thus, theories and methods of the Islamic law presented throughout the book will be analysed and evaluated based on their agreement with the *maqāṣid* of the Islamic law.

1.1. *MAQĀṢID AL-SHARIʿAH*: EARLY HISTORY OF THE IDEA

What is Maqāṣid?

The term '*maqṣid*' (plural: *maqāṣid*) refers to a purpose, objective, principle, intent, goal, end,[1] telos (Greek), finalité (French), or Zweck (German)[2]. *Maqāṣid* of the Islamic law are the objectives/purposes behind Islamic rulings.[3] For a number of Islamic legal theorists, it is an alternative expression to 'people's interests' (*maṣālih*). For example, Abd al-Malik al-Juwaynī (d. 478 AH/ 1185 CE), one of the earliest contributors to *al-maqāṣid* theory as we know it today (and as will be explained shortly) used *al-maqāṣid* and public interests (*al-maṣāliḥ al-ʿāmmah*) interchangeably.[4] Abū Ḥāmid al-Ghazālī (d. 505 AH/1111 CE) elaborated on a classification of *maqāṣid*, which he placed entirely under what he called 'unrestricted interests' (*al-maṣāliḥ al-mursalah*, as will be explained later).[5] Fakhr al-Dīn al-Rāzī (d. 606 AH/1209 CE) and al-Āmidī (d. 631 AH/1234 CE) followed al-Ghazālī in his terminology.[6] Najm al-Dīn al-Ṭūfī (d. 716 AH/1316 CE), who gave *al-maṣlaḥah* precedence even over the 'direction implication of the (specific) script' defined *maṣlaḥah* as, 'what fulfils the purpose of the Legislator.'[7] Al-Qarāfī (d. 1285 AH/1868 CE) linked *maṣlaḥah* and *maqāṣid* by a fundamental (*uṣūlī*) 'rule' that stated: 'A purpose (*maqṣid*) is not valid unless it leads to the fulfilment of some good (*maṣlaḥah*) or the avoidance of some mischief (*mafsadah*).'[8] These are a few examples that show the close link between *maṣlaḥah* and *maqāṣid* in the *uṣūlī* conception (especially between the fifth and eighth Islamic centuries, which is the period in which the *maqāṣid* theory was developed, as will be explained below).

Dimensions of Maqāṣid

Purposes, or *maqāṣid,* of the Islamic law themselves are classified in various ways, according to a number of dimensions. The following are some of these dimensions:

1. Levels of necessity, which is the traditional classification.
2. Scope of the rulings aiming to achieve purposes.
3. Scope of people included in purposes.
4. Level of universality of the purposes.

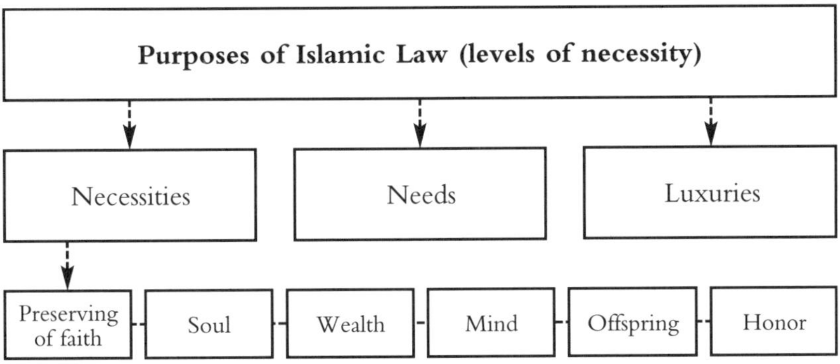

Chart 1.1. Hierarchy of the purposes of the islamic law (dimension of levels of necessity)

Traditional classifications of *maqāṣid* divide them into three 'levels of necessity,' which are necessities (*ḍarūrāt*), needs (*ḥājiyāt*), and luxuries (*taḥsīniyyāt*). Necessities are further classified into what 'preserves one's faith, soul, wealth, mind, and offspring.'[9] Some *uṣūlīs* added 'the preservation of honor' to the above five widely popular necessities.[10] These necessities were considered essential matters for human life itself. There is also a general agreement that the preservation of these necessities is the 'objective behind any revealed law.'[11] Purposes at the level of needs are less essential for human life, and purposes at the level of luxuries are 'beautifying purposes' (*taḥsīniyyāt*), in the traditional expression.[12] Chart 1.1. illustrates the hierarchy of levels of necessity. The levels in the hierarchy are interrelated, according to al-Shāṭibī. Each level serves and protects the level below. For example, the level of needs acts as a 'shield of protection' to the level of necessities.[13] That is why some scholars preferred to perceive necessities in terms of 'overlapping circles,' rather than a strict hierarchy.[14]

I find the levels of necessity reminiscent of the twentieth century's Abraham Maslow's hierarchy of human (rather than 'divine') objectives or 'basic goals,' which he called, the 'hierarchy of needs.'[15] Human needs, according to Maslow, range from basic physiological requirements and safety, to love and esteem, and to 'self-actualisation.' In 1943, Maslow suggested five levels for these needs. Then, in 1970, he revised his ideas and suggested a seven level hierarchy.[16] The similarity between al-Shāṭibī's theory and Maslow's theory in terms of the levels of goals is interesting. Moreover, the second version of Maslow's theory reveals another interesting similarity with Islamic 'goal' theories, which is the capacity to evolve.

Islamic theories of goals (*maqāṣid*) evolved over the centuries, especially in the twentieth century. Contemporary theorists criticised the above traditional classification of necessities for a number of reasons, including the following:[17]

1. The scope of traditional *maqāṣid* is the entire Islamic law. However, they fall short to include specific purposes for single scripts/rulings or groups of scripts that cover certain topics or 'chapters' of fiqh.

2. Traditional *maqāṣid* are concerned with individuals rather than families, societies, and humans, in general.

3. The traditional *maqāṣid* classification did not include the most universal and basic values, such as justice and freedom.

4. Traditional *maqāṣid* were deduced from studying '*fiqhī* literature,' rather than the original sources/scripts.

To remedy the above shortcomings, modern scholarship introduced new conceptions and classifications of *al-maqāṣid* by giving consideration to new dimensions. First, considering the scope of rulings they cover, contemporary classifications divide *maqāṣid* into three levels:[18]

1. General *maqāṣid*: These *maqāṣid* are observed throughout the entire body of the Islamic law, such as the necessities and needs mentioned above and newly proposed *maqāṣid*, such as 'justice' and 'facilitation.'
2. Specific *maqāṣid*: These *maqāṣid* are observed throughout a certain 'chapter' of the Islamic law, such as the welfare of children in family law, preventing criminals in criminal law, and preventing monopoly in financial transactions law.
3. Partial *maqāṣid*: These *maqāṣid* are the 'intents' behind specific scripts or rulings, such as the intent of discovering the truth in seeking a certain number of witnesses in certain court cases, the intent of alleviating difficulty in allowing an ill and fasting person to break his/her fasting, and the intent of feeding the poor in banning Muslims from storing meat during Eid days.

In order to remedy the individuality drawback, the notion of *maqāṣid* has been expanded to include a wider scope of people – the community, nation, or humanity, in general. Ibn Ashur, for example, gave *maqāṣid* that are concerned with the 'nation' (ummah) priority over *maqāṣid* that are concerned with individuals. Rashid Rida, for a second example, included 'reform' and 'women's rights' in his theory of *maqāṣid*. Yusuf al-Qaradawi, for a third example, included 'human dignity and rights' in his theory of *maqāṣid*. These expansions of the scope of *maqāṣid* allows them to respond to global issues and concerns, and to evolve from 'wisdoms behind the rulings' to practical plans for reform and renewal.

Finally, contemporary scholarship has introduced new universal *maqāṣid* that were directly induced from the scripts, rather than from the body of fiqh literature in the schools of Islamic law. This approach, significantly, allowed *maqāṣid* to overcome the historicity of fiqh edicts and represent the scripts' higher values and principles. Detailed rulings would, then, stem from these universal principles. The following are examples of these new universal *maqāṣid*:

1. Rashid Rida (d. 1354AH/1935 CE) surveyed the Qur'an to identify its *maqāṣid*, which included, 'reform of the pillars of faith, and spreading awareness that Islam is the religion of pure natural disposition, reason, knowledge, wisdom, proof, freedom, independence, social, political, and economic reform, and women's rights.'[19]
2. Al-Tahir ibn Ashur (d. 1325 AH/ 1907 CE) proposed that the universal *maqṣid* of the Islamic law is to maintain 'orderliness, equality, freedom, facilitation, and the preservation of pure natural disposition (*fiṭrah*).'[20] It is to be noted that the purpose of 'freedom' (*ḥurrīiyyah*), which was proposed by Ibn Ashur and several other contemporary scholars, is different from the purpose of 'freedom' (*ᶜitq*), which was mentioned by jurists.[21] *Al-ᶜitq* is freedom from slavery, not 'freedom' in the contemporary sense. 'Will' (*Mashī'ah*), however, is a well-known Islamic term that bears a number of similarities with current conceptions of 'freedom' and 'free will.' For example, 'freedom of belief' is expressed in the Qur'an as the 'will to believe or disbelieve.'[22] In terms of terminology, 'freedom' (*al-ḥurriyyah*) is a 'newly-coined' purpose in the literature of the Islamic law. Ibn Ashur, interestingly, accredited his usage of the term *ḥurriyyah* to 'literature of the French revolution, which were translated from French to Arabic in the nineteenth century CE,'[23] even though he elaborated on an Islamic perspective on freedom of thought, belief, expression, and action in the *mashī'ah* sense.[24]
3. Mohammad al-Ghazaly (d. 1416 AH/ 1996 CE) called for 'learning lessons from the previous fourteen centuries of Islamic history,' and therefore, included 'justice and freedom' in *maqāṣid* at the necessities level.[25]
4. Yusuf al-Qaradawi (1345 AH/1926 CE -) also surveyed the Qur'an and concluded the following universal *maqāṣid*: 'Preserving true faith, maintaining human dignity and rights, calling people to

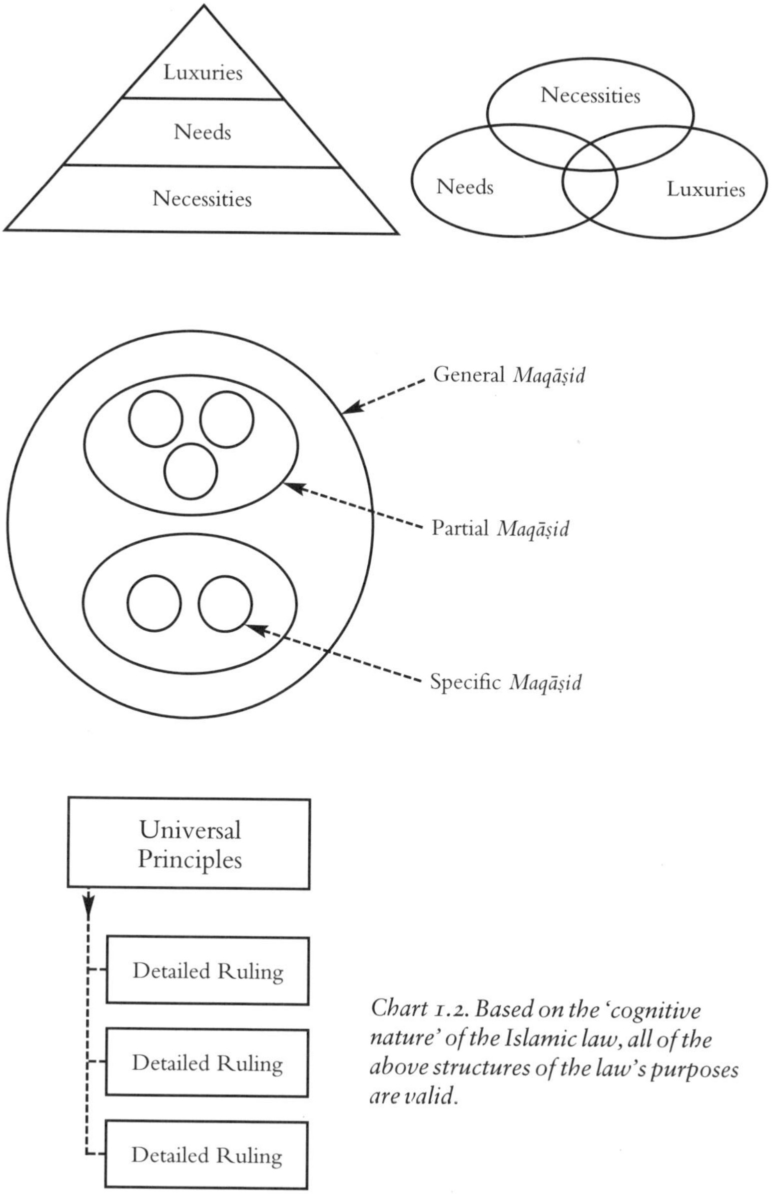

Chart 1.2. Based on the 'cognitive nature' of the Islamic law, all of the above structures of the law's purposes are valid.

worship God, purifying the soul, restoring moral values, building good families, treating women fairly, building a strong Islamic nation and calling for a cooperative world.'[26] However al-Qaradawi explains that proposing a theory in universal *maqāṣid* should only happen after developing a level of experience with detailed scripts.[27]

5. Taha al-Alwani (1354 AH/ 1935 CE -) also surveyed the Qur'an to identify its 'supreme and prevailing' *maqāṣid*, which are, according to him, 'the oneness of God (*tawḥīd*), purification of the soul (*tazkiyah*), and developing civilisation on earth (*ᶜimrān*).'[28] He is currently writing a separate monograph to elaborate on each of these three *maqāṣid*.[29]

All of the above *maqāṣid* were presented as they appeared in the minds and perceptions of the above jurists. None of the above classic or contemporary classifications and structures could claim to be 'according to the original divine will.' If we refer to nature that God created, we will never find natural structures that could be represented in terms of circles, pyramids, or boxes, as the above diagram shows. All such structures in science and humanities too, and the categories they include, are human-made for the sake of illustration for themselves and other humans.

Therefore, *al-maqāṣid* structure is best described as a 'multi-dimensional' structure, in which levels of necessity, scope of rulings, scope of people, and levels of universality are all valid dimensions that represent valid viewpoints and classifications. More elaboration on the concept of 'multi-dimensionality' is provided in the next chapter on systems theory and philosophy.

The above twentieth-century views also show that *maqāṣid al-sharīᶜah* are, actually, representations of each scholar's own viewpoint for reform and development of the Islamic law, despite the fact that all these *maqāṣid* were 'induced' from the scripts. This fusion of the scripts and contemporary needs for reform gives *al-maqāṣid* special significance. I view *maqāṣid* as one of today's most important intellectual means and methodologies for Islamic reform. It is a methodology from 'within' the Islamic scholarship that addresses the Islamic mind and Islamic concerns. This approach is radically different from projects for Islamic 'reform' and 'renewal' that come from 'without' the Islamic terminology and scholarship.

I shall now present a brief historical account of the ideas of *maqāṣid* from the companions of the Prophet's era to our current time.

Al-Maqāṣid in the Companions' Ijtihad

The history of the idea of speculating a certain underlying purpose, aim, or intent of Qur'anic or Prophetic instructions goes back to the companions of the Prophet, as narrated in a number of incidents. One clear and popular example is the multi-chained hadith of 'afternoon prayers at Banū Qurayẓah,' in which the Prophet sent a group of companions to Banū Qurayẓah,[30] and ordered them to pray their afternoon (*aṣr*) prayer there.[31] The span of time allowed for *aṣr* prayers had almost expired before the group reached Banū Qurayẓah. Thus, they found themselves divided into supporters of two different opinions, one opinion entailed praying at Banū Qurayẓah's anyway and the other opinion entailed praying on the way (before the prayer time was over).

The rationale behind the first opinion was that the Prophet's instruction was clear in asking everybody to pray at Banū Qurayẓah, while the rationale of the second opinion was that the Prophet's 'purpose/intent' of the order was to ask the group to hasten to Banū Qurayẓah, rather than 'meaning/intending to' postpone prayers until after its due time. According to the narrator, when the companions later narrated the story to the Prophet, he approved both opinions.[32] The approval of the Prophet, as jurists and Imams said, entails the permissibility and correctness of both views. The only prime jurist who disagreed with the companions who prayed on the way was Ibn Ḥazm al-Ẓāhirī (the literalist), who wrote that they should have prayed the 'afternoon prayer' after they reached Banū Qurayẓah, as the Prophet had said, even after midnight![33]

Another incident, which shows a more serious consequence of taking a 'purpose-oriented' approach to the Prophetic instructions occurred during the days of ʿUmar, the second caliph. The status of ʿUmar in Islam and his continuous and wide-ranging consultation of a large number of companions, make his opinions of special significance. In this incident, the companions asked ʿUmar to distribute the newly-'conquered' lands of Egypt and Iraq amongst them as some sort of 'spoils of war.'[34] Their argument relied on the clear and specific verses of the Qur'an that allowed fighters their 'spoils of war.' ʿUmar refused to divide whole cities and provinces over the companions by referring to other verses, with more general expressions, stating that God has a 'purpose' of 'not making the rich dominate wealth.'[35] Therefore, ʿUmar (and the companions who supported his opinion) understood the specifics of the verses of 'spoils of war' within the context of a certain purpose (*maqṣid*) of the law. This purpose was, 'diminishing the difference between economic levels,' to use familiar contemporary terms. The significance of ʿUmar's ijtihad is that it could, traditionally, be considered as a 'collective ijtihad' carried out by (a large number of) the companions. This ijtihad has its significance in fiqh, regardless of the 'authority' of a companion's opinion, which is a matter of difference of opinion within traditional schools of the law (as will be explained later).

Another telling example is ʿUmar's application of a moratorium on the (Islamic) punishment for theft during the famine of Madinah.[36] He thought that applying the punishment prescribed in the scripts, while people are in need of basic supplies for their survival, goes against the general principle of justice, which he considered more fundamental.

A third example from ʿUmar's fiqh (application of the law) is when he did not apply the 'apparent meaning' of the hadith that clearly gives a soldier the right to the spoils of war from opponents.[37] He decided to give soldiers only one-fifth of these spoils, if they were 'significantly valuable,' with a purpose to achieve fairness amongst soldiers and enrich the public trust.

A fourth example is ʿUmar's decision to include horses in the types of wealth included in the obligatory charity of zakah, despite the Prophet's clear instruction to exclude them. ʿUmar's rationale was that horses at his time were becoming significantly more valuable than camels, which the Prophet included in zakah at his time.[38] In other words, ʿUmar understood the 'purpose' of the zakah in terms of a form of social assistance that is paid by the wealthy for the sake of the poor, regardless of the exact types of wealth that were mentioned in the Prophetic tradition and understood via its literal implication.[39]

All known schools of law, except for the Ḥanafīs, are against such expansion of 'the pool of charity' (*wiʿāʾ al-zakāh*), which illustrates how literalism had a strong influence on traditional juridical methods. Ibn Ḥazm, again, asserted that, 'there is no zakah on anything except eight types of wealth, which are mentioned in the sunnah, namely, gold, silver, wheat, barley, dates, camels, cows, sheep and goats. There is no zakah on horses, commercial goods, or any other type of wealth.'[40] It is clear how such opinion hinders the institution of zakah from achieving any meaningful sense of justice or social welfare.

Based on a 'methodology that considers the wisdoms behind the rulings,' Qaradawi rejected classic opinions on the above matter in his very detailed study on zakah. He wrote: 'Zakah is due on every growing wealth ... The purpose of zakah is to help the poor and to serve the public good. It is unlikely that The Legislator aimed to put this burden on owners of five or more camels (as Ibn Ḥazm had said), and release businessmen who earn in one day what a shepherd earns in years ...'[41]

However, ʿUmar did not take this purpose-oriented approach to all rulings of the Islamic law. Bukhārī narrates that ʿUmar was asked: 'Why do we still jog around the kaʿbah with our shoulders uncovered even after Islam had prevailed in Makkah?' The story behind the question is that after the 'conquest of Makkah,' the people of Makkah claimed the Prophet and his companions lost their health during their prolonged stay in Madinah. The Prophet, therefore, ordered the companions to jog around the Kaʿbah with their shoulders uncovered in a show of strength. ʿUmar, however, did not take a purpose-oriented approach to this question. He answered: 'We do not cease doing anything we used to do at the Prophet's time.'[42] ʿUmar, thus, made a distinction between 'acts of worship' (*ʿibādāt*) and 'worldly transactions' (*muʿāmalāt*), a distinction that was later endorsed by all schools of *uṣūl al-fiqh*. Shāṭibī, for example, expressed this distinction when he wrote: 'Literal compliance is the default methodology in the area of acts of worship (*ʿibādāt*), while the consideration of purposes is the default methodology in the area of worldly dealings (*muʿāmalāt*).'[43]

The significance of ijtihad in the above incidents is that the companions did not always apply what *uṣulīs*, much later, called *dilālah al-lafẓ* (the implication of the term). Practical implications were sometimes based on the purpose, which could be termed '*dilālah al-maqṣid*.' This *dilālah* enables greater flexibility in understanding terms (*alfāẓ*) and placing them in their circumstantial contexts, as the above examples illustrate.

Nevertheless, the (neo-)traditionalist school[44] of Islamic law does not consider the above changes according to purposes to be against the direct linguistic implication (*dilālah*) of the scripts. A typical opinion claims that there were certain 'causes' (*ʿillal*) behind these rulings, and that the rulings simply no longer applied when these causes no longer existed or when they were 'specified' (that is, *mukhaṣṣaṣṣah*) by other scripts.[45] For example, the related *ʿillah* of the application of the punishment for theft is 'theft carried out by a person who is not in need.' Therefore, the punishment for theft just does not apply to the thieves that ʿUmar pardoned. If such interpretation of some of ʿUmar's ijtihad is not possible, current (neo-)traditionalism would discredit these incidents of ʿUmar's ijtihad as 'contrary to the scripts.'[46] However, I would say that such criteria included in the *ʿillah*, such as the 'in need' criterion, are not 'consistent' (*munḍabiṭ*), since they might 'change with the change of circumstances.' Therefore, the criterion is not an *ʿillah*, in the technical sense of the term, but indeed a *maqṣid*. Therefore, from a technical point of view, it is more 'appropriate' (*munāsib*) to relate the change that ʿUmar applied to the *maqṣid* of social assistance, rather than the above claimed *ʿillah*. Similarly, it is claimed that the *ʿillah* of the application of the individual spoils of war is the 'leader's consent according to public interest.'[47] However, again, this claimed *ʿillah* is not 'consistent' (*munḍabiṭah*) since it 'changes with the change of circumstances.' Thus, it is more appropriate to relate the change that ʿUmar made to the *maqṣid* of fairness amongst soldiers and the *maqṣid* of achieving public interest.

The above examples are meant to illustrate early conceptions of *maqāṣid* in the application of the Islamic law and the implications of giving them fundamental importance. The role that *maqāṣid* could play in various techniques for ijtihad and the relationship between the *ʿillah* and *maqṣid* are discussed in detail later in Chapter Six.

Early Theories of Maqāṣid

After the Companions' era, the theory and classifications of *maqāṣid* started to evolve. However, *maqāṣid* as we know them today were not clearly developed until the time of the later *uṣūlīs* of the fifth to eighth Islamic century, as I will elaborate in the next subsection. During the first three centuries, however, the idea of purposes/causes (Arabic: *ḥikam, ʿilal, munāsabāt*, or *maʿānī*) appeared in a number of reasoning methods utilised by the Imams of the classic schools of Islamic law, such as reasoning by analogy (*qiyās*), juridical preference (*istiḥsān*), and interest (*maṣlaḥah*). Purposes themselves, however, were not subjects of separate monographs or special attention until the end of the third Islamic century. Then, the development of the theory of 'levels of necessity' by Imam al-Juwaynī (d. 478 AH/ 1085 CE) took place much later in the fifth Islamic century. The following is an attempt to trace early conceptions of *al-maqāṣid* between the third and fifth Islamic centuries.

1. Al-Tirmidhī al-Ḥakīm (d. 296 AH/908 CE). The first known volume dedicated to the topic of *maqāṣid*, in which the term '*maqāṣid*' was used in the book's title, is *al-Ṣalāh wa Maqāṣiduhā* (Prayers and their Purposes) which was written by al-Tirmidhī al-Ḥakīm.[48] The book is a survey of the wisdoms and spiritual 'secrets' behind each of the prayer acts, with an obvious Sufi inclination. Examples are 'confirming humbleness' as the *maqṣid* behind glorifying God with every move during prayers, 'achieving consciousness' as the *maqṣid* behind praising God, 'focusing on one's prayer' as the *maqṣid* behind facing the direction of the Kaʿbah, and so on. Al-Tirmidhī al-Ḥakīm also wrote a similar book on pilgrimage, which he entitled, *al-Hajj wa Asrāruh* (Pilgrimage and its Secrets).[49]
2. Abū Zayd al-Balkhī (d. 322 AH/933 CE). The first known book on the *maqāṣid* of dealings (*muʿāmalāt*) is Abū Zayd al-Balkhī's *al-Ibānah ʿan ʿilal al-Diyanah* (Revealing Purposes in Religious

Practices), in which he surveys purposes behind Islamic juridical rulings. Al-Balkhī also wrote a book dedicated to *maṣlaḥah* which he entitled, *Maṣāliḥ al-Abdān wa al-Anfus* (Benefits for Bodies and Souls), in which he explained how Islamic practices and rulings contribute to health, physically and mentally.[50]

3. Al-Qaffāl al-Kabīr (d. 365 AH/975 CE). The oldest manuscript that I found in the Egyptian Dār al-Kutub on the topic of *al-maqāṣid* is al-Qaffāl's *Maḥāsin al-Sharā'iᶜ* (The Beauties of the Laws).[51] After a 20–page introduction, al-Qaffāl proceeds to divide the book into the familiar chapters of traditional books of fiqh (i.e., starting with purification, and then ablution and prayers, etc). He mentions each ruling briefly and elaborates on the purposes and wisdoms behind it. The manuscript is fairly clear and contains around 400 pages. The last page mentions the date of the book's completion, which is the 11th of Rabiᶜ 1, 358 AH (7th of February, 969 CE). The coverage of the rulings of fiqh is extensive, albeit strictly addressing individual rulings without introducing any general theory for the purposes. Nevertheless, the book is an important step in the development of *al-maqāṣid* theory. The following is my translation of an excerpt from the introduction (from the first page shown in Chart 1.3.):

> ... I decided to write this book to illustrate the beauties of the revealed Law, its magnanimous and moral content, and its compatibility with sound reason. I will include in it answers for those who are asking questions about the true reasons and wisdoms behind its rulings. These questions could only come from one of two persons. The first person attributes the creation of the world to its Creator and believes in the truth of prophethood, since the wisdom behind the Law is attributed to the Wise Almighty King, who prescribes to His servents what is best for them ... The second person is trying to argue against prophethood and the concept of the creation of the world, or maybe is in agreement over the creation of the world while in rejection of prophethood. The logical line that this person is trying to follow is to use the invalidity of the Law as proof for the invalidity of the concept of a Law-Giver ...

Chart 1.3. The first page of Egyptian Dār al-Kutub's manuscript of al-Qaffāl al-Kabīr's 'Maḥāsin al-Sharā'i'' (The Beauties of the Laws).

4. Ibn Bābawayh al-Qummī (d. 381 AH/991 CE). Some researchers claim that research on *maqāṣid al-sharīᶜah* was restricted to the Sunni schools of law until the twentieth century.[52] However, the first known monograph dedicated to *maqāṣid* was, in fact, written by Ibn Bābawayh al-Ṣadūq al-Qummī, one of the main Shia jurists of the fourth Islamic century, who wrote a book of 335 chapters on the subject.[53] The book, which was entitled *ᶜIlal al-Sharā'iᶜ* (The Reasons behind the Rulings), 'rationalises' believing in God, prophets, heaven, and other beliefs. It also gives moral rationales for prayers, fasting, pilgrimage, charity, caring for parents, and other moral obligations.[54]
5. Al-ᶜĀmirī al-Faylasūf (d. 381 AH/991 CE). The earliest known theoretical classification of purposes was introduced by al-ᶜĀmirī al-Faylasūf in his *al-Iᶜlām bi-Manāqib al-Islām* (Awareness of the Traits of Islam).[55] Al-ᶜĀmirī's classification, however, was solely based on 'criminal punishments' in the Islamic law (*ḥudūd*).

Classifications of *maqāṣid* according to 'levels of necessity' were not developed until the fifth Islamic century. Then, the whole theory reached its most mature stage (before the twentieth century CE) in the eighth Islamic century.

1.2. *AL-MAQĀṢID* AS A DEVELOPED THEORY: FIFTH TO EIGHTH CENTURIES AH

The Emergence of a Philosophy for Islamic Law

The fifth Islamic century witnessed the birth of what Abdallah Bin Bayyah called 'a philosophy of the Islamic law.'[56] Literal and nominal methods that were developed, until the fifth century, proved incapable of coping with the complexities of the evolving civilisation. This is why unrestricted interest (*al-maṣlaḥah al-mursalah*) was developed as a method that covers 'what was not mentioned in the scripts,' and thus, compensates for the limitations of *qiyās*. I had argued, however, that *qiyās* could not handle all 'new situations,' despite the *uṣūlī* attempts to develop it through the 'appropriateness' (*munāsabah*) consideration, because it was restricted with the exactness/consistency (*inḍibāṭ*) condition.[57] *Al-maṣlaḥah al-mursalah* helped to fill this gap and also gave birth to the theory of *maqāṣid* in the Islamic law. A few jurists made the most significant contributions to the *maqāṣid* theory between the fifth and eighth Islamic centuries, namely, Abū al-Maᶜālī al-Juwaynī, Abū Ḥāmid al-Ghazālī, al-ᶜIzz ibn Abd al-Salām, Shihāb al-Dīn al-Qarāfī, Shams al-Dīn ibn al-Qayyim, and, most significantly, Abū Isḥāq al-Shāṭibī.

Abū al-Maᶜālī al-Juwaynī (d. 478 AH/1085 CE)

Al-Juwaynī's *al-Burhān fi Uṣul al-Fiqh* (The Proof in the Fundamentals of Law) was the first *uṣūl* treatise to introduce a theory of 'levels of necessity,' in a way that is similar to today's familiar theory. He suggested five levels of *maqāṣid*, namely, necessities (*ḍarūrāt*), public needs (*al-ḥājah al-ᶜāmah*), moral behavior (*al-makrumāt*), recommendations (*al-mandūbāt*), and 'what cannot be attributed to a specific reason.'[58] He proposed that the purpose of the Islamic law is the protection (*al-ᶜiṣmah*) for people's 'faith, souls, minds, private parts, and money.'[59]

Al-Juwaynī's *Ghiyāth al-Umam* (The Salvage of the Nations) was, in my view, another important contribution to *al-maqāṣid* theory, even though it primarily addresses political issues. In *al-Ghayyāthī* (a popular short name for that book), al-Juwaynī makes a 'hypothetical assumption' that jurists and schools of law eventually disappeared from Earth, and suggested that the only way to salvage Islam would be to 're-construct' it from the bottom up, using the 'fundamental principles, upon which all rulings of law are based and to which all rulings of law converge.'[60] He wrote that these fundamentals of the law, which he explicitly called '*al-maqāṣid*,' are 'not subject to opposing tendencies and difference of opinion over interpretations.'[61]

Examples of these *maqāṣid*, on which al-Juwaynī 're-constructed' the Islamic law are 'facilitation' in the laws of purification, 'elevating the burden of the poor' in the laws of charity, and 'mutual agreement' in the laws of trade.[62] I view al-Juwaynī's *Ghiyāth al-Umam* as a project for the 're-construction' of the Islamic law based on *maqāṣid*, which he had to express in such a way that it would save him from academic and political persecution.[63] Certainly, this view requires more research and a more extensive analysis of the text itself.

Abū Ḥāmid al-Ghazālī (d. 505 AH/1111 CE)

Al-Juwaynī's student, Abū Ḥāmid al-Ghazālī, developed his teacher's theory further in his book, *al-Mustaṣfā* (The Purified Source). He ordered the 'necessities' that al-Juwaynī had suggested as follows: (1) faith, (2) soul, (3) mind, (4) offspring, and (5) wealth.[64] Al-Ghazālī also coined the term 'preservation' (*al-ḥifẓ*) of these necessities.

Despite the detailed analysis that he offered, al-Ghazālī, obviously under the influence of his Shāfiʿī school (which views analogical reasoning as the only valid method of ijtihad), refused to give independent legitimacy (*ḥujjiyyah*) to any of his proposed *maqāṣid* or *maṣāliḥ*, and even referred to them as 'the illusionary interests' (*al-maṣāliḥ al-mawhūmah*).[65] Yet, al-Ghazālī presented some interesting analogies (*qiyās*), in which he used the *maqṣid* as ratio legis (*ʿillah*), despite the Shāfiʿīs' critique of *maqāṣid* as 'non-exact' (*ghair munḍabiṭah*). For example, he wrote, 'all intoxicants, whether liquid or solid, are forbidden based on analogy with liquor, since liquor is forbidden for the purpose of the preservation of people's minds.'[66]

Al-Ghazālī also suggested a fundamental rule, based on the order of necessities he suggested, which implies that the higher-order necessity should have priority over a lower-order necessity if they generate opposite implications in practical cases.[67] Thus, al-Ghazālī's ijtihad diverges from the strict Shāfiʿī adherence to formality, in the logical sense, in the procedure of analogical reasoning, which he himself supported in his *al-Mustaṣfā* and his other books on the theory of the law.

Al-ʿIzz Ibn Abd al-Salām (d. 660 AH/1209 CE)

Al-ʿIzz wrote two small books about *al-maqāṣid*, in the 'wisdoms-behind-rulings' sense, namely, *Maqāṣid al-Ṣalāh* (Purposes of Prayers) and *Maqāṣid al-Ṣawm* (Purposes of Fasting).[68] However, his significant contribution to the development of the theory of *al-maqāṣid* was his book on interests (*maṣāliḥ*), which he called, *Qawāʿid al-Aḥkām fī*

Maṣāliḥ al-Anām (Basic Rules Concerning People's Interests). Beside his extensive investigation of the concepts of interest and mischief, al-ʿIzz linked the validity of rulings to their purposes. For example, he wrote: 'Every action that misses its purpose is void,'[69] and, 'when you study how the purposes of the law brings good and prevents mischief, you realise that it is unlawful to overlook any common good or support any act of mischief in any situation, even if you have no specific evidence from the script, consensus, or analogy.'[70]

Quṭb al-Dīn al-Qasṭalānī (d. 686 AH/1287 CE), following the example of al-ʿIzz, wrote two books dedicated to the topics *maqāṣid* for prayers and fasting. Both books are written in the same 'wisdoms-behind-the-rulings' approach.[71]

Shihāb al-Dīn al-Qarāfī (d. 684 AH/1285 CE)

Al-Qarāfī's contribution to the theory of *maqāṣid* is his differentiation between different actions taken by the Prophet based on his 'intents.' He writes in his *al-Furūq* (The Differences):

> There is a difference between the Prophet's actions in the capacity of a conveyer of the divine message, a judge, and a leader ... The implication in the law is that what he says or does as a conveyer goes as a general and permanent ruling ... [However,] decisions related to the military, public trust, ... appointing judges and governors, distributing spoils of war, and signing treaties ... are specific to leaders.[72]

Thus, al-Qarāfī defined a new meaning for '*al-maqāṣid*' as the purposes/intents of the Prophet himself in his actions. Later, Ibn Ashur (d. 1976 CE) developed al-Qarāfī's above 'difference' and included it into his definition of *al-maqaṣid*.[73] Al-Qarafi also wrote about 'opening the means to achieving good ends,' which is another significant expansion of the theory of *maqāṣid*. Al-Qarāfī proposed that while means that lead to prohibited ends should be blocked, means that lead to lawful ends should be opened.[74] Thus, he did not restrict himself to the negative side of 'blocking the means' method. Chapter Six explains.

Shams al-Dīn Ibn al-Qayyim (d. 748 AH/1347 CE)

Ibn al-Qayyim's contribution to the theory of *maqāṣid* was through a very detailed critique of what is called juridical tricks (*al-ḥiyal al-fiqhiyyah*), based on the fact that they contradict with *maqāṣid*. He wrote:

> *Fiqhī* tricks are forbidden acts of mischief because, first, they go against the wisdom of the legislation, and, secondly, because they have forbidden *maqāṣid*. The person whose intention is usury is committing a sin, even if the outlook of the fake transaction, which he used in the trick, is lawful. That person did not have a sincere intention to carry out the lawful transaction, but rather, the forbidden one. Equally sinful is the person who aims at altering the shares of his inheritors by carrying out a fake sale [to one of them] ... Shariʿah laws are the cure of our sicknesses because of their realities, not their apparent names and outlooks.

Ibn al-Qayyim summarised his juridical methodology that is based on 'wisdom and people's welfare' with the following strong words, which I had mentioned earlier in the introduction:

> Shariʿah is based on wisdom and achieving people's welfare in this life and the afterlife. Shariʿah is all about justice, mercy, wisdom, and good. Thus, any ruling that replaces justice with injustice, mercy with its opposite, common good with mischief, or wisdom with nonsense, is a ruling that does not belong to the Shariʿah, even if it is claimed to be so according to some interpretation.[75]

Abū Isḥāq al-Shāṭibī (d. 790 AH/1388 CE)

Al-Shāṭibī used, more or less, the same terminology that al-Juwaynī and al-Ghazālī developed. However, I argue that in his *al-Muwāfaqāt fī Uṣūl al-Sharīʿah* (Congruences in the Fundamentals of the Revealed Law), al-Shāṭibī developed the theory of *al-maqāṣid* in the following three substantial ways:

(i) From 'unrestricted interests' to 'fundamentals of law.' Before al-Shāṭibī's *Muwāfaqāt*, *al-maqāṣid* were included in 'non-restricted interests' and were never considered as fundamentals (*uṣul*) in their own right. Al-Shāṭibī started his volume on *al-maqāṣid* in *al-Muwāfaqāt* by quoting the Qur'an to prove that God has purposes in His creation, sending His messengers, and ordaining laws.[76] Hence, he considered *al-maqāṣid* to be the 'fundamentals of religion, basic rules of the law, and universals of belief' (*uṣūl al-dīn wa qawāʿid al-sharīʿah wa kullīyah al-millah*).[77]

(ii) From 'wisdoms behind the ruling' to 'bases for the ruling.' Based on the fundamentality and universality of *al-maqāṣid*, al-Shāṭibī judged that, 'the universals (*al-kulliyyah*) of necessities, needs, and luxuries cannot be overridden by partial rulings (*al-juz'iyyāt*).'[78] This is quite a deviation from traditional fundamentals, even in al-Shāṭibī's Mālikī school, which always gave precendence to 'specific' partial evidences over 'general' or universal evidences.[79] Al-Shāṭibī also made 'knowledge of *maqāṣid*' a condition for the correctness of juridical reasoning (ijtihad) on all levels.[80]

(iii) From 'uncertainty' (*ẓanniyyah*) to 'certainty' (*qaṭʿiyyah*). In order to support the new status that he gave to *al-maqāṣid* amongst the fundamentals, al-Shāṭibī started his volume on *maqāṣid* by arguing for the 'certainty' (*qaṭʿiyyah*) of the inductive process that he used to conclude *al-maqāṣid*, based on the high number of evidences he considered,[81] which is also a deviation from the popular 'Greek-philosophy-based' arguments against the validity and 'certainty' of inductive methods.

Al-Shāṭibī's book became the standard textbook on *maqāṣid al-sharīʿah* in Islamic scholarship until the twentieth century, but his proposal to present *maqāṣid* as 'fundamentals of the shariʿah,' as the title of his book suggests, was not as widely accepted.

1.3. CONTEMPORARY CONCEPTIONS OF *MAQĀṢID*

From 'Protection' and 'Preservation' to 'Development' and 'Rights'

Contemporary jurists/scholars developed traditional *maqāṣid* terminology[82] in today's language, despite some jurists' rejection of the idea of 'contemporarisation' of *maqāṣid* terminology. The following are some examples taken from the area of *ḍarūrāt*. Traditionally, the 'preservation of offspring' is one of the necessities that Islamic law aimed to achieve. Al-ᶜĀmirī had expressed it, in his early attempt to outline a theory of necessary purposes, in terms of 'punishments for breaching decency.'[83] Al-Juwaynī developed al-ᶜĀmirī's 'theory of punishments' (*mazājir*) into a 'theory of protection' (*ᶜiṣmah*) which was expressed by al-Juwaynī as, 'protection for private parts.'[84] It was Abū Ḥāmid al-Ghazālī who coined the term 'preservation of offspring' as a purpose of the Islamic law at the level of necessity.[85] Al-Shāṭibī followed al-Ghazālī's terminology, as explained above.

In the twentieth century, writers on *maqāṣid*, significantly, developed 'preservation of offspring' into a family-orientated theory. Ibn Ashur, for example, made 'care for the family' to be a *maqṣid* of the Islamic law, in its own right. In his monograph 'The Social System in Islam,' Ibn Ashur elaborated on family-related purposes and moral values in the Islamic law.[86] Whether we consider Ibn Ashur's contribution to be a sort of re-interpretation of the theory of 'preservation of offspring,' or a replacement of the same theory with a new one, it is clear that Ibn Ashur's contribution had opened the door for contemporary scholars to develop the theory of *maqāṣid* in new ways. The orientation of the new views is neither al-ᶜAmiri's theory of 'punishment' nor is it al-Ghazālī's concept of 'preservation,' but rather the concepts of 'value' and 'system,' to use the terminology of Ibn Ashur. Nevertheless, some contemporary scholars are against the idea of incorporating new concepts, such as justice and freedom, in *maqāṣid*. They prefer to say that these concepts are implicitly included in the classic theory.[87]

Similarly the 'preservation of mind' which until recently was restricted to the purpose of the prohibition of intoxicants in Islam, is currently evolving to include 'propagation of scientific thinking,' 'travelling to seek knowledge,' 'suppressing the herd mentality,' and 'avoiding brain drain.'[88]

Likewise, the 'preservation of honor' and the 'preservation of the soul' were at the level of 'necessities' in al-Ghazālī's and al-Shāṭibī's terms. However, these expressions were also preceded by al-ᶜĀmirī's 'punishment' for 'breaching honor' and al-Juwaynī's 'protection of honor.' Honor (*al-ʿirḍ*) has been a central concept in the Arabic culture since the pre-Islamic period. Pre-Islamic poetry narrates how ʿAntarah, the famous pre-Islamic poet, fought the Sons of Damdam for 'defaming his honor.' In the hadith, the Prophet described the 'blood, money, and honor of every Muslim' as 'sanctuary' (*ḥarām*) that is not to be breached.[89] Recently, however, the expression of 'preservation of honor' is gradually being replaced in the Islamic law literature with 'preservation of human dignity' and even the 'protection of human rights' as a purpose of the Islamic law in its own right.[90]

The compatibility of human rights and Islam is a topic of a heated debate, both in Islamic and international circles.[91] A Universal Islamic Declaration of Human Rights was announced in 1981 by a large number of scholars who represented various Islamic entities at the United Nations Educational, Scientific and Cultural Organisation (UNESCO). Supported by a number of Islamic scripts mentioned in its references section, the Islamic Declaration essentially includes the entire list of basic rights that were mentioned in the Universal Declaration of Human Rights (UDHR), such as rights to life, freedom, equality, justice, fair trial, protection against torture, asylum, freedom of belief and speech, free association, education, and freedom of mobility.[92]

However, some members of the United Nations High Commission for Human Rights (UNHCHR) expressed concerns over the Islamic Declaration of human rights because they think that it 'gravely threatens the inter-cultural consensus on which the international human rights instruments were based.'[93] Other members believe that the declaration 'adds new positive dimensions to human rights, since, unlike international instruments, it attributes them to a divine source thereby adding a new moral motivation for complying with them.'[94] A *maqāṣid*-based approach to the issue of human rights supports the latter opinion, while addressing the concerns of the former, especially if *al-maqāṣid* terminology is to be 'contemporarized' and made to play a more 'fundamental' (*uṣūlī*) role in juridical reasoning, as this book is suggesting in Chapter Six. The topic of human rights and *maqāṣid* requires further research in order to resolve the 'inconsistencies' that some researchers have suggested in terms of the application level.[95]

In the same way, the 'preservation of religion,' in al-Ghazālī's and al-Shāṭibī's terminology, had its roots in al-ʿĀmirī's 'punishment for giving up true faith.'[96] Recently, however, the same theory for that purpose of the Islamic Law has been re-interpreted to mean a dramatically different concept, which is 'freedom of faiths,' to use Ibn Ashur's words,[97] or 'freedom of belief,' in other contemporary expressions.[98] Presenters of these views often quote the Qur'anic verse, 'No compulsion in matters of religion,'[99] as the fundamental principle, rather than what is popularly, and inaccurately, called 'punishment for apostacy' (*ḥadd al-riddah*) that used to be mentioned in traditional references in the context of the 'preservation of religion.'

Finally al-Ghazālī's 'preservation of wealth,' along with al-ʿĀmirī's 'punishments for theft' and al-Juwaynī's 'protection of money' had recently witnessed an evolution into familiar socio-economic terminology, such as 'social assistance,' 'economic development,' 'flow of money,' 'wellbeing of society,' and 'diminishing the difference between economic levels.'[100] This development enables utilising *maqāṣid al-Sharīʿah* to encourage economic growth, which is much-needed in most countries with a majority of Muslims.

'Human Development' as a Maqṣid in its Own Right

'Human development,' the development concept that the UN Development Reports adopt, is much more comprehensive than economic growth. According to the latest United Nations Development Program (UNDP) reports, most countries with a Muslim majority rank lower than the 'developed' range of the comprehensive Human Development Index (HDI). This index is calculated using more than 200 indexes, including measures for political participation, literacy, enrolment in education, life expectancy, access to clean water, employment, standard of living, and gender equality. Nevertheless, some countries with majority of Muslims, especially oil-rich Arab states, show 'the worst disparities,' the UN Report says, between their levels of national income and measures for gender equality, which includes women's political participation, economic participation, and power over resources.[101]

In addition to Muslim minorities who live in developed countries, a few countries with Muslim majorities were ranked under 'high human development,' such as Brunei, Qatar, and the United Arab Emirates. However, the above groups collectively represent less than one percent of Muslims. The bottom of the HDI list includes Yemen, Nigeria, Mauritania, Djibouti, Gambia, Senegal, Guinea, Ivory Cost, Mali, and Niger (which collectively represent around 10 percent of Muslims).

I suggest 'human development' to be a prime expression of *maṣlaḥah* (public interest) in our time, which *maqāṣid al-sharīʿah* should aim to realise through the Islamic law. Thus, the realisation of this *maqṣad* could be empirically measured via the UN 'human development targets,' according to current scientific standards. Similar to the area of human rights, the area of human development requires more research from a *maqāṣid* perspective. Nevertheless, the evolution of 'human development' into 'purposes of Islamic law' gives 'human development targets' a firm base in the Islamic world, instead of presenting them, according to a number of (neo-)literlists, as merely 'tools for western domination.'[102]

In this book, all of the above traditional and contemporary conceptions of *maqāṣid* will be used as guiding fundamentals and criteria for the systems based analysis and evaluation of the Islamic law. In other words, *maqāṣid* will be presented as a philosophy of Islamic law.

2

Systems as Philosophy and Methodology for Analysis

Overview

Before taking a 'systems approach' to the analysis of the fundamentals (*uṣūl*) of Islamic law and its philosophy, the following questions shall be answered:

- What are systems? Are they 'real' or 'mental' creations?
- What is 'systems philosophy' and how does it relate to Islamic and modern philosophies?
- What is a 'systems approach'?
- How does a systems-based analysis compare to other types of analysis?

This chapter explains what a system is in terms of 'systems philosophy.' A systems philosophical approach views the creation and functionality of nature and all its components in terms of a large holistic system that is composed of an infinite number of interacting, opened, hierarchical, and purposeful sub-systems. Then, the advantages of a systems approach to analysis, versus traditional methods of analysis, broadly labelled as 'decompositional,' are outlined. I shall, finally, define a systems approach to analysis based on my definition of what defines a systems, or 'system features.' The language of this chapter is rather technical, since 'systems' is a multi-disciplinary field that had emerged from the realm of science, rather than the realm of humanities.

2.1. SYSTEMS AND SYSTEMS PHILOSOPHY

Teleology, Causality, and Irrationality

Major advancements in science often lead the way to major shifts in philosophical paradigms. Ancient, and especially Greek, alchemy, geometry, and astronomy were breakthroughs that taught humans how much they do not know. Thus, teleological theories of a universe with a 'purpose' were born and eventually dominated philosophy of religion. Philosophy of religion, until medieval times, 're-interpreted' teleological theories to be theories for the purposes of God. Islamic philosophy also re-interpreted ancient teleological theories in an Islamic sense. In addition, Islamic philosophers/scientists developed the ancient concepts of causality, not only from the scientific side but from the theological side as well, as Chapter Six will explain. Islamic philosophy's developments of the Greek philosophy paved the way for the renaissance and modernist philosophy, and was largely responsible for the 17th century's paradigm shift from teleology to causality.

When alchemy, geometry, and astronomy eventually gave birth to the seventeenth century modern science, philosophers started to call for dealing with natural phenomena through its own principles (*juxta propria principia*), with an increasingly popular pre-assumption that nature is nothing but a big mechanical machine that has no final purposes outside the realm of 'science.' The one grand 'purpose' that remained was for humans to 'control' the universe for their own benefit. Thus, modernist philosophy replaced the metaphysical idea of anthropocentrism (centrality of man), which was the basis of ancient teleological thinking, by another anthropocentrism idea, in which humans occupy the center due to their own activities and not to Providence. Teleology was seen as an idea that would hinder the progress of science. Hence, 'causality' started to play the role of the 'logical' and dominant method of thinking, and everything in nature, it was believed, was explainable through piecemeal cause-and-effect explanations. This meant that producing an effect is 'nothing but' the natural result of applying its cause. Modernist piecemeal analysts labelled any theory of purposeful or goal-seeking natural behavior or phenomenon as 'metaphysical,' mysterious, and outside the circle of logic and science.

'Islamic modernism,' which was by and large a reaction to European modernism, also endorsed the ideas of the centrality and supremacy of science. Yet, the Islamic mind was ready for the idea of causality more than any other mind, thanks to the pre-renaissance Islamic contributions to philosophy. Thus, Islamic modernism worked within the framework of modern science and the concept of causality in order to re-interpret or re-word the Islamic philosophy of religion. Thus, Islamic articles of faith were 're-interpreted' in order to fit the conclusions of (pre-twentieth century) science, and causality was the logic of modernist *kalām* (philosophy of religion). Mohammad Abdu's *Risālah al-Tawḥīd* is the clearest example of all the above changes in Islamic methodology (Chapter Five elaborates on Islamic modernism).

In the west, the second half of the twentieth century witnessed post-modernism's complete rejection of all modernist 'meta-narrations.' As Chapter Five explains, all streams of postmodernism agreed on the 'deconstruction of centricm.' Thus, according to postmodernists, the center should remain void of anything, whether it is science, man, the west, or even God. 'Rationality' itself, according to postmodernists, became an undesirable form of centrism and marginalization. 'Irrationality' became a desirable and 'moral' alternative.

'Islamic postmodernism,' in turn, utilised deconstructionist concepts in order to criticise central and basic Islamic articles of faith in a radical way. The 'centricity' of the Qur'an and the Prophet in Islam and the Islamic law was made subject to a 'free play of the opposites,' to borrow an expression from Derrida. Chapter Six will also elaborate on the different streams of 'Islamic' postmodernism and as well how they influenced some twentieth century Islamic Studies.

Towards an 'Islamic' Systems Philosophy

What concerns us in this chapter is systems philosophy as a rational and non-eurocentric 'post-postmodern' philosophy, and how Islamic philosophy and theory of Islamic law could make use of the progress in this new philosophy. Systems theory and philosophy emerged in the second half of the twentieth century as an anti-thesis of both modernist and postmodernist philosophies. Systems theorists and philosophers reject the modernist 'reductionist' view that all human experience could be analysed into indivisible causes and effects. On the other hand, systems philosophy also rejects postmodernist irrationality and deconstruction, which are 'meta-narrations' in their own right. Thus, according to systems philosophy, the universe is neither a huge deterministic machine nor a totally unknown being, complexity can be explained neither via a series of 'nothing-but' cause-and-effect operations nor via claims of 'non-logocentric irrationality,' and the problems of the world could be solved neither via more technological advances nor via some sort of nihilism. Hence, thanks to systems philosophy, the concept of 'purposefulness,' with all of its teleological shadows, was back to philosophical and scientific discourses.

'Islamic systems philosophy' is an idea that this book is trying to propose and promote. The proposed new Islamic philosophy could benefit from systems philosophy's critique of both modernism and postmodernism, in order to critique the Islamic versions of modernism and postmodernism.

As Chapter Six explains, a number of systems philosophical theories rejected the concept of God altogether, just because medieval and modernist theologians had proposed some cause-and-effect arguments for God. It is fair to say that arguments could be 'historicised,' if you wish, without necessarily historicising what was argued for. Hence, an Islamic systems philosophy could build on the conclusions of systems philosophy for the sake of 'updating' Islamic theological arguments. In my view, an updated proof of God's perfection of His creation should now rely on a systems approach rather than previous causality-based arguments. A systems approach is a holistic approach, in which an entity is dealt with as a whole system that consists of a number of sub-systems. There is a number of system features that govern the analysis of a system into its sub-system components, and also define how these sub-systems interact with each other and the outside environment.

The following arguments for the existence and magnificence of God, which I prefer to call proofs, are proposed briefly here, and are certainly opened to further investigation and exploration in light of Islamic scripts and universal concepts.

1. The proof of complexity: The 'inherent complexity' in the design of the universe cannot be explained without a Synthesiser.
2. The proof of purposeful behavior: The directed and purposeful physiochemical behavior in nature, which all of its systems and sub-systems illustrate, is a proof of a Designer of this system.
3. The proof of regulation: Living creatures' mechanisms of regulation despite the infinite number of 'disturbances,' is another proof for inherent design and intelligence in the universe.
4. The proof of order: The high-level design in the order of natural processes and the many steps in each of these processes is another proof.
5. The proof of organismic analogy: The incredible similarities between tiny organisms, animals, plants, human bodies, societies, and large-scale civilizations, is another systematic proof for God's creation. This concept is already known in the Islamic literature as *al-sunan al-ilāhiyyah* (the divine natural laws).

The above systems approach to the Islamic *ʿaqīdah* (creed), however briefly mentioned here, is a basis for the systems approach to the Islamic law and its philosophy, which is proposed later in this book.

Are Systems 'Real' or Mental Creations?

Since the concept of systems is going to be of ultimate importance for us, the following question should be asked: What is a system; is the world created in terms of 'systems' or is a system a matter of constructed imagination? Another way to put this ontological question is to ask about the relationship between the 'physical' and the 'mental' in our human experience. The two typical answers to this question reflect typical realist and nominal tendencies, where physical 'reality' is objective and external to individual consciousness, or, otherwise, subjective and a product of individual mental consciousness, respectively.[1] Therefore, a typical 'identity' answer implies that our experience with systems represents the 'truth' about the world, and a typical 'duality' answer entails that systems are only in our minds and are completely unrelated to the physical world.[2]

Systems theory presents a middle road between the above two views by proposing 'correlation' as the nature of the relation between systems and the world, i.e., our mental cognition of the outside world in terms of systems 'correlates' with what is there.[3] Therefore, according to this theory, a system does not necessarily identify with existing things in the real world but is rather a 'way of organising our thoughts about the real world.'[4] Accordingly, a system would be 'anything unitary enough to deserve a name.'[5] This is not a 'fictionalist view of reality,' as some people describe it,[6] because any view of what we call 'reality' in terms of any system is a matter of 'cognition,' systems theory proposes.[7] After all, that is how we are able to change our theories on science over the centuries, without necessarily representing actual changes in physical realities. And this is how some critique is proposed here based on what I will call 'the cognitive nature of the Islamic law.'

2.2. A SYSTEMS APPROACH TO ANALYSIS

Traditions of 'Decompositional' Analysis

The word 'analysis' has its roots in the ancient Greek term '*analusis*,' which means 'loosening up' or 'dissolution.'[8] Common understanding of the meaning of 'analysis,' as most dictionaries show, entails some 'resolution into simpler elements' or 'breaking into more simple parts.'[9] In philosophy, however, analysis is a central philosophical concept that has been defined in as many ways as the number of distinct schools of philosophy. Some attempts were made in order to classify methods of analysis into distinct categories. For example, the *Stanford Encyclopaedia of Philosophy* classified methods of analysis into decompositional, regressive, and interpretive modes.[10] However, none of these modes was explicitly endorsed by any philosopher or school of philosophy, and each of these modes could rightly be explained in terms of any of the other two.[11] Therefore, I will mention classic methods of analysis below in terms of a tradition of 'decomposition,' which is part of the cause-and-effect tradition that was explained above.

The concept of 'decomposition' has its roots in ancient methods of Greek philosophy and geometry. In Pappus's *Mathematical Collection* which was composed based on centuries of development in Geometry after Euclid's *Elements*, analysis was described as follows: 'we suppose the thing sought as being and as being true, and then we pass through its concomitants[12] in order, as though they were true and existent by hypothesis, to something admitted; then, if that which is admitted be true, the thing sought is true, too, and the proof will be the reverse of analysis.'[13] The central tool here is the decomposition of the required-to-prove into its basic constituents in a number of iterative steps. Then, the 'regressive' proof presented is based on these decomposition steps.

In Plato's version of analysis, 'classificatory trees' were developed. Plato created these trees by 'dividing a genus into its constituent species' through a series of dichotomies.[14] Aristotle's *Analytics* was an in-kind development in the method of division or decomposition, in which he developed the concept of 'structure.'[15] He started his analyses by constructing classificatory trees of arguments into their various logical elements. Then, he studied their structure by elaborating on the elements' 'syllogistic' relationships.[16]

Plato's and Aristotle's methods of decomposition had a great impact on human thought over the past two millennia, which was manifested in various ways. Examples are Ibn Rushd's 'divisions of categories,'[17] Aquinas's '*resolutio*,'[18] Descartes's 'reduction to simplest terms,'[19] Locke's resolution of ideas into simple 'sense impressions,'[20] Leibniz's reduction of propositions into 'self-evident truths,'[21] Kant's subclasses of 'synthetic *apriori* truths,' Fredge's 'logical analysis,' Russell's 'deductive chains,' and even Wittgenstein's 'grammatical investigation.'[22]

Despite the wide variety and sophistication of the above-mentioned philosophical analysis methods, all forms of the decompositional tradition are criticised, by contemporary systems theorists/philosophers, for their (1) partial/atomistic orientation, (2) traditional logic, and (3) static perspective. Partial views (1) represent a general feature of philosophy and science up until systems approaches were proposed in modern time. Some holistic views appeared occasionally, for example, in Aristotle's metaphysical vision of nature's 'hierarchic order' or Hegel's proposition that 'the whole is more than the sum of its parts.'[23] However, the general orientation of philosophical analysis was partial rather than holistic which makes it subject to a great deal of inaccuracy in its drawn conclusions. In terms of logic (2), when 'structure' was included in philosophical analysis, the focus was on the simple logical relations between specific elements rather than the logic, function, or purpose of the structure as a whole. It is true that Russell's deductive chains brought the logic of Aristotle's syllogistic structures up to date with modern times. However, logic, since the time of Russell, had undergone major changes that ought to be included in analytical studies.[24] Moreover, structure today is understood in terms of one form or the other of 'synergy,'[25] rather than mere linear logical relations. Finally, decompositional analysis focuses on static relationships (3) between elements and often overlooks their dynamics of change, which have a great impact on the overall performance of any paradigm. Contemporary systems analysis gives the 'dynamics of change' specific attention.[26] Next, I will introduce systems analysis as a more effective alternative to decompositional analysis.

Systems Analysis

Systems analysis is based on the definition of systems itself,[27] i.e., the analyst assumes that the analysed entity is 'a system.' Thus, analysis entails identifying the entity's features, as pre-defined in the analyst's theory for systems. This is how systems theory and systems analysis are related. A common definition of a system is, 'a set of interacting units or elements that form an integrated whole intended to perform some function.'[28] Thus, systematic analysis typically involves the identification of units, elements, or sub-systems, and how these units are interrelated and integrated in processes or functions.[29] Whitehead, for example, describes the concept of analysis as, 'the evocation of insight by the hypothetical suggestions of thought, and the evocations of thought by the activities of direct insight. In this process, the composite whole, the interrelations, and the things related, concurrently emerge into clarity.'[30] Uncovering these interrelations is what will reveal 'the whole' of the analysed system and take analysis beyond the atomistic and static views of 'decompositional analysis.' Systems analysis is gaining popularity and has been recently applied to a large number of fields of knowledge.[31]

However, I argue that despite its advantages over decompositional analysis and the large number of applications it now deals with, systems analysis is still underdeveloped compared to systems theory itself. There is a wealth of research on the concept of 'system' in systems theory that has not been utilised in systematic analysis. Current methods are still based on the above simple and common definition of a system as a 'set of interacting units,'[32] and hence missing a large number of system features that could be of great use to analysis. Next I will elaborate on a number of these definitions and features, with a purpose of presenting new criteria for systems analysis that are best suited to the analytical task at hand.

Now, given the assumption that the analysed entity is a 'system,' the analysis process proceeds to examine the features of that system. There are numerous theories of the general features of systems. I will outline some of these theories next. The system features surveyed below are rather abstract and written in a 'natural sciences' language. Yet, I find this survey necessary in order to be able to elect a few system features that are most suitable to this book's objectives.

Theories of System Features

I had previously proposed that 'efficient' systems must maintain the features of goal-orientation, openness, cooperation between sub-systems, hierarchical structure, and balance between decomposition and integration.[33] However, I will propose in this section a more comprehensive set of systems features based on the following survey of related literature. Keep in mind the relationship between these features and the (Islamic) theological arguments and the concepts of 'Designer' and 'Synthesiser' (with a capital D and S) of the majestic system of this universe, which I had proposed in the previous section of this chapter.

Bertalanffy, the 'father of systems theory,' outlined a number of features or characteristics for systems.[34] The following is a summary.

1. Holism: Holistic properties, which are not possible to detect by analysis, should be possible to define in a system. Holism is an important feature of systems that was also extensively explored by Smuts,[35] Litterer,[36] and de Saussure.[37]

2. Goal-seeking: Systemic interaction must result in reaching some goal or final state, or arriving at some equilibrium.
3. Interrelationship and interdependence of objects and their attributes: unrelated and independent elements can never constitute a system.
4. Inputs and outputs: In a closed system, the inputs are determined once and for all. In an open system, additional inputs are admitted from its environment. A 'living system' has to be an open system.
5. Transformation: All systems, if they are to attain their goal, must transform some 'inputs' into some 'outputs.' In living systems, this transformation is mainly of a cyclical nature.
6. Regulation: The interrelated objects constituting the system must be regulated in some fashion so that its goals can be realized. Regulation implies that necessary deviations will be detected and corrected. Feedback is therefore a requisite of effective control. Surviving open systems should maintain a stable state of dynamic equilibrium.
7. Hierarchy: Systems are generally complex wholes made up of smaller subsystems. This nesting of systems within other systems is what is implied by hierarchy.
8. Differentiation: In complex systems, specialised units perform specialised functions. This is characteristic of all complex systems that is also called specialisation or division of labor.
9. Equifinality and multifinality: This feature entails attaining the same objectives via equally valid alternative ways, or from a given initial state, and obtaining different and mutually exclusive objectives.
10. Entropy: This is the amount of disorder or randomness present in any system. All non-living systems tend towards disorder; left alone they will eventually lose all motion and degenerate into an inert mass. When this permanent stage is reached and no events occur, maximum entropy is attained. A living system can, for a finite time, avert this process by importing energy from its environment. It is then said to create what is called 'negentropy,' which is characteristic of all kinds of life. Hence, Hitchins defined a system to be a 'collection of interrelated entities such that both

the collection and the interrelationships together reduce local entropy.'[38]

Katz and Kahn defined an open system according to the following set of features: importation of energy, information input, throughput, output, cycles of events, negative entropy, coding process, equilibrium, differentiation (elaboration), integration (coordination), and equifinality (as defined by Bertalanffy).[39]

Ackoff defined systems in terms of sets of two or more elements that satisfy the following three conditions:[40]

1. The behavior of each element has an effect on the behavior of the whole.
2. The behavior of the elements and their effects on the whole are interdependent.
3. However subgroups of the elements are formed, all have an effect on the behavior of the whole, but none has an independent effect on it.

Churchman, who was another leading systems theorist, proposed the following characteristic features of a system:[41]

1. It is teleological (purposeful).
2. It has parts (components) that in themselves have purpose.
3. Its performance can be determined.
4. It has a user or users.
5. It is embedded in an environment.
6. It includes a decision maker who is internal to the system and who can change the performance of the parts.
7. There is a designer who is concerned with the structure of the system and whose conceptualisation of the system can direct the actions of the decision maker and ultimately affect the end result of the actions of the entire system.
8. The designer's purpose is to change a system so as to maximise its value to the user.
9. The designer ensures that the system is stable to the extent that he or she knows its structure and function.

Boulding elaborated on the feature of 'order,'[42] which was proposed as a theological argument in the previous section. Boulding proposed that order, regularity and non-randomness are 'naturally' preferable to lack of order, irregularity and randomness, and that orderliness makes the world good, interesting and attractive to the systems theorist. He further considered the search for order and law, via quantification and mathematisation, to be valuable aids for establishing order. Bowler focused on hierarchy and levels in his proposed general system features, which are presented below.[43]

1. The universe is a hierarchy of systems; that is, simple systems are synthesised into more complex systems from subatomic particles to civilisations.
2. All systems, or forms of organisation, have some characteristics in common, and it is assumed that statements concerning these characteristics are universally applicable generalisations.
3. All levels of systems have novel characteristics that apply universally upward in the hierarchy to more complex levels but not downward to simpler levels.
4. It is possible to identify relational universals that are applicable to all systems at all levels of existence.
5. Every system has a set of boundaries that indicates some degree of differentiation between what is included and excluded in the system.
6. Everything that exists, whether formal, existential, or psychological, is an organised system of energy, matter, and information.
7. The universe consists of processes synthesising systems of systems and disintegrating systems of systems. It will continue in its present form as long as one set of processes does not eliminate the other.

Maturana and Varela proposed that a necessary feature for a living system is its capacity for 'autopoiesis,' or self-renewal. This feature allows living systems to be autonomous. The activities of autonomous systems are mainly directed inwards, with the sole aim of preserving its autonomy.[44] Luhmann utilised the autopoiesis concept in his proposal for 'law as a social system,' in order for the law to respond to 'the part of its environment selected by its norms,' and changes itself 'through internally linked communications,' and hence, 'preserves its autonomy.'[45] Gharajedaghi proposed five systems principles that he learnt through management of business organisations, namely, openness, purposefulness, multidimensionality, counter-intuitiveness, and emergent properties.[46] Hitchins proposed that the 'philosophy of systems engineering' is based on the fundamentals of 'holism,' 'openness,' and 'synthesism.'[47]

Koestler presents a hierarchic view, expressed in the *holon* (wholeness) feature, which entails that wholes and parts do not have separate existences in living organisms or social organisations. Their integrative and self-assertive tendencies exist side by side and are reflected in their 'cooperative' behavior.[48] I had previously proposed that this 'cooperative behavior' results in maximizing the utilization of the information available inside systems.[49]

Weaver classified systems according to the feature of complexity, as follows:

1. Organised complexity: A typical form of organised complexity is a living system.
2. Unorganised complexity: This type refers to non-living systems where the number of variables is very large and each variable has a totally unpredictable or unknown behavior.
3. Organised simplicity: This type refers to simple systems, such as machines, which have a small number of components.[50]

Simon classified systems in terms of the feature of 'decomposition,' as follows:[51]

1. Decomposable system: subsystems can be regarded as independent of one another.
2. Near-decomposable system: interaction between subsystems is weak but not negligible.
3. Non-decomposable system: directly dependent on other systems or explicitly affect them.

Ackoff classified systems in terms of their goals, as follows[52]:

1. Goal-maintaining system, which attempts to fulfil a pre-determined goal.
2. Goal-seeking system, which considers choices concerning how to deal with variable behavior in the system. Previous behavior stored in a simple memory permits changes based on learning.
3. Multigoal-seeking system, which is capable of choosing from an internal repertoire of actions in response to changed external conditions. Such automatic goal changing demands distinct alternatives; generally the system decides which means of achievement are best.
4. Goal changing system, which reflects upon decisions made. Information collected and stored in the memory is examined for the creation of new alternatives for action. Will, purpose, autonomy, 'feedforward' mechanism, learning, and consciousness define this process, existing only within living systems.

Jordan also classified systems based on three features, namely, structural versus functional, purposive versus non-purposive, and mechanistic versus organismic, as follows:[53]

1. Structural, purposive, mechanistic, such as a road network.
2. Structural, purposive, organismic, such as a suspension bridge.
3. Structural, non-purposive, mechanistic, such as for instance, a mountain range.
4. Structural, non-purposive, organismic, such as a bubble (or any physical system in equilibrium).
5. Functional, purposive, mechanistic, such as a production line (where a breakdown in one machine does not affect the other machines).
6. Functional, purposive, organismic, such as a living organism.
7. Functional, non-purposive, mechanistic, such as the changing flow of water as a result of a change in the river bed.
8. Functional, non-purposive, organismic, such as a the space/time continuum.

Beer presented a 'viable system model' based on four principles of organisation.[54]

1. The first principle of organisation: Variety, diffusing through an institutional system, tends to equate; it should be designed to do so with minimum cost.
2. The second principle of organisation: Channels carrying information between the management unit, the operation and the environment must each have a higher capacity than the generating subsystem.
3. The third principle of organisation: Whenever the information carried on a channel crosses a boundary, it undergoes transduction; the variety of the transducer must be at least equivalent to the variety of the channel.
4. The fourth principle of organisation: The operation of the first three principles must constantly recur through time, and without lag.

Skyttner proposes the following twenty general features, which he argued are valid for all kinds of systems:[55]

1. System holism principle: A system has holistic properties not manifested by any of its parts. The parts also have properties not manifested by the system as a whole.
2. Suboptimalisation principle: If each subsystem, regarded separately, is made to operate with maximum efficiency, the system as a whole will not operate with utmost efficiency.
3. Darkness principle: No system can be known completely.
4. Eighty-twenty principle: In any large, complex system, eighty percent of the output will be produced by only twenty percent of the system.
5. Hierarchy principle: Complex natural phenomena are organised in hierarchies wherein each level is made up of several integrated systems.
6. Redundancy of resources principle: Maintenance of stability under conditions of disturbance requires redundancy of critical resources.

7. Redundancy of potential command principle: In any complex decision network, the potential to act effectively is conferred by an adequate concatenation of information.
8. Relaxation time principle: System stability is possible only if the system's relaxation time is shorter than the mean time between disturbances.
9. Negative feedback causality principle: Given negative feedback, a system's equilibrium state is invariant over a wide range of initial conditions.
10. Positive feedback causality principle: Given positive feedback in a system, radically different end states are possible from the same initial conditions.
11. Homeostasis principle: A system survives only so long as all essential variables are maintained within their physiological limits.
12. Steady-state principle: For a system to be in a state of equilibrium, all subsystems must be in equilibrium. All subsystems being in a state of equilibrium, the system must be in equilibrium.
13. Self-organising systems principle: Complex systems organise themselves, and their characteristic structural and behavioral patterns are mainly a result of interaction between the subsystems.
14. Basins of stability principle: Complex systems have basins of stability separated by thresholds of instability. A system dwelling on a ridge will suddenly return to the state in a basin.
15. Viability principle: Viability is a function of the proper balance between autonomy of subsystems and their integration within the whole system, or of the balance between stability and adaptation.
16. First cybernetic control principle: Successful implicit control must be a continuous and automatic comparison of behavioral characteristics against a standard. It must be followed by continuous and automatic feedback of corrective action.
17. Second cybernetic control principle: In implicit control, control is synonymous with communication.
18. Third cybernetic control principle: In implicit control, variables are brought back into control in the act of, and by the act of, going out of control.
19. The feedback principle: The result of behavior is always scanned and its success or failure modifies future behavior.

20. The maximum power principle: Those systems that survive in competition between alternative choices are those that develop more power inflow and use it to meet the needs of survival.

The feature of hierarchy in systems inspired a range of general classifications of systems and sub-systems, where specific features were given to each level of the hierarchy. I shall now explain further.

Theories of System Hierarchies

Systems theorists attempted to define abstract levels of hierarchy in systems in general, and studied the relationship between these levels. Fivaz puts the knowledge about levels in an 'evolutionary paradigm,' in which the understanding of systemic qualities and behavior on a certain level entails the study of the levels above and below the chosen level.[56] According to Boulding, the levels in the 'hierarchy of systems complexity' are mechanical, cybernetic, positive feedback, creodic, reproductive, demographic, ecological, evolutionary, human, social, and transcendental, in this sequence.[57] Miller viewed the levels in the hierarchy of 'living systems' as: cells, organs, organisms, groups, organisations, communities, societies, and supranational systems.[58] Miller also proposed a general hierarchy of 'information processing systems,' which includes: reproducer, boundary, ingestor, distributor, converter, producer, storage, extruder, motor, supporter, input transducer, internal transducer, channel, timer, decoder, associator, memory, decider, encoder, and output transducer.[59] Lovelock has a similar classification, which he called 'processing levels.'[60] Kirchner proposed a theory for the whole universal/Gaia system, in which levels of the hierarchy are organised from weak to strong as follows: influential Gaia, co-evolutionary Gaia, homeostatic Gaia, teleological Gaia, and optimising Gaia.[61] De Chardin has an alternative mind/noosphere theory, in which the levels in the hierarchy are energy, matter, life, instincts, thoughts, and noosphere.[62] Laszlo proposed parallel levels, which extend across space, technology, science, communication, and forms of government, as Chart 2.1 (a) shows.[63] Salk divided 'categories of nature' into units, binary components, and disciplines (Chart 2.1. (b)).[64]

Klir proposed an 'epistemological systems hierarchy,' in which the levels are concerned with data, models, structure, and meta-systems, in order.[65] Cook proposed 'control centers' on the five following levels: the atomic level, the cellular level, the brain level, the family level, and the government level.[66] Checkland proposed a systems typology of subatomic systems, atomic systems, and molecular systems. These levels give rise to non-living systems (crystals, rocks and minerals), and living systems (single cells, plants, animals, and ecologies).[67] Powers proposed a 'control theory' that defines the levels of 'core of control' from intensity to spiritual phenomena, passing through the levels of sensation, configuration, transitions, sequence, relationships, programmes, principles, and system concepts.[68]

From a systems theoretical, cognition-based, and multidimensional point of view, all of the above theories for features and hierarchies are valid views of systems. As such, this book is dealing with fundamentals of Islamic law as a 'system' which interacts with the scripts and life realities, and produces rulings and guidelines. This system includes a hierarchy of sub-systems which deal with various topics of the 'fundamentals.' Nevertheless, none of the above theories could be fully endorsed for the sake of the analysis carried out in this work, for the following reasons.

(a)

	Space	**Technology**	**Science**	**Communi-cations**	**Goverment**
1.	Cave/tent	Human energy		Pictograms	Family, hunting
2.	Village	Animal energy	Protoscience	Ideograms	Tribal level
3.	Town	Metal tools	Mathematics	Writing	Theocratic politics
4.	City	Machine technology	Newtonian	Machine transmission	National state system
5.	'Ecumenopolis'	Cybernetics	Einsteinian relativity	Electrical transmission	Sovereignty invested in global mankind

(b)

Unit	Binary Components	Discipline
Collective mind	Culture/society	Sociometabiology
Mind	Intuition/reason	Metabiology
Organism	Species/individual	Socio-biology
Cell	Gene/soma	Biology
Atom	Nucleus/electrons	Chemistry
Particle	Energy/mass	Physics
Form	Continuous/discrete	Mathematics
Order	Non-manifest/manifest	Metaphysics

Chart 2.1. (a) Laszlo's parallel hierarchies. (b) Salk's hierarchy of the 'categories of nature.'

First, most of the above theories were primarily oriented to the physical world of matter and, hence, not applicable to our investigation in the world of philosophy and law. Examples are Katz and Kahn's 'importation of energy' and 'coding,' Bowler's 'matter' component of 'any system,' Beer's principles which involved 'cost' and 'management units,' and Boulding's search for order via 'quantification and mathematisation.' Similarly, Churchman assumed a 'human designer' for all systems. Skyttner's features, which he argued are 'valid for all kinds of systems,' involved features that do not apply to many systems, including our proposed system of Islamic law. Example features are redundancy of resources, physiological limits, internal communication, and power inflow. Maturana and Varela's idea of 'self-renewal' for living systems does apply to the Islamic law, as far as this book is concerned. However, as will be shown later, this renewal (*tajdīd*) comes from the law's openness to and interaction with the outside environment, not from 'autonomous activities that are directed inwards,' as was the case in the *autopoiesis* process, which Luhmann adopted for his theory of the law. Furthermore, there are numerous proposed 'universal' system levels that do not apply to our topic, such as the levels of mechanical, reproductive, demographic, ecological, cells, organs, organisms, memory, channel, timer, decoder, and motor.

Second, many of the above classifications were binary and one-dimensional, contrary to the multidimensional universal feature of systems, rightly proposed by Gharajedaghi and others. One example is Weaver's 'complex' versus 'simple' dichotomy, even though 'degrees of complexity' could present a more realistic feature. Another example is Bertalanffy's, Jordan's, Salk's and Checkland's classification of all systems into living (i.e., in a biological sense) versus non-living, neither of which applies to systems in the realm of social sciences or humanities. Finally, systems theories that addressed one aspect only, such as holism, interrelationships, hierarchy, or decomposition, do not capture all the dimensions that analysis is supposed to tackle. Therefore, I decided to propose a novel set of system features that will be utilised in this work's systematic analysis, and which could also be useful in other analyses of theological, social, and legal systems.

Proposed System Features

This book will assume that the set of fundamentals of Islamic law (*uṣūl al-fiqh*) is a 'system,' which will be analysed according to a set of features. Here I am suggesting a number of features for this system and will argue for each from two perspectives: systems theory and Islamic theology. The systematic analyses presented here will, then, revolve around the six following system features: cognitive nature of systems, wholeness, openness, interrelated hierarchy, multi-dimensionality, and purposefulness.

Cognitive Nature of the System of Islamic Law

From a systems theory perspective, 'correlation,' as explained previously, is the systems' philosophical middle ground between realists' 'identity' and nominalists' 'duality,' i.e., in order to best describe the relationship between mentally hypothesised systems and reality. The 'cognitive nature of systems' is another expression of this correlation. A hypothesised system of the Islamic law, in our case, is a construction in the jurist's cognitive faculty, or '*fī dhihn al-faqīh*,' to use Ibn Taymiyah's expression of the same concept.[69]

From an Islamic theological perspective, Islamic law (fiqh) is a result of human reasoning and reflection (ijtihad) upon the scripts attempting to uncover its hidden meanings or practical implications. Islamic jurists and theologians maintained that, 'God is not to be called a *faqīh* (jurist or lawyer), because nothing is hidden from Him.'[70] Therefore, Islamic law (fiqh, that is) is a matter of human cognition (*idrāk*)[71] and understanding (*fahm*),[72] rather than a literal manifestation of God's commands. Al-Eini explains: 'Fiqh is an understanding. Understanding requires good perception. And perception is a force by which one could associate holistic pictures and meanings to mental cognition (*idrāk ᶜaqlī*).'[73] Al-Bayḍawī wrote: 'Precisely, fiqh is a probable perception (*ẓann*) rather than confirmed knowledge (*ᶜilm*), which is at a different level, because the belief that a certain ruling is so and so according to God is a claim that is impossible to verify.'[74] The feature of the 'cognitive nature of the Islamic law' is necessary for validating a much-needed pluralistic view towards all schools of Islamic law, as will be elaborated later.

Wholeness of the System of Islamic Law

From a systems theoretic perspective, it was explained above that the main advantage of systematic analysis over 'decompositional' analysis is its holistic, versus partial/atomistic, approach. Partial cause-and-effect thinking was a general feature of human thinking until modern time, as explained in the previous section. Currently, however, research in natural and social sciences is widely moving from 'piecemeal analysis,' classic equations, and logical statements, to the explanations of all phenomena in terms of holistic systems.[75] Even basic physical phenomena, such as space/time and body/mind, cannot be split empirically, according to today's science.[76] Systems theory views every cause-and-effect relation as one part of a whole picture, in which groups of relations result in new emerging properties and combine to form a 'whole' that is more than a simple 'sum of the parts.'

Based on theological and 'rational' arguments, the juridical authority (*hujjiyyah*) of what jurists called 'the holistic evidence' (*al-dalīl al-*

kullī) is considered one of the fundamentals (*uṣūl*) of the Islamic law[77] which jurists had given priority over 'single and partial rulings.'[78] Developing systematic and holistic thinking for the fundamentals of Islamic law (*uṣūl al-fiqh*) will be useful for Islamic philosophy of law, in order to develop the semantics of causes-and-effects into a more holistic language. A holistic approach will also be useful for Islamic philosophy of religion (*ʿilm al-kalām*), in order to develop its language of causes-and-effects into a more systematic language, including proofs for the existence of God, as outlined earlier.

Openness of the System of Islamic Law

Systems theorists differentiated between open and closed systems. 'Living systems' must be open systems, they maintained.[79] This applies to living organisms as well as any system that is to 'survive.'[80] It was mentioned above that Bertalanffy linked the features of openness and purposefulness with his system feature of 'equifinality,' which means that open systems have the ability of reaching the same objectives from different initial conditions via equally valid alternatives. These 'initial conditions' come from the environment. Thus, an open system interacts with the environment outside the system, unlike closed systems which are isolated from the environment.

The system of the Islamic law is an 'open' system, in the above sense. A few jurists, however, are still calling for the 'closure of the door of ijtihad (new juridical reasoning) on the *uṣūl* (theoretical) level,'[81] which would, effectively, transform the Islamic law into a 'closed system,' and which would eventually cause the Islamic law to 'die,' to go along with the metaphor. However, all known schools of Islamic law and the vast majority of jurists over the centuries have concurred that ijtihad is necessary for the Islamic law because '(specific) scripts are limited and events are unlimited.'[82] Thus, the fundamental methodology of Islamic law has developed certain mechanisms for dealing with new events or, in systems theoretical terminology, 'interacting with the environment.' Examples of these mechanisms are analogical reasoning (*qiyās*), interest (*maṣlaḥah*), and accommodating customs/traditions (*iʿtibār al-ʿurf*). However, it will be shown that these mechanisms are in need of more development in order to give the Islamic law enough 'flexibility' to be able to deal with today's rapidly changing circumstances. Hence, the mechanisms and degrees of 'openness' will be one of the features used in developing and critically analysing the Islamic *uṣūl* system and its subsystems.

Interrelated Hierarchy of the System of Islamic Law

Analysing entities in terms of hierarchy is a common approach between systematic and decompositional methods. The previous subsection surveyed a number of suggested 'universal' levels in hierarchies and concluded that they were tailored to specific environments. I will refer here to the theory of 'categorisation' in cognitive science, in an attempt to outline a universal classification strategy that is suitable for the subject at hand. Categorisation is the process of treating distinct entities, scattered over a multi-dimensional 'feature space,' as equivalent and belonging to the same group or category.[83] It is one of the most fundamental cognitive activities, through which humans understand information they receive, make generalisations and predictions, and name and assess various items and ideas.[84] According to cognitive science, there are two alternative theoretical explanations of human categorisations, which represent, in my view, two alternative methods of categorisation itself. These alternative methods are categorisations based on 'feature similarity' and 'mental concepts.'[85]

Feature-based categorisations attempt to discover 'natural' similarities and differences between categorised entities. Similarity or difference between two entities is measured according to how much they match or differ in terms of certain pre-defined 'features' or characteristics.[86] Items are judged to belong to a certain category via matching their features with the features of an 'ideal prototype.'[87]

On the other hand, concept-based categorisations define categories based on mental concepts, rather than feature similarities. A mental concept is an underlying principle or theory in the classifier's perception, which includes a complex combination of causal and explanatory links represented in a structured framework. A concept is not a simple true-or-false feature, but a group of multidimensional criteria, which could create a number of simultaneous categorisations for the same number of entities. A concept also implies a range of 'rough,' 'vague' or 'soft,' rather than 'hard' categories,[88] i.e., the line between categories is not a clear number or measure, but a perception that could differ, within a 'reasonable' range, from one person to another.[89]

Feature-based classifications are criticised for a number of limitations that concept-based classifications do not have. The following are theoretical reasons behind preferring concept over feature-based categorisation methods, which will be used, later, in criticising traditional (feature-based) categorisation of schools of Islamic law.

i) Concept-based methods are integrative and systematic methods, unlike feature-based methods, which deal with entities as lists of unconnected attributes or features, and hence, miss a lot of significant analytical information.
ii) Feature-based methods might lead to overgeneralisations by abstracting a great deal of information into simplistic decisions of existence or non-existence of one or more features.
iii) Feature-based classifications do not allow ranges, or multi-level rankings, because they are based on a 'pigeon-hole' true-or-false method.
iv) In order to keep the homogeneity of the categorising features, important non-binary factors could sometimes be ignored.

In this book, concept-based categorisations will be applied to the fundamentals of Islamic law and feature-based categorisations will be criticised. However, analysis will not stop at the resulting 'tree-structure' hierarchy, but will also extend to analyse the interrelationships between the resulting sub-concepts. This consideration of 'structure' will not abide by formal logical analysis, such as Aristotle's syllogism and Russell's deductive chains, but will focus on 'decision-making procedures' in the practical *fiqhī* implementation of these concepts.

Multi-Dimensionality of the System of Islamic Law

Dimensionality in systems terminology has two 'dimensions,' namely, rank and level. Rank of dimensionality is the number of dimensions in the 'space' under consideration. Level of dimensionality is the possible number of levels/intensities in one dimension. Popular philosophical investigation tends to think in terms of one dimension and two levels. Phenomena and even ideas with 'opposing tendencies' are usually seen in terms of one factor only, and hence, appear 'contradictory' rather than 'complementary,' and are analysed as 'zero-sum' games rather than 'win-win' games.[90] Thus, phenomena and ideas are always expressed in terms of dichotomies that seem to be 'opposite,' such as, religion/science, empirical/rational, physical/metaphysical, realist/nominalist, deductive/inductive, universal/specific, collectivity/individuality, teleological/deontological, mind/matter, objective/subjective, and so on. The above dichotomies represent one-dimensional single-rank thinking, in which consideration is given to one factor only, even though these pairs could be seen 'complementary' in other dimensions. For example, science and religion, in their popular conceptions, could be contradictory in terms of the centrality of the concept of the 'Divine command,' but they could be complementary in terms of aiming to achieve human happiness, in terms of attempting to explain the origins of life, and so forth. Mind and matter could be viewed as contradictory in terms of their relation with sensual data, but they could also be viewed as complementary in terms of theories of cognitive/ brain science and 'smart' machines, or artificial intelligence. And so on.

Additionally, lack of multi-dimensionality manifests in popular two-level judgements of opposing tendencies, which are better viewed

Chart 2.2. A gray-scale picture distorts the variety of detail of a colored picture. Its two-color 'distortion,' however, filters out a great deal of information. In this example, viewing the two-color picture alone creates an interesting puzzle.

as furthermost points on a continuum or spectrum of points. Hence, human thinking is often confined to false binary choices, such as, certain/uncertain, win/lose, black/white, low/high, or good/bad. In a single-rank dimension of color, for example, white and black should rather be seen as the extreme ends of an infinite number of grey levels (refer to Chart 2.2 for an illustration).

Systematic analysis, presented later, will show that reasoning in traditional schools of Islamic law involved a great deal of one- dimensional and binary thinking. One-dimensional methods consider only one factor in a given juridical case (*mas'alah*). Hence, the vast majority of legal opinions (*fatāwā*) were issued based on single evidences (often called: *dalīl al-mas'alah*, or 'the evidence of the case'), even though there is always a variety of evidences (*adillah*) that could apply to the same case and imply different outcomes or rulings. This is a standalone topic that is discussed in traditional and contemporary literature on fundamentals of fiqh under the title, 'disagreement between evidences' (*taᶜāruḍ al-adillah*). The method of 'conciliation between evidences' (*al-jamᶜ bayn al-adillah*) is an example of multi-dimensional methodology, which will be further developed in Chapter Six.

On the other hand, binary judgements, such as, obligatory/unlawful (*wājib/ḥarām*), abrogating/abrogated (*nāsikh/mansūkh*), truthful/fraudulent (*ṣaḥīḥ/fāsid*), exact/illusionary (*munḍabiṭ/mawhūm*), and so on, limited the ability of Islamic law to take into consideration cases in the 'grey area' between these extreme points. Analysis will show how some schools of Islamic law suggested 'intermediate categories' to expand popular binary classifications, and how they contributed to a sense of realism and flexibility in the Islamic law.

Purposefulness of the System of Islamic Law

Goal-orientation and purposefulness were common features in the system theories presented above. However, Gharajedaghi, following Ackoff, differentiated between goals (Arabic: *ahdāf*) and purposes (Arabic: *ghāyāt* or *maqāṣid*). He considered an entity to be purposeful if it can produce '(1) the same outcome in different ways in the same environment, and (2) different outcomes in the same or different environments.'[91] Therefeore, goal-seeking systems mechanically produce their outcomes following the same means, given the same environments, and do not have choices or options to change their means in order to reach the same goal. Purpose-seeking systems, on the other hand, could follow a variety of means to achieve the same end or purpose. Moreover, goal-seeking systems could not produce different outcomes for the same environment because their outcomes are more or less 'pre-programmed.' Nevertheless, purpose-seeking systems could produce different outcomes for the very same environment as long as these different outcomes achieve the desired purposes. 'Purposefulness,' in the above sense, will be endorsed in this book as one of the features that apply to the fundamentals of Islamic law, as a whole, as well as to all of its levels and elements.

From a theological perspective, 'causation' in 'divine actions' was the subject of long philosophical/theological (*kalāmī*) debates. The question was whether 'God's actions have to have causes behind them' (*taʿlīl afʿāl Allāh*) or not. It is important to note that the concept of 'causes' (*ʿilal/asbāb*) was not differentiated, as far as *kalām* literature was concerned, from the concept of 'purposes' (*aghrāḍ/maqāṣid/ ḥikam*)[92]. These two concepts were differentiated, however, in the area of practical rulings (fiqh)[93]. *Taʿlīl* theological debates are relevant to our study since the Islamic law itself is theologically a result of one of these 'divine actions,' which is revelation and the '*aghrāḍ*' behind the law are, then, *maqāṣid al-sharīʿah*. Thus, the question is: Did God have a purpose behind revealing the law? *Kalāmiyyūn*/Theologians gave three different answers to this question.

(i) Divine actions 'must' have causes/purposes. Muʿtazilīs and Shia (with some exceptions) divided all actions into 'embellished' (*ḥassan*) and 'repugnant' (*qabīḥ*) actions.[94] Most of them believed that one of these two features is 'intrinsic' (*dhātī*) in every action and not subject to changing circumstances. They believed that human reason is capable of 'judging' embellishment and repugnance (*al-taḥsīn wal-taqbīḥ*) independently. And since these definitions are the result of 'rationality,' Muʿtazilīs considered them universal and, thus, applied them to human beings and to God too (based on their 'principle of justice'). For human beings, embellished actions are 'obligations' and repugnant actions are 'forbidden.' In terms of God, embellished actions are actions that 'He must do,' and repugnant actions are 'impossible for Him to do,' in their words. They also believed that an action without a purpose (*gharaḍ*) is nonsense/meaningless (*ᶜabath*) and, thus, repugnant. Therefore, they judged that all of God's actions are necessarily 'purposeful.'[95]

(ii) Divine actions are above causes/purposes. Ashᶜarites (and Salafīs, including Ḥanbalīs) took a position that is a reaction to and the radical opposite of the above Muᶜtazilī position. They believed that an action could be 'embellished' or 'repugnant,' but they judged that this classification should be based on the 'revealed law' (shariᶜah) and not reason. Without the shariᶜah, for Ashᶜarites, actions are equally 'embellished' and 'repugnant;' good and bad (precisely, with the exception of knowledge/ignorance and justice/injustice[96]). Thus, they judged that God never 'has to' do anything, and what He does, regardless of what it is, is 'good' and 'embellished.' Therefore, Ashᶜarites believe that God's actions are 'above purposes,' because the performer of an action for a purpose is 'in need' of that purpose and God is above needs.[97] They also argued that God is the 'Cause of the causes and the Creator of the causes and their effects too,' and hence, does whatever He wills without having to 'abide by any of our causation rules.'[98] Ashᶜarites based their whole fundamentals of law and moral philosophy on the above argument. Al-Ghazālī, for example, judged that the 'theory of mean' (which is also called Aristotle's principle of moderation) is valid because 'the scripts had prescribed it, not because rationality approved it as the philosophers had said.'[99]

(iii) Divine actions have causes/purposes out of God's grace. Maturidites (a section of Ḥanafīs), who had fewer followers than the above schools, took a middle ground. They believed that Muᶜtazilīs were correct in assigning purposes to God's actions, but mistaken in placing 'obligations' on God. Maturidites also believed that Ashᶜarites were correct in saying that God does not 'need' purposes, but believed that purposes and benefits are the 'needs' of humans, not God. Maturitides believed in the principle of *al-taḥsīn wa al-taqbīḥ*. However, for them, 'reason' does not have 'authority to judge' what is embellished and what is repugnant, but rather, reason is a God-given 'tool' by which humans could only 'know' what is embellished and what is repugnant.[100]

Many jurists who were 'officially' Ashᶜarites, according to their school of law, did not accept the Ashᶜarites's radical position on divine purposes and took a position that is closer to the Maturidi position on this issue. However, and for political reasons and fear of persecution, when these jurists expressed their views on purposefulness, they all ensured a safe distance from Muᶜtazilism by rejecting the Muᶜtazilī 'embellishment and repugnance' doctrine. Examples are al-Āmidī (d. 631 AH/1234 CE),[101] al-Shāṭibī (d. 790 AH/1388 CE),[102] Ibn Taymiyah (d. 728 AH/ 1328 CE),[103] Ibn al-Qayyim (d. 748 AH/1347 CE),[104] and Ibn Rushd (Averröes, d. 584 AH/ 1189 CE).[105] Ibn Rushd's attack on the Ashᶜarite position was the harshest. He wrote in his critique of Ghazālī's *Tahāfut* (Incoherance) that, 'those who reject *asbāb*, reject reason itself.'[106] Al-Shāṭibī, significantly, considered the purposes of the Islamic law (*maqāṣid al-sharīᶜah*) to be more basic than the 'fundamentals of law' (*uṣūl al-fiqh*) themselves. He counted amongst the 'fundamentals of religion and universals of belief' (*uṣūl al-dīn wa kulliyyah al-millah*) the purposes/*maqāṣid* behind God's actions.[107]

Finally, the six system features, proposed above, namely, cognitive nature, wholeness, openness, interrelated hierarchy, multidimensionality, and purposefulness, are highly interrelated. However, the one feature that spans across all other features and represents the core methodology of systematic analysis in this book is purposefulness. The following is a brief outline of the relationships between purposefulness and other features of the system of Islamic law.

i) Purposefulness is related to the cognitive nature of the Islamic law because various proposals for the nature and structure of the purposes of the Islamic law (*maqāṣid al-sharīᶜah*) reflect cognitions of the nature and structure of law itself.
ii) Universal purposes of the Islamic law (*al-maqāṣid al-ᶜāmmah*) represent the law's holistic characteristics and universal principles.
iii) Purposes of the Islamic law play a pivotal role in the process of ijtihad, in all of its various forms, which is the mechanism by which the system of Islamic law maintains its 'openness.'

iv) Purposes of the Islamic law are perceived in a number of hierarchical ways, which correspond to the hierarchies in the system of Islamic law.

v) Purposes provide multiple dimenions that help resolve and understand 'apparent contradictions' and 'opposing tendencies' in the scripts and the fundamental theories of the law.

Therefore, I will consider the purposes of the Islamic law (*maqāṣid al-sharīʿah al-islāmīyah*) to be the basic fundamental principle and methodology in the systems-based analysis presented in this book. Since the effectiveness of a system is measured based on its fulfilment of its (manmade or 'natural') purpose, the effectiveness of the system of Islamic law is assessed based on its fulfilment of its purposes (*maqāṣid*).

Before we move to the next chapter on Islamic law, it is necessary to note that the previous two chapters presented the methodology utilised in this work, which is actually based on two sets of theories, namely, systems theories and theories of *maqāṣid al-sharīʿah*. In the rest of this book, the system features of cognition, wholeness, openness, hierarchy, multi-dimensionality, and purposefulness, as defined in this chapter, will form the tools and criteria of the presented analysis. Nevertheless, the analysis presented in Chapters 3, 4 and 5, for classic and contemporary theories, respectively, will primarily rely on the features of cognition and hierarchy. Then, in Chapter 6, the fundamentals of Islamic law will be defined as a 'system' whose feature of wholeness, openness, multi-dimensionality, and purposefulness is realised through the realisation of *maqāṣid al-sharīʿah*.

3

Islamic Law, Imams, & Schools: A Historical Survey

Overview

This chapter presents an analysis of classic/traditional schools of Islamic law (*madhāhib al-fiqh*) in terms of their history and fundamental sources. The concept of Islamic law and the various uses of the term in the English language is discussed in the first section. The second section briefly outlines the evolution of schools of Islamic law from the post-prophetic era until what was referred to as 'the declination era,' and criticises the 'feature-based' method used in traditional categorisation of *madhāhib*. Nine classic/traditional schools of Islamic law are considered, namely, Mālikīs, Ḥanafīs, Shafiᶜīs, Ḥanbalīs, Shia Jaᶜfarīs, Shia Zaydīs, Ẓahirīs, Ibāḍīs, and Muᶜtazilīs.

3.1. WHAT IS 'ISLAMIC LAW?'

Fiqh and Shariᶜah

The term 'Islamic law' is commonly used in literature written in the English language in reference to four different Arabic terms, namely, *fiqh, shariᶜah, qānūn,* and *ᶜurf*.[1] The word fiqh is used in the Qur'an and hadith in various forms to refer to understanding, comprehension, and gaining knowledge of the religion in general.[2] Eventually, and since the end of the era of the imams of the Islamic schools of law/

thought, the word fiqh has been typically defined as, 'knowledge of practical revealed rulings extracted from detailed evidences' (*al-ᶜilmu bi al-aḥkām al-sharᶜiyyah al-ᶜamaliyyah min adillatihā al-tafṣīliyyah*).[3] Thus, fiqh is limited to 'practical' (*ᶜamaliyyah*) versus theological (*iᶜtiqādiyyah*) issues. 'Detailed evidences' are verses from the Qur'an and narrations of hadith.

On the other hand, the term 'shariᶜah law' has negative connotations in the English language, because it is normally used to refer to various corporal punishments used in some countries. Statistically speaking, these punishments have been applied predominantly on the weak and marginalised in these societies.[4] This partial application raises serious questions about the political motives behind applying these punishments, regardless of the juridical/theological debates over them. Nevertheless, the word shariᶜah is used in the Qur'an to mean a 'revealed way of life,' for example, the word '*shirᶜah*' in Surah *al-Mā'idah*, and the word shariᶜah in Surah *al-Jāthiyah*. Yusuf Ali translated them as 'Law' and 'Way,' respectively. Picktall translated them as 'divine law' and 'road.' Irving translated them as 'code of law' and 'highroad.' My translation of the word shariᶜah to mean 'a way of life' is similar to Ramadan's.[5]

It is necessary, for a number of theoretical and practical reasons, to clearly distinguish the concept of fiqh from the concept of shariᶜah. Theoretically speaking, the two terms refer to two different meanings. Fiqh represents the 'cognitive' part of the Islamic law, to use a systems term, while shariᶜah, by definition, represents the 'heavenly' part of this law. Thus, the term *faqīh* is used for people with 'understanding' (*fahm*),[6] 'perception' (*taṣawwur*),[7] and 'cognition' (*idrāk*),[8] and is not to be used for God. On the other hand, the term *al-shāriᶜ* is a name for God,[9] which means 'The Legislator,'[10] and could not be used for humans, except for the Prophet, when he 'conveys a message from God.'[11]

Qānūn and ᶜUrf

The word *qānūn* is a Farsi word, which was 'arabised' to mean principles or *uṣūl*,[12] and since the nineteenth century to mean written laws.[13] Written laws, in countries which endorse Islam as a (or the) source of legislation, could be directly derived from *fatāwā* of fiqh (that is, opinions from one or more of the schools of Islamic law, taken *verbatim*). This is specifically true in the family and inheritance laws in a number of countries. For example, Egyptian family law number 25/1925, amended by law number 100/1985, borrowed many of its statutes from the Ḥanafī fiqh.[14] However, many written laws in these countries are also borrowed from other (secular) systems of law, or are purely based on local custom, tradition, or *ᶜurf*. For example, article 66 of the same law (25/1925) is based on an Egyptian custom that 'commits the bride to buying her own furniture at a level that is comparable to the dowry that she received,'[15] which is a stipulation that has no *fiqhī* basis in any classic school of law.

On the other hand, *ᶜUrf* literally means custom or, more accurately, a 'good' custom that the community approves.[16] *ᶜUrf* is sometimes claimed to be 'Islamic law' in some societies in order to approve some customary practices,[17] even if they were clearly prohibited in the Islamic schools of law, such as honor killings that take place in some Arabic Bedouin areas and south-east asian areas.[18] In the schools of fundamentals of law, most scholars consider custom to be an effective factor only in the application of the Islamic law, rather than a source of law in its own right.[19]

Chart 3.1 summarises all of the above (classic) relations between fiqh, shariᶜah, *ᶜurf* and *qānūn*. Traditionally, 'shariᶜah' is believed to include the Qur'an, the prophetic tradition, and rulings of *fiqh/sharᶜ* deduced from them.

Traditionally, *ᶜurf* (custom) only affects the application of fiqh in some cases, hence the slight contact between their circles, as

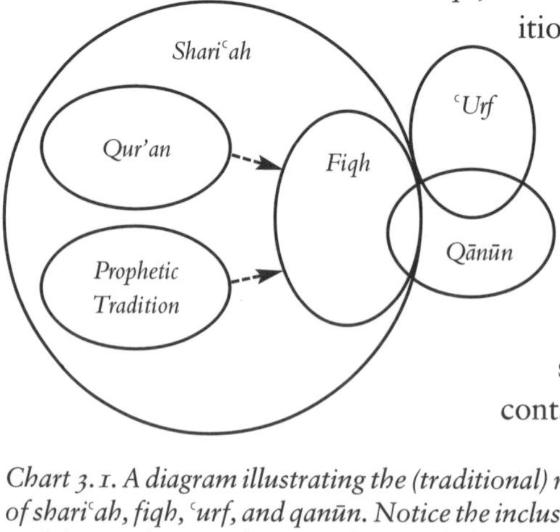

Chart 3.1. A diagram illustrating the (traditional) relations between the concepts of shariᶜah, fiqh, ᶜurf, and qanūn. Notice the inclusion of fiqh with the Qur'an and the prophetic tradition in 'the revealed.'

shown in the chart. Finally, *qānūn* is the written law that could be borrowed from fiqh, *ᶜurf*, and other sources, hence, the intersection between the three circles, as shown.

The Importance of Differentiating Between Fiqh and Shariᶜah

Practically, blurring the line between fiqh and shariᶜah gives way to claims of 'divinity' and 'sanctity' in human juridical ijtihad. Historically these claims have resulted in two serious phenomena, namely, mutual accusations of heresy and resistance of renewal of the Islamic law.

Mutual accusations of 'heresy' or 'apostasy', not just error or sin, have frequently occurred between groups of scholars who had different opinions about what they held as fundamental/essential/divine parts of the law. A large number of bloody conflicts throughout the Islamic history were instigated by such accusations between followers of different *madhāhib*. One example is the violent conflict between the Ashᶜarite and Muᶜtazilī schools of thought during the Abbasids reign, in the eighth century CE. A second example is the fierce battles, in Khurasan (1000 CE), Nisapur (1159 CE), Esfahan (1186 CE), and Jerusalem (1470 CE), between followers of the Shāfiᶜī and Ḥanafī schools of law over their minor discrepancies. In Khurasan, around 1000 CE, the battle started after the Caliph, impressed by Abū Ḥāmid al-Ghazālī's knowledge, decided to change the official school of law in courts from the Ḥanafī to the Shāfiᶜī school, to which al-Ghazālī belonged. *Fiqhī* differences between the two schools might explain the seeming cause of the conflict, but it is obvious that politics of power played a key role.

A third example is 'the sword' that Ibn al-Ṣalāḥ recommended his students to use on teachers of philosophy in the thirteenth century CE. The numerous battles between Sunni and Shia that lead to the repeated 'destruction, looting, and burning' of the cities of Baghdad, Basra, Karkh, and Rayy (for example, in 962, 972, 974, 981, 1008, 1015, 1031, 1041, 1047, 1079, 1184 CE) is yet a fourth example.[20] Similar accusations of heresy over differences of opinion in the Islamic law continue to breed ideologies of violence and intolerance, and suppress freedoms and a culture of co-existence in our present time.

On the other hand, inflexibility and resistance of renewal in the Islamic law has continued to intensify as the circle of the 'sanctified,' and hence 'unchangeable,' widened throughout the centuries. Gradually, the circle of the 'sanctified and unchangeable' started to include opinions of imams from various schools of law. Eventually, the 'door of ijtihad' was claimed to have been closed and the Islamic law, in general, lagged behind real-life changes that occurred since the medieval era.

3.2. SCHOOLS OF ISLAMIC LAW: A BRIEF HISTORY

Overview

The purpose of this section is to present a brief account of the historical development of the nine schools of law under consideration, from the 'post-prophetic era' until the 'declination era.' This account represents the 'historical context' of the development of the fundamental theories which will be presented in the following sections. This section also presents a critique of the traditional 'one-dimensional' and 'feature-based' categorisation of classic schools of Islamic law.

Post-Prophetic Era

In the beginning of the post-prophetic era, various historic accounts of the companions' reasoning (ijtihad) show a general tendency to reach agreements on juridicial matters based on direct citations of Qur'anic verses or accounts of prophetic decisions made in similar situations. Examples are the companions' famous debates over the 'inheritance of the grandmother' (*mīrath al-jaddah*), 'seeking permission for entering people's homes' (*al-isti'dhān*), 'the waiting period for a widow' (*ʿiddah al-armalah*), fasting while travelling (*al-ṣawm fī al-safar*), and also a number of other issues.[21]

Then, with the expansion of the 'Islamic State' and new experiences that the companions developed through their interactions with people from different civilisations, the companions started to face new questions with no available direct answers. In these cases, they clearly applied their own sense of public interest (*maṣlaḥah*), especially those who were in government positions, for instance, the issues of the 'conquered land' (*al-arḍ al-maftūḥah*), that of 'laborer liability' (*taḍmīn al-ṣunnāʿ*), 'collecting the Qur'an' (*jamʿ al-muṣḥaf*), and 'ʿUmar's *ijtihādāt*' (previously discussed in Chapter One).

However, several factors contributed to a divergence of juridical opinions within the community of companions and, eventually, the formation of the first categorisation of schools of law based on their methodology of juridical reasoning (ijtihad). The schools, or rather 'tendencies,' were the 'supporters of opinion' (*ahl al-ra'ī*) and the 'supporters of narration' (*ahl al-athar*), and they are briefly discussed in various contemporary accounts of the 'evolution of fiqh.' The factors that led to the formation of these two 'tendencies' could be summarised in three factors, namely, political/sectarian conflicts, migration of the companions, and personalities of the imams of the time.

First, major conflicts followed the assassination of ʿUthmān ibn ʿAffān (d. 35 AH/655 CE), the third Caliph, which divided the community of companions into a number of political rivals. Political rivals quickly became fighting parties,[22] and political conflicts became 'sectarian divisions' when political differences generated philosophical differences over 'matters of faith,' as far as rivals claimed.[23] Political/Sectarian rivalism gave birth to a phenomenon that had a major impact on the law, which is 'forging of narrations' (*waḍʿ al-ḥadīth*). According to some narrators who took part in this process themselves, various sectarian/political rivals attempted to give legitimacy to their sectarian convictions or even political leaders by forging supporting prophetic narrations.[24]

Second, the personalities of the teachers of the time affected their students and the schools that eventually developed in their regions. A typical example is the difference between ʿAbdullāh ibn ʿUmar and ʿAbdullāh ibn ʿAbbās. When Abū Jaʿfar al-Manṣūr requested Mālik ibn Anas to write '*al-Muwaṭṭa*'' (The Well-Trodden Path), it is narrated that he outlined a methodology for Mālik by saying: 'Put together a book that benefits people, in which you avoid Ibn ʿAbbās's provisions (*rukhaṣ*) and Ibn ʿUmar's strictnesses (*shadā'id*).'[25] ʿAbdullāh ibn ʿUmar was known for a sense of strictness. He, for example, hurt his eyes by washing the inside of his eyelids during ablution. The effect of his personality was obvious on the opinions of some of his students, such as, Nāfiᶜ, Sālim, and Sulaymān ibn Yasār. On the contrary, ᶜAbdullāh ibn ᶜAbbās was known for a sense of leniency and magnanimity, which showed in his *fatāwā* and his students, such as, Jābir ibn Zayd, Ibrāhīm al-Nakhᶜī, and Saᶜīd ibn al-Musayyab. ᶜĀ'ishah (the Prophet's wife), for another example, was a strong and independent woman. Her character showed on a number of her *fatāwā* and opinions, in which she advocated women's independence and rights, notably against some of the other companions' direct narrations. Badr al-Dīn al-Zarkashī wrote a book dedicated to ᶜĀ'ishah's critiques to the other companions' narrations, which he called, '*ᶜAyn al-Iṣābah fī Istidrāk ᶜĀ'ishah ᶜalā al-Ṣaḥābah*' (The Accurate Account on ᶜĀ'ishah's Amendments to the Companions' Narrations).[26] I noticed that ᶜĀ'ishah's opinions found their way especially to the Ḥanafī school. This is perhaps the effect of ᶜĀ'ishah's students, al-Shiᶜbī and Ḥammād, who were both teachers of Abū Ḥanīfa.[27]

Finally, the first Islamic century witnessed a wide movement of migration, starting with the companions, especially to Iraq, Syria, and Egypt, and ending with Arabian soldiers who travelled to far off lands and, eventually, decided to stay in these places. Chart 3.2 shows a map of seventh century Muslim Caliphate and how the 'battles' of the time shaped the migration paths. Iraq became home to a large number of companions, such as ᶜAlī ibn Abī-Ṭālib and his children, ᶜAbdullāh ibn ᶜAbbās, Moḥammad ibn Maslamah, Usāmah ibn Zayd, and Abū Masᶜūd al-Anṣārī. Egypt became home to ᶜAmrū ibn al-ᶜĀaṣ and his sons, Qays ibn Saᶜad, Moḥammad ibn Abū Bakr, ᶜAmmār ibn Yāssir, and others. Yemen became home to Muᶜādh ibn Jabal, ᶜUbayd Allāh ibn al-ᶜAbbās, and others. Syria became home to Muᶜāwiyah and many other Ummayyads, ᶜAbdullāh ibn ᶜUmar, Shuraḥbīl, Khālid ibn al-Walīd, al-Ḍaḥḥāk ibn Qays, and others. Oman became home to Hudhayfah ibn al-Yamān and others. Abū Ayyūb al-Anṣārī went as far as today's Istanbul, where he died. Yet, many of the companions remained in Makkah and Madinah.[28] Thanks to the civilisations in which the new immigrants merged, Islamic law began to incorporate new geographical and cultural dimensions.

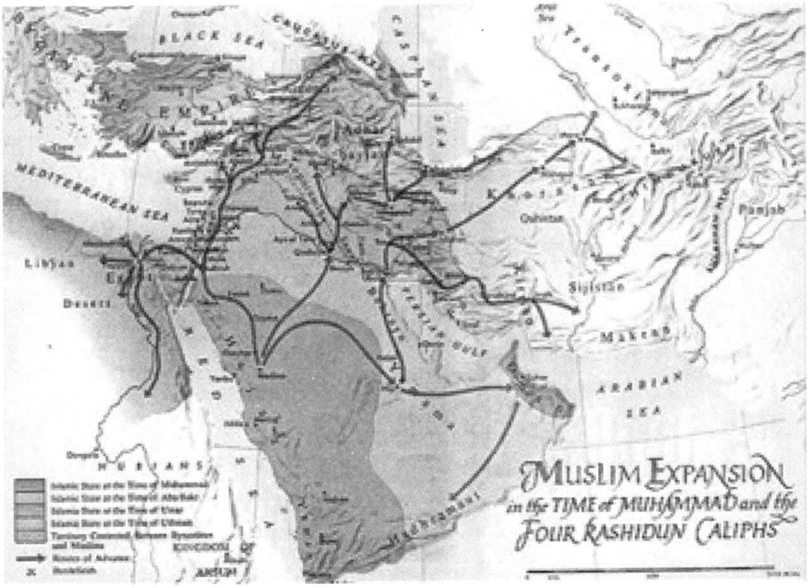

Chart 3.2. This map illustrates the seventh-century paths that battles, and immigrants, took. Scanned from: R. Roolvink et al., Historical Atlas of the Muslim Peoples (Amsterdam, 1957). Available in soft form on: http://www.princeton.edu/thumcomp/dimensions.html (visited: April 13, 2006).

Ahl al-ra'ī (Supporters of Opinion) and *ahl al-athar* (Supporters of Narration) generally reacted in two different ways with the above factors. The following is an outline of these reactions.

1. *Ahl al-Ra'ī*: The 'Supporters of Opinion' generally reacted to the phenomenon of forging of prophetic narrations by showing significant reluctance to accept 'single-chained' (*āḥād*) and especially 'disconnected-end' (*mursal*) chains of narrators. They tended to resort to principles mentioned in the general expressions (*ʿumūm*) of the Qur'an in their search for answers to new questions. Eventually, this method evolved into the (formal) procedures of reasoning by analogy (*qiyās*) and juridical preference (*istiḥsān*). Jurists of Iraq were famous for relying on 'reason' in their methods to the extent of being accused by some of the jurists of Madinah of, 'preferring their opinions over the Prophet's tradition.'[29]

2. *Ahl al-Athar*: 'Supporters of Narration' dealt differently with the phenomenon of forging prophetic narrations and with new questions. Their hadith approach was to verify the narrators' honesty via studying their biographies more carefully, and to intensify the search for any hadith that applies, via direct or indirect linguistic implications, to the unanswered questions they had. 'Supporters of Narration' generally preferred to resort to 'weak' (*ḍaʿīf*) narrations over analogical reasoning and over the principles 'deduced' from the general expressions of the Qur'an.[30]

Ahl al-ra'ī li ahl al-athar tendencies were not simply a matter of geography, as some researchers had thought.[31] It is true that the migration factor, explained above, played a role in the tendency of those who lived in Iraq towards opinion (perhaps also due to the influence of ʿAlī and Ibn ʿAbbās) and the tendency of those who lived in al-Hijaz and Syria towards narration (perhaps also due to the influence of Ibn ʿUmar and Abū Hurayrah).

However, while the Iraqi school practiced '*al-ra'ī*' through the methods of *qīyās* and *istiḥsān*, the Ḥijāzī school, especially in Madinah also practiced *al-ra'ī* through the method of interest/*maṣlaḥah*, especially in the fiqh of Mālik and his students. Nevertheless, Ḥijāzīs generally used 'unrestricted' *maṣlaḥah* in, what they called, the 'absence of a script', by which they mean the absence of a specific script that addresses the issue at hand. On the other hand, Iraqis generally used *qīyās*, and especially *istiḥsān*, even in the presence of scripts that they considered 'conflicting with reason.' These reasoning methods will be discussed in more detail in the next chapter.

Finally, the difference between *ahl al-ra'ī* and *ahl al-athar* was not a matter of 'traditionists' versus 'liberals,' over the 'effectiveness of the scripts,' as some current researchers thought.[32] It is clear that both methods were clearly 'traditional,' in being solely script- and narration-based. Nevertheless, *ahl al-ra'ī* were dealing with traditions in a more rational way, while *ahl al-athar* were more literal. In other words, the two schools represented two alternative methodologies of applying the scripts.

The Imams' Era

The second and third Islamic centuries could be called the 'era of imams.' Traditional schools of Islamic law (*madhāhib*), as we know them today, were named after a number of imams who lived at that time. The schools of Shāfiʿīs, Mālikīs, Ḥanafīs, Ḥanbalīs, Shia (I will consider Jaʿfarīs and Zaydīs here), and Ibāḍīs, were named after Moḥammad ibn Idrīs al-Shāfiʿī (d. 240 AH/854 CE), Mālik ibn Anas (d. 179/ 795 CE), Abū Ḥanīfa al-Nuʿmān ibn Thābit (d. 150/767 CE), Aḥmad ibn Ḥanbal (d. 241/855 CE), Jaʿfar al-Ṣādiq ibn Moḥammad al-Bāqir (d. 148 AH/765 CE, the sixth of the 'Twelve Imams'),[33] Zayd ibn ʿAlī Zayn al-ʿĀbidīn (d. 121 AH/ 739 CE), and ʿAbdullāh ibn ʿIbād (d. 86 AH/705 CE), respectively.[34] There are a few other Imams, who also lived in the second era, after whom some (extinct) *madhāhib* had been named, such as Sufyān al-Thawrī(d. 161AH/778 CE), Abū Thawr (d. 240AH/854 CE), al-Awazāʿī (d. 157 AH/774 CE), and al-Layth ibn Saʿad (d. 175 AH/791 CE). The only exception in this nomenclature was *al-ẓāhiriyyah* (the literalists or Ẓāhirīs). Their odd literal method and the modest charisma and popularity of its founder (Dāwūd ibn ʿAlī, d. 268 AH/881 CE) is perhaps the reason behind not naming the school in the same manner.

Imams left behind legacies and large numbers of narrations, *fatāwā*, and students. Each imam had developed procedures of ijtihad, which he followed consistently – according to his students – in issuing *fatāwā* and authenticating hadith. However, imams left behind only oral or written narrations of hadith and collections of *fatāwā*, and not theoretical accounts of their methodology in ijtihad, with the exception of al-Shāfiʿī's '*Risālah*' (The Message).[35] The following is a brief account of the formation of each of the above schools of fundamentals of Islamic law, in which 'chains' of imams of each school are traced. I based this account on a survey of each *madhhab*'s currently familiar 'textbooks,' which are presently studied in traditional Islamic universities and institutes and considered 'authentic references' for these schools' opinions.

The Ḥanafī 'fundamentals of law' (*uṣūl*) were developed two generations after the founder of the school, Abū Ḥanīfa. From what we know, Abū Ḥanīfa himself did not write specific volumes on fiqh. He wrote on issues related to Islamic creed and education, such as, *al-Fiqh al-Akbar* (The Most Important Law),[36] *al-Radd ᶜAlā al-Qadarīyyah* (Refuting Pre-Destinationists),[37] and *al-ᶜĀlim wa al-Mutaᶜallim* (Teacher and Student).[38] Abū Ḥanīfa narrated hadith, which Abū Yūsuf (d. 182 AH), his chief student, collected in his '*Kitāb al-Āthār*' (The Book of Recounts).[39] Later, Abū Yūsuf wrote a book on *al-Kharāj* (Taxes),[40] in which he explained Abū Ḥanīfa's *fatāwā* regarding various financial issues, in addition to Abū Yūsuf's own positions, which were sometimes different from his teacher's. Abū Yūsuf also compiled, *Ikhtilāf Ibn Abī Laylā* (The Disagreement of Ibn Abū Laylā),[41] on the rulings of Ibn Abū Laylā, who was Baghdad's Chief Judge, which Abū Ḥanīfa disagreed with. Moḥammad ibn al-Ḥasan al-Shaybānī (d. 187 AH/ 803 CE), Abū Ḥanīfa and Abū Yūsuf's best student, narrated '*Ikhtilāf*' after Abū Yūsuf. Then, Moḥammad ibn al-Ḥasan wrote a number of comprehensive volumes on fiqh, which are now considered the main Ḥanafī references in fiqh, the most significant of which is, *al-Jāmiᶜ al-Kabīr* (The Large Compendium).[42] Up to that point, the Ḥanafī school was studied and applied based on large collections of hadith and fatwa, rather than specific methodology. It was the next generation of students who elaborated on what came to be known as *uṣūl al-ḥanafiyyah* (fundamental methodology of the Ḥanafīs). Both al-Sarkhasī (d. 489 AH/1096 CE) and al-Bazdawī (d. 542 AH/1147 CE) wrote books called, *al-Uṣūl* (The Fundamentals),[43] in which they explained formal issues of methodology, such as commands (*al-amr*), specific and general expressions (*al-khāṣ wa al-ᶜām*), juridical authority (*al-ḥujjiyyah*), analogical reasoning (*al-qiyās*), and abrogation (*al-naskh*). Al-Sarkhasī wrote in his introduction that, 'it was time to elaborate specifically on the fundamental concepts (*uṣūl*), on which Moḥammad ibn al-Ḥasan's detailed rulings (*furūᶜ*) were based, in order for future generations to build their fiqh on these *uṣūl* when they face unprecedented matters.'[44] In my view, subsequent generations of Ḥanafīs built their fatwa and ijtihad, even in unprecedented matters, on Abū Ḥanīfa, Abū Yūsuf, and Ibn al-Ḥasan's precedents and opinions, rather than al-Sarkhasī and al-Bazdawī's detailed *uṣūlī* methodology.

The Mālikī *madhhab* followed a similar course of development. Mālik left behind a large collection of *fatāwā* and hadith, especially in his '*al-Muwaṭṭa*'' (The Well-Trodden Path).[45] Ibn Waḥb (d. 197 AH/813 CE), Mālik's student, wrote '*al-Mujālasāt*' (The Meetings),[46] in which he narrated the fiqh that he heard from Mālik during their meetings. Saḥnūn (d. 695 AH/ 1296 CE), another student of Mālik, wrote, '*al-Mudawwanah al-Umm*' (The Mother Account),[47] in which he also recorded a large number of Mālik's opinions. The methodology that Mālik and consequent generations of his students developed was not articulated until the time of Abū Bakr ibn al-ʿArabī (d. 545 AH/1150 CE) and Shihāb al-Dīn al-Qarāfī (d. 684 h /1285 CE), who wrote '*al-Maḥṣūl*' (The Harvest) and '*al-Qawāʿid*' (The Basic Rules), respectively.[48] However, Mālik's books of fiqh and hadith, especially '*al-Muwaṭṭa*'' remained to be the school's primary references.

Likewise, the Ḥanbalī *madhhab* started with Aḥmad ibn Ḥanbal's large volume of narrations, followed by collections of his *fatāwā* narrated by his students, such as that of his sons, Ṣāliḥ (d. 266 AH/879 CE) and ʿAbdullāh (d. 290 AH/903 CE), in addition to Abū Bakr al-Athram (d. 261 AH/875 CE), ʿAbdullāh al-Maymūnī (d. 274 AH/887 CE), Ḥarb (d. 280 AH/893 CE), and Abū Bakr al-Marwazī (d. 275 AH/888 CE). Abū Bakr al-Khallāl (d. 311 AH/923 CE), al-Marwazī's student, wrote an encyclopaedia on Aḥmad's fiqh that he called, *Kitāb al-Sunnah* (The Book of Traditions).[49] However, the theory of the Ḥanbalī school was articulated in the usual *uṣūl* manner much later by Ibn Taymiyah (d. 728 AH/ 1328 CE) and his student, Ibn al-Qayyim (d. 748 AH/1347 CE),[50] who both built on the contributions of Najm al-Dīn al-Ṭūfī (621 AH/1224 CE), Ibn Rajab (d. 795 AH/1393 CE), and Ibn al-Lahhām (d. 803 AH/1400 CE).

Zayd ibn ʿAlī Zayn al-ʿĀbidīn narrated hadith and issued a large number of *fatāwā*, which his student, Abū Khālid al-Wasīṭī compiled in his, '*al-Majmūʿ*' (The Anthology).[51] His student Ibrāhīm ibn al-Zabarqān (d. 183AH/ 799 CE) narrated it after him.[52] The consequent generations of Zaydīs elaborated on Imam Zayd's methodology, notably his grandson, Aḥmad ibn ʿĪsā ibn Zayd (d. 389 AH/999 CE), in addition to al-Qāsim (d. 242 AH/856 CE) and Imam al-Hādī (d. 298 AH/911 CE).[53]

Ibāḍīs are related by their name to ʿAbdullāh ibn Ibāḍ (d. 86 AH/705 CE), but they started to be known by this name and develop a distinct school of law in the third century AH (ninth century CE).[54] The chief contributor to this school of law was Jābir ibn Zayd al-Azdī (d. 93 AH/711 CE), a student of a number of companions, including Ibn Masʿūd, ʿĀ'ishah, Ibn ʿUmar, Ibn ʿAbbās, and Anas ibn Mālik. The 'chain of students' after Jābir were Muslim ibn Abū Karīmah, al-Rabīʿ ibn Ḥabīb, Maḥbūb ibn al-Raḥīl, Moḥammad ibn Maḥbūb, in consequent generations.[55] Jābir wrote a large book of traditions and juridical opinions known as, *Diwan Jābir Ibn Zayd* (The Collection of Jābir Ibn Zayd), which Ibāḍīs followed and upon which they based their school of law.[56]

Jaʿfar al-Ṣādiq narrated hadith and issued *fatāwā*, in addition to practicing a number of other sciences, such as chemistry and mathematics.[57] Jaʿfar al-Ṣādiq taught a distinct group of students who conveyed his narrations and opinions, especially his son Mūsā al-Kāzim (also one of the Twelve Imams), in addition to Abū Ḥanīfa, Mālik, Sufyān, Ibn Isḥāq, Ibn Abū Ḥāzim, Yaḥyā ibn Saʿīd, and Jābir ibn Ḥayyān, whose name was used in coining the term 'Algebra.'[58] There are different opinions as to whether Imam al-Bāqir (Imam Jaʿfar's father) had written the first known book on *uṣūl al-fiqh*, even before al-Shāfiʿī's '*Risālah*,' or whether theorisation in the Jaʿfarī *madhhab* had taken place much later.[59] In any case, there is general agreement in the Jaʿfarī *madhhab* that 'independent ijtihad' only started after the twelfth Imam (ninth century CE), because before that time, the followers of this school were only following the subsequent twelve imams in *taqlīd* (imitation).[60]

Finally, the Shāfiʿī school was exceptional in the sense that Imam al-Shāfiʿī wrote/dictated his own accounts of hadith, fiqh, and even methodology of juridical reasoning (*uṣūl al-fiqh*). In fact, it was al-Shāfiʿī, according to most scholars, who laid the foundations of *uṣūl al-fiqh* as a separate branch of knowledge in Islamic law, in his book, '*al-Risālah*' (The Message).[61] The influence of Greek philosophy on al-Shāfiʿī's *uṣūl* is a matter of speculation amongst researchers. Some claim that al-Shāfiʿī was never exposed to Greek philosophy, and others claim that he was fluent in the Greek language and that Greek influence 'shows in his writings.'[62] I found no historical evidence for any of the opposing arguments. However, based on my own exposure to both al-Shāfiʿī's writings and Greek philosophy, I would say that al-Shāfiʿī's methodology in *uṣūl*, especially as illustrated in '*al-Risālah*' and '*al-Umm*,' shows no direct influence from Greek logic or philosophy. Nevertheless, it is possible that he had read what was available from the Greek heritage at his time, as his biographers had claimed. In any case, the *uṣūl* of the Shāfiʿī school itself were developed a great deal through the works of later scholars/philosophers, such as, al-Qaffāl al-Shāshī (d. 336 AH/947 CE), Abd al-Malik al-Juwaynī (d. 478 AH/1085 CE), and Abū Ḥāmid al-Ghazālī (d. 504 AH/1111 CE), who were all clearly and indisputably influenced by Greek philosophy.[63]

A Formal Critique of Madhāhib Categorisation

	Qur'an	Sunnah	Consensus	Analogy	Interest	Juridical preference	Custom	Imam's opinion	Companion's opinion	Continuity
Mālikīs	√	√	√	√	√		√		√	√
Ḥanafīs	√	√	√	√		√	√		√	√
Shāfiʿīs	√	√	√	√					√	
Ḥanbalīs	√	√	√	√	√	√			√	√
Jaʿfarīs	√	√	√					√		√
Zaydīs	√	√	√					√		√
Ẓāhirīs	√	√								√
Ibāḍīs	√	√	√	√	√	√				√
Muʿtazilīs	√	√	√	√	√	√				

Chart 3.3. A summary of the 'sources of legislation' that are used as 'classifying features' between the schools of Islamic law. This classification approach has a number of limitations, including single-dimensionality and overgeneralisation.

Below is a formal analysis and critique of the traditional *madhāhib* categorisation, from a cognitive science point of view.[64] In Chapter Two, the concept of categorisation/classification was introduced, and feature- versus concepts-based categorisations were compared. Based on the above historical survey, one could conclude that *madhāhib* categorisation started as a 'concept-based categorisation' and ended up as a 'feature-based categorisation.' When jurists were classified according to how much opinion (*ra'ī*) versus narration (*athar*) they relied upon in their *fatāwā*, the classifying criterion was the 'concept' of reason (*al-ᶜaql*), which *ahl al-ra'ī* trusted more than *ahl al-athar* in the formation of their opinions. However, this categorisation eventually evolved into a categorisation that derived its labels from the names of imams and derived its classifying features from a list of 'sources of legislation' that were articulated by the second or third generation students of these imams. Hence, categorisation of Islamic schools of law became a feature-based process (the features being: Qur'an, prophetic tradition, consensus, analogy, interest, juridical preference, custom, imam's opinion, companion's opinion, and presumption of continuity).

The following is a critique of the above feature-based categorisation of *madhāhib*, based on the theoretical analysis presented in Chapter Two.

1. Missing significant analytical information: The above feature-based classification of schools misses the similarity between 'sources' that have different names in different schools, for example, the Ḥanafī *qiyās* (analogy) and the Jaᶜfarī *istiṣḥāb* (continuity) and the Mālikī purposes of law (*maqāṣid*) and the Shāfiᶜī 'unrestricted interests' (*maṣlaḥah mursalah*). It also misses the significant differences between the Ẓāhirī, Mālikī, and Jaᶜfarī 'ijmāᶜ' (consensus) and the Ḥanafī, the Mālikī, and Muᶜtazilī '*istiḥsān*' (preference).
2. Overgeneralisations: Schools of law were identified or differentiated based on whether or not they endorse one feature or another, such as, 'consensus' or 'preference.' However, the very definition of these features varies greatly from one school to another, and hence, cannot be accurately used as bases for classification.

3. 'Pigeon-hole' binary choices: Despite the fact that al-Ṭūfī is classified as 'Ḥanbalī,' his method of 'giving interest precedence over (specific) scripts' makes him radically different from Ḥanbalī methodology and actually closer to the Muʿtazilīs. Likewise, al-Ghazālī is classified as 'Shāfiʿī' even though his analogies based on unrestricted interests and opinions on *maṣlaḥah* could put him somewhere between the Shāfiʿī and Mālikī schools. Ibn Taymiyah from the Ḥanbalī school, endorsed the Mālikī 'tradition of the People of Madinah.' Al-Naẓẓām, from the Muʿtazilī school, rejected reasoning by analogy, which is a Ẓāhirī and Shia position. And so on.
4. Multidimensional factors ignored: Historically, *madhāhib* were largely shaped by factors such as geography, politics, and court systems, as briefly outlined earlier. However, these factors were not accounted for in the classification of *madhāhib*, as were other (binary) factors.
5. In addition to the above limitations of the traditional feature-based method, the nomenclature of traditional Islamic schools of law reflects a general orientation towards the authority of their charismatic imams, rather than their detailed methodologies. In my view, the effect of the imams went further than nomenclature, and theories of fundamentals (*uṣūl*) were not as strictly observed as the individual opinions of the imams.

Chapter Five will present a categorisation of current theories in the Islamic law, in which an attempt to avoid the above drawbacks of feature-based categorisations will be made.

Chains of Studentship and Narration

To put all of the above jurists in one historical perspective, I designed Chart 3.4 in order to analyse some key teacher-student relations/connections in the *madhāhib*'s history. The chart shows a selective group of six companions (names in double-bordered boxes), 12 of their students (*tābiʿīn*), seven imams of popular *madhāhib* (names in boxes), and a few of their students.

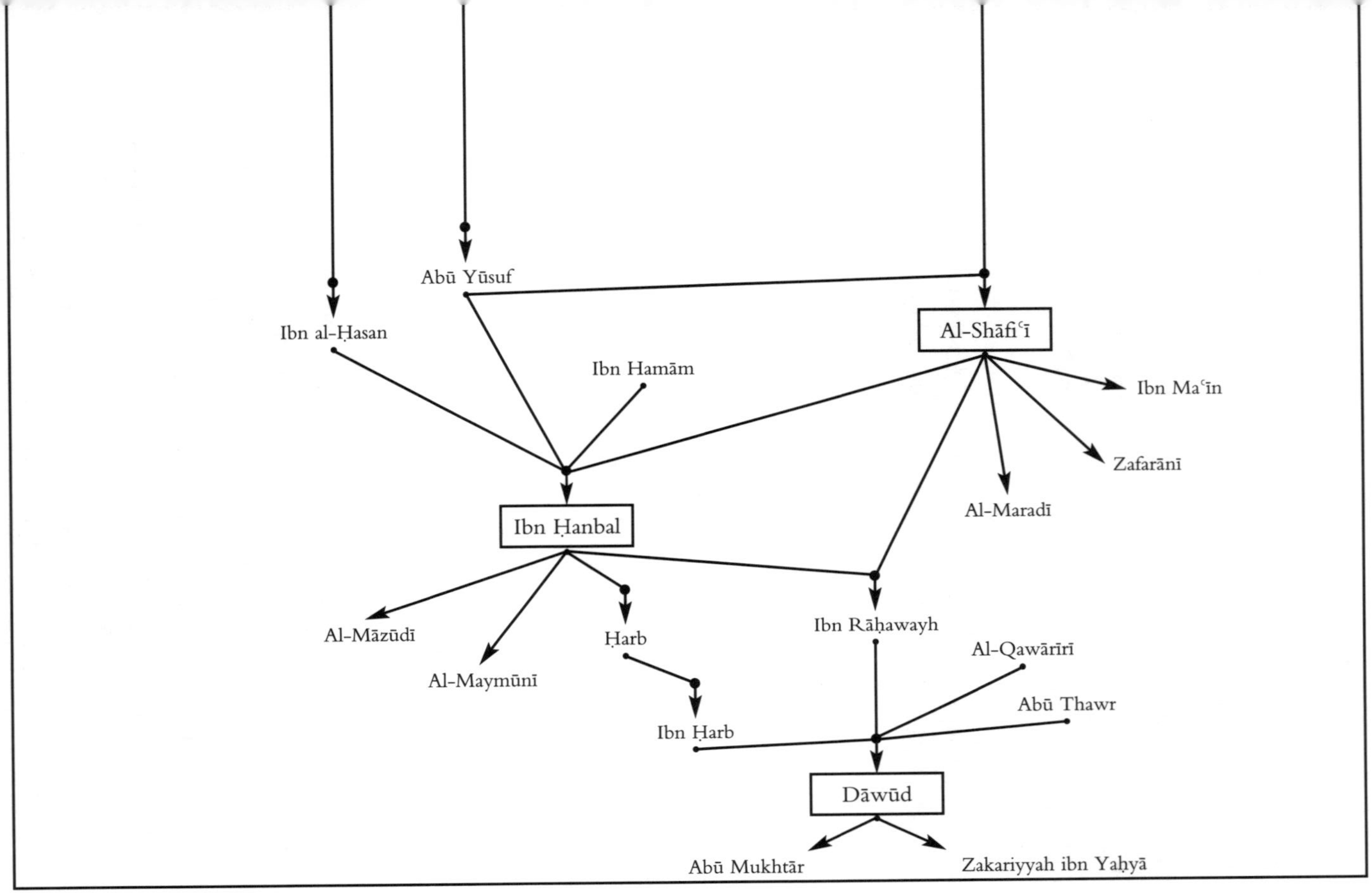
Abū Yūsuf
Ibn al-Ḥasan
Al-Shāfiʿī
Ibn Hamām
Ibn Maʿīn
Zafarānī
Ibn Ḥanbal
Al-Maradī
Al-Māzūdī
Al-Maymūnī
Ḥarb
Ibn Rāḥawayh
Al-Qawārīrī
Abū Thawr
Ibn Ḥarb
Dāwūd
Abū Mukhtār
Zakariyyah ibn Yaḥyā

Chart 3.4. Chains of students who eventually formed the schools of Islamic law, starting with (a selected group of) the companions and ending with (a selected group of) the uṣūlīs.

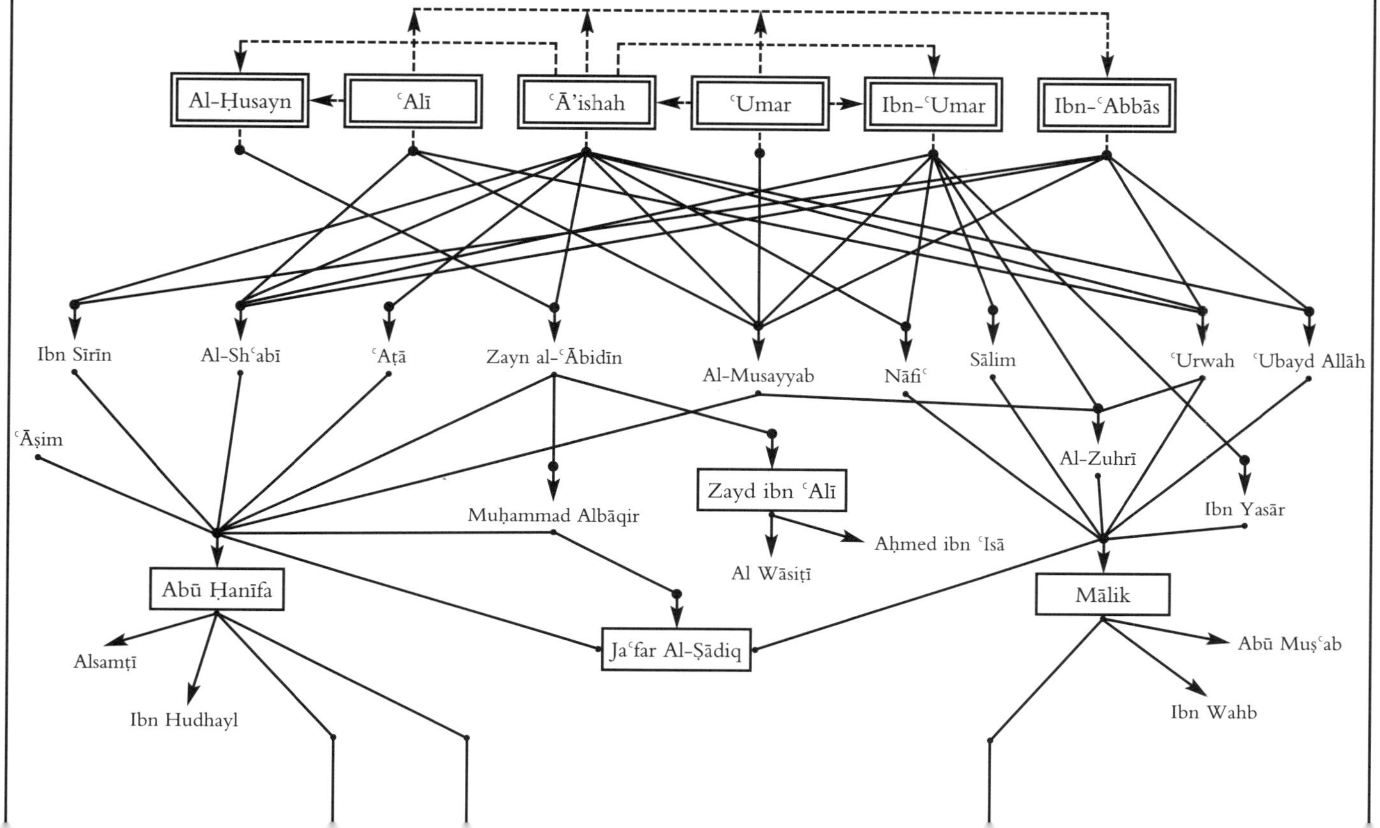

This specific group is selected for illustrative purposes. In all levels, the arrows go from each teacher to his/her student. This chart was compiled through recourse to a number of sources,[65] and the observations below were made based on the chart.

1. Learning and narration 'chains' of the companions and their students were highly interconnected. Students of the companions and the school imams were interconnected too, even though to a lesser extent. The chart illustrates how the level of interconnectivity decreased, generation after generation, until the schools of law became practically isolated in their evolution. I believe that lack of interaction between schools of law contributed to their lack of creativity and dominant partial views. It also resulted in different schools assigning different terms for similar concepts.
2. ʿĀ'ishah, Ibn ʿAbbās, and Ibn ʿUmar had great influence on the generation of *tabiʿīn*, as illustrated by the examples shown in the chart. However ʿĀ'ishah's influence and narrations through ʿAlī's lineage, narrated in Sunni sources, are disputed by the Shia school. ʿUmar and ʿAlī had a great influence on many of the companions, such as Ibn ʿAbbās and Ibn ʿUmar.
3. Jaʿfar al-Ṣādiq (the prime contributor to Shia fiqh, after whom the Jaʿfarīs/Imāmīs/Twelvers were named) influenced all Sunni schools through Mālik and Abū Ḥanīfa.
4. Each of al-Shiʿbī and Ibn al-Musayyab had learned from a large number of companions and influenced Mālik (through al-Zuhrī) and Abū Ḥanīfa, who, in turn, influenced all other imams.
5. Al-Shāfiʿī was influenced by Mālik and Abū Ḥanīfa (through Abū Yūsuf), Ibn Ḥanbal was influenced by Mālik (through al-Shāfiʿī) and Abū Ḥanīfa (through Abū Yūsuf and Moḥammad ibn al-Ḥasan), and Dawūd was influenced by Ibn Ḥanbal and al-Shāfiʿī (through Ibn Rahawayh). Both Jaʿfar and Zayd, the two main Shia imams, developed their knowledge through ʿAlī Zayn al-ʿĀbidīn ibn al-Ḥussain.
6. Finally, I cannot account fully for the diversity of methods and influences of the above key personalities via simple teacher-student chains, such as the ones drawn in this chart. For example,

ᶜĀ'ishah, Ibn ᶜUmar, and Ibn ᶜAbbās taught a number of *tabiᶜīn*. However, the strength and nature of their influence on each student were subject to a number of social factors. For example, ᶜUrwah ibn al-Zubair was ᶜĀ'ishah's nephew and hence was closer to her than many of her other students and was affected the most by her views and personality. ᶜAbdullāh ibn ᶜUmar had freed Nāfiᶜ and Ibn Yasār from slavery and, hence, they had a special relationship with him. Ibn ᶜAbbās was the Prophet's (and ᶜAlī's) cousin, which gave him wide 'connections' and a special status in all schools of law.

The 'Era of Declination'

Eventually, what is known as the 'Era of Declination,' in the Islamic civilization in general and in the theory of Islamic law in specific, started in the middle of the seventh Islamic century (13th century CE) with the 'fall of Baghdad' to the Tatarians in 656 AH.[66] Afterwards, scholars started to develop the practice of calling the imam and his students' opinions '*naṣṣun fī al-madhhab*' (a 'script' in the school). These 'scripts' were practically given precedence over the original scripts, i.e., the Qur'an and prophetic tradition. Jurists in the 'era of declination' were not allowed to make ijtihad, except when they found no related opinion narrated after their imam or his students.[67] Thus, they busied themselves with summarising the previous books in the form of exceedingly abstract exposés and complex pieces of poetry. Eventually what is known as the 'door of ijtihad' was closed, despite Wā'il Ḥallāq's tracing of some remnants of independent ijtihad in various schools.[68] The factor that contributed most to the survival of certain *madhāhib* of fiqh in particular regions was courts, which had to belong strictly to one school. Divisions between schools reached every aspect of social and religious life, including prayer areas in major mosques, which were divided into separate areas for different schools of law.[69] Competition between *madhāhib* was so strong that it, eventually, resulted in major violent disputes and the destroying of a number of major cities numerous times, as explained before.[70]

4

Classic Theories of Islamic Law

Overview

The purpose of this chapter is to provide a wide-ranging survey and analysis of the juridical theories of the nine classic schools of law under consideration, namely, Mālikīs, Ḥanafīs, Shāfiʿīs, Ḥanbalīs, Jaʿfarīs, Zaydīs, Ẓāhirīs, Ibāḍīs, and Muʿtazilīs. The presented analysis will focus on the hierarchical classifications of the various methods, in a comparative style. Some *fiqhī* examples are given, only for the sake of illustration. The language of this chapter is rather abstract, due to the specific nature of *uṣūl al-fiqh*, or the juridical theories of the Islamic law. References in the endnotes are meant to enable interested readers to refer to more detailed explanations.

The first section introduces the fundamental sources of Islamic jurisprudence, namely, the Qur'an and the Prophet's traditions. The second section surveys the script-based linguistic evidences that various schools have applied. Section Three surveys rational evidences, which were also 'script-based,' as will be argued. Finally, the fourth section presents a critical analysis of the different types and levels of 'rulings' and 'legal capacities.'

4.1. FUNDAMENTAL SOURCES/SCRIPTS

'Evidences' are the sources and procedures that a school of law endorses in order to derive rulings. They include two sources that are agreed upon (in principle) by all the schools of Islamic law, despite many differences over details of interpretation. These are the Qur'an and the Sunnah (prophetic tradition), which are considered by all traditional schools of law as the primary sources of jurisprudence. 'Evidences' also include other sources of normative judgements, such as customs and 'previous legislations,' as well as other juridical procedures that are traditionally called secondary sources of legislation, such as reasoning by analogy, consensus, or blocking the means. Differences of opinion amongst schools of law are due to their differences over evidences and/or their legitimacy.

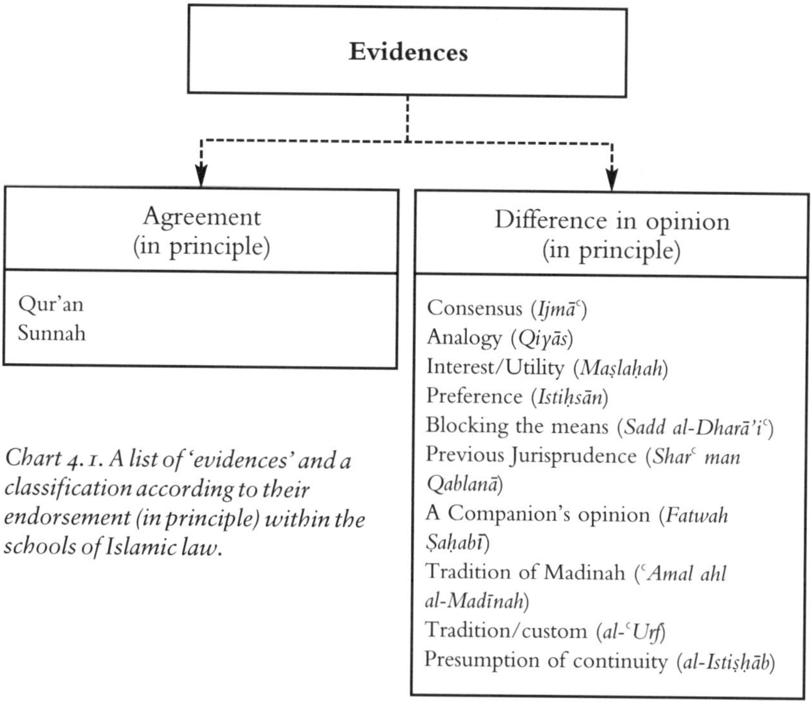

Chart 4.1. A list of 'evidences' and a classification according to their endorsement (in principle) within the schools of Islamic law.

Qur'an

The Qur'an that we know today is an exact copy (except for the dots and vocalisation marks) of the copies that were endorsed by the third Caliph, ʿUthmān, after the 'collection committee,' which he had formed, endorsed it. The idea of collecting the whole Qur'an in one book started to gain popularity amongst the companions shortly after the death of the Prophet. However, at the time of ʿUthmān, Muslims' disputes over various versions/readings of the Qur'an had reached a level that necessitated ʿUthmān's decision to collect and endorse one version of the Qur'an and order all others to be destroyed. In the endorsed version, ʿUthmān gave Quraish's dialect priority over other dialects, since it was the mother dialect of the Prophet. The popular 'ten readings' (*al-qirā'āt al-ʿashr*) of the Qur'an are all written according to the ʿUthmānī script. Their differences are all differences in dots and vocalisations added (at later stages) to the ʿUthmānī script.[1] Thus, there is an agreement over what is called "ʿUthmān's copy' in all schools of Islamic law.

There is one exception to this agreement, which is the opinion held by a handful of Shia Jaʿfarī jurists during the 'declination era.' They asserted that there is a number of missing Qur'anic verses, all related to the succession of ʿAlī ibn Abī-Ṭālib. These jurists hold some of the companions responsible for hiding these verses, for political reasons. According to all of the sunni and shia historical sources known today, none of the Shia Imams had made such allegations. Nor did any Shia Reference (*marjiʿ taqlīd*) of today, from Imams al-Khomeini and al-Sadir to Shams al-Din and Fadhlallah, endorse that opinion and, in fact, they all spoke strongly against it.[2] Furthermore, I have not come across any *fiqhī* opinion in various Shia schools of law that is based on 'verses' or 'chapters' outside the Qur'an, as we know it today. Therefore, it is accurate to say that the ʿUthmānī version, according to all schools of law, is the only version that is approved as the 'Holy Qur'an' and as authentic. Ibn al-Jazrī, for example, accounted for more than eighty narrations for each 'reading' (*qirā'ah*) of the ten known readings of the Qur'an.[3] Therefore, the 'most famous' (*mutawātir*) status that all schools of law give to the verses of the Qur'an is a result of a wide consensus over the level of authenticity of their narrations.

As far as fiqh is concerned, all schools refer to the current verses of the Qur'an for rulings, except for the Ḥanafī's referral to Ibn Masʿūd's version of some verses, and referrals by various schools to single-chained variations of some other verses (such as ʿAlī's, Ubay's,

ʿĀ'ishah's, and Sālim's versions). These versions of a handful of verses (whose narrators chose to keep after ʿUthmān's endorsement of the official copy) do not introduce any significant change in the verses' meanings. In terms of schools of law, these verses are treated as *āḥād* (hadith) sources, rather than Qur'anic verses.[4] ʿAbdullāh ibn Masʿūd's version is endorsed by the Ḥanafī School, only for the purposes of the law and not as recitable Qur'an, based on its famous (*mashhūr*) authenticity level. However, the Ḥanafī opinions that were based on them are not radically different from the rest of the opinions.[5]

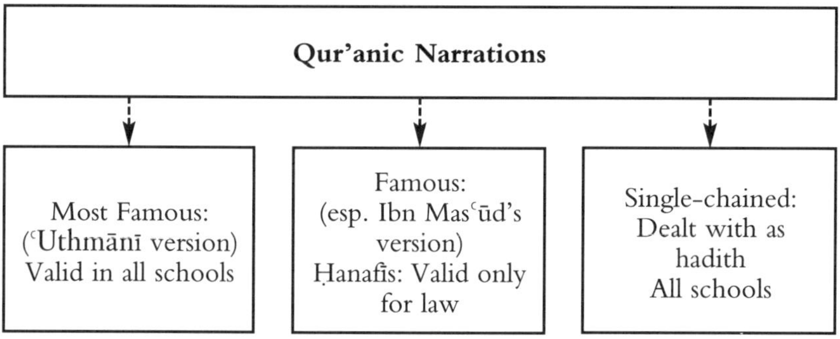

Chart 4.2. A classification of the Qur'anic narrations according to their 'level of authenticity.'

On the other hand, the Muʿtazilī school and a few scholars of fundamentals (*uṣūlī*s) gave 'reason' (*al-ʿaql*) the status of 'the most fundamental' source of legislation, even relative to the verses of the Qur'an.[6] Muʿtazilīs argued that reason is more fundamental than the scripts because it leads us to belief in the scripts themselves. However, after a Muslim believes in the Qur'an, Muʿtazilīs asserted that the Qur'an becomes 'a judging criterion over reason itself.' Therefore, the Muʿtazilī school of law is, practically, very similar to all other schools, especially the Shāfiʿī school (as will be explained later). 'Giving priority to reason over scripts' is, thus, a Muʿtazilī philosophical idea rather than a theory of juridical reasoning.

Sunnah

Sunnah (literally, tradition) is what is narrated at the authority of the companions about the Prophet's sayings, actions, or approvals. The

Prophet's witnessing of certain actions without objection is considered an approval from him, by definition. The Sunnah, in relation to the Qur'an (refer to Chart 4.3), implies a meaning that is (1) identical to the Qur'an's, (2) an explanation or elaboration on a general meaning mentioned in the Qur'an, (3) a specification of certain conditions for rulings implied in the Qur'an, (4) an addition of certain constraints to the general expressions of the Qur'an, or finally, (5) an initiation of independent legislation. Schools of law approve the first three of the above five relations and differ over the last two, as follows.

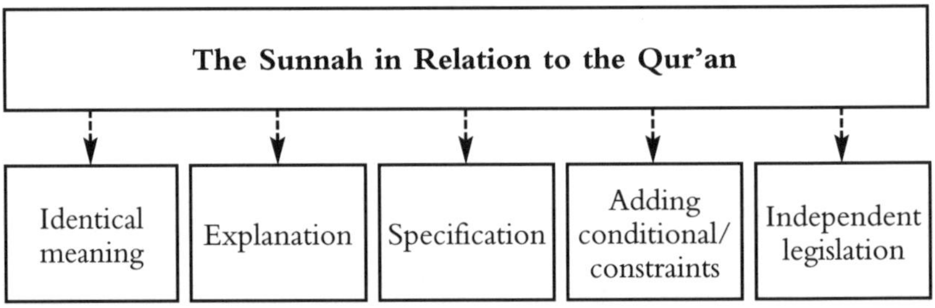

Chart 4.3. A classification of the possible relationships between the traditions of the Sunnah and the Qur'anic verses.

If the Qur'anic expression is 'general' and the Sunnah expression is 'specific' regarding the same topic, Shāfiʿīs, Ḥanfīs, Ẓahirīs, Zaydīs and Jaʿfarīs consider the (single-chained) Sunnah to be 'specifying' the general expression of the Qur'an and, thus, restricting its general expression. Ḥanafīs consider this 'specification' to be a sort of invalidation of the 'confirmed and absolute' general expression of the Qur'an and, therefore, reject the single-chained narration that place constraints on the Qur'an's general expressions.

Malik's opinion on this issue is to look for supportive evidence to the single-chained hadith that specifies the general meaning of the verse before rejecting it. His additional supportive evidence should be some ʿ*amal* (tradition) of the people of Madinah (an evidence which is invalid to all other schools), or a supporting analogy (*qiyās*). Otherwise, Malik applies weighed preference (*tarjīh*) and invalidates the single-chained narration.

If the hadith implies a ruling that has no relation with the Qur'an, all schools of law accept it as legislation on condition that it does not fall under actions that are specific to the Prophet. Actions specific to the Prophet could be actions exclusive to him out of prophethood considerations or actions that he did out of custom (*ʿādah*) of a 'man living in seventh century's Arabia.' Chart 4.4 shows this classification.

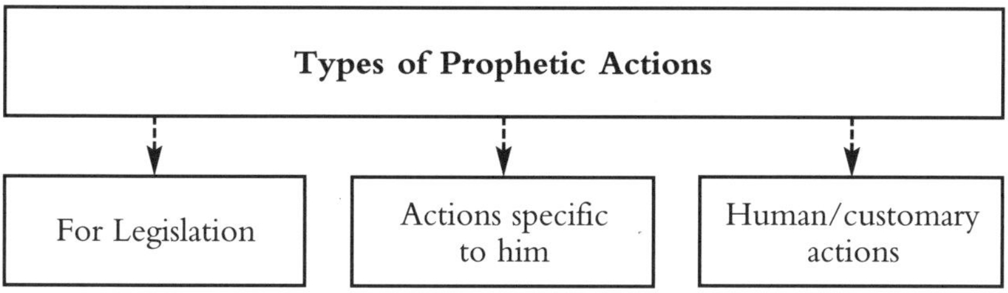

Chart 4.4. Types of Prophetic actions according to their implications on 'legislation.'

Some Mālikīs and Ḥanbalīs had added two other types to the Prophet's actions that do not fall under generally abiding 'legislation,' namely, actions 'out of being a leader' and actions 'out of being a judge.' Al-Qarāfī, for example, included all of the Prophetic actions during wars in his 'leadership actions', as well as governance-related decisions, as explained in Chapter One. He said that identifying the type of the Prophet's action according to his classification has 'implications for the law.' For example, he considered the Prophet's actions 'out of being a judge' to be valid legislations 'only for judges' when they assume their role in courts, rather than for every Muslim. Recently, following al-Qarāfi's example, al-Tahir ibn Ashur (also from the Mālikī school) added other types of actions for 'specific intents,' which are not meant to imply universal legislation, such as, advice, conciliation, discipline, and 'teaching high ideals' to specific people (Chapter Six explains in detail).

Ibāḍīs include 'acts of worship' in actions 'specific to the Prophet'. These are actions that he did not practice regularly. Other schools of law consider such actions 'recommended.' A few Muʿtazilīs differentiated between the Prophet's 'acts of worship' (*ʿibādāt*), which they considered the only type that is 'abiding to all Muslims,' versus all of his other actions, which they considered matters of 'worldly judgements' (*muʿāmalāt*). The question of how to differentiate *ʿibādāt* from *muʿāmalāt* remains an open question, even in the Muʿtazilī theory.

The scope of the Prophet's 'independent judgements' (ijtihad) is a topic of difference of opinion, and in my view, an open question. Literalists/Ẓāhirīs, and a few scholars from other schools of law, disagreed with the majority opinion that confirms the Prophet's ijtihad is possible.[7] Ibn Hazm based his disagreement on the 'uncertainty' of human reasoning, as opposed to the 'certainty' of the revelation which was available to the Prophet any time.[8] Al-Ghazālī's counter-argument is that, 'the Prophet's description of the revelation entails that it did not occur based on his requests but rather as an occasional contact initiated by The Angel.'[9]

The other basis of disagreement with the principle of the Prophet's ijtihad is the scope of *waḥī* (revelation) mentioned in the Qur'an.[10] Some exegetes interpreted the verses to mean that, 'whatever speech the Prophet utters is a revelation.'[11] This interpretation was rejected by the majority of schools, which defined a class of 'worldly affairs' and 'specifities' in the Prophet's hadith, as explained above.

There is related debate among jurists, who agreed to the principle of prophetic ijtihad, on whether or not this ijtihad was subject to error. Although the Qur'an mentioned that God did correct the Prophet on a number of occasions,[12] a number of jurists rejected the possibility of erring in the independent prophetic judgements based on the concept of infallibility (*ʿiṣmah*).[13] Most schools, however, acknowledged the possibility of error in the prophetic deliberation on the condition that, 'it would be immediately corrected by a revelation', unless it is concerned with some 'worldly affair.'[14] Differentiating between what is a 'worldly affair' and what is not proves to be an open question! The following is an example of such error in a matter of worldly affairs, which was narrated in the hadith known as the hadith of the pollenating of palm trees.'[15] Muslim's narration states: Ṭalḥah narrates:

> I was walking with the Prophet peace be upon him when he passed by some people at the tops of their palm trees. He asked: 'What are they

doing?' They answered: 'Pollenating the male into the female.' He replied: 'I do not think that this will be of benefit.' When they were told about what the Prophet said, they stopped what they were doing. Later, when the trees shed down their fruits prematurely, the Prophet was told about that. He said: 'If it is good for them they should do it. I was just speculating. So, pardon me. But if I tell you something about God, then take it because I would never lie about God.' Another narrator added: 'You know your worldly affairs better than me.'

Another hadith that adds to the dilemma of defining the sphere of 'worldly affairs' is the hadith of '*al-ghīlah*.'[16] Muslim and Mālik report that the Prophet said: 'I had almost intended to forbid *ghīlah*. Then, I noticed that the Byzantines and Persians do that without it causing any harm to their children.'[17] These hadiths, in my view, keep the question of 'what is to be considered a worldly affair' an open question.

On the other hand, valid hadiths are classified into most famous, famous, and single-chained. Most famous narrations are as absolute as the Qur'an, according to all schools, since they are narrated after a large number of companions (there are various estimates of the number 'large'), who could not possibly and logically agree to lie. Hadith included in this category are related to Islam's most famous acts of worship (basic actions of prayers, pilgrimage, and fasting).

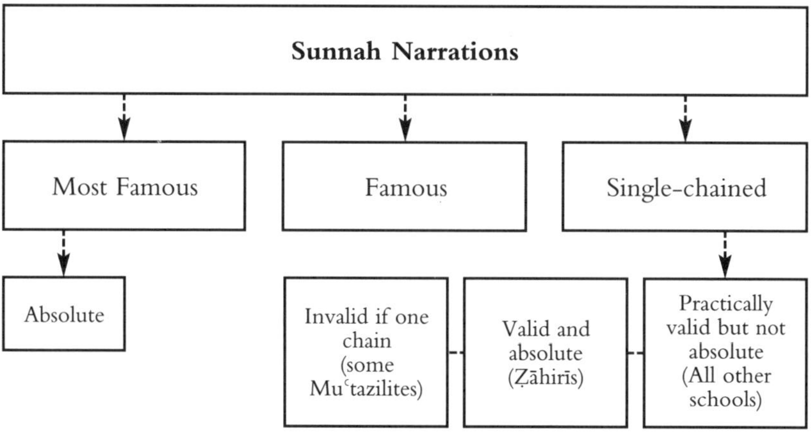

Chart 4.5. Types of Prophetic narrations in terms of their number of narrators.

However, it does not include hadith in the form of sayings. The absoluteness of these narrations, according to all schools, imply an obligation on every Muslim to believe in them, in addition to practice them. The most famous narrations are very few. Estimates range from a dozen to eighty narrations.

There comprises a category of 'famous narrations' narrated by a number of narrators not numerous enough to define it as 'logically impossible' for them to agree on lying. This category includes a small number of the hadith available in traditional sources (less than one hundred hadith according to all accounts), which makes its impact on the law limited, from a practical point of view.

The category of hadith which includes the vast majority of narrations is the *āḥād* (single-chained) category. All schools of Islamic law, except for some Muʿtazilīs, relied on this type in their derivation of their fiqh. These are narrations conveyed via one or a few 'chains of narrations,' usually with slightly different wordings. The verification procedures of the narrators and narrations are detailed extensively in the Sciences of Hadith.[18] The narration has to be valid in terms of its chain of narrators (*al-sanad*) and its content (*al-matn*). For the content of a hadith to be acceptable, the main criteria is to be linguistically correct and not to be in 'opposition' with another hadith, 'reason,' or 'analogy,' in a way that cannot be reconciled.[19] However, practically speaking, authenticity of hadith (*al-ṣiḥḥah*) was merely judged based on the chain of narrators (*al-sanad*). Differences of opinion in judging the *sanad* had implications on the law. Chart 4.6 summarises basic criteria for accepting *sanad* and *matn*.

Acceptable narrations by the Ẓāhirīs are 'certain' and 'absolute,' i.e., 'valid for juridical derivation' and 'required for correct belief,' even if they were single-chained. All other schools consider single-chained narrations to be juridically valid but not part of the Islamic creed. Some Muʿtazilīs differentiate between sayings and actions (including approvals) narrated in hadith. They do not consider actions to be valid evidences of legislation (that are abiding to every Muslim), except in the area of acts of worship (*ʿibādāt*). On the other hand, they consider 'sayings' to be valid evidences of legislation in *ʿibādāt* as well as *muʿāmalāt* (worldly transactions). The question of how to differentiate *ibādāt* from *muʿāmalāt* is another open question. Most schools believed that *ibādāt* are the issues that 'cannot be rationalised,' which still keeps the question open.[20]

Trusting a narration entails a group of conditions for bearing (*ḥaml*) or learning the hadith and another group for conveying or narrating the hadith, which all schools agreed upon, in principle. For being accepted as a bearer of a hadith, a narrator has to be mature

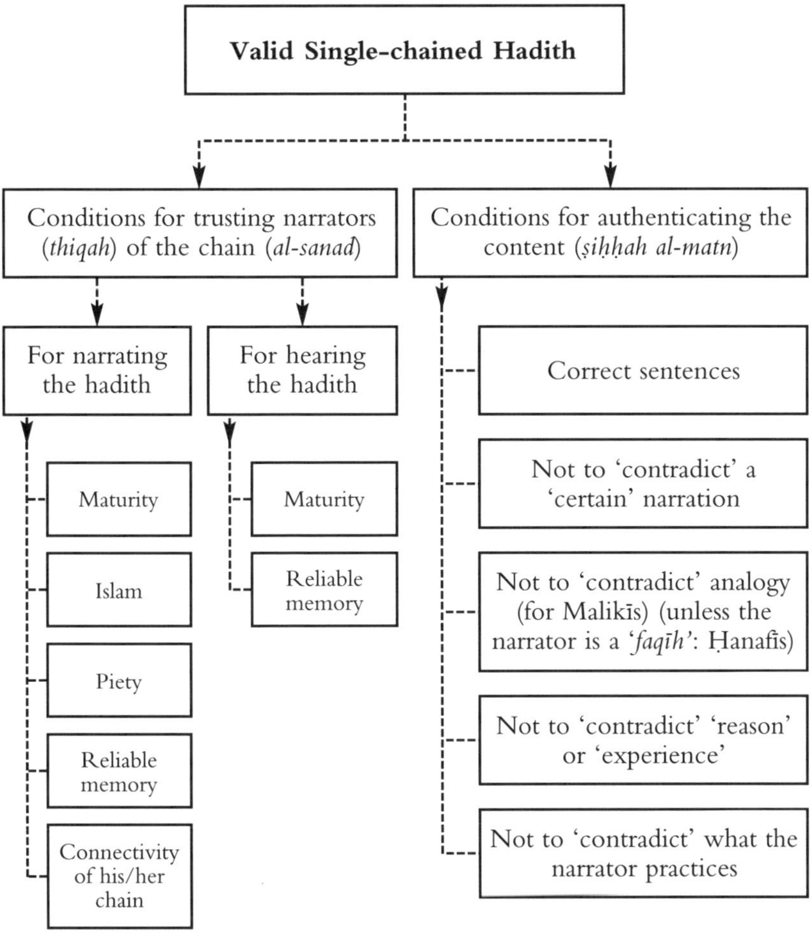

Chart 4.6. Conditions for validating single-chains narrations in traditional Sciences of Hadith.

(most estimates for his/her age is seven years old) and known to have a reliable memory (*al-ḍabṭ*). For narrating a hadith, a narrator has to be mature, Muslim, pious, has a reliable memory, and has a connected (*muttaṣil*) chain of narrators/teachers between him/her and the Prophet. The exact specifications of each of these conditions are subject to many differences of opinion amongst scholars of hadith, even within each school. Moreover, there are clear divisions in terms of trusted narrators between the Sunni schools (Mālikīs, Shāfiʿīs, Ḥanafīs, Ḥanbalīs, and Ẓāhirīs), and the Shia schools (Jaʿfarīs and Zaydīs). Ibadis have their own group of trusted narrators as well. Sunni schools accepted all companions and their students, including the 'Shia' imams and the 'Ibāḍī' students of the companions (who were much later labelled as Shia and Ibāḍī after the establishment of these parties, as explained before). For Sunnis, however, later generations of Shia, Ibāḍīs, and Muʿtazilīs are not generally acceptable as trustworthy narrators of hadith because of their alleged 'innovations' (*bidʿah*). On the other hand, Jaʿfarīs and Zaydīs do not accept the companions' narrations (except for the companions who were considered part of the Prophet's household or *āl al-baīt*). This is largely due to the conflict between ʿAlī on one side and Muʿawiyah and ʿĀ'ishah on the other, which became the civil war and Battle of the Camel (*Mawqiʿah al-Jamal*) in 37AH/ 657CE. Nevertheless, narrations from the Shia sources produced juridical rulings that are quite similar to other Sunni rulings (except for some minor differences in fiqh, which are as much as the differences between any other two Sunni schools). In my view, differences between Sunni and Shia schools were and remain to be in the area of *kalām* and politics, that is, political positions over the companions' post-ʿUthmān civil war. Ibadis also ended up with a fiqh that is quite similar to the rest of the schools, despite the historic political differences between them and the rest of the schools.[21]

The last condition for accepting a narrator, which is the ability to relate a connected chain of narrators/teachers up to the Prophet, is a matter of significant differences amongst schools of Islamic law. A chain with missing narrators from the beginning, the middle, or the end of the chain has various levels of credibility and different terminologies in the Sciences of Hadith, and has contributed to many differences of opinion. For example, the *mursal* hadith (which is a narration related directly to the Prophet without mentioning intermediate narrators/companions) had a significant impact on differences in *fiqhī* opinions. Schools of law took different positions on *mursal* hadith (refer to Chart 4.7). Mālikīs and Ḥanafīs accept it from the students of the companions only. Al-Shāfiʿī did not accept such hadith except when there was supporting evidence, such as other narrations of the same hadith (even if they were also *mursal* narrations). Jaʿfarīs and Zaydīs accept it from the Imams on their authority. Aḥmad ibn Ḥanbal considers the *mursal* narration to be 'weak,' in terms of authenticity, and therefore, would not use it unless no other narration was available. However, he gives the *mursal* hadith priority over other secondary evidences (such as analogy).

Regarding the narrations themselves (of the degree *aḥād*), they have to be conveyed in complete sentences. Moreover, they cannot contradict with other 'certain' narrations or analogy (according to Mālikīs, and unless the narrator is considered a '*faqīh*,' according to Ḥanafīs). Nor can they contradict the narrator's practices or 'reason,' according to Muʿtazilīs.[22] However, in my view, the very definitions of 'contradiction,' 'certainty,' and 'reason' in traditional schools of law require 'philosophical updating,' as this book will argue. Moreover, the condition that 'reason' should not contradict with narrations is problematic, since al-Ghazālī, amongst other jurists, included in their definition

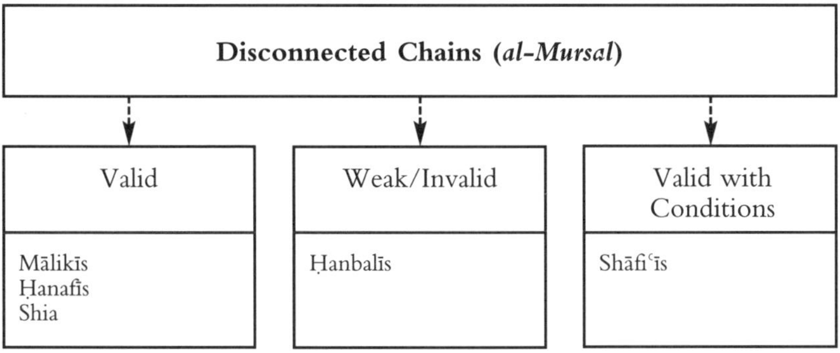

Chart 4.7. Positions of some schools of law regarding the mursal hadith.

of reason, which was 'what is acceptable according to common sense and experience.'[23]

The next section studies the linguistic tools that various schools of law used in deriving rulings from the primary scripts/sources introduced in this section.

4.2. SCRIPT-BASED LINGUISTIC EVIDENCES

Overview

When jurists talk about 'an evidence' from the Qur'an or the prophetic tradition, they actually mean a ruling that is derived from a specific expression of a verse or hadith, according to one of the categories of linguistic expressions explained in this section. Expressions, or 'terms' are categorised in terms of clarity (*wuḍūḥ*), implication (*dilālah*), and scope (*shumūl*). These expressions and the methods of deriving meanings/rulings from them is a shared concern for all schools of the Islamic law. With the evolution of the schools of law and the increasing popularity of Greek philosophy in jurists' circles, these classifications ended up resembling the 'conceptions' (*taṣawwurāt*) sections within medieval treaties on logic, in content and structure, as this section explains.

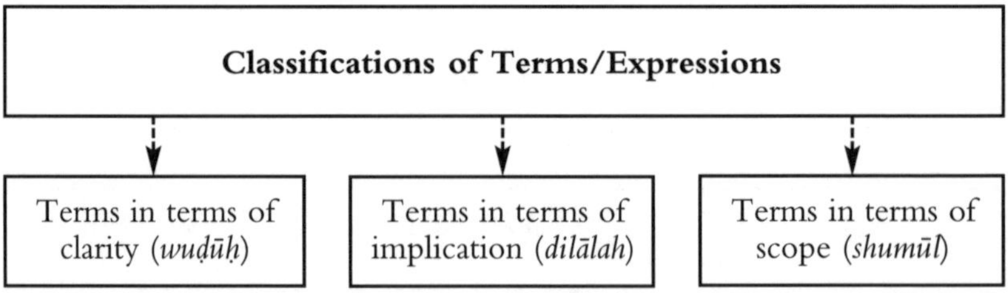

Chart 4.8. Classification of terms/expressions in terms of clarity, implication, and scope.

Clarity

A binary classification of clarity is agreed upon amongst schools, in which expressions are classified into 'clear' and 'unclear' rulings.[24] Jurists further divided clear terms into into four levels of clarity, which are ordered from clearest to least clear. They are 'firmly constructed' (*muḥkam*), 'text' (*naṣṣ*), 'apparent' (*ẓāhir*), and 'explained' (*mufassar*). This division is made based on three criteria, namely, the possibility of specification (*takhṣīṣ*), interpretation (*ta'wīl*), and abrogation (*naskh*).

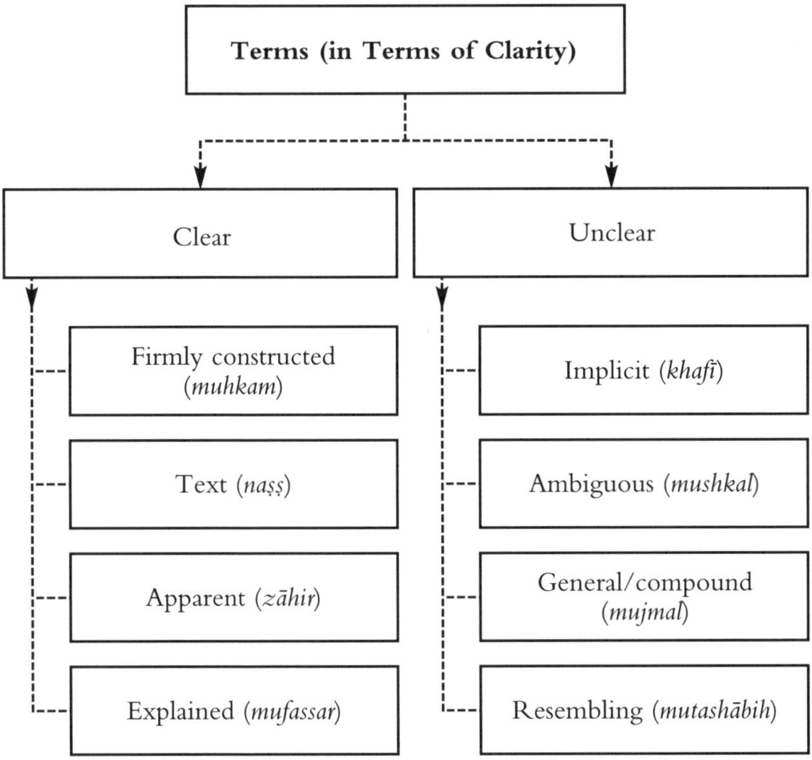

Chart 4.9. Classification of 'clear' and 'unclear' terms.

	Possibility of Specification	Possibility of Re-interpretation	Possibility of Abrogation
Firmly constructed	No	No	No
Text	Yes	Yes	No *except with evidence*
Apparent	Yes	Yes	Yes
Explained	Depending on the 'explaining' evidence		

Chart 4.10. Classification of clear terms according to the possibility of their specification, re-interpretation, and abrogation.

A firmly constructed term is a clear expression that 'does not need any specification or interpretation,' and is 'proven not to have been abrogated' (i.e., cancelled during the time of the Prophet).[25]

The implication of this type of terms is considered stronger than all other terms, i.e., it specifies, interprets, or even abrogates 'opposing' expressions. The conditions of 'proven' not to be 'abrogated' or 'in opposition' are problematic, since abrogation and opposition are unjustifiably and inconsistently claimed, as will be explained later.

A 'text' (*naṣṣ*) is a clear expression, but could be specified via some other expression. It could also be abrogated with an 'opposing' evidence.[26] The evidence that has the capacity to specify, interpret, or abrogate a *naṣṣ* has to be another *naṣṣ* or a *muḥkam* expression. This purely linguistic approach to the prioritisation and the application of evidences is endorsed by most schools of law. However, some jurists suggested evidences outside *al-naṣṣ* that has the capacity to 'oppose' *al-naṣṣ*, such as, interest (*maṣlaḥah*) and custom (*ᶜurf*). For example, al-Ṭūfī, a leading Ḥanbalī jurist, gave precedence of *al-maṣlaḥah* over a specific *naṣṣ*. Ibn ᶜĀbidīn, a leading Ḥanafī jurist, restricted the meaning of *al-naṣṣ* with *al-ᶜurf*. These opinions raise a serious question about the 'absoluteness' of the direct implication of *al-naṣṣ* that is claimed in all schools of law, which had resulted in a great deal of inflexibility in dealing with evolving realities (*al-wāqiᶜ*). This point is of special importance and will be dealt with in the context of 'openness' of the system of Islamic law.

The next level of 'clarity' is the 'apparent meaning' (*al-ẓāhir*), which is defined as a separate category from *al-naṣṣ* only in the Ḥanafī school. According to Ḥanafīs, the difference between *al-naṣṣ* and *al-ẓāhir* is in: 'the meaning of *al-naṣṣ* is intended in the script, while the meaning of *al-ẓāhir* is understood as a secondary implication.'[27] The implication of *al-ẓāhir* in the law is also 'certain,' it is claimed, unless a *naṣṣ* or a *muḥkam* 'opposes' it. The lowest level of clarity is what is called the 'explained' term (*al-mufassar*). Jurists mean by an 'explained' expression an unclear expression that is explained by other clear ones. The level of clarity after the explanation depends on the level of the explaining term, whether *muḥkam*, *naṣṣ*, or *ẓāhir*.

Similarly, *uṣūlīs* divide 'unclear term' (*ghayr al-wāḍiḥ*) into four categories, depending on whether the 'lack of clarity' comes from the structure of the term itself or from its scope, i.e., its capacity to include certain meanings. The four categories are implicit (*khafī*), ambiguous (*mushkal*), general (*mujmal*), and resembling (*mutashābih*).[28]

An implicit term is unclear in terms of what should be included in its scope.[29] For example, jurists had differences of opinion over whether the expression of 'thief,' which is mentioned in verse 5:38, includes 'fraudulents' and 'shop lifters' or not. Schools of law resulted in providing different answers to this question based on their methodologies

	Reason for Non-clarity	
	Structural	Scope
Implicit		√
Ambiguous	√	
Whole		√
Resembling	√	

Chart 4.11. Classification of types of unclear expressions, based on the reason behind their non-clarity.

in dealing with implicit expressions. Ḥanafīs (except Abū Yūsuf) did not include 'shop lifters' in the category of 'thieves' because of the 'difference in the names,'[30] they said. There is clearly a great deal of literalism (*ḥarfiyyah*) in this view. On the other hand, Mālik, Shāfiʿī, and Aḥmad considered what they called 'the meaning of theft' to be the criteria of considering someone a 'thief.' They further asserted that this 'meaning' should be 'defined according to custom.'

A similar example is the word 'killer' in the hadith, 'a killer does not inherit [from the murdered].' A difference of opinion arose as to whether a 'killer by mistake,' 'by instigation,' or 'by association' is implicitly included in that term. For example, al-Shāfiʿī included everybody that could be 'called' a killer in the term, with or without intention to kill. Mālik, on the other hand, insisted that the 'purpose/intent' of the person should be to kill and, therefore, did not include 'killing by mistake' in the term. Ḥanafīs took a rather literal opinion on this issue, and decided that the implicit meaning in the word 'killer' is the action of killing itself. Thus, if the person himself/herself carried out the action of killing, whether or not intentionally, then he/she is included in the hadith. Otherwise, he/she is not included in the term, even if he/she had helped the murderer, even intentionally, with the action of the killing! These are example of incomprehensible rulings that jurists sometimes issue just to keep in line with their fundamental linguistic theories. The negative implications of the resulting 'rulings' on the higher objectives (*maqāṣid*) of justice and social order are clear in the above two examples.

An ambiguous term (structurally) implies more than one meaning and 'could not be understood except with outside evidence.'[31] A classic example is the word 'periods' (Arabic: *qurū'*), mentioned in verse 2:228. Schools of law differ over this expression due to their differences over outside evidences that they used to explain the ambiguity. Thus, their difference of opinion in this example, boils down to their difference over the methodology of dealing with, again, 'opposing evidences.'

A 'whole' term (*mujmal*) is an expression that includes a number of situations and rulings in its meaning, which are in need of other expressions or evidences for clarification.[32] Examples are 'prayer' or 'pilgrimage' mentioned in the scripts, which imply a number of detailed rulings known from other scripts. Jurists claimed that after illustrating this *mujmal* expression, it becomes clear, i.e., either *naṣṣ*, *muḥkam*, or *mufassar*.[33]

Finally, the 'resembling' (*mutashābih*) term is an Arabic expression that could not be understood 'rationally,' jurists said.[34] Examples are individual Arabic letters mentioned at the beginning of some chapters of the Qur'an, and expressions used to describe God in 'human-like' terms. In this case, some form of interpretation or *ta'wīl* has to be carried out in order to clarify the 'resembling' expression.

In my view, the above classifications of clear and unclear expressions are arbitrary! My reason behind this 'radical' view is that the difference between the levels of *muḥkam*, *naṣṣ*, and *ẓāhir* depends on specification, interpretation, and abrogation, as jurists maintained. However, countless instances in the *fiqhī* literature of various schools prove that almost every *muḥkam* or *naṣṣ* expression is in fact subject to difference of opinion on whether it is actually 'specified,' 'interpreted,' or 'abrogated' by other expressions. Therefore, the categories of *muḥkam*, *naṣṣ*, and *ẓāhir* converge to one category of *al-ẓāhir*, which if interpreted or explained, will depend on the 'level of clarity' of the explaining expression. Similarly, most scriptural expressions could be 'whole' and in need of clarification as to its components, or ambigious/implicit and in need of clarification as to its meaning, and so on. There are no 'natural' differences between these categories.

Implication

The second classification of terms is according to the implications or meanings (*dilālāt*) implied by them. The two classifications of implications, which are endorsed by all other schools in similar terms, are the Ḥanafī's and the Shāfiʿī's. After analysing both, I realised that the two schools endorse very similar categorisation of implications, albeit in slightly different means of articulation. Chart 4.12 and Chart 4.13 summarise the Ḥanafī and Shāfiʿī classifications, respectively.

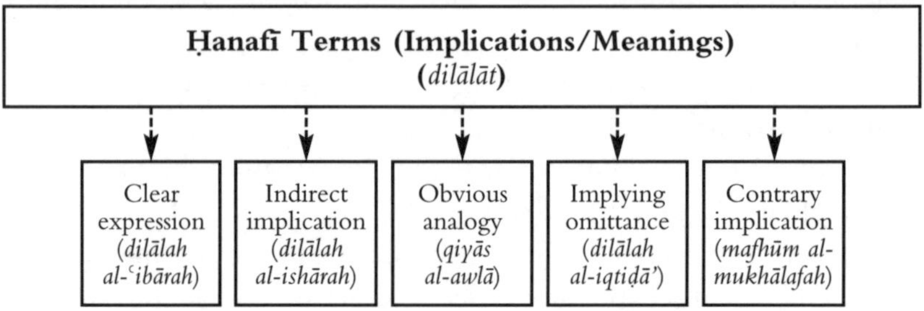

Chart 4.12. Implications of expressions according to the Ḥanafīs.

The Ḥanafī Classification of Implications

According to Ḥanafīs, a 'clear expression' (*ʿibārah*) implies a certain meaning in a direct and straightforward manner, which could be *muḥkam*, *naṣṣ*, *ẓāhir*, and *mufassar*, as explained above. On the other hand, an 'indirect implication' (*ishārah*) implies a meaning based on an understanding of a relationship between an (indirect) meaning and another (direct) meaning. For example, the 'verse of debts' implies (directly) that the consent has to be written according to the parties' agreement, but it also implies (indirectly) that the contract is legally binding to both parties in front of a court, even though this is not directly stated in the verse. Another example is the 'verse of consultation' (or *shūrā*), which directly implies a governing system that is based on people's consent, but could indirectly imply 'accountability' and 'transparency.' These two examples are meant to show how extending direct implication (*ʿibārah*) to indirect implication (*ishārah*) could contribute to a much-needed expansion and 'contemporisation' of the interpretations of the scripts. However, direct *ʿibārah* has absolute priority over indirect *ishārah*, according to all schools. Moreover, clear direct *ʿibārah* is considered definitive/certain, while indirect *ishārah* is probable (*ẓannī*) and, thus, does not, formally speaking, entail juridical 'obligation' of its implied rulings, such as 'legal abidance' or 'transparency.' The 'levels of rulings' are introduced and discussed later.

Obvious analogy (*qiyās jalī*) is an implication that is derived from the expression by 'common sense.' Some jurists call it the 'implication[35] of the implication.' For example, forbidding 'eating' what belong to the orphans without a right to do so, as verse 4:10 states, also implies wasting this wealth in any other way. Another example is the implication of the verse that orders a son or daughter not to say a 'word of grumbling' to their parents. The 'obvious analogy' implies an order not to harm parents by any means. This form of analogy is less formal than syllogistic analogy and its implication is used by most jurists. In addition, Ibn Taymiyah used the validity of the 'obvious analogy' to criticise the claimed 'certainty' of Aristotle's syllogistic analogy.

A final implication in the Ḥanafī classification is an implication of an omitted word (*iqtiḍā'*), or words that are also concluded, again, by 'common sense' from the expression. Omittance is a form of eloquency in Arabic expressions and a form of ambiguity, too, which could result in juridical flexibility and, also, differences of opinion. For instance, 'forbidden upon you is anything that dies by itself,'[36] implies ommitance of either the word 'eating,' i.e., it is forbidden to eat dead animals, or the word 'using,' i.e., it is forbidden to use a dead animal's bones or skin in any way.[37] In this example 'using' is more general than 'eating.' Thus, schools of law differed over whether to give priority to the 'general substitution' or the 'specific substitution' for the ommited word. Shāfiʿīs endorsed the 'general' choice while Ḥanafīs endorsed the 'specific.'

The Shāfiʿī Classification of Implications

The Shāfiʿī's classification of implications (Chart 4.13) show direct similarities with the Ḥanafī's, namely, 'clearly stated' (*ṣarīḥ*), which in similar to the Ḥanafī's *ʿibārah*, '*mafhūm*' (understood by implication), which is similar to the Ḥanafī's *qiyās al-awlā* (obvious analogy), and *iqtiḍā,* (implying ommitance). The difference between the two classifications is a level that the Shāfiʿīs added to determine whether the 'unclearly-stated' expression is 'intended' (by the expression) or not, and therefore, whether the 'indirect meaning' will be considered an indirect implication (*ishārah*) or implicit implication (*īmā'*). The technical difference between *ishārah* and *īmā'* is that *īmā'* is directly related to the *ʿillah* (appropriate 'cause') of the expression, while *ishārah* is concluded by 'the language sense' without following the

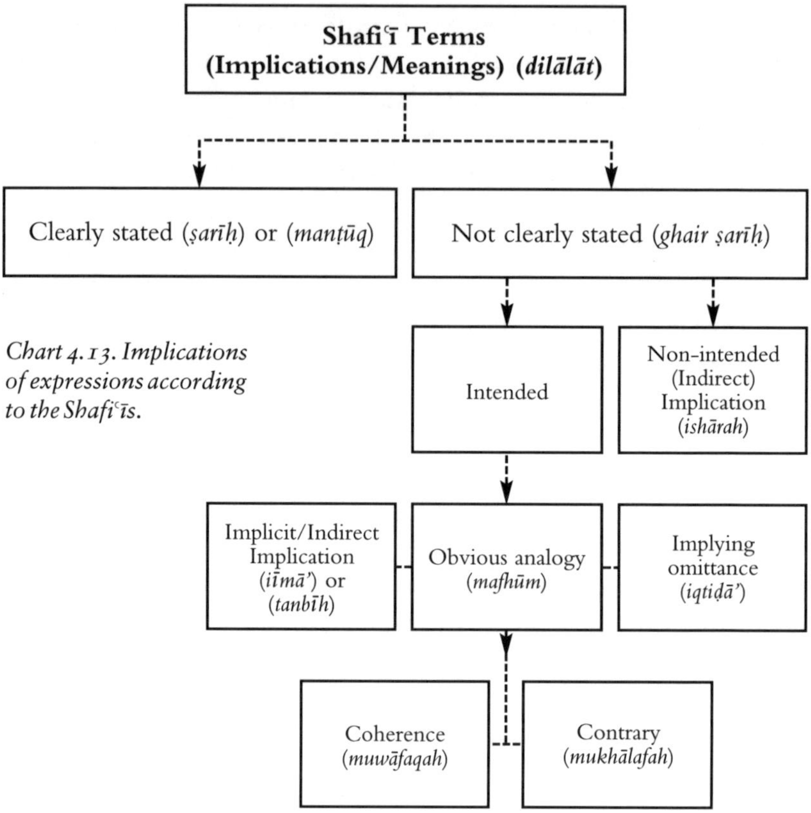

Chart 4.13. Implications of expressions according to the Shafiᶜīs.

formal procedure of extracting the ᶜ*illah*.[38] However, in terms of juridical implications, the Shāfiᶜīs' extra category does not make any practical difference.

Jaᶜfarīs and Zaydīs had introduced a different classification of 'firmly constructed' (*muḥkam*) terms that is also similar to the Shāfiᶜī and Ḥanafī classification. Jaᶜfarī and Zaydī categories of terms are: 'clear' (*jalī*), 'apparent' (*ẓāhir*), 'implied' (*mafhūm*), 'specific' (*khāṣ*), 'rationally embellished' (*taḥsīn ᶜaqlī*), and 'allegorical' (*majāz*), in that order.[39] The definition of each of these categories is similar to the corresponding categories of Ḥanafī and Shāfiᶜī. The only significant addition in this categorisation is the 'rationally embellished' category, which opens the door for free ijtihad, on condition that there is no related clear, apparent, implied, or specific script.[40]

However, there are two other differences between the Ḥanafī and Shāfiʿī classifications that do have juridical implications. They are the interrelations between the categories of implications and the 'contrary implication.'

The Ḥanafī and Shāfiʿī classifications differ in terms of the prioritisation of these implications, i.e., which implication to apply first in case there is more than one in the expression(s) at hand. The Ḥanafī's order is:

1. *ʿIbārah.*
2. *Ishārah.*
3. *Qiyās al-awlā.*
4. *Iqtiḍā'.*

The Shāfiʿī's order is as follows (using the Ḥanafī terms, while disregarding the difference between the two types of indirect implications):

1. *ʿIbārah.*
2. *Qiyās al-awlā.*
3. *Ishārah.*
4. *Iqtiḍā'.*

This difference in the order of *qiyās al-awlā* and *ishārah* had resulted in a number of differences in *fiqhī* rulings between Ḥanafīs and the rest of schools of law (which generally followed the Shāfiʿī classification). For example, one verse of the Qur'an states: 'But whoever deliberately slays another believer, his requital shall be hell.'[41] This verse implies (indirectly, i.e., *bi al-ishārah*) that hell is the (only) punishment for murderers.[42] However, another verse states: 'Upon him who has slain a believer by mistake there is a duty of freeing a believing soul from bondage and paying an indemnity to the victim's relations.'[43] Shāfiʿīs made an obvious analogy or *qiyās al-awlā* between a killer with intention and the killer without intention who is mentioned in this verse. Therefore, Shāfiʿīs judged that an intentional killer should pay a indemnity equal to the indemnity that a mistaken killer pays, in addition to the default punishment.

Shāfiʿīs gave priority to obvious analogy over indirect implication because it is the 'closest implication to the direct implication of *al-naṣṣ* (or *al-ʿibārah*),' while Ḥanafīs gave priority to *al-ishārah* because it is 'closest to the structure of the wordings since it is an integrative part of *al-naṣṣ*.'[44] Therefore, both schools are in fact endeavoring to be as close as possible to the literal meaning of *al-naṣṣ*. This book suggests, however, that greater weight should be given to the rationale/purpose of *al-naṣṣ*, rather than its literal meaning.

Contrary Implication

All traditional schools of Islamic law, except for the Ḥanafīs, agree with the Shāfiʿīs in dividing the *mafhūm*/implication into *mafhūm al-muwāfaqah* (coherence implication, which include the examples of 'obvious analogy,' mentioned above), and *mafhūm al-mukhālafah* (contrary implication). Contrary implication means that the 'existence of a fact implies the absence of the contrary.' In formal logic, it is the proposition that 'α' is equal to 'NOT NOT α.' Schools of law which endorsed contrary implication divided it into five different types, namely, title (*al-laqab*), attribute (*al-waṣf*), condition *(al-sharṭ*), limit/end (*al-ghāyah*), and number (*al-ʿadad*). This means that the mention of one of these types in a script implies, according to contrary implication, the logical absence and juridical invalidity of its opposite. Ḥanafīs rejected this type of implication since 'a ratio legis (*ʿillah*) of a script cannot imply two opposite rulings simultaneously.'[45]

An example of a 'title' is the word 'pastured' (*sā'imah*) mentioned in the hadith: 'there is zakah charity due on pastured cattle.'[46] Therefore, non-pastured cattle are not included in zakah, according to all schools of law, except for the Ḥanafī school, which did not endorse contrary implication.[47]

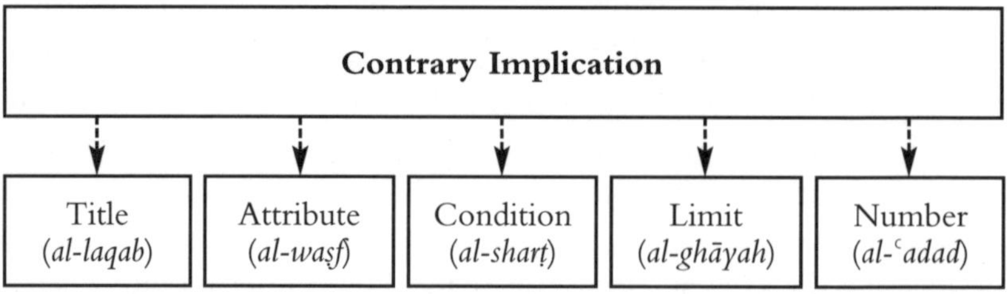

Chart 4.14. Types of contrary implication.

An example of an attribute is 'believer' associated with the women mentioned in verse 4:25 (in the context of marriage). Therefore, al-Shāfiʿī made believing a 'condition' for that marriage to be valid and so did not allow marriage with non-believers. Ḥanafīs, who do not endorse contrary implication, allowed Muslim men to marry 'believer' and 'non-believer' women.

An example of a condition is the verse, 'if they [i.e., your divorcees] happen to be with child, spend freely on them until they deliver their burden.'[48] According to contrary implication, if the divorcee does not have a child, then she is not entitled to the support mentioned. Ḥanafīs disagreed.[49]

An example of a 'limit' is found in verse 2:187 on fasting: 'eat and drink until you can discern the white streak of dawn against the blackness of night.'[50] This verse implies that eating and drinking are allowed until the stated time limit is reached and not allowed afterwards. Ḥanafīs agree on the same conclusion but consider 'eating and drinking' in this example to be a default ruling that is 'restricted' by fasting, rather than by contrary implication.[51]

Contrary implication was also applied to numbers. If a verse or hadith mentions a number, then all other numbers are invalid, and no other number could replace the number mentioned in the text. An example is the percentages and thresholds mentioned in the hadith on zakah (obligatory charity). Ḥanafīs also do not allow changing the numbers, but base their opinion on the direct implication of the text (*al-naṣṣ*), rather than on contrary implication.

It is true that all schools of law exclude attributes that are mentioned for the sake of other 'allegorical purposes' from 'contrary implications.' They also exclude contrary implications that 'oppose' other scripts.[52] However, this method (illustrated by the examples mentioned) show a sort of 'Exclusive-OR,' to use a logical term,[53] that is implicit in the very reading of the scripts and, thus, does not allow a range or a variety of rulings to be applied according to different situations. This method added to the inability of traditional Islamic law to change with changing circumstances and, thereby, hindered the scripts from contributing to that change. For example, the 'implication of numbers' resulted in an 'opposition' (*taʿāruḍ*) between a number of hadith narrations regarding certain kinds of zakah, which varied within a certain range.[54] This forced jurists to cancel/abrogate certain narrated numbers in order to apply the method of implication of numbers consistently. For example, there is a difference between the 'Book of Abū Bakr,' the 'Book of ʿAlī,' and the 'Book of ʿAmr ibn Ḥazm' in terms of the numbers for what should be taken as zakah out of camel herds.[55] Due to these differences in narrations and the implication of numbers, jurists were divided over which numbers to endorse (and, thus, which to reject based on contrary implication). A few scholars including al-Tabari, however, decided that a valid choice could be based on any of the above narrations.[56]

Nevertheless, if we consider a different dimension, other than the implication/counter implication dimension, we will not have to face or resolve any contradiction. The purposes (*maqāṣid*) of zakah include facilitation, as jurists had concluded. Some contemporary jurists maintained that the principle of facilitation implies that numbers differed based on considerations regarding the circumstances of the donors themselves.[57]

Scope

Expressions/Terms were also categorised according to their 'scope,' and theoretical differences over the relationship between the resulting

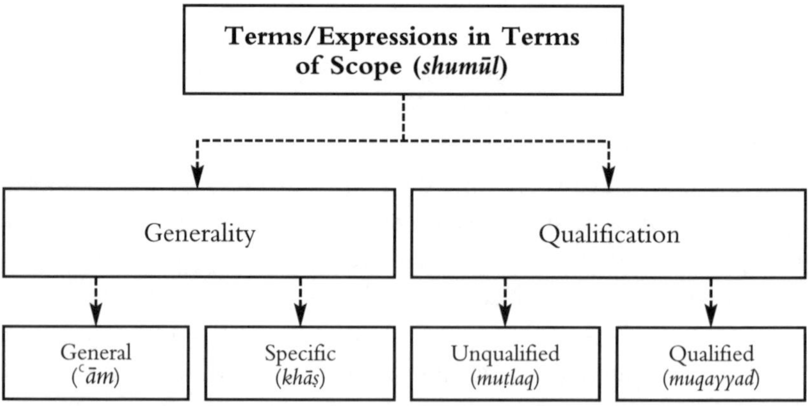

Chart 4.15. Classification of expressions in terms of their scope.

categories generated some difference of opinion on the practical *fiqhī* level. Once more, reminiscent of some Greek categorisations, terms were classified in terms of 'generality' and 'qualification.' Thus, terms were further classified into the binary categories of 'general' versus 'specific,' and 'unqualified' versus 'qualified.'

Generality

A general (*ᶜām*) term includes more than one entity in its expression, while a specific term includes only one entity, whether it is a person or an attribute. Jurists agree that a specific term is 'certain' (*qaṭᶜī*) in its implication, and thus cannot be probable (*ẓannī*) based on any speculated hypothesis.[58] However, jurists differed over the 'certainty' of the scriptural general term. Ḥanafīs considered it 'certain' (*qaṭᶜī*), while all other schools considered it to be 'probable' (*ẓannī*) and, thus, 'specifiable.' This difference of opinion had an impact on scripts that were thought to be in 'opposition.' For example, a difference of opinion occurred over the implication of general verses of the Qur'an versus the

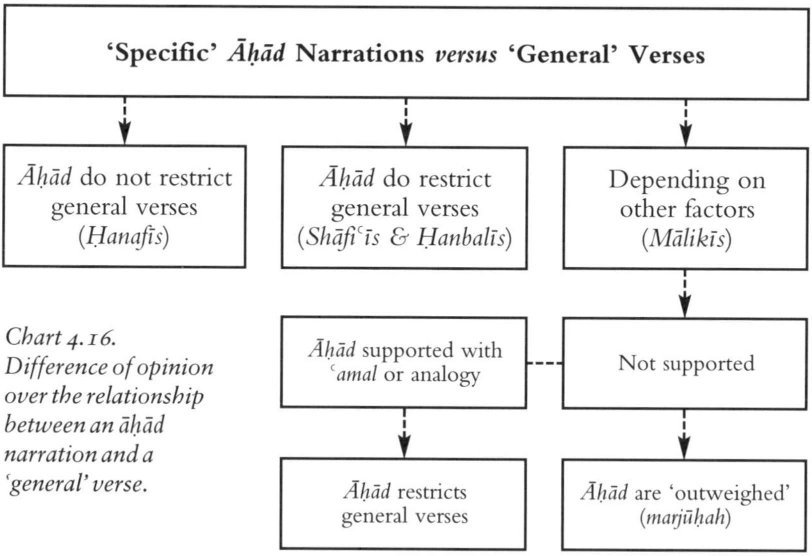

Chart 4.16. Difference of opinion over the relationship between an āḥād narration and a 'general' verse.

implication of *āḥād* specific terms that could theoretically restrict them. One classic example is verse 5:6 that states: 'When you are about to pray, wash your face, and your hands and arms up to the elbows,' which is a 'general' expression that is not specified by any specific order of washing. However, a number of narrations describe how the Prophet had consistently followed a certain order in his ablution. Ḥanafīs rejected the 'requirement' of order in ablution (and considered it a 'recommendation') based on their theory that general expressions are 'certain' and not to be specified by 'probable' *āḥād* narrations. All other schools of law required ordering, since they considered the specifics mentioned in the hadith to be 'restrictions put on the general meaning of the verse.'[59] Mālik, on the other hand, agreed with the restrictions based on the tradition of the people of Madinah (*ʿamal ahl al-madīnah*), which supported the above-mentioned *āḥād* narrations. Without that *ʿamal* (or alternatively, a valid analogy), Mālik would have considered the hadith 'in opposition' (*muʿāriḍ*) with the verse and, therefore, outweighed (*marjūḥ*).

Qualification

A similar difference of opinion occured in the way different schools of law dealt with 'qualified' verses 'unqualified' expressions (Chart 4.17).

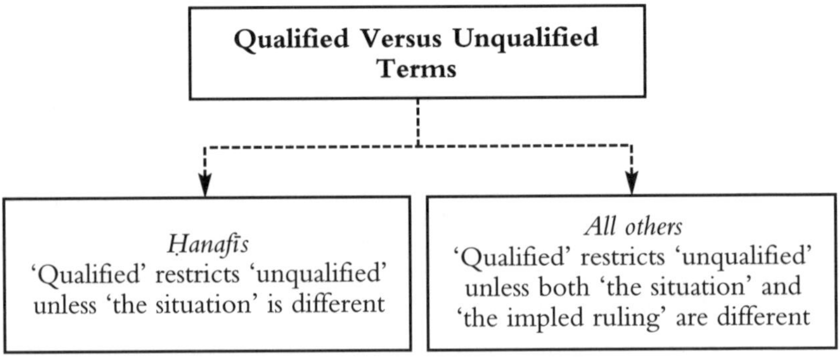

Chart 4.17. Difference of opinion over qualified versus unqualified terms/ expressions.

When jurists studied qualification of a certain expression, they looked into two factors, (1) the 'situation' or the case that the script is dealing with, and (2) the ruling that the script implies (which ranges from 'obligation' to 'prohibition'). They defined the relationship between a 'qualified' and a 'non-qualified' term based on the following four logical possibilities of similarity and difference:

1. A similar case and a similar ruling.
2. A similar case and different ruling.
3. A different case and similar ruling.
4. A different case and a different ruling.

The following are four illustrative examples for the above four possibilities, respectively:[60]

1. The hadith in which a man broke his fast intentionally and asked the Prophet how he could compensate for it. The Prophet asked him to fast for two months. In a different narration of a similar situation, the Prophet asked the enquirer to fast for two 'consecutive months.' All schools of law apply the specification of sequence here and, thus, restrict the first general expression with the second (specific) expression.
2. Two narrators addressed zakah (obligatory charity) of camels. The first narration mentioned 'camels' with no further qualification and the second mentioned 'pastured camels,' which means that non-pastured camels are not included in the ruling of zakah. However, because of the similarity of the 'situation,' i.e., camels' zakah, all schools agreed to restrict the unqualified expression with the 'pastured' qualification.
3. Several verses addressed the issue of witnesses in various situations, such as verse 2:282, 'have witnesses whenever you trade with one another,' and verse 65:2, 'let two persons of [known] probity from among your own community ...' The first verse, which mentions an 'unqualified' witness, is addressing the situation of a trade transaction, while the second verse, which mentions a witness 'qualified' with 'probity,' is talking about witnesses of

divorce. Yet, all schools of law (except for the Ḥanafīs) restricted the unqualified expression of the first verse with the qualification mentioned in the second verse and, thus, required a 'proof of probity' for all witnesses.

4. An example of two verses with two different cases and two different rulings is the verse, 'fast for three days' (related to the ruling of breaking an oath) and the verse, 'fast for two consecutive months' (related to the ruling of *ẓihār*).[61] Because of the difference in the situation and in ruling, all schools agreed on not restricting the first verse with the 'consecutive' qualification mentioned in the second verse.

As we can see from the above analysis of 'scope,' there is a general trend amongst classic jurists to encourage 'specification' and 'qualification.' This trend added to the already inflexible and restricted methods of literal linguistic derivations. In these pure linguistic theorisations of 'extracting rulings,' little consideration, if any, is given to the underlying circumstances or the intended objective/*maqṣid* of the *naṣṣ*. For example, rulings for 'compensations' (*kaffārāt*), similar to the one mentioned above, are supposed to remain open and are not 'qualified' or 'restricted.' This gives the muftī a chance to address various people according to their educational needs, which is the purpose behind these *kaffārāt*, to start with. Restricting this area to the strictest possible ruling (such as requiring two consecutive months of fasting) defeats this purpose, and also goes against the well-known general purpose of facilitation and magnanimity in matters of worship.

Similarly, much of the juridical deliberations on zakah were focused on issues such as whether the cattle is supposed to be 'pastured' or not, whether gold should be 'ring-shaped' (*muḥallaq*) or not, whether a 'needy' (*miskīn*) person could also be 'poor' (*faqīr*) or not, whether glass, copper, or salt are considered 'metals' or not, and so on. All of these zakah debates miss the real point/purpose behind zakah as a social welfare system. Similarly, rulings related to courts and procedures should not be merely tied to linguistic derivations and terms, but should, rather, consider the society and its evolution and the 'absolute' objective of achieving justice. However, in addressing the issues above, jurists resorted to the fundamentals of specifity and qualification, rather than the fundamentals of social justice and common good. Linguistic derivations are perhaps necessary for defining pure acts of worship, but they should not be considered sufficient sources for judgement on issues related to public interest. These issues should be dealt with according to a value- and purpose-oriented methodology. Chapter Six elaborates on a 'purposefulness-based' approach.

Linguistic Evidence: The Impact of Greek Philosophy

The general categorisation of knowledge, according to Islamic medieval philosophies, follows the 'conception' and 'assent' scheme (Chart 4.18). Conception is divided into terms (*alfāẓ*), meanings (*maʿānī*), and definitions (*taʿārīf* or *ḥudūd*).[62] Terms are studied in terms of their implication of meanings, generality, degrees of being, composition, and the relationship between words and meanings.

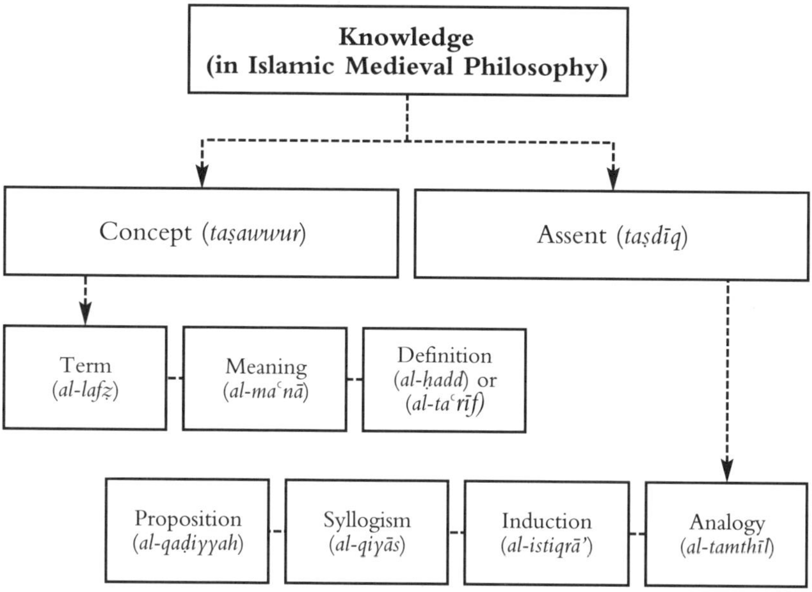

Chart 4.18. Classification of knowledge in Islamic philosophy.

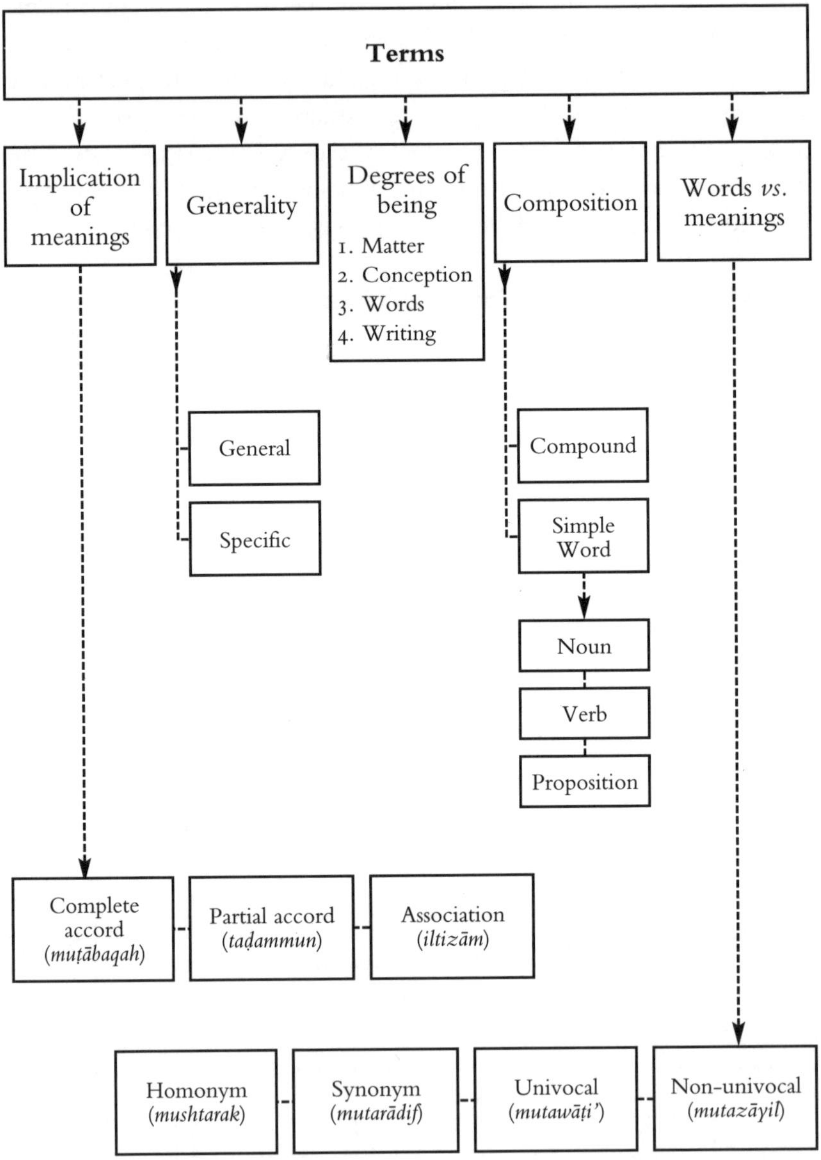

Chart 4.19. Classification of terms in Islamic philosophy.

Words imply meanings in complete accord (*muṭābaqah*), partial accord (*taḍammun*), or association (*iltzām*). Terms, in reference to generality, could be divided into 'general' and 'specific.' Terms could be simple non-dividable words (such as nouns, verbs, or prepositions), or otherwise compound. Finally, words could be homonyms, synonyms, univocal, or non-univocal.

The effect of Greek philosophy, especially Aristotle and the Peripatetics, on the above categorisations is obvious, from the 'conceptions' and 'assents,'[63] to 'homonyms' and 'synonyms.'[64] It is clear that later Islamic philosophers and juridical theorists generally followed Ibn Sīnā (Avicenna) in his commentaries on Greek philosophy. Islamic philosophers also viewed 'meanings' through Aristotle and Ibn Sīnā,[65] as shown by their studies of essence (*dhāt*) versus accident (*ʿaraḍ*), definite (*yaqīnī*) versus uncertain (*ʿadam yaqīnī*), and so on.

The impact of Greek philosophy on Islamic fundamentals of law, via Islamic philosophy, is obvious. Jurists were either 'philosophers,' such as al-Ghazālī, Ibn Rushd, and Ibn Taymiyah, or influenced by philosophers, directly or indirectly. Thus, the way 'terms' are categorised, and how they are related to 'meanings,' is quite 'Greek.' Under this influence, traditional Islamic fundamentals of law, despite its different streams, followed a Greek 'logic' (in Arabic: *manṭiq*, which literally means, utterance), hence, its essence-based definitions, binary classifications, and syllogistic analogies. Chapter Six will revise these Greek influences, from various angles, in light of contemporary systems theory.

4.3. SCRIPT-BASED RATIONAL EVIDENCES

Overview

Scholars differentiated between 'primary sources,' which are the Qur'an and prophetic traditions, and 'secondary sources,' which they only applied 'if there is no evidence from a *naṣṣ*,' i.e., specific (*khāṣṣ*) Qur'anic verse or hadith. This section introduces the following secondary sources: namely, consensus, analogy, interest, juridical preference,

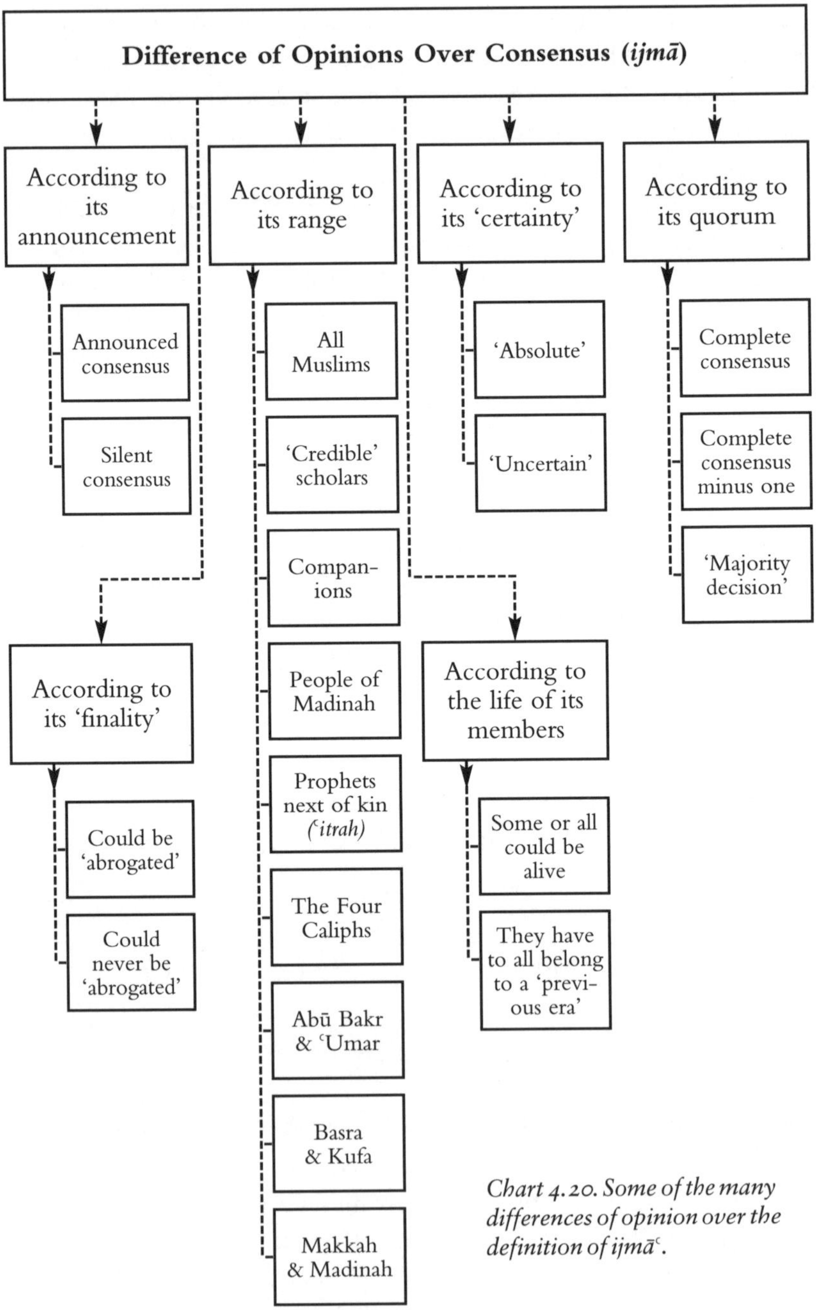

Chart 4.20. Some of the many differences of opinion over the definition of ijmāʿ.

blocking the means, custom, imam's opinion, companion's opinion, traditions of people of Madinah, and presumption of continuity. Jurists who endorsed any of these sources, based their endorsement on evidence from 'the scripts,' too. Thus, in my view, the differentiation between 'scripts' and 'secondary evidences' is actually a differentiation between 'linguistic' and 'rational' evidences, both of which are script-based.

Consensus

The ironic fact about 'consensus' (ijmāᶜ), which most schools of law count as an 'absolute' source of legislation, is that there is no 'consensus' over its very definition. In fact, there are dozens of different definitions and conditions for its occurrence, even within each school of law. Al-Ghazālī, from the Shāfiᶜī school, defined it as the consensus of the whole 'ummah of Islam' over a certain religious matter.[66] Most scholars, however, defined it as the consensus of 'credible' scholars, who reached the level of *mujtahid* (independent deliberator). There are several definitions, however, for that level of credibility of scholars, which range from 'learning Qur'an, Sunnah and analogy,' to many more requirements, including 'memorising four hundred thousand hadith.' Charts 4.20 and 4.21 compares some of these opinions.

Traditional classifications of schools of law contributed to the difference of opinion over ijmāᶜ, since some schools did not count scholars from some other schools as worthy of being part of a legitimate consensus.[67] Some definitions of consensus restricted it to the 'consensus of the companions,' as, for example, the Ẓāhirī definition. However, there are several views on what makes a person – who saw or met the Prophet – a 'companion.' Some scholars consider every person who met the Prophet to be part of a legitimate consensus. Others, like Ibn Ḥazm and the Ḥanafī school, limited the number of such companions to a number less than one hundred and thirty.[68] Mālikīs expanded the definition to include the consensus of the 'People of Madinah,' and considered this consensus to be a legitimate source of legislation.[69] More details on this evidence is provided later, since it has been used interchangeably with ᶜ*amal* (custom) of the people of Madinah.[70]

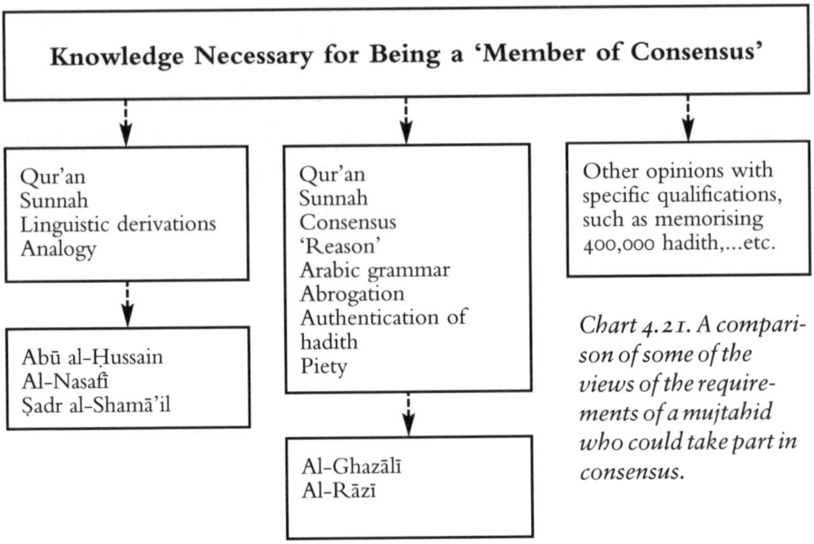

Chart 4.21. A comparison of some of the views of the requirements of a mujtahid who could take part in consensus.

Jaʿfarīs and Zaydīs both consider the Prophet's next of kin (ʿAlī, Faṭimah, al-Ḥasan and al-Ḥusain) to form a legitimate consensus.[71] However, some Jaʿfarī *uṣūlī*s rendered consensus 'redundant' because, 'a consensus is supposed to reveal the opinion of the infallible Imams,' the first of whom is ʿAlī, in any case.

A narration related to Aḥmad ibn Ḥanbal and Abū Ḥāzim (a leading Ḥanafī scholar) considers the consensus of the first four Caliphs (Abū Bakr, ʿUmar, ʿUthmān, and ʿAlī) legitimate consensus. No other school of law endorsed this type of consensus. Some comparative *uṣūl* books mentioned some opinions which approved the 'consensus' of Abū Bakr and ʿUmar, Makkah and Madinah, and even Kufa and Basra. No school of law had endorsed these opinions.

There is also a difference of opinion regarding whether consensus has to be 'complete,' i.e., an agreement by each and every member of the consensus, or it could be achieved by some form of 'majority decision.' All schools of law endorsed the condition of complete consensus for its validity. However, al-Ṭabarī and Abū al-Ḥusain al-Khayyāṭ believed that it could be achieved with 'one individual disagreement.' The whole issue seems to be hypothetical, rather than something that ever really happened. Portraying consensus as some form of collective decision-making is inaccurate, because it was not narrated in any historical account that a process of 'consensus-testing' was ever carried out amongst jurists.

Another difference of opinion occurred over whether the 'era' of the members of consensus has passed or not. Most schools endorsed the opinion that ijmāᶜ should count once scholars at any time reach it.[72] Aḥmad ibn Ḥanbal and some Muᶜtazilīs considered the fact that, 'one or more of the consensus members might change his/her opinion as long as they are alive.' And since they view ijmāᶜ as a binding and 'non-changeable' authority, they judged that members of ijmāᶜ should all be deceased so that it is guaranteed that none of them will change his/her opinion and render their ijmāᶜ void. Al-Juwaynī, from the Shāfiᶜī school, differentiated between consensus over 'certain' and 'uncertain' matters. He held the same opinion of Ibn Ḥanbal regarding the 'era of consensus' in case of 'uncertain' matters, which, according to him, are subject to changing of one's opinion, versus 'certain' matters.[73] However, al-Juwaynī did not provide criteria to differentiate between 'certain' and 'uncertain' matters.

One classification of ijmāᶜ is whether it has to be announced by each and every member of it, an opinion that many scholars deemed 'practically impossible.'[74] Thus, some schools of law endorsed what they called 'silent consensus,' which means that members of the ijmāᶜ whose opinions are not known could be considered in agreement with all other members who made their opinion known. There is neither announced nor silent consensus over this form of consensus. In fact, there are twelve different opinions about its validity.[75]

Finally, regarding whether or not a ruling that is based on consensus could ever be changed or 'abrogated,' all schools of law (except for a few scholars) took the opinion that such a ruling could never be changed.[76] This view was actually based on the *uṣūlī* rule that states that, 'no abrogation could be valid after the prophetic era,' and the 'logical' contradiction between the authority of the first consensus and the subsequent ones.[77] However, I think that, according to this rule, rulings that were directly connected to a certain time, because of certain circumstances, are unjustifiably made 'eternal.'

Ibn Ḥazm's critique of ijmāᶜ was as follows: 'matters of consensus are either explicitly mentioned in the Qur'an or most famous hadith, or otherwise, matters of difference of opinion over some interpretation or *āḥād* narration. In the first case, the verses or hadith do not need consensus for evidence, since they are primary evidences in their own right. In the second case, consensus is untruly claimed.' He argued: 'consensus could never be proven, even if it were to be restricted to the companions, whose number was in the thousands.'[78]

Despite all of the above differences of opinion, most *uṣūlīs* in various schools of law consider consensus to be an 'absolute/certain' (*qaṭᶜī*) evidence that generates 'absolute' knowledge. Examples are, al-Baghdādī, al-Juwaynī, al-Ghazālī, Abū al-Ḥussain, al-Shirāzī, al-Samarqandī, al-Nasafī, al-Farra, al-Sarkhasī, among others. A few *uṣūlī*s, including al-Rāzī and al-Āmidī, considered consensus an 'uncertain' evidence.[79]

Analogy

Analogy (*qiyās*) is a secondary source of legislation that is viewed as legitimate by the four Sunni schools of law, Muᶜtazilīs, and Ibāḍīs. Jaᶜfarīs, Zaydīs, Ẓāhirīs, and some Muᶜtazilīs, describe analogy as 'legislation according to whims.' Imam Jaᶜfar al-Ṣādiq, reportedly,

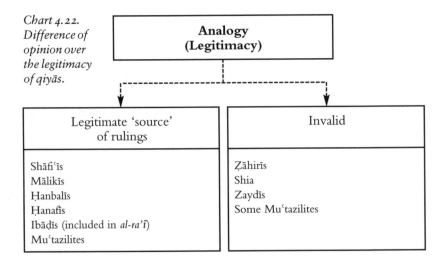

Chart 4.22. Difference of opinion over the legitimacy of qiyās.

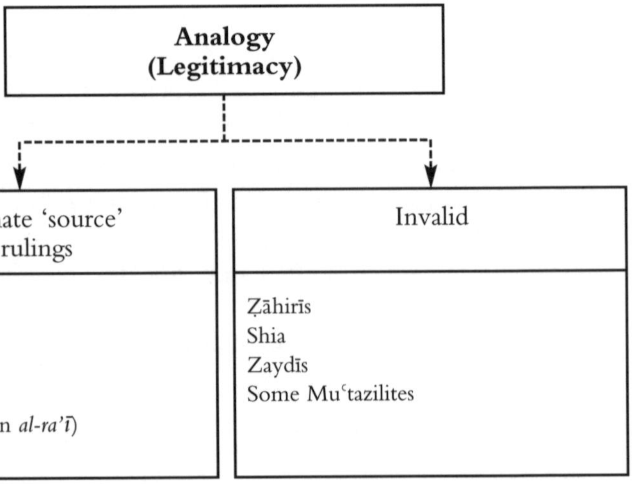

(a)

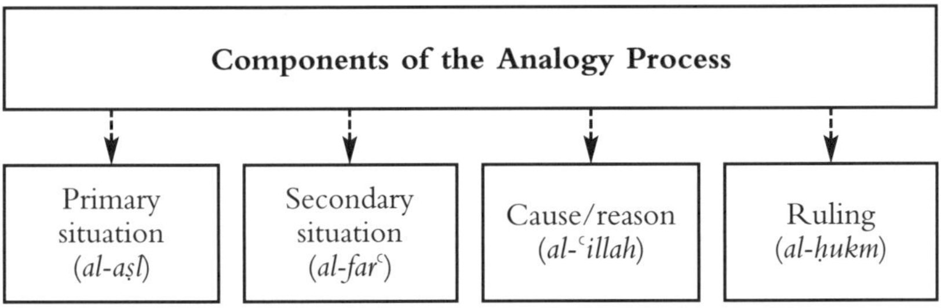

(b)

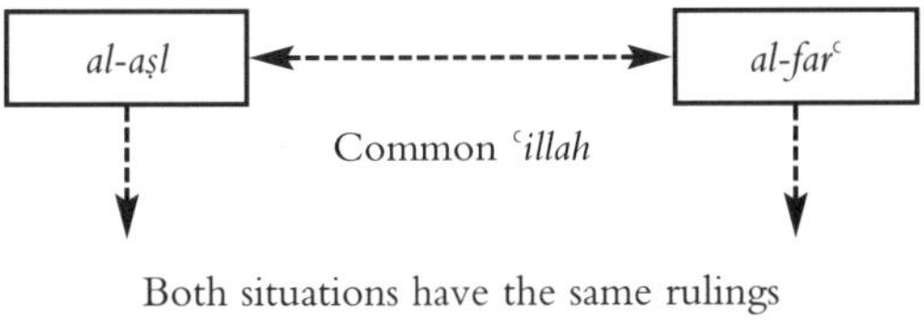

Chart 4.23. (a) The four components/units of analogy and (b) how the components interact in the analogy process.

asserts that, 'there is no question without a direct answer from the Book or the Tradition.'[80] However, analogy is actually a process of juridical decision making, rather than a 'source' of legislation.

The analogy process has four components, namely, primary situation (*al-aṣl*), secondary situation (*al-farʿ*), cause/reason (*al-ʿillah*), and the ruling (*al-ḥukm*). Analogy (*qiyās*) is carried out between two situations/cases, the ruling of the first (primary) situation has been previously decided, while the ruling of the second (secondary) situation is unknown. *Qiyās* entails that if there is a (speculated) common cause (*ʿillah*) between the two situations, then, by analogy, the ruling in the first situation applies to the second.[81]

However, *qiyās*, according to Ẓāhirīs, Shia Jaʿfarīs, Zaydīs and some Muʿtazilīs, is 'uncertain' and an 'innovation in the religion.' Ibn Ḥazm articulated this stand by referring to *qiyās* as, 'a judgement without confirmed knowledge following uncertain evidences.'[82] Ibn Ḥazm also criticised those who supported the legitimacy of *qiyās* based on ijmāʿ, based on his view that 'ijmāʿ could never be proven.'[83]

Ibn Ḥazm, and Ẓāhirīs in general, consider the literal meaning of only the Qur'an or hadith to carry any legitimacy in the Islamic law. His point of view is that human 'reason' is basically some sort of 'whim and speculation' that could be 'useful in worldly matters but not in matters of faith.'[84] The Ẓāhirīs rejection of analogy resulted in a number of strange *fatāwā* that are often cited as amusing stories. These *fatāwā*, which were based on the rejection of analogy, caused the Ẓāhirī school a great deal of unpopularity on a public level. For example, Ibn Ḥazm narrated a hadith in which the Prophet is reported to have said: 'A virgin's consent [to a marriage proposal] is to stay silent [when asked for her opinion].' Ibn Ḥazm commented: 'Therefore, if she says "yes" then her marriage contract is void!'[85] Ibn Ḥazm did not wish to make an analogy between an agreement by means of 'silence,' as mentioned in the hadith, and an agreement by means of 'saying yes.' Other schools made it a matter of 'options' for the bride to give a silent or oral consent. Ḥanafīs made the whole procedure subject to custom, since, they explained the hadith, it is 'shameful for an (Arab) woman to say yes in such a situation.'

Jaʿfarīs, Zaydīs, and Muʿtazilīs accept analogy if the cause (*ʿillah*) is stated in the script and not 'speculated.' Other schools considered this form of reasoning to be a direct linguistic derivation of rulings from scripts, rather than a valid form of analogy. Ibadis include *qiyās* in a general category of reasoning that they call *al-ra'ī* (using opinion).[86]

Despite the high status that he attributed to 'reason,' al-Naẓẓām, a leading Muʿtazilī jurist, rejected reasoning by analogy. He said that rulings of the Islamic law 'do not necessarily follow a rational line of thought.'[87] He mentioned many examples of rulings of the Islamic law that are 'irrational' because they, 'did not equate in judgement between equal entities and did not differentiate in judgement between different entities.' Two examples, according to al-Naẓẓām, are, 'requiring two witnesses to prove murder and four witnesses to prove adultery,' and 'ablution by washing certain organs of the body that were not the cause of uncleanness.'[88] In my view, the inconsistencies that al-Naẓẓām had pointed out are not evidences for 'irrationality,' but rather, for the 'change of rulings according to their purposes.' A '*maqāṣidī*' approach to these rulings show that the whole purpose of seeking witnesses is to confirm certain incidents (the act of murder, in the first incident, and the act of 'public adultery,' in the second). Therefore, the numbers are not prime purposes of the rulings in their own right, but rather tools for the sake of correct court procedures. In the second example, ablution has a pure ritual purpose. Ḥanafīs among others did not allow analogy in cases of *ʿibādāt* (rituals or pure acts of worship).[89] They defined these acts as 'acts which cannot be rationalized,' and gave examples such as acts of worship and procedures for pilgrimage.[90] This book argues for the utilisation of such *maqāṣidī* (that is, purpose-oriented) approaches as the basis of analogical reasoning itself.

Finally, Mālikīs allowed the 'primary situation' in analogy to be an analogy in its own right. This means that a ruling for a situation could be generated from an analogy, without need of an actual 'primary situation.' Then, a ruling could be generated from the new ruling, and so on. This extension of the definition of *qiyās* in the Mālikī school opens possibilities for relying solely on 'causes' for generating a sequence of valid analogies, rather than relying on primary situations that must necessarily be 'mentioned in the scripts.'

A 'cause' (*ʿillah*) is at the heart of the analogy process. Schools of law agreed upon three specifications for a valid *ʿillah*. Schools of law that endorsed analogy agreed on visibility (*ẓuhūr*), extension (*taʿaddī*), and validity (*iʿtibār*). Visibility entails 'the ability to perceive the cause' and to 'confirm its existence in a situation.' Extension entails the ability to extend the cause to other situations, whereas there is a lack of a script that restricts that extension. Validity means the lack of an 'invalidating statement' by a script which rejects the consideration of the 'cause.'[91]

However, schools of law differed over a condition/specification, which they called 'consistency' or 'exactness' (*inḍibāṭ*) of the cause. Exactness of a cause means 'not to change significantly with changing circumstances.'[92] The reason behind the controversy over the consistency/exactness criteria is the controversy over whether or not analogy is allowed according to the 'wisdom behind the ruling' (*ḥikmah*). The following are examples which illustrate the difference between *ʿillah* and *ḥikmah* in classic schools of law.

An exemption (*rukhṣah*) from fasting is granted to Muslims who are 'ill or are travelling.' Illness or travelling for a certain distance (concluded from related hadith) are valid *ᶜillal* or causes behind this exemption. The wisdom (*ḥikmah*) behind this exemption is 'facilitation.' For the elderly, scholars granted the same exemption from fasting based on analogy with the illness 'cause,' not based on the 'wisdom' of facilitation. That is why, in most schools of law, this exemption is not given to a laborer, for example, who has a great deal of hardship in keeping up with fasting while carrying out a physically demanding job. Scholars, from various schools, claimed that illness or travel is 'measurable' and 'deterministic' and, therefore, are exact causes for *qiyās*, while 'facilitation' is not measurable and 'changes with circumstances.' Therefore, '*ḥikmah*' was considered too 'lucid' to be a valid criterion of juridical analogy. One could argue here that this 'causal,' rather than 'teleological,' view of *qiyās*, misses the point behind the exemption ruling, even if it achieves *inḍibāt* (exactness) and formality on a procedural level. Chapter Six discusses the importance of considering *maqāṣid* in the process of *qiyās* in more detail.

In order to carry out a correct analogy, *uṣūlis* outlined a multiple-step process (*maslak)*, which is outlined below. A *manāṭ* is the ratio legis, grounds, effective cause, the prime criterion, or the 'reason' behind the rule.

1. Extraction of the grounds (*Takhrīj al-manāṭ*): It is a process of reflection upon the primary script in order to extract as many possibilities as possible for grounds (*ᶜillah* or effective causes) for the primary ruling. These possibilities for grounds are the 'attributes' that the subjects or materials mentioned in the primary script, which represent possible candidates for being the *ᶜillah* behind the ruling.

2. Eliminating the alternatives (*Tanqīḥ al-manāṭ*): In this step, jurists apply some form of *ratio decidendi*, to use a term from the British philosophy of law. The different attributes that resulted from step number one are examined one by one, in an Exclusive-OR manner, to use a logical term, in order to determine one chosen attribute, after excluding/clearing out all others. Despite the superficiality in this attribute-based process, scholars had made a condition for the winning attribute, which will be called '*ᶜillah*' afterwards, which is to be an

'appropriate' attribute (*waṣf munāsib*). Appropriateness (*munāsabah*) is generally defined as the 'fulfilment of interest' (*taḥqīq al-maṣlaḥah*). This *maṣlaḥah* was not clearly defined in early literature on *uṣūl al-fiqh*. However, in later literature of Sunni *uṣūl* (which are the schools that endorsed analogy anyway) one could notice a growing tendency to relate 'appropriateness' with 'purposefulness,' i.e., to relate *munāsabah* with *maqāṣid al-sharīʿah*. This tendency is most evident in al-Shāṭibī's theory on *maqāṣid*, and to a lesser degree in the earlier theories of al-Ghazālī's, al-ʿIzz's, and al-Qarāfī's theories on *qiyās*.[93] Al-Ṭūfī defined *al-waṣf al-munāsib* as, '*al-maṣlaḥah* that leads to the legislator's purpose (*maqṣid*).'[94] The vast majority of the *uṣūlī* schools had not endorsed equating the 'cause' of the ruling with the 'purpose' of the ruling, since the 'purpose' is not '*munḍabiṭ*.'[95] Chapter Six presents a different perspective.

3. Asserting the realisation of the ratio legis (*Taḥqīq al-manāṭ*): This is the final step in the *qiyās* process, in which the *mujtahid* jurist verifies whether the *ʿillah* applies to the real-life situation under consideration. For example, intoxication is the ratio legis behind the 'prohibition of liquor' (which is the prime ruling). When an ijtihad is made regarding a certain substance, the question would be: Is intoxication realised in this substance or not? Another example: the intention to kill is the ratio legis behind the persecution of a killer. However, in the case of murder, the question would be: Was the intention of killing verified or not? A final example: 'poverty' and 'need' is the ratio legis behind receiving zakah (obligatory annual charity). The question of *taḥqīq al-manāṭ*

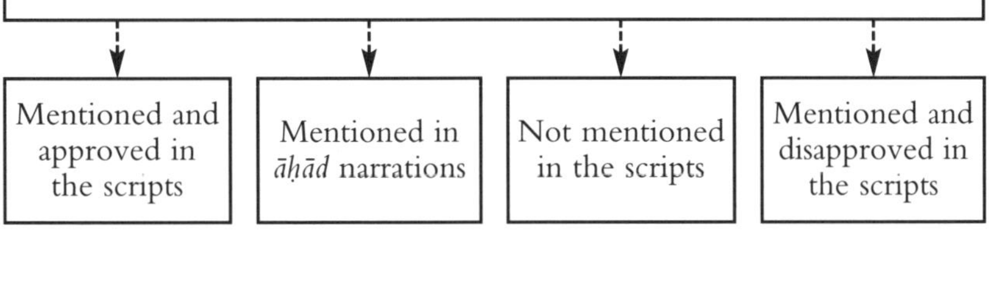

Chart 4.24. The four categories of appropriate attributes.

would be: Is that specific person 'poor' and 'in need' or not? Therefore, I would say that *taḥqīq al-manāṭ* (asserting the realisation of the ᶜ*illah*) is on the borderline between fiqh and science, and should not depend solely on the *mujtahid* (as is the case in traditional *uṣūl*). To illustrate, one could ask the question, 'how' is the *mujtahid* going to prove, assert, or verify that a certain substance is an 'intoxicant,' a certain suspect has a certain 'intention,' or a certain person is 'poor'? In nowadays world, these kinds of questions have to be referred to the 'specialists' in related branches of science, and not to jurists. Chapter Six elaborates.

Jurists from various schools differentiate between the ᶜ*illah* that 'is supported by the script' and the ᶜ*illah* that is conceived by the *mujtahid* but could not be proven to have the script's support.[96] Based on this, they divide the 'appropriate' attribute into the four categories shown in Chart 4.24.

Schools of law agree that if an attribute is 'disapproved' by a script, despite its apparent benefits, then it cannot be used in *qiyās*. For example, the benefits of increasing one's wealth by means of usury are mentioned and disapproved of in the related scripts. Similarly, the benefits of trade in liquor and gambling are also mentioned and disapproved of in the scripts. If the attribute is explicitly mentioned in the scripts, such as the intoxication of liquor or intention (ᶜ*amd*) in killing, then *qiyās* based on it is valid, even according to the schools which did not endorse *qiyās*, namely, the Jaᶜfarīs, Zaydīs, Muᶜtazilīs, and Ẓāhirīs. These schools, however, consider the attribute/ᶜ*illah* to be an 'implication of the script' (*dilālah al-naṣṣ*), rather than an implementation of analogy.

If the attribute is implied in general terms in the scripts, under some other section or related to some other ruling, then it is a valid 'appropriate attribute' according to the Shāfiᶜīs and Ḥanafīs. Shāfiᶜīs call it *al-mulā'im* (the 'suitable' attribute), while the Ḥanafīs refer to it as *al-munāsib* (the 'appropriate' attribute), and consider it a 'rational evidence.'[97]

What jurists meant by an attribute that is 'not mentioned in the scripts' is an attribute that cannot be concluded by direct linguistic derivations from specific verses or hadith, as described earlier. Interests (*maṣāliḥ*) that could be 'speculated' from the scripts but lack the

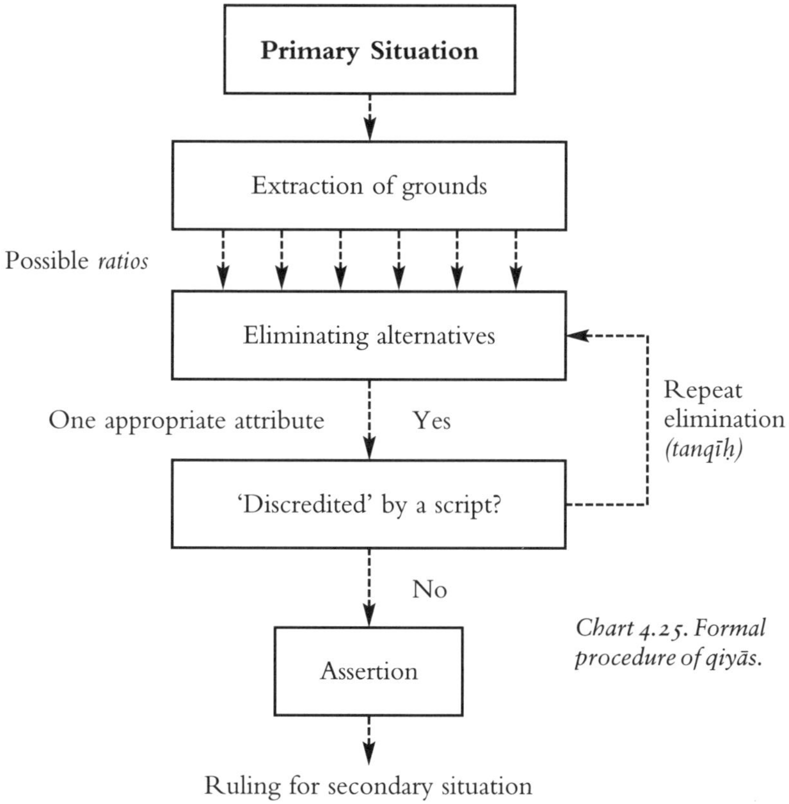

Chart 4.25. Formal procedure of qiyās.

endorsement of an explicit language that states their validity or invalidity are classified, according to all schools of law, as *maṣāliḥ mursalah* ('non-restricted' interests). The next section discusses this point under the general secondary source of legislation that the jurists called '*istiṣlāḥ*' (bringing interests), the validity of which was also the subject of difference of opinion.

Jurists also discussed causes where the result of *qiyās* 'contradicts the implication of another script that is specific about the (secondary) situation.' Al-Shāfiʿī, Mālik, and Ibn Ḥanbal agreed that, 'there is no place for *qiyās*' if there is a related verse or hadith. They applied this rule even if they deem the verse 'probable' in its implication or the hadith 'probable' in its authentication or implication. However, if the implication of the verse or hadith is 'probable,' they allow *qiyās* to 'restrict the probable meaning.'[98]

However, Mālik added that if the hadith is 'probable' (for example, *āḥād*), and contradicts 'multiple *qiyās*' (i.e., more than one *qiyās* that imply a ruling that is 'opposing' to the linguistic implication of the hadith), then the 'multiple *qiyās*' is called an '*aṣl*' (a fundamental ruling), and is given priority over the 'probable' hadith.[99] For example, Mālik rejected the 'authenticity' of the *āḥād* hadith, 'if a dog drinks from your bowl then wash it seven times,' based on several analogies/*qiyās* with other verses and hadith that permitted eating from animals caught by hunting dogs. Therefore, Mālik concluded an *aṣl* that, 'dog saliva is clean.'[100]

The above difference between Mālik and the other schools of law over the capacity of an *aṣl* (fundamental rule) to invalidate an 'authentic' *āḥād* narration is similar to their difference over the role of *maṣlaḥah* (interest). The next subsection explains.

Interest

The classification of *maṣlaḥah* (interest, good, benefit, utility) into *maṣlaḥah* that is 'supported by scripts,' 'discredited by scripts,' and 'not mentioned in the scripts,' imply a special literal definition of what jurists called 'script.'

Some Muʿtazilīs disputed the existence of a category of unrestricted interests (*maṣlaḥah mursalah*), based on their fundamental concepts of

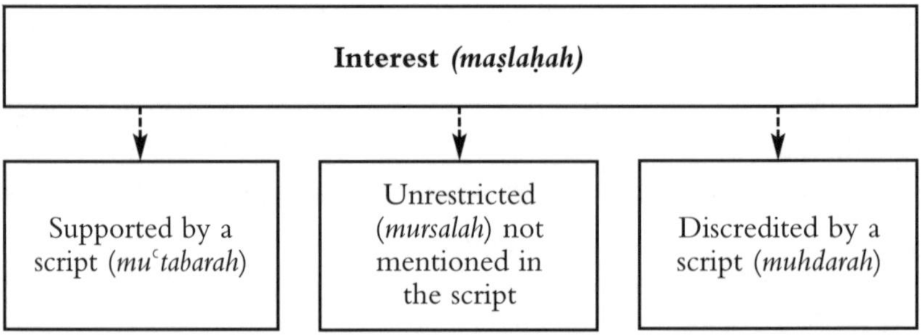

Chart 4.26. Classification of interests based on their (literal) mention in the script.

rational 'embellishment and repugnancy' (*al-taḥsīn wa al-taqbīḥ al-ʿaqlī*). They argued that because the Islamic way of life is comprehensive, everything has to be either an embellished and encouraged good or a repugnant and discouraged evil, whether mentioned in direct or indirect terms in the scripts. This is a typical Muʿtazilī opinion that no other school shared, despite its strong argument.

Jurists differed over the legitimacy of *al-maṣlaḥah al-mursalah*. Mālikīs and Ḥanbalīs accepted this *maṣlaḥah* to have legitimacy, based on the Qur'an, prophetic tradition, ijmāʿ, and *qiyās*. That is why they did not allow such *maṣlaḥah* to 'contradict' with any of the above evidences.[101] Ibāḍīs included it in their *ra'ī* (using opinion).[102]

Mālik, according to al-Shāṭibī, endorsed *al-maṣlaḥah al-mursalah* under a number of conditions, which could be summarised in three points as follows.[103]

1. To fall under the areas of worldly dealings (*muʿāmalāt*) and of customs (*ʿādāt*), and not in the area of acts of worship (*ʿibādāt*).
2. Not to contradict any specific script or fundamental *aṣl*.
3. To lead to a higher interest or a general purpose that is mentioned in the script.

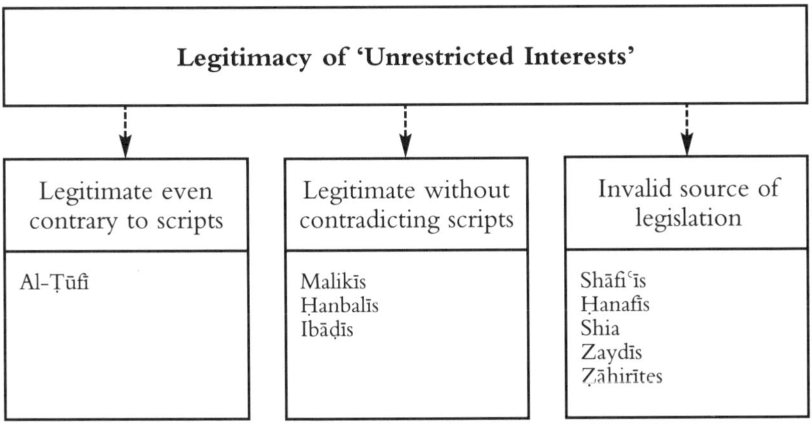

Chart 4.27. Difference of opinion over al-maṣlaḥah al-mursalah.

Later Ḥanbalīs included *al-maṣlaḥah al-mursalah* in their rule of 'the change of fatwa according to change of circumstances,' for which Ibn Taymiyah and Ibn al-Qayyim were most famous of and wrote extensively about.[104]

Al-Ṭūfī, a leading Ḥanbalī scholar, took a controversial position, which is still causing a heated debate until today.[105] He judged that *al-maṣlaḥah* is the purpose of the Islamic law, in principle, and that the (specific) scripts that contradict with *al-maṣlaḥah* should simply be disregarded. His definition of *maṣlaḥah* was even more controversial, because he said it was up to 'the judgement of custom and reason.'[106]

The rest of the schools of law judged that *al-maṣlaḥah al-mursalah* is an invalid source of legislation. However, in my view, all schools applied their own methods of considering *al-maṣlaḥah* in their ijtihad, one way or the other. Shāfiʿīs, for example, include '*maṣlaḥah*' in the concept of *munāsabah* in *qiyās*, as previously discussed.[107] Ḥanafīs include *maṣlaḥah* in their *istiḥsān*.[108] Jaʿfarīs and Zaydīs, on the other hand, invalidated *maṣlaḥah* based on the fact it is 'uncertain,' and 'does not 'represent the infallible Imam's opinion.'[109] Nevertheless, there is a great deal of '*maṣlaḥah*' in the Jaʿfarī and Zaydī juridical method of 'rational evidence' (*al-dalīl al-ʿaqlī*), which they apply, 'after the Qur'an, Sunnah, and consensus.'[110] Finally, the Ẓāhirī school is the only school that rejected *maṣlaḥah* and did not replace it with any alternative evidence.

Juridical Preference

Positions over juridical preference (*istiḥsān*) were also divided in a binary manner. Shāfiʿīs, Jaʿfarīs, Zaydīs, and Ẓāhirīs, consider *istiḥsān* an illegitimate and 'uncertain' evidence.[111] Al-Shāfiʿī and Ibn Ḥazm defined it as, 'choice according to desires,' and 'a source of contradiction.'[112] On the other hand Ḥanafī, Mālikī, ʿIbāḍīs, Ḥanbalī, and Muʿtazilī schools endorsed *istiḥsān* as a source of legislation.

What is common amongst all versions of *istiḥsān* is that the *mujtahid* judges a certain situation based on a certain basis, which is different from the usual basis/principle upon which similar situations are judged (Chart 4.28).

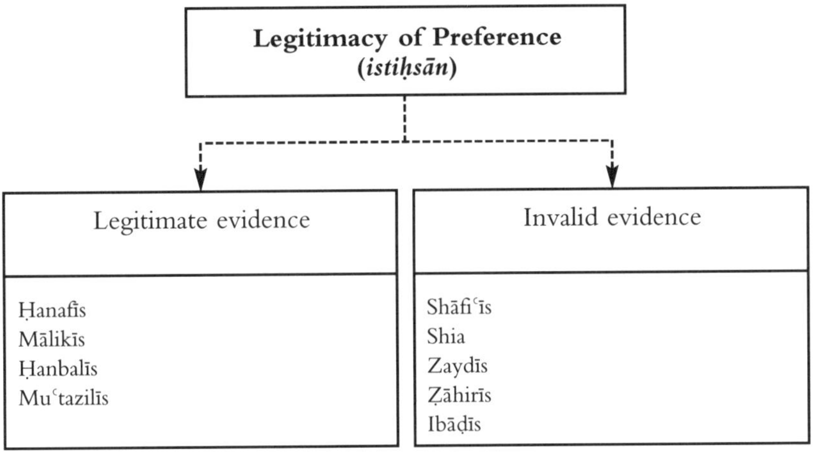

Chart 4.28. Difference of opinion over istiḥsān.

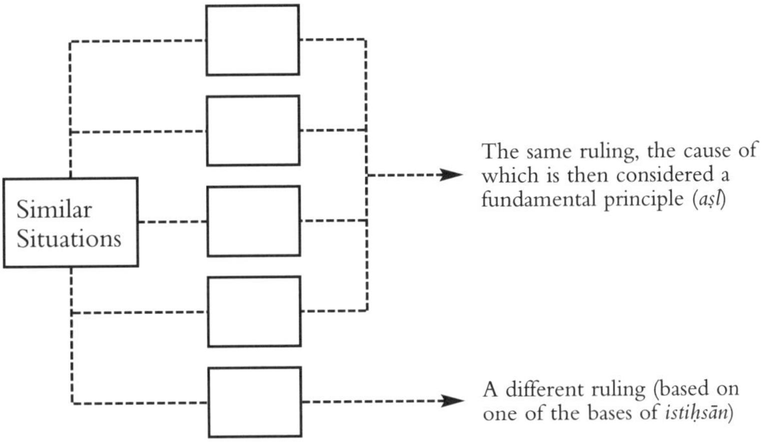

Chart 4.29. Judging a certain situation based on a basis that is different from the principle upon which similar situations are judged.

Contrary to al-Shāfiʿī's description of *istiḥsān* as 'judging according to desire,' his teacher, Mālik, had described it as 'nine-tenth of knowledge.'[113] For Mālik, *istiḥsān* entails a deep consideration of certain factors which should change a jurist's usual judgement. These factors, which are called the bases of *istiḥsān*, could be divided into six categories, namely, script, consensus, necessity, analogy, public interest, and custom.[114]

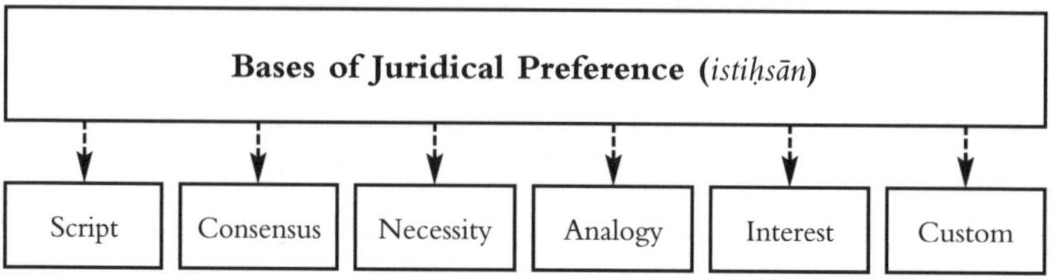

Chart 4.30. Classification of the bases of istiḥsān.

The following are illustrative examples of these bases from various schools that endorsed *istiḥsān*:

1. *Istiḥsān* based on the script: Narrated hadith forbids exchange of 'similar goods' unless the exchange is done instantly. Otherwise, it is considered a kind of 'deferred usury' (*ribā al-nasī'ah*). However, other scripts allow interest-free loans, which would fall under *ribā al-nasī'ah*. Mālikīs classify the ruling that allows loans under '*istiḥsān* based on the script.'[115] For all other schools, the above case falls under linguistic 'specification' (*takhṣīṣ*).
2. *Istiḥsān* based on consensus: Similar to the loan's *istiḥsān*, *istiṣnāʿ* (purchase with order, i.e., with deferred delivery) is considered lawful according to *istiḥsān*. The default rule in deferred delivery, according to all schools, is prohibition. A fundamental rule states: 'It is prohibited to sell what you do not possess' (based on the related narration). However according to Ḥanafīs, there is a 'consensus' on the lawfulness of such transaction, which is grounds for an exception from the fundamental rule.[116] 'Consensus,' which Ḥanafīs claimed in this case, is rather a social agreement over a certain custom, as Ibn ʿĀbidīn, a later Ḥanafī scholar, noted.[117] This observation raises an interesting question on the relationship between 'custom' and 'fundamental rules' that are derived from scripts, which will be discussed later.
3. *Istiḥsān* based on necessity (*darūrah*): Some jurists mentioned the example of allowing medical doctors to see patients' private parts, for the necessity of treatment, under this category.

4. *Istiḥsān* based on analogy (*qiyās*): In this case, two analogies contradict and one of them is selected. For a traditional example, Ḥanafīs decided that the saliva of birds of prey, such as eagles, is clean. Two analogies contradicted: the first is with the saliva of meat-eaters, such as lions, which they view as forbidden. The second analogy is with the saliva of humans, who also eat meat. Ḥanafīs chose the second analogy, based on *istiḥsān*.
5. *Istiḥsān* based on public interest: The traditional example in fiqh literature is the 'liability of craftsmen' (*taḍmīn al-ṣunnāᶜ*), despite the well-known hadith which states that, 'a craftsman is trusted.' The hadith implies that a craftsman is not liable for damage of crafted goods. However, several schools of law held craftsmen liable based on *istiḥsān* of 'public interest.'
6. *Istiḥsān* based on custom: Traditional examples mentioned under this category are the same examples mentioned under '*istiḥsān* based on consensus.' This, again, raises the question of the relationship between 'consensus' and 'custom' in the fundamentals of the Islamic law.

Blocking the Means

Blocking the means (*sadd al-dharā'iᶜ*) is another 'reasoning procedure' that some jurists considered to be a 'source of legislation,' especially in the Mālikī school.[118] Most jurists do not mention blocking the means as separate evidence, but included its meaning in '*al-maṣlaḥah*.'[119] *Sadd al-dharā'iᶜ* entails forbidding or blocking a lawful action because it could be means that lead to unlawful actions.[120] Jurists from various schools mentioned that 'leading to unlawful actions' should be 'more probable than not,' but they differed over how to systemise the comparison of probabilities. Jurists divided 'probability' of unlawful actions into four different levels (Chart 4.32).[121]

The following are examples that jurists mentioned to illustrate the above categories:

1. An example of an action that results in a 'certain' harm is 'digging a well on a public road,' which will certainly harm people. Jurists agreed to block the means in such case, but had a difference of

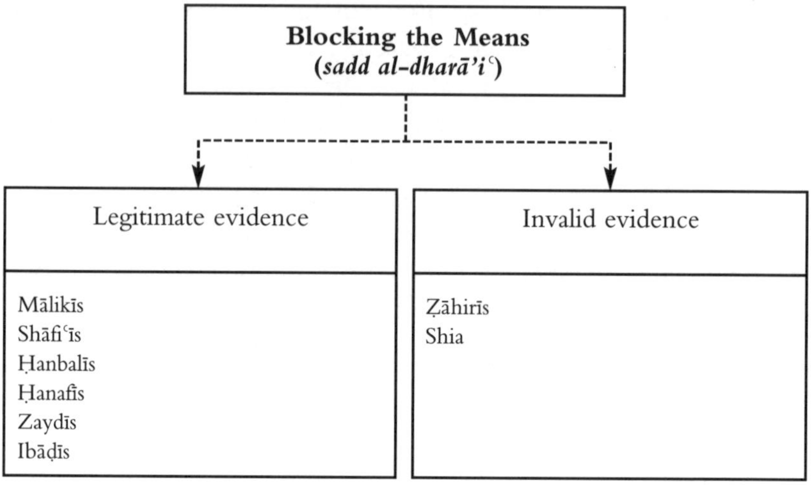

Chart 4.31. Difference of opinion over sadd al-dharā'iʿ.

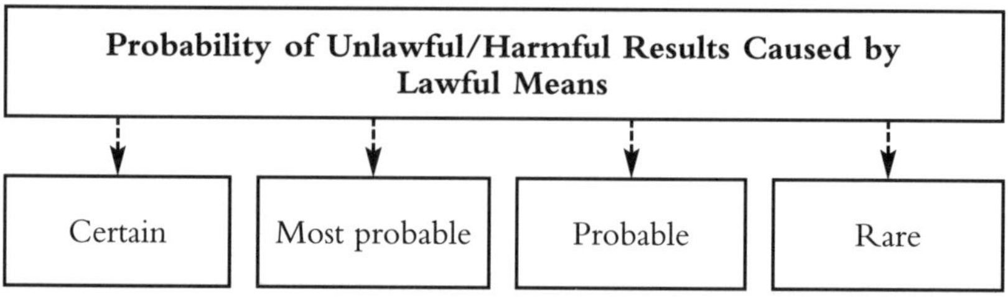

Chart 4.32. Four 'categories' of probability, according to jurists who endorsed blocking the means, namely, certain, most probable, probable, and rare.

opinion over whether the well-digger, in this example, is liable for any harm that happens to people because of his/her action. The difference of opinion is actually over whether prohibiting some action entails making people liable for the resulting damage if they carry that action out, or not.

2. An example of an action that results in a 'rare' harm, according to al-Shāṭibī, is selling grapes, even though a small number of people will use them to make wine. 'Blocking the means' does not apply to such action, jurists agreed, 'since the benefit of the action is more than the harm, which happens in rare cases in any case.'[122]

3. Harm is 'most probable,' jurists argued, when 'weapons are sold during civil unrest or grapes are sold to a wine-maker.'[123] Mālikīs and Ḥanbalīs agreed to block these means, while others disagreed because, as they argued, harm has to be 'certain' to justify blocking its means.
4. Harm is 'probable,' some jurists claimed, 'when a woman travels by herself,' and 'when people use legally-correct contracts with hidden tricks as means to usury.'[124] Again, Mālikīs and Ḥanbalīs agreed to block these means, while others disagreed because the harm is not 'certain' or 'most probable.'

The above examples show that means and ends are subject to variations in economic, political, social, and environmental circumstances, and not constant rules. 'A woman travelling by herself,' 'the selling of weapons,' or 'selling of grapes' could lead to probable harm in some situations, but could definitely be harmless or even beneficial for people in other situations. Therefore, it is inaccurate to classify actions according to probabilities of harm in 'hard' categories, as shown above. Chapter Six will suggest a 'continuous spectrum' of probabilities, in order to allow the jurist to move along that spectrum, according to the underlying circumstances, without assigning specific categories of probability to any specific action.

Finally ethically speaking, 'blocking the means' is a consequentialist approach.[125] It could be useful in some situations, but could also be misused by some pessimistic jurists or politically-motivated authorities. Some examples are provided and explained in Chapter Six.

Previous Jurisprudence

Based on the Qur'an, God had revealed a shariᶜah to prophets before Muhammad similar to the Islamic shariᶜah.[126] Therefore, some schools of Islamic law included 'previous jurisprudence' (*sharᶜu man qablanā*) within valid evidences of the Islamic law. However, jurists who agreed to apply rulings from *sharᶜu man qablanā* stipulated that these rulings must be mentioned in the Qur'an or the prophetic traditions.[127] Their rationale behind this stipulation is to confirm that the rulings were not abrogated by new (Islamic) rulings.

Ẓāhirīs and Jaʿfarī's rejected *sharʿu man qablanā* as a source, also based on the concept of abrogation. Their view is that the Islamic law had abrogated all laws before it. A few jurists decided not to give an opinion on this issue because, they said, 'they do not have enough basis to judge.'[128]

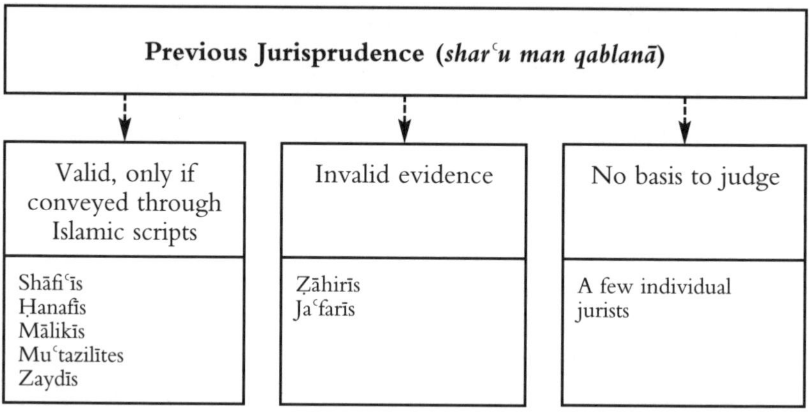

Chart 4.33. Difference of opinion over sharʿu man qablanā.

A Companion's Opinion

In addition to the difference of opinion over what defines a 'companion,'[129] there is a difference of opinion over the juridical validity of a companion's opinion or *ra'ī al-ṣaḥābī* (Chart 4.34). A companion's opinion, for Ibn Ḥanbal, is valid evidence that applies if the jurist 'cannot find a (direct) evidence in the Qur'an or Sunnah.'[130] Abū Ḥanīfah held the same position, but later Ḥanafīs gave *qiyās* a higher priority over a companion's opinion. Al-Shāfiʿī gave priority to consensus and analogy, in addition to the Qur'an and Sunnah, over applying a companion's opinion.[131] Mālik set a condition for the validity of *ra'ī al-ṣaḥābī*, which is to agree with Madinah's tradition (*ʿamal ahl al-madīnah*).[132]

Some jurists mentioned that there is a 'consensus' over the validity of this evidence,[133] which is inaccurate for two reasons. First, later jurists from various schools did not accept a companion's opinion as evidence in its own right, such as al-Ghazālī, al-Āmidī, al-Subkī, al-

Shawkānī, and Ibn Taymiyah.[134] Secondly, Ibn Ḥazm (and the Zaydīs) 'prohibited' the 'imitation of anyone other than the Prophet', including the companions.[135] Jaʿfarīs and Zaydīs take only the opinions of the companions from the *ʿitrah* (Prophet's next of kin).[136]

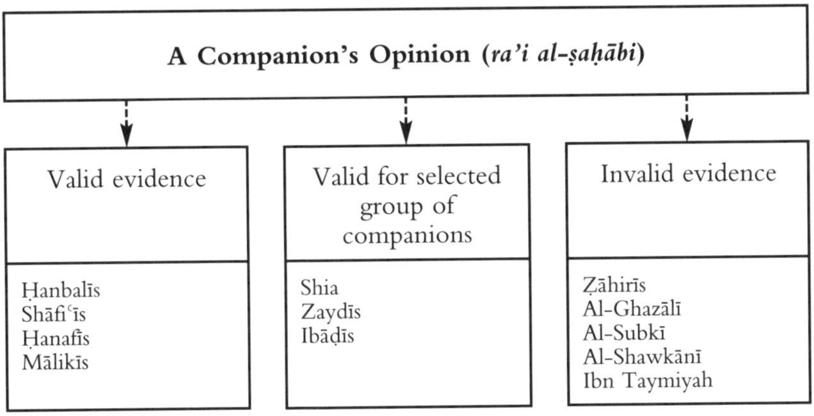

Chart 4.34. Difference of opinion over ra'ī al-ṣaḥābī.

Tradition of People of Madinah

The tradition (*ʿamal*), also called the consensus (ijmāʿ), of the people of Madinah is a key evidence/source in the Mālikī school. Based on *ʿamal*, Mālik had judged everything in the methods of the law, from the interpretation of verses to the authenticity of single-chained (*āḥād*) narrations and other secondary evidences.

A few scholars from other schools of law, such as Ibn Taymiyah and Ibn al-Qayyim from the Ḥanbalī school, agreed with the legitimacy of this evidence in principle because they considered it a form of 'collective narration after the Prophet'.[137] All other schools disagreed with consensus of the people of Madinah based on their own definitions of consensus. Al-Shāfiʿī disapproved any specific status for Madinah and argued that this kind of consensus opens the door for 'everybody to claim some consensus for their own region.'[138]

Ibn Ḥazm, and a number of other jurists, disputed the idea of claiming a consensus of a whole city the size of Madinah, on a 'logical' basis.

Ibn Ḥazm cited many cases in which Mālik had claimed a Madinan consensus, despite different opinions endorsed by other students of companions who also lived in Madinah at the time of Malik.[139]

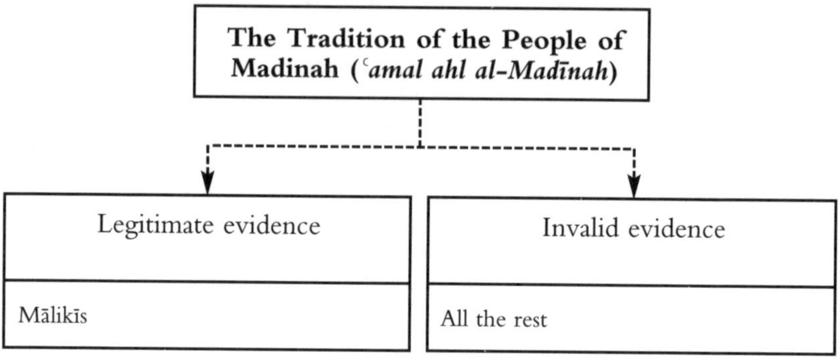

Chart 4.35. Difference of opinion over ʿamal ahl al-Madīnah.

Custom

All schools of law consider custom, or *al-ʿurf*, in their theories one way or another (Chart 4.36). However, there is a basic difference between jurists who considered *al-ʿurf* to be a standalone evidence (with some conditions they stipulated), and those who considered it to be merely a 'consideration' that is only effective in the applications of rulings (which are decided based on other evidences, in any case).

Ḥanfīs and Mālikīs endorsed a fundamental rule that made custom an 'evidence' similar to a scriptural evidence (*al-thābitu bi al-ʿurfi kal-thābiti bi al-naṣṣ*).[140] However, Ḥanafīs and Mālikīs consider it to be valid only if it 'does not contradict an evidence from the Qur'an or Sunnah.'[141] Al-Ṭūfī differed with his Ḥanbalī school over this issue, and considered *al-ʿurf* to be a method of defining *al-maṣlaḥah* (in addition to 'reason'). Therefore, al-Ṭūfī practically gave *al-ʿurf* priority over specific evidences from the Qur'an and Sunnah. Ḥanafīs and Mālikīs did not go as far as al-Ṭūfī in giving such authority to people's social evolution, but considered *al-ʿurf*, nevertheless, to be an evidence that 'specifies the scriptural general evidences.'[142] For example, an 'authentic' narration entails 'forbidding every sale with a condition.'[143] However, Ḥanafīs and Mālikīs allow sales with conditions that are 'customarily agreed upon.' Ibn ᶜĀbidīn articulated their position by writing: 'Does this mean that *ᶜurf* can judge a hadith? The answer is, no. *ᶜUrf* judges the analogy/*qiyās* based on the hadith, not the hadith itself. The reason behind the hadith (of forbidding sales with conditions) is to reduce people's disputes. Therefore, *ᶜurf* is coherent with the meaning of the hadith.' I, however, argue that this mechanism of interpretation of the scripts, based on how much people's traditions fulfil the 'meaning,' or the 'purpose,' behind them, is a flexible mechanism that enhances both 'openness' and 'purposefulness' in the Islamic law, as will be explained in Chapter Six.

Moreover, to be able to judge situations based on 'what is customarily agreed upon,' scholars from the Ḥanafī and Ḥanbalī schools of law put a condition for a jurist to have an 'understanding of the status quo' (*fiqh al-wāqiᶜ*).[144] This is another point of interaction between the law and social sciences, in which verified statistical data or sound sociological analysis play an effective role in deciding whether the desired 'meaning' or 'purpose' is met in reality.

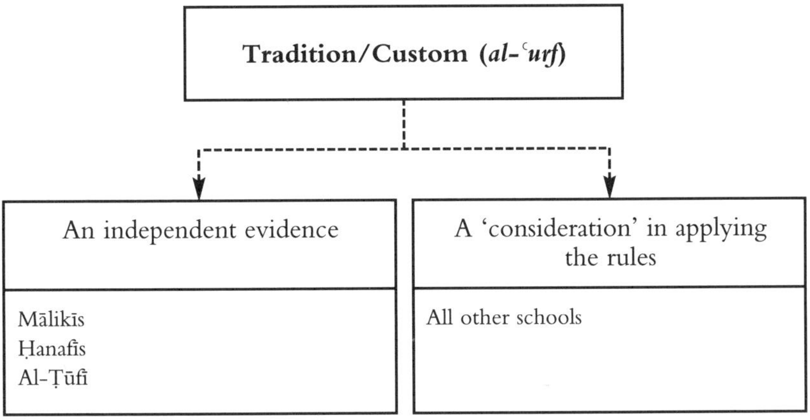

Chart 4.36. Difference of opinion over al-ᶜurf.

Presumption of Continuity

Presumption of continuity (*istiṣḥāb*) is a reasoning principle, rather than an 'evidence' or a source of legislation in its own right. It entails the continuation of a current status (permissibility, innocence, and so on) until some event entails otherwise. Presumption of continuity is an 'evidence' that is approved by all various schools of law. However, some Muʿtazilīs object to giving it a separate name on the basis that it is included in the 'judgement of reason.'[145] Jaʿfarīs do include *istiṣḥāb* in the 'judgement of reason,' but also establish its legitimacy based on (interpretations of) a number of narrations.[146] Jurists defined presumptions or *istiṣḥāb* in a variety of ways. The following are four examples of these definitions.[147]

1. The presumption of permissibility until proven forbidden.
2. The presumption of innocence until proven guilty.
3. The presumption of attributes until proven otherwise.
4. The presumption of duty until proven fulfilled.

Chapter Six will argue that the above fundamental rules are in effect a *maqāṣid*-based understanding and application of the Islamic law.

Prioritisation of Evidences

To outline the relationship between all the evidences mentioned in this section, the following chart 4.37 how each school 'prioritised' its valid evidences. The rankings are based on the school's main books of *uṣūl al-fiqh*, in addition to my observation of each school's mainstream trend. Some re-ranking applies subject to certain conditions (as the arrows on the chart illustrate).

Ḥanafīs give priority to Qur'anic evidences over all other evidences, including the Sunnah. They do not 'specify' or 'qualify' a general or unqualified expression of the Qur'an with a hadith. If they could not find evidence in the Qur'an, they search for a hadith that applies to the case in hand. A companion's opinion is next, in validity, after the Prophet's saying. Then, they carry out analogy. Ḥanafīs give analogy priority over hadith if it is an *aḥād* narration. But juridical preference, which comes next to analogy, overrides analogy if it is 'inappropriate,' i.e., if it misses the purpose of the law. Then, consensus is the evidence that comes next in rank, theoretically, even though I have not personally come across a ruling in the Ḥanafī school that is built exclusively on

Ḥanafī

1. Qur'an
2. Sunnah
3. Companions opinions
4. Analogy
5. Preference
6. Consensus
7. Custom
8. Presumption of continuity

If narration is *āḥād* (4. Analogy → 2. Sunnah)

If analogy is 'inappropriate' (5. Preference → 4. Analogy)

Shia (and Zaydīs)

1. Qur'an
2. Sunnah
3. Consensus (of *ʿitrah*)
4. Companions opinions (*ʿitrah*)
5. Presumption of continuity

Shāfiʿīs

1. Qur'an
1. Sunnah
2. Consensus (of companions)
3. Companions opinions
4. Analogy
5. Presumption of continuity

At one level (1. Qur'an, 1. Sunnah)

If narration is *āḥād* (4. Analogy → 1. Sunnah)

Ḥanbalīs

1. Qur'an
2. Sunnah
3. Companions opinions
4. Consensus
5. Analogy
6. Interest
7. Preference
8. Blocking the means
9. Presumption of continuity

Mālikīs

1. Qur'an
2. Sunnah
3. Companions opinions
4. Madinah's tradition
5. Analogy
6. Interest
7. Blocking the means
8. Custom
9. Presumption of continuity

If narration is *āḥād* (4. Madinah's tradition, 5. Analogy → 2. Sunnah)

via preference, if applies (6. Interest → 5. Analogy)

Ibāḍīs

1. Qur'an
2. Sunnah
3. Consensus
4. Analogy
5. Presumption of continuity
6. Preference
7. Interest

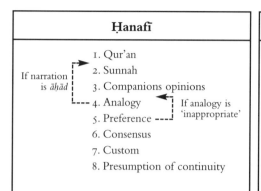

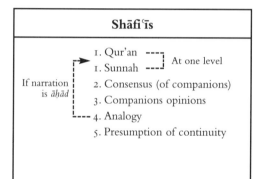

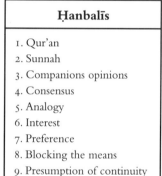

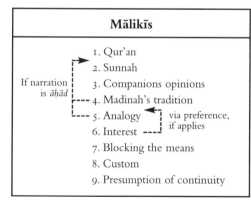

Muʿtazilītes	Ẓāhirīs
1. Qur'an	1. Qur'an ┐ At one level
2. Sunnah	2. Sunnah ┘
3. Consensus	3. Presumption of continuity
4. Analogy	
5. Interest	
6. Preference	

Chart 4.37. An overview of the prioritisation of evidences in various schools of Islamic law.

some 'consensus.' Custom and presumption of continuity are evidences in their own right that apply if none of the above is valid. Ḥanafīs give custom, however, priority over the literal implication of narrations if it achieves the same interest.

Shāfiʿīs place the Qur'an and Sunnah at the same level, i.e., a hadith is as valid as a verse, and if they 'contradict,' the more 'specific' and 'qualified' expression restricts the more 'general' and 'unqualified' expression. Consensus (of the companions) is applied in the Shāfiʿī methodology, on condition that it does not contradict with the implication of the Qur'an or hadith. If the companions do not have consensus over a certain issue, the opinion of one of them is applied. Then, if none of the above is available, they will apply analogy. Finally, Shāfiʿīs apply presumption of continuity as a last resort.

The Jaʿfarī and Zaydī procedures of ijtihad are quite similar. They apply the Qur'an, then the Sunnah. The opinion of one member of the Prophet's *ʿitrah*, or their consensus comes next. The Shia definition of presumption of continuity includes a variety of 'rational' procedures that they apply if they do not find any of the above *nuṣūṣ* and narrations. The Ẓāhirī/Literal school endorsed only the linguistic evidence of the Qur'an and Sunnah (at the same level of authority or *ḥujjiyyah*), and presumption of continuity as a reasoning procedure. They did not approve any other source of legislation.

Mālikīs apply the Qur'an, the Sunnah, a companion's opinion, Madinah's tradition, analogy, and interest, in that order. However, Madinah's tradition is given priority over *āḥād* narrations if they 'contradict.' Analogy is also given priority over *āḥād* narrations if they 'contradict,' given that they do not contradict Madinah's tradition. Moreover, Malik had frequently given interest (*maṣlaḥah*) priority over analogy, in the name of *istiḥsān* (juridical preference).

Imam Aḥmad ibn Ḥanbal mostly resorted to the evidences of the Qur'an, Sunnah, and the companion's opinion. He considered analogy to be a last resort, and rarely applied it. Later Ḥanbalī jurists developed the following list of evidence: Qur'an, Sunnah, companion's opinion, consensus, analogy, interest, preference, blocking the means, and presumption of continuity, in that order. This Ḥanbalī ranking is quite similar to the Ḥanafī ranking except for giving 'consensus' a higher priority over analogy, and counting 'blocking the means' as separate evidence.

Ibāḍīs apply the Qur'an, their narrations of hadith, 'consensus,' and analogy, in that order. They give *istiṣḥāb* priority over *istiḥsān* and *maṣlaḥah*.

Finally, since the Muʿtazilī school gave authority to reason (*al-ʿaql*) as, 'an independent source and the law's most fundamental evidence,'[148] some scholars are inclined to giving 'rational implication' (*al-dilālah al-ʿaqliyyah*) precedence over all other implications.[149] However, the Muʿtazilī process of juridical reasoning is quite similar to the rest of the traditional schools of law. In my view 'reason' is a theory in the Muʿtazilī philosophy of religion (*kalām*), rather than a method of ijtihad in the Muʿtazilī philosophy of law.

4.4. RULINGS

Overview

This section analyses both types of Islamic juridical rulings, accountability (*taklīfī*) and declaratory (*waḍʿī*) rulings. Accountability rulings are analysed in terms of their levels and issues related to legal capacity. The three types of declaratory rulings are discussed, namely, causes,

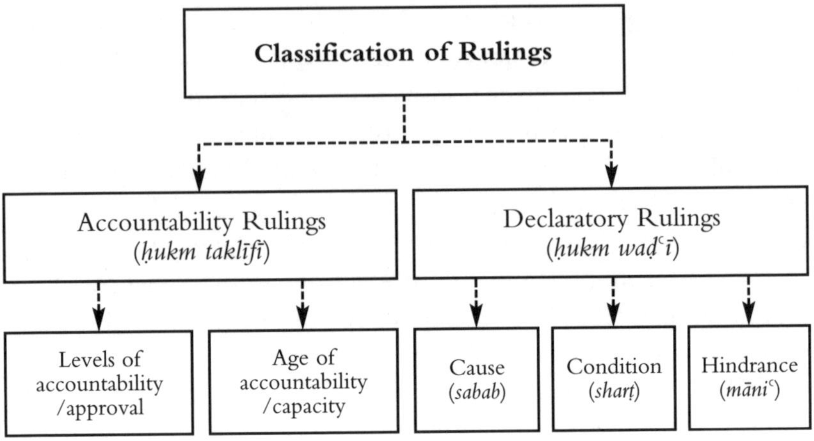

Chart 4.38. Classification of rulings into accountability and declaratory rulings.

conditions, and hindrances. Chart 4.38 presents a summary of the classification of rulings in traditional schools of Islamic law.

Levels of Approval

Schools of Islamic law, except for Ḥanafīs and some Muʿtazilīs, divide the juridical 'levels of accountability' into five levels, namely, obligation (*wājib*), recommended (*mandūb*), lawful (*mubāḥ*), discouraged (*makrūh*), and prohibited (*ḥarām*). Ḥanafīs added two levels to the five-level classification based on 'certainty' of the evidences. Some Muʿtazilīs divide all actions into 'obligation' and 'prohibition,' and rejected all intermediate levels of approval. This is in accordance with the Muʿtazilī fundamental theory that all actions are 'naturally' and 'intrinsically' divided into 'embellished' (*ḥassan*) and 'repugnant' (*qabīḥ*) actions, which could be understood rationally. Chart 4.39 summarises the above differences of opinion, which will also be further explained.

Obligations and Prohibitions

Schools of Islamic law agree on identifying obligations based on orders/imperatives in the scripts. A fundamental rule states that, 'the

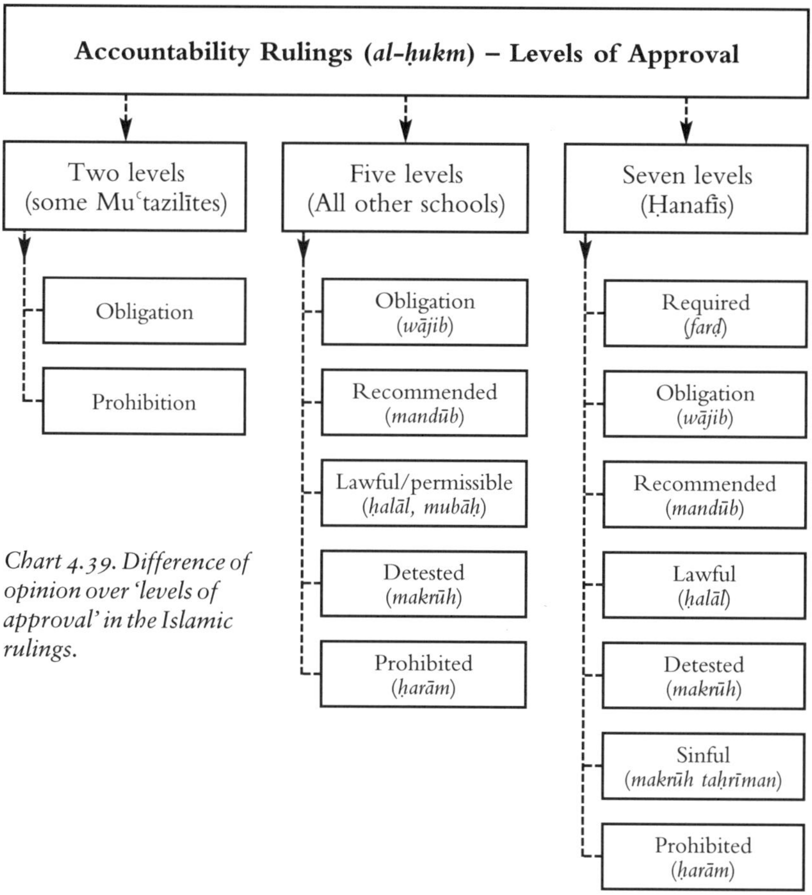

Chart 4.39. Difference of opinion over 'levels of approval' in the Islamic rulings.

default implication of an order (*amr*) is obligation.' Likewise, the default implication of a negative order (*nahī*) is prohibition.[150] Jurists theoretically classified obligations in various ways depending on their timing, alternatives/choices, scope, and whether they are 'precisely measured.' Chart 4.40 is a summary.

Optional Levels

If there is evidence that an order in not meant to be abiding, i.e., that it is permissible not to carry out the action, then the related action will

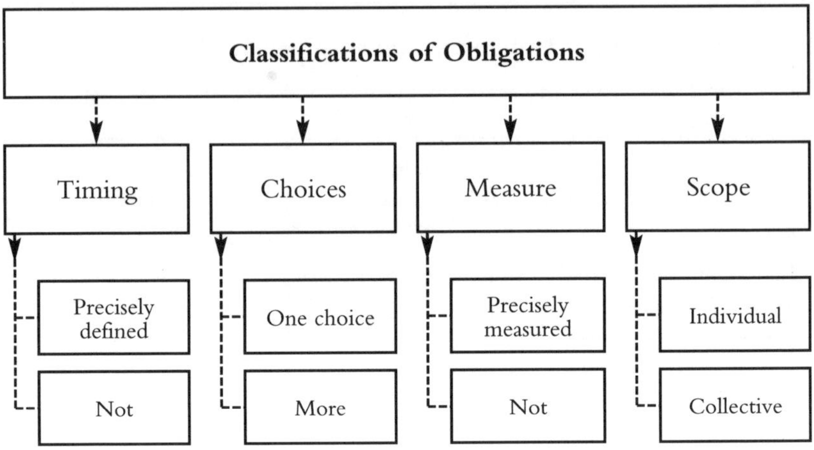

Chart 4.40. Classifications of obligations.

fall into a different category which most jurists call 'recommended.'[151] This evidence is usually a hadith that demonstrates that the Prophet had approved or carried out an action that is 'contrary' to the order. Similarly, a 'contrary' evidence in case of prohibition moves the action from the level of 'sin' (*ḥarām*) to the level of 'detested' (*makrūh*).

Ḥanafīs differentiate between two levels of obligation and two levels of prohibition, based on the level of 'certainty' of the evidence. Thus, Ḥanafīs differentiate between 'requirement' and 'obligation,' and 'prohibition' and 'sinful.' Narrations via *āḥād* are an example of 'uncertain' evidences.

The practical implication of this differentiation is that 'requirements' and 'prohibitions' become integral parts of the religion (*maʿlūm min al-dīn bi al-ḍarūrah*), which means that they are part of not only the Islamic practice code but also the Islamic belief system. This means that 'denying' any of the 'requirements' or 'prohibitions' puts one's faith in jeopardy, while denying matters of 'obligation' or 'sin' is not a matter of creed. All other schools of law make the same differentiation, in terms of the 'integrative parts of the religion,' without giving the two levels of obligation separate names. The relationship between the concept of 'certainty' and 'sanctifying human opinions' will be discussed in Chapter Six.

Also according to Ḥanafīs, if the evidence supporting the obligation is 'certain,' then the related action is required for 'legal correctness.' Otherwise, there are no legal consequences of the action and it becomes 'void.' For example, according to Ḥanafīs, if a trade transaction is carried out without one of the *farḍ* or required conditions, such as the lawfulness of the goods, then it is legally 'void,' as if never happened. But if the missing condition is a *wājib*, such as witnesses, then the transaction is still correct and legally abiding, despite the deficiency. All other schools do not make this differentiation, and thus render both actions invalid, whether the missing condition, for example, is *farḍ* or *wājib*.

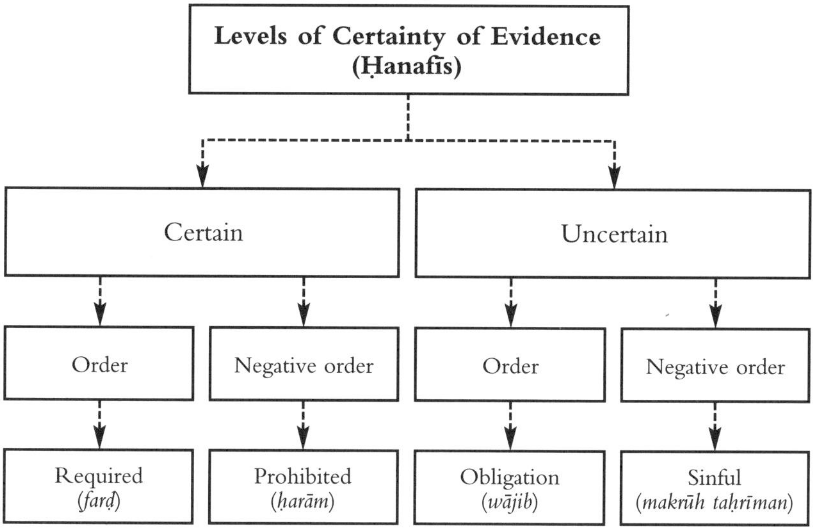

Chart 4.41. The Ḥanafī classification of levels of obligation and prohibition based on the evidence's 'certainty.'

Declaratory Rulings

Declaratory rulings are reasons, conditions, and hindrances. A ruling applies if its reasons exist, conditions are met, and hindrances are absent, as applicable. A 'reason' (*sabab*) is similar to a 'cause' or ʿ*illah*, as discussed earlier. A condition (*sharṭ*) could be either defined by the scripts or agreed upon by people (in the field of transactions). A hindrance (*māni*ᶜ) is a situation that renders the legal effect of the reason invalid. 'Correctness' (*al-ṣiḥḥah*) is reached if reasons exist, conditions are met, and hindrances are avoided. Otherwise, the transaction or action is void/incorrect (*fāsid* or *bāṭil*).

For example, prayers are obligatory if the 'reason' of prescribed timing is reached, the condition of ablution is met, and hindrances, such as mental incapacity, are absent. A second example: death is the 'reason' behind inheritance, life of the heir is a condition, and the heir killing the deceased is a hindrance from inheritance. A final example: a contract is the 'reason' behind certain financial obligations, witnesses are conditions, and the prohibition of goods is a hindrance from maintaining legal consequences for that contract.

Legal Capacity

Accountability or legal capacity (*ahlīyah*) in the Islamic law is classified by jurists into two levels, active legal capacity (*ahliyyah al-adā'*) and receptive capacity (*ahliyyah al-wujūb*). Active legal capacity entails rights, obligations and legal qualification, while receptive legal capacity entails rights without obligations or qualifications.[152] Jurists differentiated between the following four stages of human life, namely, from conception to birth, from birth to age of differentiation (*tamīyz*) to puberty (*bulūgh*), and from puberty to death.

The receptive legal capacity of an embryo only entails a right for what is of benefit to the embryo and its anticipated life. The 'period of pregnancy' is a topic that is discussed in fiqh in the context of rights

	Conception to birth	Birth to 'differentiation'	'Differentiation' to puberty	Puberty to death
Active legal capacity	—	—	√ (partial)	√ (full)
Receptive legal capacity	√ (partial)	√ (full)	√ (full)	√ (full)

*Chart 4.42. The jurists' classification of legal capacities in terms of human life stages (from Hasaballah's Uṣūl al-Tashrī*ᶜ*).*[153]

entailed because of pregnancy (for the baby and the mother). Jurists agreed on a minimum period of six months based on the 'implication of numbers' (*dilālah al-ᶜadad*) in verses 46:15, 'and her bearing him and his utter dependence on her took thirty months,' and 2:233, 'mothers may nurse their children for two whole years.'[154] However, there is a 'difference of opinion' regarding the maximum period of pregnancy, ranging from nine months to seven years! The evidences that jurists depended on in these judgements were either 'companion's opinion' or 'custom,' which is determined by 'asking people with experience in such matters.'[155]

Age of 'differentiation,' according to jurists, is the age at which a child is able to 'know what buying and selling is.'[156] Jurists had a difference of opinion as to whether the limit (*ḥadd*) of differentiation is the age of five, of seven, or eight. Again, all opinions are based on a 'companion's opinion' or 'experience.'[157]

Between birth and differentiation, a subject (*mukallaf*) lacks 'active legal capacity' but has a (full) 'receptive legal capacity,' i.e., capacity for receiving and giving inheritance, charity, and so on.[158] This full receptive capacity continues until death, and it takes on an 'active legal capacity' from the time of puberty (Chart 4.32).

The age of puberty is also a matter of a 'difference of opinion,' whether it is 'nine years,' 'seeing hair on the (boy's) face,' 'twelve years,' or 'the ability to conceive (for girls) and cause conception (for boys).'[159] Evidences presented depended on 'people's experience' and various indirect linguistic implications from the scripts.[160]

Active legal capacity entails responsibility of the subject/*mukallaf* for his/her own decisions, and independence from the approval of others in transactions. However, from the age of differentiation to the age of puberty, this capacity is partial, i.e., some decisions taken by the *mukallaf* have to be approved by guardian(s).[161]

Finally, the 'sign of death' is also a matter of a similar 'difference of opinion' in classic schools of Islamic law. Also based on 'custom,' signs of death, according to jurists, are 'collapsing cheeks,' 'inclined nose,' 'relaxed palm and legs,' or 'ceasing to move.'[162]

This subsection, which discussed various issues related to 'legal capacity,' included a number of issues that fell within the realm of what we call today 'science' rather than the realm of what we call 'law,' such as, 'period of pregnancy,' 'age of differentiation,' 'sign of puberty,' and 'sign of death.' Thus, in my view, these issues are not supposed to be determined according to a scholar's opinion or 'what people say,' but rather according to sound statistical conclusions based on some representative sample of medical and social records. Chapter Six will discuss 'openness' in the systems of Islamic law, and will elaborate on the important role that natural and social sciences could play in a systems approach to the Islamic law.

5

Contemporary Theories in Islamic Law

Overview

This Chapter attempts to answer the following questions:

- Are the classic schools of law that the previous chapter surveyed still strictly followed?
- And if the map of schools and theories of the Islamic law had changed, as many researchers maintain, what names can we give to the new schools and theories in the Islamic law?
- What are the principal features that define each contemporary school?
- And how much do they agree or disagree with classic schools?

This chapter attempts to answer the above questions. It starts with a survey of contemporary classifications of the theories of Islamic law and presents a new concept-based and multi-dimensional classification. The proposed concept-based classification attempts to overcome some of the drawbacks of feature-based classifications. The analysis presented in this chapter will show how contemporary theories endorse or criticise classic theories of Islamic law. The next chapter will build upon this chapter and the previous chapter's analysis in developing a systems approach to the Islamic law.

5.1. CONTEMPORARY CLASSIFICATIONS AND LABELS

Background

The twentieth century CE witnessed radical changes in the map of theories/schools of Islamic law. By the end of the nineteenth century, the most powerful modern countries had colonised the vast majority of countries with large Muslim populations.[1] The invading modernity, despite its many failures, is largely responsible for a revival in Islamic ijtihad in two different ways: (1) colonisation brought with it new problems which required new solutions, and (2) colonisation brought with it new perspectives and ideas in every field of knowledge.

By the beginning of the twentieth century, scholars and muftis realised that new *fatāwā* were needed, and historical collections of opinions within each traditional *madhhab* proved inadequate to deal with problems that modernity created. Thus, many muftīs began to widen their horizons to include other *madhāhib* in their *fatāwā*. As a result comparative studies of fiqh started to gain popularity. Eventually influential Islamic institutions considered reform in the theory of Islamic law necessary. On the other hand, modernity brought new philosophies and new ideas to traditional Islamic institutions, especially via some talented Muslim lawyers and jurists who were directly influenced by western scholarship. Examples are Rifaa al-Tahtawi, Mohammad Iqbal, and Mohammad Abdu. Eventually, western philosophical ideas started to find their way to Islamic thought in general and Islamic law in particular, and new fundamental methodologies began to emerge.

Today's classification of contemporary theories in Islamic law is by and large no longer along the lines of Shāfiʿī, Ḥanbalī, Jaʿfarī, and other traditional schools of law, as will be illustrated. However, there is still a general clear division between Sunni, Shia, and Ibāḍī schools of law, and a minority of Sunni scholars still adhere to one of the four Sunni *madhāhib* in all aspects of jurisprudence. This book will classify the tendency to remain within the historic boundaries of specific *madhāhib* as 'scholastic traditionalism.'[2] Nevertheless, I will argue that most contemporary scholars use traditional schools of law as 'supporting arguments' rather than 'original authorities.' This section proposes a new 'typology' of current theories of Islamic law, which represents today's landscape of fiqh more comprehensively than traditional *madhāhib* classification. The scope of the new classification includes all researchers and scholars of Islamic law, regardless of their backgrounds and geographical locations. First, current alternative classifications of Islamic schools of thought (or 'ideologies') will be introduced critically.

Islamic 'Ideologies'

Current studies on Islam and society, especially on what is called 'political Islam,' typically start with a 'typology of Islamic ideologies.' The purpose of these typologies is to define and assign certain labels to various groups, politicians, and thinkers, in order to decide strategies for 'dealing' with each. In these studies, 'ideology' is defined in a number of ways, perhaps depending on the 'ideology' of the writers and the goals of their studies. 'Classic' classifications, such as H. Gibb's, W. Smith's, A. Hourani's, L. Binder's, H. Mintjes's, and R. Humphrey's, divide these 'ideologies' into the popular threefold typology of 'traditionalism/fundamentalism,' 'modernism,' and 'secularism.'[3] This classic classification is merely a classification of reactions to Western political domination in the Islamic world, rather than a classification of theories of the Islamic law. Moreover, this threefold classification itself is a reflection of the above writers' concepts of 'fundamentalism,' 'modernity,' and 'secularism,' in their own environments. John Esposito preferred to analyse 'attitudes towards modernisation and Islamic socio-political change,'[4] which he classified into 'conservative,' 'neo-traditionalist,' 'Islamic reformist,' and 'secularist' attitudes. Yvonne Haddad also refers to 'attitudes' or 'tendencies,' which she divided into 'neo-normativist,' 'normativist,' and 'acculturationist.'[5] William Shepard considered the Islamic ideologies to be 'responses to the western impact and of proposals for rehabilitating Muslim history,' and came up with eight categories in a two-dimensional classification of 'Islamic totalism' and 'modernity.'[6] John Voll analysed 'styles of action' in Islamic history, and classified them into 'adaptionist,' 'conservative,' and 'fundamentalist.'[7] Fazlur Rahman contrasted 'neo-fundamentalism' with 'Islamic modernism,' which in his opinion, meant 'the induction of change into the content of the shariᶜah.'[8] He also defined a 'postmodern fundamentalist' trend, whose 'basic élan is anti-Western.'[9] Despite the variations in the above classifications, I would say that they still revolve around the old three-class typology of fundamentalism, modernism, and secularism. There is also a general tendency in the above studies to divide modernism into two distinct levels, and hence, wind up with four classes. Chart 5.1 summarises the expressions/labels that were used for these four classes.

1	2	3	4
Fundamentalism	Apologetic modernism	Modernism	Secularism
Traditionalism	Neo-fundamentalism	Reformism	Liberalism
Literal Salafism	Neo-traditionalism	Neo-modernism	Modernism
Radical fundamentalism	Conservativism	Salafi reformism	Acculturationism
Conservative traditionalism	Neo-normativism	Normativism	Adaptionism
Conservatism	Rejectionist neo-traditionalism	Accomodationist neo-traditionalism	Rational reformism
Normativism	Salafi reformism	Reformist traditionalism	
Rejectionist traditionalism	Reformist traditionalism	Traditionalism	
Postmodern fundamentalism			

Chart 5.1. A summary of the expressions used in typologies of 'Islamic ideologies.'

Tariq Ramadan's typology does not follow the 'classic' three-fold classification. It rather identifies 'tendencies' in 'Islamic thought' and, hence, represents the streams of Islamic thought of various groups/movements more accurately than the other (classic) classifications.[10]

RAND's Classification

Another significant classification is provided in RAND Corporation reports on Islamism.[11] The 2004 report stated its objective, which is to contribute to the efforts of those who 'want to prevent a clash of civilisations.' Similar to the above-mentioned typologies, the RAND report presents a four-class typology of four 'essential positions,' namely, fundamentalism, traditionalism, modernism, and secularism. Yet, RAND's typology is of particular relevance to our research because these 'positions' represent, more or less, *fiqhī* positions over a number of contemporary issues. These issues, which the report says 'have become contentious in the Islamic world,' are related to 'political and individual freedom, education, the status of women, criminal justice, the legitimacy of reform and change, and attitudes towards the west.' Examples of these issues are polygamy, *ḥijāb*, flogging, public participation of women, and jihad.

The following is a brief summary of RAND's typology, followed by my comments.

1. Fundamentalism was divided into scriptural fundamentalism and radical fundamentalism:
(a) Scriptural fundamentalists believe in an expansionist and aggressive version of Islam that is grounded in theology, imposes a strict public observance of Islam, and resorts to violence. In terms of Islamic law, their sources are defined as the Qur'an, Sunnah, charismatic leaders, and radical authors. Iranian revolutionaries, Saudi-based Wahhabis, and the Turkish Kaplan congregation were all included in this category.
(b) Radical fundamentalists believe in an expansionist and aggressive version of Islam, and they can resort to violence and 'terrorism.' In terms of Islamic law, their sources are defined as the Qur'an, Sunnah, charismatic leaders, and Islamic philosophy. Al-Qaeda, Taliban, Hizb-ut-Tahrir, and other Islamic movements, are given as examples.
2. Traditionalism was divided into conservative traditionalism and reformist traditionalism.

(a) Conservative traditionalists support a literal and strict form of Islam, but do not resort to violence. They resist modernity and change. Those who live in a traditional society are also described as less educated and less capable of distinguishing local customs from Islamic doctrine. In terms of Islamic law, their sources are defined as the Qur'an, Sunnah, local customs, and opinions of local clerics. Akbar Ahmad and Abdur-Rahman Doi are given as examples.

(b) Reformist traditionalists are described as 'more ready to make some concessions' in the literal application of orthodoxy through reform and re-interpretation, with an objective to conserve the 'spirit of the law.' In terms of Islamic law, their sources are defined as the Qur'an, Sunnah, scholars (including secular philosophers), modern laws and ethics, and community consensus. Yusuf al-Qaradawi and Ruqaiyyah Maqsood are provided as examples.

3. Modernism was not divided into further classes, and modernists are described as 'ready to make far-reaching changes in the current orthodox understanding of Islam.' They are also described as believers in the 'historicity of Islam,' i.e., the report says, 'Islam as practiced during the time of the Prophet is no longer valid.' In terms of Islamic law, their sources are also defined as the Qur'an, Sunnah, scholars (including what the report called 'secular philosophers'), and modern laws and ethics. Khaled Abou El-Fadl, Mohammad Shahrur, Serif Mardin, Bassam Tibi, and Nawal Saadawi were given as example modernists.

4. Secularism was divided into mainstream secularism and radical secularism.

(a) Mainstream secularists 'want the Islamic world to accept a division of church and state in the manner of western industrial democracies, with religion relegated to the private sphere.'

(b) Radical secularists are essentially 'anti-American' and 'extremely hostile.'

The following are my comments on the above categorisation in point form.

1. This classification is by and large based on the above groups' current political positions on the United States' foreign policy, especially its 'war on terror' policy. The typology is not clearly related to Islamic law, 'western values,' the 'international community,' or 'modernity,' as the report claims.
2. Despite numerous practical and 'lifestyle' examples given in the report, the comparison does not capture the basic theoretical differences in these groups' versions of the fundamentals of Islamic law (*uṣūl*), upon which they build their ideological stances.
3. The Qur'an and prophetic tradition are mentioned amongst the sources for all trends (except for the secularists). However, it is essential to consider the detailed methodology of dealing with these two sources and the role of other sources (such as *maṣlaḥah* and *ᶜurf*). In extreme/conservative groups, for example, patriarchal traditions do override the script on all practical levels, as the next subsection demonstrates. This also explains part of the report's surprise with the conservatives' 'considerable liberties' with the 'literal substance of Islam.' In modernist trends, for another example, the concept of *maṣlaḥah* often generates new approaches to politics that are rather pragmatic.
4. The differentiation between scriptural fundamentalists (for example, Wahhabis) and radical fundamentalists (for example, Al-Qaeda and Taliban) based on 'theology' is not accurate. All these groups have the same theological positions, which are based on the 'Salafi creed' (*ᶜaqīdah al-salaf*). On the other hand, the positions of many 'Iranian revolutionaries' differ from the above groups on a number of theological issues (except for their general ideological stances from the United States). 'Iranian revolutionaries' themselves are divided across the spectrum of the Islamic positions, despite, again, their similar political stands on the current United States' foreign policies. The next subsection will illustrate how some of them contributed to 'modernist approaches' to the Islamic law, such as Mohammad Khatami and Abdul-Karim Soroush.
5. Despite the accurate analysis of the 'reformist traditionalist' strategy of 're-interpretation,' 'secular philosophers, modern laws

and ethics' are certainly not amongst their 'sources of Islamic law.' However, the inclusion of secular philosophers and modern ethics amongst modernist scholars' sources is accurate. In fact, modern values are the essential core of the modernists' positions, based upon which scriptural re-interpretation itself is carried out.

6. The concept of 'historicity of Islam' is mentioned in the report as a 'modernist' feature. However, in this section, various forms and degrees of 'historicisation' will be analysed, based on postmodern, rather than modern, philosophy. This Chapter will stress the importance of differentiating between modern and postmodern critical positions.
7. It is more accurate to divide the modernist category into at least two categories, based on the difference between 're-interpretation' and 'radical criticism' strategies, as this section will suggest.
8. It would be more accurate to identify Islamic positions in terms of theories, rather than specific personalties and names. Many of the names associated with specific categories in the report actually shift their positions along two or more of the proposed categories, depending on the issue. For example, Shaykh al-Qaradawi takes what could be classified as a 'traditionalist' position on issues he classifies as 'constant fundamentals' (*uṣūl thābitah*), a 'modernist re-interpetation' position on issues that he classifies as 'variable' (*mutaghaīrāt*), and yet, what could be called a 'secular position' on issues he classifies as belonging to the 'field of no legislation' (*majāl al-farāgh al-tashrīʿī*).[12]
9. Despite the report's classification of the three of them under 'modernists,' Nawal Saadawi's position is radically different from Mohammad Shahrur's or Khaled Abou El-Fadl's. While Saadawi denounces 'Islam, and all religions,' for being patriarchal and restrictive towards women,[13] Shahrur and Abou El-Fadl are clearly working within the Islamic juridical tradition, despite their feminist and modernist 're-interpretations.'[14]

'Script-Based' Classifications

Apart from the typologies that are based on 'Islamic ideologies,' there are a few typologies of approaches based on the Islamic primary sources, namely, the Qur'an and prophetic traditions. Scholars who suggested these typologies assert their belonging to a 'centrist' trend. Centrism (*Waṣaṭiyyah*, often translated as 'moderation') argues a position of 'revitalisation' or 'reform' (*iḥyā'*, *nahḍah*, or *iṣlāḥ*) between two 'extremes,' typically called 'literalism' (*ḥarfiyyah*) and 'westernisation' (*taghrīb*).[15] The following is a summary of the features of these three-class categorisations, which are becoming increasingly popular in juridical literature written in the Arabic language.

1. *Literalism or Stagnation*: Literalists (often called 'neo-literalists') are usually described as considering the literal meanings of the scripts and 'ignoring their purposes.'[16] Stagnation refers to the strict following of one of the Islamic *madhāhib*, which is, in the 'neo-literalist' case, the Ḥanbalī school in its modern Salafi/ Wahhabi version. Wahhabism is an Islamic movement that was named after Imam Mohammad ibn Abdul-Wahhab, who led a movement in Arabia in order to 'retain the pure and original form of Islam and purify it from all the Sufi innovations.'[17] Abdul-Wahhab allied with Abdul-Aziz al-Saud, the founder of today's Saudi Arabia, and followed the Hanbali school, especially Ibn Taymiyah's opinions.
2. *Secularisation or Westernisation*: This is a label for 'radical critiques' of mainstream Islamic thought/law based on contemporary philosophy or methodology. Secularists are 'emerging from a fundamental philosophical reference to western civilisation.'[18] They are also accused of abandoning the Islamic scripts (*nuṣūṣ*) for the sake of their own reasoning.[19]
3. *Centrism or Renewal*: This is a new school of Islamic law that argues a position between the above two positions. Generally, centrists do not restrict themselves to a specific traditional school of Islamic law, but choose from amongst their opinions in order to achieve people's interest (*maṣlaḥah*) in real life situations.[20]

The following are my comments on the above categorisation.

1. This categorisation is, also, a 'pigeon-holes' division of methods that assumes consistency in its 'ideal types.' However, there is more than one identifiable trend within each of the above-mentioned trends. 'Literalism,' sometimes uses methods that do not strictly abide by the literal meanings of the scripts, but rather by the popular traditions/customs, first and foremeost.
2. It is more accurate to classify methods rather than scholars, for the reason that many scholars shift their theoretical positions based on circumstances.
3. The 'centrist/moderate school,' contributed an important departure from the strict adherence to traditional Islamic *madhāhib*. It also endorsed forms of contemporary re-interpretation of the scripts that aimed to keep with the 'spirit of the law.' However, there is a large variety of methods of (re)interpretation of *madhāhib* and scripts, some of which could also be rightly classified as 'modernist' or even 'secularist.'
4. 'Westernisation' and 'modernisation' are incorrectly used as synonyms, as Mohammad Khatami has rightly noted.[21] Despite the fact that modernism emerged from 'the west,' it was 'interpreted' in a variety of ways in various parts of the world.
5. 'Western' philosophy did have a significant impact on the 'moderate' stream itself, via the influence of Mohammad Abdu and others.
6. 'Secularism' is a label given to a variety of methods, some of which are unrelated to the concept of the 'separation of religion and state,' which is the original definition of secularism.
7. Dividing the entire world into an 'Islamic domain' and 'the West' is a remnant of the old land of war/land of Islam division. It is unfortunate, however, that the current international political situation only gives credit to these binary classifications. We began the twenty first century with a number of conflicts that further enforced an antagonistic approach towards the 'Islamic world' in many western countries, and a parallel defensive approach in the other direction.
8. There is a difference between 'modernist' approaches, which were influenced by modernism one way or the other, and what this

book will call 'postmodernist' approaches to the Islamic law, which were influenced by postmodern theory/philosophy one way or the other.

Next, I will propose a classification that is focused on contemporary schools/theories of Islamic law, based on a number of dimensions that include 'levels of authority' and sources of the law. The next section begins with an explanation of these dimensions.

5.2. A PROPOSED CLASSIFICATION

Levels of Authority

Much of the *uṣūlī* debates drew upon two levels of legitimacy or authority (*ḥujjiyyah*), namely, authority/sound/proof (*ḥujjah*) and invalid/unsound/radically criticised (*bāṭil*). A *ḥujjah* is a base for a ruling while a '*bāṭil*' evidence/argument is 'radically criticised' and does not have authority, as a matter of principle and under all circumstances. Examples are the books/articles that were written by imams about the invalidity of some evidences and methods, such as, al-Shāfiʿī's '*Ibṭāl al-Istiḥsān*' (Invalidating Legal Preference), Dāwūd's '*Ibṭāl al-Qīyās*' (Invalidating Analogical Reasoning), Ibn Taymiyah's three volumes on '*Ibṭāl Qawl al-Falāsifah*' (that is, Invalidating the Philosophers's Arguments), Ibn al-Rāwandī's '*Ibṭāl al-Tawātur*' (Invalidating Most-Famous Narrations), Ibn al-Qayyim's '*Buṭlān al-Kīmyā*" (Invalidity of Chemistry), and so forth.[22] Chart 5.2 illustrates this popular binary classification of authorities.

Chart 5.2. Traditionally, evidences/arguments are always divided between two categories, sound (ḥujjah) and unsound (bāṭil).

ḥujjah	*bāṭil*

In a few cases, jurists from various schools referred to evidences that do not have direct and definite authorities, but are rather 'supporting evidences' (*li al-isti'nās*). This is a level of authority that is good for 'additional justification' rather than being *ḥujjah* in its own right.[23]

For example, al-Shāfiʿī accepted narrations with disconnected-ends (*marāsīl*) from Ibn al-Musayyab, 'as supporting evidence (*isti'nās*), not because they were valid (*ḥujjah*) in their own right' (Chart 5.3).[24] Moreover, there are a number of evidences that jurists, especially from the Shāfiʿī school, endorsed at the level of *isti'nās*, such as, 'applying the minimum denominator' (*al-akhdh bi-aqall mā qīl*), 'inspiration' (*al-ilhām*), 'the implication of the context' (*dilālah al-sīyaq*), and 'taking precautions' (*al-iḥtīyāṭ*).[25] However, in today's theories of Islamic law, there are several juridical evidences, which were classically 'original' evidences, that had been moved to the level of 'supporting' (*isti'nās*) evidences, as explained in the next subsections.

Chart 5.3. Supporting evidence (isti'nās) is an intermediate level of ḥujjīyah that appears in a few rulings.

ḥujjah	*isti'nās*	*bāṭil*

In some cases, jurists applied '*ta'wīl*' (literally, interpretation) to verses of the Qur'an or narrations.[26] I will translate *ta'wīl* as 're-interpretation,' however, since it is always an interpretation that is different from the usual interpretations offered in usual accounts of exegesis. Jurists put some conditions for the validity of *ta'wīl*, which al-Zarkashī summarised as follows:

1. not to contradict the linguistic rule of correctness in Arabic,
2. not to contradict the normal/customary use of the Arabic language,
3. and not to contradict the general principles of the Islamic law.[27]

Ta'wīl usually entailed some form of restricting the meaning (*takhṣīṣ*). For example, Shāfiʿīs ruled that the pool of zakah includes vegetables, despite the hadith that states that, 'there is no charity (*ṣadaqah*) on vegetables.' They 're-interpreted' the word '*ṣadaqah*' to restrict it to optional charity, rather than the obligatory charity of

Chart 5.4. Ta'wīl is a level of ḥujjiyyah between ḥujjah and isti'nās.

ḥujjah	*mu'awwal*	*isti'nās*	*bāṭil*

zakah.[28] Thus, this re-interpreted evidence is '*mu'awwal*,' and not up to the level of *ḥujjah* (Chart 5.4).

In a few other cases, some jurists criticised evidences in a way that does not totally discredit them in the usual (binary) manner. They used expressions such as, '*fīhi shaī*'' (there is something wrong about it), or '*fīhi maghmaz/khadshah*' (there is a flaw in it).[29] For example, al-Laknawī al-Ḥanafī used this expression to criticise his Ḥanafī school's method of giving precedence to abrogation (*al-naskh*) over conciliation (*al-jam*ᶜ) in resolving opposing narrations (*al-muta*ᶜ*āriḍāt*).[30]

ḥujjah	*mu'awwal*	*isti'nās*	*fīhi shaī'*	*bāṭil*

Chart 5.5. Fīhi shaī' is a minor criticism between isti'nās and buṭlān.

Recently, however, two new types of *ta'wīl* became common in the field of Islamic law, namely, apologetic (re)interpretation and radical (re)interpretation. Apologetic interpretations introduce 'sensible explanations' for traditional rulings that are thought to contradict 'reason' or 'acceptable behavior,' without entailing any change to the ruling itself on a practical level. Examples include: re-interpreting polygamy, mentioned in verse 4:3, to mean that it is meant to be a solution for the 'natural' imbalance between the numbers of men and women; re-interpreting verse 2:282, which equated a man's testimony with the testimony of two women, to be 'better than legal systems which did not accept the testimony of women at all,' or to be 'particular to economic transactions;'[31] and re-interpreting verse 4:34, which mentioned 'chastisement' (*ḍarb*) of women, to mean that 'chastising is allowed only using a toothbrush.'[32] On the other hand, radical interpretations do not contradict possible dictionary meanings of words in the Arabic language, in accordance to what jurists had allowed for acceptable interpretations. However, they are unprecedented and usually at odds with the customary usage of these words in the Arabic language, contrary to what jurists had allowed. In the above examples, some radical re-interpreters of verse 4:3 argued that polygamy in the Islamic law is restricted to marrying widows.[33] Similarly, verse 2:282

on a woman's testimony is to be linked to 'historical practical considerations.'[34] They also re-interpret verse 4:34, which mentions 'chastising' (*ḍarb*) of women, to mean 'mentioning a similie to them' (*ḍarb al-mithāl*),[35] as a sort of advice. Chart 5.6 summarises all of the above suggested 'levels of authority.'

Proof (*ḥujjah*)	Apologetic interpretation	Interpreted (*mu'awwal*)	Supportive evidence (*isti'nās*)	Minor criticism (*fīhi shaī'*)	Radical re-interpretation	Void (*bāṭil*)

Chart 5.6. This book suggests five additional levels of 'authority' between 'proof' and 'void.'

A multidimensional systems approach, as explained in Chapter Two, entails a shift from the usual binary categorisation of authority into a multi-level categorisation, as explained above. Thus, it is more 'systematic' to present the above categories on an open scale rather than the pigeonhole boxes of Chart 5.6. The practical advantage that a 'spectrum' offers is openness to, yet, more levels of *ḥujjiyyah* between the presented levels. Chart 5.7 illustrates how I view the different levels of *ḥujjiyyah* in a continuous spectrum between proof (*ḥujjah*) and radically criticised/void (*bāṭil*).

Direction of decreasing *ḥujjīyah* →

Proof (*ḥujjah*)	Apologetic interpretation	Interpreted (*mu'awwal*)	Supportive evidence (*isti'nās*)	Minor criticism (*fīhi shaī'*)	Radical re-interpretation	Void (*bāṭil*)

Chart 5.7. A multi-valued spectrum of ḥujjiyyah, from 'proof' to 'void.'

Current 'Sources' in Islamic Law

In Chapter Four, traditional sources/evidences of Islamic law were briefly mentioned, namely, the Qur'an, prophetic tradition, consensus, analogy, interest, juridical preference, custom, the imam's opinion, the companion's opinion, and presumption of continuity. However, contemporary theories of Islamic law draw on a different set of sources/

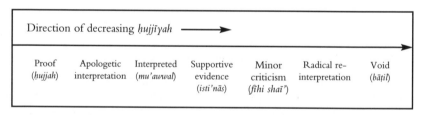

evidences, which this subsection attempts to identify based on a survey carried out on a large number of contemporary references, including those that are mentioned in this chapter's endnotes.

Today's jurists basically refer to Qur'anic verses, prophetic narrations, and rulings issued by the traditional schools of Islamic law. However, perceptions of Qur'anic exegesis, hadith collections, and various rulings issued by schools of law are shaped by available edited-manuscripts. The twentieth century witnessed a broad movement of manuscript editing and publication, particularly Arabic books related to Islamic law and its sources. Publishing houses, especially in Beirut and Cairo, printed and widely publicised books that were only accessible to a few scholars/students of Islamic law in traditional Islamic universities. The selection of these manuscripts depended on the (traditional) curricula in these universities, in addition to what was available in major manuscript libraries around the world. Recently, a large number of Islamic internet websites and software companies have contributed to even much wider distribution of these books.[36] Moreover, manuscript editing is becoming a trend in graduate studies related to Islamic law in Islamic universities and in departments/programs of Islamic Studies outside these universities.

It is not possible to keep track or carry out a full survey of all the edited/printed manuscripts around the world that are related to Islamic law. Yet, from my frequent visits and dealings with university libraries, book fairs, and publishing houses in various countries, I could identify the main scholars/jurists (between the second and twelvth Islamic centuries), whose edited-manuscripts are shaping current research in Islamic law and the perception of its 'literature.' The following is a list of these scholars in the areas of exegisis, hadith, and fiqh and *uṣūl* in various schools of law.

1. Qur'anic exegesis. Today, the most well known exegetes from various schools are: Ibn Kathīr, al-Ṭabarī, al-Bayḍawī, al-Zamkhsharī, al-Rāzī, al-Shanqīṭī, al-Baghawī, Abu al-Saud, al-Saadi, al-Nasafī, al-Ṭabṭaba'i, al-Qummi, al-Ṭusi, Ṣadr al-Mut'allihīn, al-Waḥidi, al-Thaʿalibi, al-Suyuṭi, al-Qurṭubi, al-Alusi, al-Samarqandi, al-Kashāni, al-Janābidhi, Abdul-Jabbar, al-Samʿani, al-Sanʿani, Ibn Taymiyah, al-Shawkānī, al-Mawardi, al-Ḥabri, al-Kūfi, al-Hawwari, Iṭfeesh, and al-Khalīli.

2. Hadith collections. The most popular compilers of standard hadith collections from various schools are: al-Bukhārī, Muslim, al-Ḥākim, Ibn al-Jārūd, Ibn Ḥibbān, Ibn Khuzaimah, al-Bayhaqī, al-Nassā'ī, Abū Dāwūd, Ibn Mājah, al-Tirmidhī, al-Dārquṭnī, al-Dāramī, Ibn Bābawayh, al-Ṭaḥnawī, Mālik, al-Shāfiʿī, Abū Ḥanīfa, Abdul-Razzaq, al-Ṭabarī, al-Ṭabarānī, Ibn Abī-Shaybah, al-Bazzār, al-Rabīʿ Ibn Ḥabīb, al-Killīnī, al-Majlisī, and al-ʿĀmilī.
3. Fiqh and *uṣūl*. The following jurists are the most prominent in their respective schools of Islamic law, and their edited-manuscripts are now considered 'textbooks' for studying these schools.

(a) The Ḥanafī school: Abū Ḥanīfa, Abū Yūsuf, Moḥammad ibn al-Ḥasān, al-Sarkhasī, al-Bazdawī, Ibn Nujaym, al-Rāzī, al-Merghayānī, al-Kasānī, al-Zaylaʿī, al-Samarqandī, al-Ṭaḥāwī, al-Sīwāsi, Ibn Mūsā, al-Laknawī, Shaikhizādah, Ibn al-Humām, and Ibn ʿĀbidīn.

(b) The Mālikī school: Mālik, Ibn Wahb, Saḥnūn, Ibn al-ʿArabī, al-Qarāfī, al-Mawwāq, al-Abdarī, al-Thalabī, al-Qayrawānī, al-Ghirnāṭī, Ibn ʿAbdul-Barr, al-Kurdī, al-Adawī, Ibn Rushd, al-Shāṭibī, al-Dardīr, Ibn Farḥūn, al-Kharshī, al-Wansharīsī, al-Shādhilī, and al-Sunūsī.

(c) The Ḥanbalī school: Ibn Ḥanbal, al-Marwazī, al-Khallāl, Ibn Taymiyah, Ibn al-Qayyim, al-Ṭūfī, Ibn Rajab, Ibn al-Lahhām, Ibn Baṭṭah, al-Mirdawī, al-Bahwatī, al-Maqdisī, Ibn Mufliḥ, Ibn Qudāmah, al-Baghawī, al-Zarkashī, al-Marwazī, al-Baʿlī, and al-Kharqī.

(d) The Zaydī school: Zayd, al-Wāsiṭī, Ibn al-Zabarqān, Ibn Muzāḥim, Aḥmad Ibn ʿĪsā, al-Qāsim, al-Hādī, Ibn Isḥāq, al-Ansī, Ibn al-Murtaḍā, Ibn Muftaḥ, and recently, al-Shawkānī.

(e) The Ibāḍī school: Jābir ibn Zayd, al-Busaidī, Iṭfeesh, al-Bahlawī, Ibn Jaʿfar, al-Ḥawarī, al-Salīmī, al-Shamakhī, al-Autabī, and al-Shaqsī.

(f) The Jaʿfarī school: Jaʿfar, al-Killīnī, Ibn Bābawayh, Ibn Qawlawayh, Ibn al-Junaid, al-Ṣadūq, al-Mufīd, al-Murtadā, al-Ṭūsī, al-Khū'ī, al-Ḥasan al- Ḥillī, al-Muḥaqqiq al-Ḥillī, al-Muṭahhar al-Ḥillī, al-ʿĀmilī, al-Ṭabṭaba'i, and al-Najafī.

(g) The Shāfiʿī school: Al-Shāfiʿī, al-Qaffāl al-Shāshī, al-Juwaynī, al-Ghazālī, al-Māwardī, al-Shirbīnī, al-Fairūzabādī, al-Ṣanʿānī, al-Nawawī, al-Ḥaḍramī, al-Haithamī, al-Bijirmī, al-Shirāzī, Ibn al-Ṣālaḥ, al-Anṣārī, Ibn Raslān, al-Subkī, Qalyūbī, ʿUmayrah, and al-Ramlī.

(h) The Ẓāhirī school: Dawūd and Ibn Ḥazm.

(i) The Muʿtazilī school: ʿAbdul-Jabbār, al-Bājī, Abū al-Ḥussain al-Baṣrū, Abū Hāshim, al-Kaʿabī, al-Jubba'i, Ibn Khallād, al-Naẓẓām, Ibn al-Hudhail, and Abū Muslim.

The twentieth century also witnessed a great deal of research and writing on issues related to the Islamic law, written in all known languages. Authors/Researchers gave the above-mentioned classic jurists and their works a 'level of authority' that ranged from '*ḥujjiyyah*' to 'radical criticism.'

In addition, some other 'sources of law' were considered to have 'authority' in their own right, such as, higher principles and interests, 'rational' arguments, and 'modern' universal values and rights.

Therefore, the following is a list of current sources on the Islamic law. The next subsection will explain how various theoretical approaches considered these sources at different levels of authority.

1. Verses of the Qur'an, usually interpreted according to one of the exegeses mentioned above.
2. Prophetic traditions, usually cited in one of the collections that are mentioned above.
3. 'Islamic' higher interests (*maṣāliḥ*), which are induced from the scripts and narrations, as explained in Chapter One.
4. Rulings from traditional schools of Islamic law, according to one of the schools' jurists mentioned above.
5. 'Rational' arguments, or rationality, which could mean a number of things. However, the common feature of all 'rational' arguments is their reliance on pure human reasoning, rather than an outside (divine) source of knowledge.
6. Modern values, the reference of which is usually the Universal Declaration of Human Rights and similar international and national declarations.

Chart 5.8 illustrates how I view these sources as a representation of a dimension of human experience versus revelation. Qur'anic verses are at the right end of the spectrum, even though its interpretation is subject to human experiences, as obvious from the science of exegesis. The prophetic traditions range from 'pure conveyance of the message' to 'pure human judgements,' as will be elaborated in the next chapter. Interests represent human cognition of the higher objectives of the revelation. It was also explained in Chapter One how perceived interests are subject to each jurist's 'worldview' and agenda of reform. Rulings made by jurists, who belonged to traditional *madhāhib*, are legal opinions (*fatāwā*), which were given in certain geographical and historical contexts. Thus, on the spectrum shown, they are closer to 'human experience' than 'revelation.' What some Muslims view as a 'rational norm' is an expression of human experience, even though it is also shaped, in part, by popular perceptions of Islam. Finally, politicians compiled modern declarations of universal human rights in order to preserve 'human intrinsic dignity.' Thus, these declarations represent the ultimate human experience in deciding the law. Some current scholars of Islamic studies have suggested them as the most justifiable sources of 'Islamic' law for today. The following subsections will elaborate on these sources.

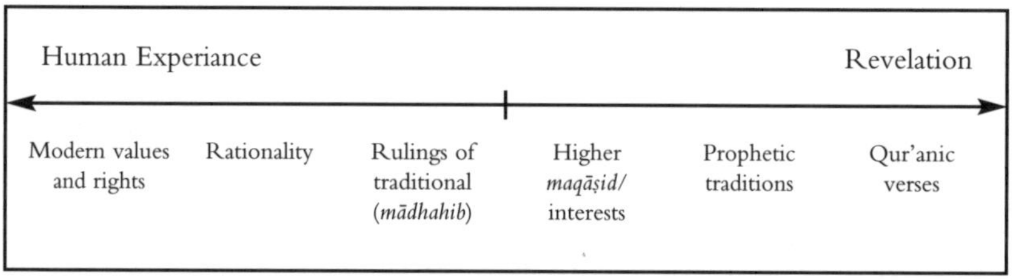

Chart 5.8. A multi-valued spectrum of sources according to a dimension of 'human-experience' versus 'revelation.'

Current 'Tendencies' in Islamic Law

Chart 5.9 presents a two dimensional classification that illustrate the current various sources of Islamic law versus the current various levels of authority given to them. In other words, verses of the Qur'an, prophetic traditions, rulings from traditional schools of Islamic law, Islamic higher principles/interests, rationality, and modern values, were given 'authority' that ranged from 'proof' (*ḥujjah*) to 'radically criticised' (*buṭlān*), including various degrees of interpretation and criticism. Within this two-dimensional space, I identified three major 'tendencies' in various contemporary theories of Islamic law, namely, traditionalism, modernism, and thirdly, postmodernism. The hypotheses presented by these tendencies are marked by regions on the

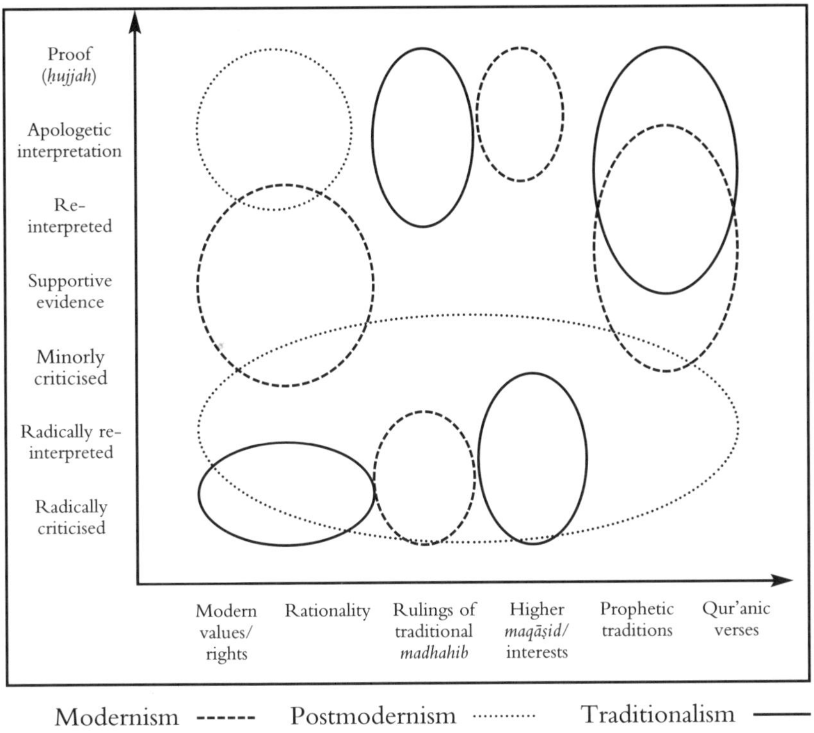

Chart 5.9. A two-dimensional illustration of where the proposed tendencies stand in terms of sources of the Islamic law versus 'levels of authority.'

chart. 'Tendencies' do not necessarily represent specific schools with exclusively defined theories, nor do they necessarily represent specific scholars/researchers, since scholars often change positions and move between 'tendencies' over time and subject to the topic at hand.

The intersections of these regions explain the similarity in positions and arguments that one might notice between scholars coming from quite different angles. For example, traditionalists and postmodernists use similar 'anti-eurocentrism,' 'anti-rationality,' and 'anti-purposefulness' arguments. Traditionalists and modernists both use similar 'apologetic re-interpretations' of the scripts and traditional *madhāhib* rulings. Likewise, modernist and postmodernist approaches sometimes use the literal meanings of the scripts for 'supportive evidence,' and the 'historicity' radical critique for Islamic schools of law, all in very similar ways. And so on.

I propose that each of the above 'tendencies' is the result of a number of theoretical 'streams' that contributed to it. The next three subsections will elaborate on these streams that formed the tendencies of traditionalism, modernism, and postmodernism, respectively.

5.3. TRADITIONALISM

Traditionalism includes a few streams that address different sources of the law in their endorsements or critiques. I will identify them as scholastic traditionalism, scholastic neo-traditionalism, neo-literalism, and ideology-oriented theories.

Scholastic Traditionalism

Scholastic traditionalism[37] holds the opinions of one classic school of Islamic law (for example, Shāfiʿī, Mālikī, Ḥanafī, Ḥanbalī, Shia, or Ibāḍī) as 'text addressing the issue at hand' (*naṣṣun fī al-mas'alah*).[38] Verses from the Qur'an or narrations of hadith that agree with the conclusions of the *madhhab* are used, in effect, for 'supportive evidence' (*li al-isti'nās*). They are seldom used as proof in their own right. When the verse or a hadith contradicts with the conclusions of the *madhhab*, they are re-interpreted (*yu'awwal*) or considered 'abrogated' (*yunsakh*) in order to fit the conclusions of the *madhhab*.[39] Scholastic traditionalism allows ijtihad only if there is no previous ruling in the chosen *madhhab*, and in this case ijtihad is based on analogy with some related previous rulings in the literature of the school.

One illustrating example of scholastic traditionalism is a graduate thesis on fiqh, presented to Imam Saud Islamic University in Riyadh, entitled, 'Leadership of Women in the Islamic Law' (*Wilāyah al-Mar'ah fī al-Fiqh al-Islāmī*).[40] The thesis starts with the Ḥanbalī interpretation (especially, Ibn Taymiyah's) of the hadith narrated in Bukhārī, 'Those who entrust their affairs to a woman will never know prosperity.'[41] The writer rejects, without much explanation, traditional and contemporary objections to the Hanbali interpretation of this hadith, which are based on the effect of the political context of the

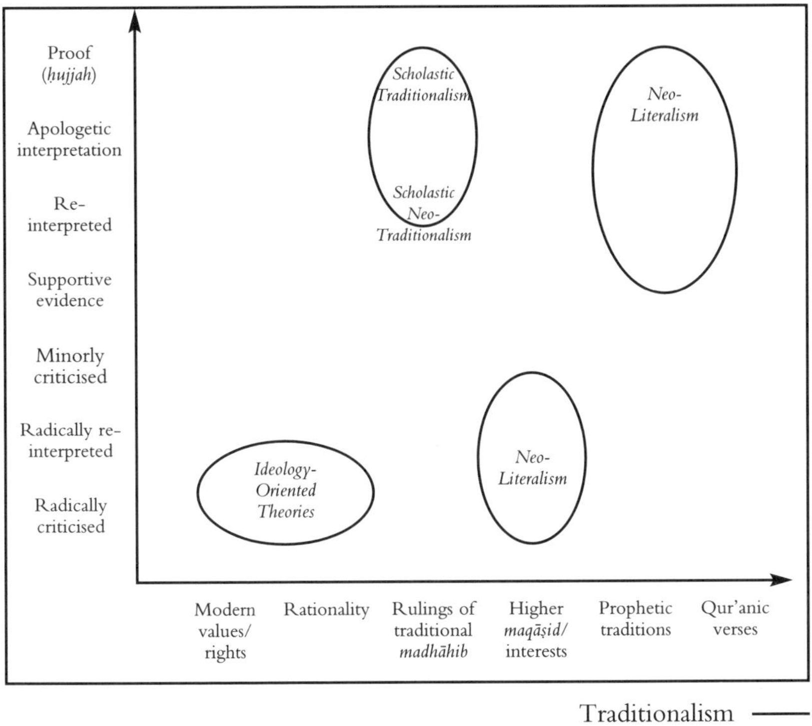

Chart 5.10. Traditionalism tendency in terms of its contributing streams.

narration, in addition to questioning the narrator's integrity.[42] Then, the thesis discusses at length all shapes and forms of '*wilāyāt*' (leadership responsibilities) that a woman could possibly assume. They are all rendered 'unlawful,' except for three 'leadership' roles, which are women's responsibility over their own money, women working in specific educational and medical jobs, and women leading other women in prayer. All other leadership roles that a woman could ever assume in any other social, legal, political, judicial, media, economic, military, or educational domain are said to be unlawful in 'Islam.' The opinions presented in this thesis are typical and even legalised in some countries, and clearly illustrate how scholastic traditionalism fails to achieve justice and equality in that it takes certain narrations and opinions out of every historical and geographical context and applies them to today's world.

Scholastic Neo-Traditionalism

Scholastic neo-traditionalism[43] is opened to more than one school of law for reference on valid rulings and not restricted to one school. There are various degrees of this openness, the highest of which is openness to all schools of law mentioned above, as well as opinions of companions and other pre-*madhāhib* scholars. A lesser degree of openness is to accept opinions only within the circle of either the four Sunni schools (in addition to Ibāḍīs) or the Shia schools. The reason behind the neo-traditionalism insistence on choosing one *madhhab*'s opinion, rather than creating a new one, is the abiding of its adherents by the fundamental (*aṣl*) of consensus (ijmāᶜ). Despite the many theoretical differences in defining ijmāᶜ itself, as explain before, compliers with it insist that a chosen opinion must be supported by at least one school.[44] For Shia and Ibāḍī schools, however, ijmāᶜ is the consensus of jurists in their own school.[45]

The criteria of choosing amongst these schools also vary. One criterion is the 'authenticity' of the schools' evidences, judged based on a contemporary revision of chains of narrators carried out by Shaykh al-Albānī, for example.[46] Another criterion is some sort of 'majority vote,' which supports the chosen opinion by showing that a majority of the currently popular schools accepts it.[47] Yet, a third criterion for choosing one traditional opinion over the others is the 'best interest' of people (or *maṣlaḥah*),[48] or the purposes of the law (*maqāṣid al-sharīᶜah*).[49] This is where I think that scholastic neo-traditionalism intersects with modernist reformism (refer to Chart 5.9). Modernist reformism refers to the Qur'an and prophetic tradition as the 'only sacred Islamic *nuṣūṣ*,'[50] even though they are always understood, in this particular stream, through the opinions of scholars from one of the traditional schools, as the next subsection explains.

I would argue that scholastic neo-traditionalism is currently the mainstream approach in traditional Islamic academic institutes, such as universities and fiqh academies. Typically, issuing a fatwa or researching an issue (*mas'alah*) involves a descriptive comparison of one or more opinions from traditional schools of law, usually followed by a recommendation of one of them through resorting to one of the criteria outlined above. In this circle, ijtihad is restricted to the area of fatwa, but not fundamental sources or methodology (*uṣūl*), which are generally considered fixed (*thawābit*).[51] Given the enormous breadth of Islamic juridical literature and the element of rationality/*maṣlaḥah* in the neo-traditionalist approach, it is always possible to find some historical opinion that answers a contemporary question, however different the context or circumstances are.[52] Nevertheless, because neo-traditionalists restrict themselves to historic *fatāwā* for contemporary issues, the premises upon which these *fatāwā* are based are sometimes outdated. One example is the fatwa given by the European Fiqh Council for Fatwa and Research (EFCR) on allowing house mortgages for Muslim minorities in the West for the sake of their public interest (*maṣlaḥah*). The fatwa was 'supported' by a classic Ḥanafī fatwa that allowed Muslims to deal in usury (*ribā*) outside the 'land of Islam.'[53] The concepts of 'land of war' and 'land of Islam' are historic constructs that described a world once divided into two distinct fighting campaigns – Muslims and the 'others.'[54] Basing a contemporary fatwa in Europe on such concept is highly counter-productive, for a number of obvious reasons, and goes against the 'Muslim-integration' mission of EFCR itself. Another example is the deliberation of the same council regarding women who convert to Islam while their husbands choose to remain non-Muslim.[55] Several council members stated in their papers that the couple should be divorced if one of them is in the 'land of war' while the other is in the 'land of Islam.'

An additional example that shows how deep the same binary land of Islam/land of war classification is in neo-traditionalist methodology is a graduate thesis presented to the High Institute of Judges in Riyadh, which discusses the issue of 'different lands' (*ikhtilāf al-dāraīn*).[56] The thesis studied rulings related to the dealings between two people, one of them living in the 'land of Islam' while the other is living in the 'land of war.' The researcher takes this classification for granted and goes on to discuss other related concepts, such as 'enslavement' (*istirqāq*), 'apostasy' (*riddah*), and the contract of protection for non-Muslim minorities (*dhimmah*). The researcher did not restrict himself to his specific Ḥanbalī stream, but made his choices from amongst the opinions endorsed by classic (Sunni) schools based on, more or less, a 'majority decision.' However, restricting the scope of research to the classic schools of law, despite the obvious historical difference in underlying circumstances, hindered the researcher from addressing the above issues from a contemporary and realistic perspective.

The concept of ijmāᶜ, in the above sense, prevents contemporary jurists from having direct contact with the Islamic primary scripts and, hence, practically rendering them 'supportive evidences.' This contributes to 'inflexibility' in the Islamic law, in terms of new circumstances and questions. For example, all classic schools do not allow Muslim women to carry out their marriage contracts/vows by themselves (except for the Ḥanafī's opinion which gives an exception to widows and divorcees). According to classic schools, the girl has to delegate a close male relative,[57] which is a traditional Arabic practice that 'protects the girl from being called shameless.'[58] The juridical opinion that supports this practice is based on an isolated narration that states: 'A woman's marriage without the permission of her male guardian is void, void, void.'[59] In addition to the debate on the authenticity of this hadith in traditional sources,[60] several verses of the Qur'an are clearly against this opinion and set a general principle of equality in 'legal capacity.'[61] Neo-traditionalism does not break the ijmāᶜ on this ruling and, therefore, finds apologetic justifications for placing such restrictions on every woman's legal capacity, despite their contradiction with a number of scripts.[62]

Neo-Literalism

Neo-literalism[63] is another stream of traditionalism that is named in relation to the (extinct) Ẓāhirī school.[64] However, literalism is not only a Sunni phenomenon but a Shia phenomenon as well. One medieval Shia group, *al-madrasah al-akhbāriyyah* (Narration school), was against not only analogical reasoning but all forms of ijtihad.[65] However, the effect of the Narrationists (*al-akhbāriyyīn*) on the Shia thought has significantly decreased since Imam Bahbahānī's reform movement in the late eighteenth century.[66] The difference between the old Literalist school (for example, Ibn Ḥazm's version) and the Neo-literalist school is that literalists were open to a wide collection of hadith narrations (as clearly appears from Ibn Ḥazm's '*al-Muḥallā*,' for example).[67] However, contemporary (neo-)literalism depends mostly on the hadith collection of one school of law (for example, the Wahhabi version of the Ḥanbalī school, or the Shia hadith collections). Moreover, the old literalist school endorsed *istiṣḥāb* (presumption of continuity) as a fundmanetal source of jurisprudence that has a component of 'purposefulness' (*maqāṣidiyyah*) to it, as the next chapter explains. However, neo-literalists are against the idea of the purposes/ *maqāṣid* being a legitimate source of jurisprudence. In fact, neo-literalism radically criticises the theory of *maqāṣid* as 'secular ideas in disguise,'[68] which is, interestingly, the same criticism, word for word, of some 'postmodernists' to the same approach.[69]

'Blocking the means' is a recurring theme in current neo-literalist approaches, which is utilised by some authoritarian regimes for their own ends, especially in the areas of laws related to women. For example, in the name of blocking the means, women are prohibited from 'driving cars,' 'traveling alone,' 'working in radio or television stations,' 'serving as representatives,' and even 'walking in the middle of the road.'[70] To illustrate one such mis-application of 'blocking the means,' the following is a fatwa issued by the Saudi High Council of Fatwā regarding women driving cars.[71]

> [Question]: Under circumstances of necessity is it permissible for a woman to drive an automobile by herself, without the presence of a legal guardian, instead of riding in a car with a non-*maḥram* man [stranger]?
>
> [Fatwa]: It is impermissible for a woman to drive an automobile, for that will entail unveiling her face or part of it. Additionally, if her automobile were to break down on the road, if she were in an accident, or if she were issued a traffic violation she would be forced to co-mingle with men. Furthermore, driving would enable a woman to travel far from her home and away from the supervision of her legal guardian. Women are weak and prone to succumb to their emotions and to immoral inclinations. If they are allowed to drive, then they will be freed from appropriate oversight, supervision, and from the authority of the men of their households. Also, to receive driving privileges, they would have to apply for a license and get their picture taken. Photographing women, even in this situation, is prohibited because it entails *fitnah* [mischief] and great perils.

The next chapter will elaborate on the Mālikī juridical method of 'opening the means' (*fatḥ al-dharā'iᶜ*), which has not been adequately utilised in current theories of the Islamic law.

Ideology-Oriented Theories

A stream of traditionalism overlaps with postmodernism in criticising modern 'rationality' and values for their biased 'euro-centricity' and 'internal contradictions.' Perhaps this is why Fazlur Rahman categorised its advocates as 'postmodernist fundamentalists.'[72] Their arguments are usually used against 'the west,' and especially democracy and democratic systems, which is rendered 'fundamentally contrary to the Islamic system.'[73] The main argument of this stream is that 'governance, legislation, and sovereignty' (*al-ḥākimiyyah wa al-tashrīᶜ wa al-sīyādah*) is a 'right for God alone,' and is not to be given to people based on any contract or right. A number of other supportive arguments are used, for popular consumption, based on the 'consequences' of democracy, such as, 'the west's freedom of disbelief ... promiscuity ... immorality ... usury ... monopoly ... double-standard policies ... secularism.'[74] This stream's 'basic élan is anti-Western,'[75] as Fazlur Rahman notes. Thus, they are supported by a number of dictatorships for their own political interests. I agree with Abdullah An-Naᶜim that, 'Islam, like any religious tradition, can be used to support human rights, democracy, and respect among different communities, or oppression, authoritarianism, and violence ... There is no inherent or inevitable "clash of civilisations;" all depends on the choices we all make, everywhere, Muslims and non-Muslims alike.'[76]

The next section will analyse the various streams that form 'Islamic modernism,' according to the new classification.

5.4. ISLAMIC MODERNISM

The terms 'Islamic modernism' and 'Islamic modernists' have been used recently by several scholars. Charles Kurzman uses it to identify a movement that 'sought to reconcile Islamic faith and modern values, such as constitutionalism, as well as cultural revival, nationalism, freedom of religious interpretation, scientific investigation, modern-style education, women's rights, and a bundle of other themes.'[77] Ebrahim Moosa uses the term to identify a group of Muslim scholars who 'were tremendously impressed by both the ideals and reality of modernity,' and 'truly believed that Muslim thought as they imagined it from their medieval incarnation' was 'sufficiently flexible to foster innovation and adapt to change commensurate with time and space.'[78] Ziauddin Sardar uses the term to categorise a group of twentieth century reformers who 'made a serious attempt at ijtihad,' to 'modernise Islam' in terms of 'western modes of thought and social organisation,' and especially 'using *maṣāliḥ* (interests).'[79] Neil Robinson mentions how modernists 'called for a new ijtihad which would disregard the established schools.'[80]

While agreeing, in principle, with the above definitions, I do not restrict modernists to early twentieth century scholars. As a matter of fact, the popularity of modernist approaches, as described below, is currently growing in both Islamic and western academic institutes. Moreover, I will present modernism in terms of theories rather than specific scholars. The examples presented below are meant to illustrate modernism, rather than to classify certain scholars as 'modernists.' As mentioned before, scholars often shift their approaches based on the issue they address and due to their own development throughout their lives.

I will discuss Islamic modernist approaches to Islamic law in terms of a number of 'streams,' namely, reformist re-interpretation, apologetic re-interpretation, dialogue-oriented re-interpretation, *maṣlaḥah*-oriented theories, and *uṣūl* revisionism. These streams have dealt with juridical sources in a variety of ways. The following is an outline of these ways, which Chart 5.11 summarises.

Two key contributors to Islamic modernism, in its various streams, were Mohammad Abduh (1849–1905 CE), the Chief Egyptian Mufti at his time, who was influenced by both his Islamic and French juridical studies, and Mohammad Iqbal (1877–1938 CE), who wsa an Indian poet-lawyer-philosopher, educated in both England and Germany, in addition to India. Both scholars, from both geographical sides of the

Islamic world, integrated their Islamic and western studies into new proposals for Islamic reform. 'Re-interpretation' of Islam and its classic knowledge was a common theme in both proposals. Iqbal distinguished between universal principles of the Qur'an, on one hand, and their relative interpretation in practical life, on the other hand.[81] Abduh wrote some exegesis based on his own direct understanding of the Qur'anic Arabic language and without quoting any previous exegete, for the first time in Islamic scholarship history.[82] Although Abduh did not mention in explicit terms any influence of French theories of law on his juridical methodology, one could draw a link between Abduh's 're-interpretation' methodology and the French 'exegetical school,' which was powerful at the time he studied law in France in the late nineteenth century. Abduh wrote in his autobiography that before he went to France, he perfected the French language 'in order to be able to study the French law directly from its sources.'[83] At that time, French exegetes were 're-interpreting' the French code in terms of 'themes,' regardless of the articles' order[84] which is identical to the methodology that Abduh endorsed, as he explained in the introductory notes of his exegesis.[85]

Abduh's student, Rashid Rida, made similar 'reformist interpretations' in his exegesis, *al-Manār* (The Lighthouse),[86] which is now a standard reference in contemporary Qur'anic studies, even though it was left incomplete. Then, another student of Abduh's, al-Tahir ibn Ashur, the Shaykh of the Zaitunah Mosque at his time, wrote a full exegesis of the Qur'an, *al-Taḥrīr wa al-Tanwīr* (Liberation and Enlightenment). In his introduction, he explained how he believed in interpretation 'according to the meanings one directly derives from the Qur'anic language.'[87] These pioneering exegeses paved the way to new methods and schools of interpretation/re-interpretation, which have contributed to modern reformist streams.[88]

Abduh's re-interpretation aimed to prove that 'Islam is coherent with modern science and rationality.'[89] This is reminiscent to the old debate in Islamic philosophy on resolving the 'contradiction between reason and revelation' (*taʿāruḍ al-ʿaql wa al-naql*). However, what Abduh called 'science' was actually late nineteenth century experimental physics and biology, which lead Abduh to seek metaphorical interpretations for all Islamic 'metaphysical' matters, in the nineteenth century sense, such as the tree of Adam and Eve, the existence of angels, and the harm of envy. Perhaps under the effect of Darwinian grand theories, which were popular at that time, Abduh re-interpreted the verses that narrated the story of Adam and Eve to be a 'metaphoric story that is mentioned in the Qur'an not as a scientific fact, but merely as a lesson and example for human beings.'[90] He further re-interpreted 'the tree' from which Adam and Eve ate to be a metaphor for human 'evil and disobedience,'[91] and re-interpreted the angels, to whom the Qur'an attributed some actions, to simply mean 'forces of nature.'[92] He also re-interpreted 'the evil of envy' to be the evil plots that an envious person carries out against the envied,[93] rather than any special metaphysical power, which he excluded as unscientific.

Mohammad Abduh's support for 'experimental logic,'[94] which he expressed in his new interpretation of the Qur'an, reminds me of Abū Ḥamid al-Ghazālī's support for Aristotle's deductive logic through his innovative interpretation of some Qur'anic verses to prove the validity of basic inference principles, such as logical implication and exclusive-OR.[95] While both interpretations might be valid linguistically, neither should necessitate that the Qur'an is meant to endorse a specific system of logic. Science and its bases of logic are 'human' and both are ever changing. This takes us back to the 'cognitive nature' of human reasoning that was explained in Chapter Two.

On the other hand, today's science says that it neither has proofs nor counterproofs for metaphysical hypotheses such as 'angels' and 'the power of an envious eye.' In fact, New Age literature suggests the actual useful and harmful physical effects of human 'energy' without any physical contact, and this movement can even back its hypotheses with the 'science' of sensitive energy photography.[96]

Reformist Re-interpretation

A new approach to interpretation, which I will call 'reformist re-interpretation,' is popularly known as the 'contextual exegesis school' (*madrasah al-tafsīr al-mawḍūʿī*), 'thematic exegesis school' (*madrasah al-tafsīr al-miḥwarī*) or to use Fazlur Rahman's expression, 'systematic interpretation.'[97] Early contributors were Imams Abduh, al-Tabtabai,

Ibn Ashur, and al-Sadir. This method reads the Qur'an, as a whole, looking for general themes across its entirety, its chapters, and groups of verses. Traditional exegetes used to put all their emphasis on the explanation of single words or verses, but rarely on a group of verses in a specific context. Abduh and Ibn Ashur stressed the importance of thematic interpretation in the introduction of their exegeses and hinted to several new links between particular Qur'anic stories and sections.

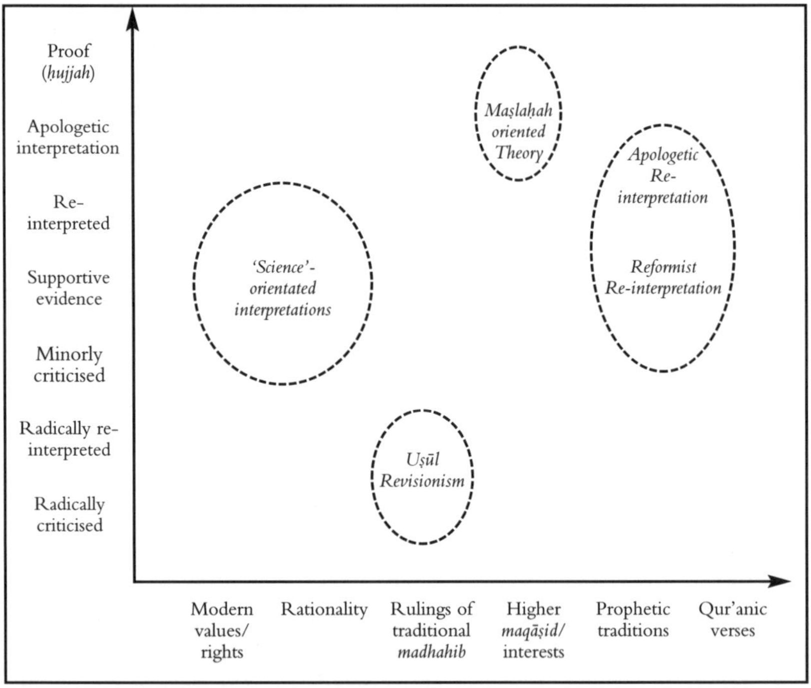

Chart 5.11. Modernism tendency in terms of its contributing streams.

However, neither wrote exclusively on the subject. Later, Ayatollah al-Sadir gave an important series of lectures in Najjaf, Iraq, on the methodology of thematic interpretations and applied it to interpret how the Qur'an presented the concepts of history and ideal society.[98] Later, Mohammad al-Ghazaly, Hasan al-Turabi, Fazlur Rahman, Abdullah Draz, Sayyid Qutb, Fathi Osman, and al-Tijani Hamed, all suggested new interpretations based on the new methodology.[99]

More recently, Taha J. al-Alwani called for a new reading of the scripts that 'acknowledges that people's rational faculties, cultures, experiences, and knowledge, completely shape what they understand from the scripts.'[100] Abdul-Karim Soroush highlighted the merits of al-Tabtabai's new interpretation of the Qur'an using the Qur'anic language itself, in a 'hermeneutical circle,' while not focusing on the 'meanings of the words, only their functions.'[101] Based on these 'functions,' Soroush further suggested differentiating between the verses that are 'functions of cultural, social and historical environment' and other verses that are not.[102] Fazlur Rahman criticised medieval Islamic thought for not producing 'a single work of ethics squarely based upon the Qur'an, although there are numerous works based on Greek philosophy.'[103] He wrote that a new interpretation of the Qur'an based on ethics is necessary to derive a workable Islamic law,[104] which places emphasis on the 'purposes' rather than the 'quantified actions.'[105] Salwa El-Awa took a modern linguistic approach to the Qur'an, though not in a 'deconstructionist' sense (as the following subsection will explain). Following the modern London Linguistic School, she stressed the importance of considering the emotional, situational and cultural context or 'brackets' while interpreting the Qur'an. She further proposed that these contexts were the reason behind the occurrence of multiple-meanings (*wujūh* or *taʿaddud dilālī*) that traditional exegesis scholars suggested in several Qur'anic expressions.[106] Recently she proposed a 'systematic approach to exegesis.'[107] The above re-interpretation streams ended the monopoly on Qur'anic interpretation, which had been held by traditional exegetes.[108] The significance of reformist re-interpretations is the new paradigms and positions they produced on practical everyday issues, such as family issues, economy, and politics. The following is an illustration of these new positions in the area of 'Islam and politics.'

Ali Abdel-Raziq, an Azhari judge, sparked a heated discussion in 1925, which is still alive up till now, on whether Islam is a 'religion that has a political character' or not. In a re-interpretation style, he quoted numerous Qur'anic verses and prophetic traditions to argue that Prophet Muhammad only had 'authority as a prophet' and not dominion as 'king, caliph or sultan' and that he established 'religious unity' and not 'a political state.'[109] Abdel-Raziq's point, as I see it, is that the Islamic law is neutral about political systems, i.e. Muslim societies are free to choose any political system they wish, without making any system an Islamic obligation. Abdel-Raziq's opinion is actually quite similar to traditional *fiqhī* opinions that made political leadership (*imāmah*) 'an obligation based on rationality (*bi al-ᶜaql*) rather than revealed knowledge (*bi al-sharᶜ*).'[110] Although these interpretations are not new, they costed him a trial and the revocation of his Azhari degree.[111]

Apologetic Re-interpretation

The difference between reformist re-interpretations and apologetic re-interpretations is that reformist re-interpretations have a purpose of making real changes in the practical implementation of the Islamic law, while apologetic re-interpretations are justifying a certain status quo, 'Islamic' or 'non-Islamic.' The following are examples of re-interpretations in the area of 'Islam and politics' after Abdel-Raziq, which I classify as 'apologetic.' Mahmoud Mohamed Taha supported the idea of 'socialism' in Islam,[112] through a different interpretation of, ironically, the same verse that Abdel-Raziq quoted: 'You [Muhammad] have no dominion over them' (Qur'an 88:22). He goes further to interpret the verses requiring *shūrā* (consultation) and zakah (obligatory charity) to be 'necessary stages in preparation' for socialism. Sadek Sulaiman concluded from the same script on *shūrā* that 'democracy and *shūrā* are synonymous in conception and principle ... and are thus one and the same.'[113] Mohammad Khalaf-Allah interpreted the same *shūrā* concept, in light of the Prophet's implementation of it, as the authority of 'majority vote.'[114] Abdulaziz Sachedina explored the 'Islamic roots of democratic pluralism' in the Qur'an and evidences of 'civil society' in Madinah's early Muslim community in order to 'legitimise modern *secular* ideas of citizenship in the Muslim political culture' (italics mine).[115]

Although all of the above interpretations are linguistically valid, given the flexible nature of the Arabic language, none of them should necessitate that the Qur'an must support a specific political system or voting system. Rachid Ghannouchi was more cautious than other modernists when he supported democracy and democratic principles not based on a direct interpretation of the scripts, but rather on the fact that 'the essence of God's laws, for which all divine messages were sent, is the establishment of justice for mankind.'[116] Mohammad Khatami, Iran's fifth president, followed the same line of argument and added that he supports democracy because the only available alternative is dictatorship, which goes against Islam's principles.[117]

The above argument is, obviously, not meant to demean a British-style democracy, majority vote, party systems, or an American model of civil society. I am arguing here that this level of detail about any 'worldly matter' should not be given a sacred halo by forcefully reading them into the Qur'an or hadith. Direct democracy, for example, could very well be as successful as, if not actually better than, a multiparty democratic system,[118] and they both aim at the same set of 'higher values.' Approval voting systems, pair-wise elections, multilevel voting systems, and (the Swedish style) multiple-member district systems are equally valid alternatives to majority vote systems in achieving fair representation in a 'multi-participant decision making environment.'[119] Transparency, tolerance, volunteerism, teamwork, reciprocity, and mutual respect do not have to happen in a society exclusively through the American model of non-governmental organisations.[120] And so on. The point here is that scripts should be read in terms of higher values (or *maqāṣid*) rather than specific detailed political structures, as apologetic modernists do.

The same suggestion applies to the Muslim feminist re-interpretation of the scripts.[121] For the same reasons, they should be in terms of the higher human and social values that the scripts advocate, rather than specific preconceived egalitarian models.[122] Women's issues, however, make a much more complex case since, in this area, long-established interpretations that were made to support medieval traditions are deep-rooted in the fabric of the Islamic law.

Scripts should neither be (a) used for the sake of powerful people nor (b) hindered from playing an effective role in future generations when people discover better ways of carrying out their affairs. This is precisely what happened with early (apologetic) interpretations that were meant to support certain prevailing political structures. In our day, these interpretations are considered integral parts of the 'Islamic law' that are difficult to challenge, and had impeded political development and modern reform in Islamic societies. One illustrative example is al-Māwardī's '*al-Aḥkām al-Sulṭāniyyah*' (The Rulings of the Kings).

Al-Māwardī legitimised the Abbasid tribal and monarchic system, which he found most excellent at his time, through his book '*al-Aḥkām al-Sulṭāniyyah*.' Al-Māwardī's book is now a standard textbook in '*al-sīyāsah al-sharʿiyyah*' (that is, Islamic political theory). Al-Māwardī 'interpreted' the scripts to imply 'protecting people with noble lineages [such as the Abbasids] from having a governor over them unless he comes from more noble roots,'[123] 'legitimising a caliph who is appointed by another of his own,'[124] 'giving people money from the trust according to their tribal lineages,'[125] and giving the caliph the right to 'have a monopoly over decision making' (*al-istibdād bi al-amr*).[126] Al-Māwardī's views obviously do not realise justice, good governance, or civility in any contemporary sense. Yet, they are considered 'Islamic law' rather than 'history of Islamic law.' Any attempts to modernise them, in order to realise the (Islamic) principles of justice and consultation, are labeled by popular traditionalist voices as 'acts of deviance.'[127]

Maṣlaḥah-Based Theories

A *maṣlaḥah*-based approach, which is also one of the approaches classified here under 'modernism,' attempts to avoid the shortcomings of apologetics by reading the scripts in terms of the interests they achieve, rather than specific pre-conceived policies. Mohammad Abdu and al-Tahir ibn Ashur paid special attention to interests and purposes in the Islamic law and considered them components of their fundamental reform in the Islamic law.[128] Ibn Ashur's proposal for the revitalisation of the Islamic law was based on 'paying much less attention to the *uṣūl* discipline altogether and focusing on a new methodology that is based on *al-maqāṣid*.'[129] He harshly criticised the traditional schools of Islamic law for 'ignoring the purposes of the Islamic law,'[130] which in his opinion were 'the only shared reference that deals effectively with the dilemmas of change of circumstances and differences of opinion[131] However, the form of imperfect inductive reasoning that Ibn Ashur used was previously criticised in western philosophy since the time of Aristotle, and also in traditional Islamic fundamental references, because of its 'uncertainty.'[132]

Al-Sadir's contribution on the methodology level, was to legitimise induction as 'an established basis for both science and theology.'[133] He studied inductive reasoning extensively in his '*al-Usus al-Manṭ iqiyyah li al-Istiqrā*' (Logical Bases of Induction). Al-Sadir maintained that, 'induction was the main reasoning tool that the Qur'an had used to prove the existence of God.'[134] After an interesting and careful mathematical analysis, al-Sadir acknowledged induction's 'uncertainty' but proposed that this uncertainty decreases as more 'empirical evidence' is found, based on the theory of probability. However, despite Ibn Ashur and al-Sadir's contributions to the *maqāṣid*-based project of reform in the Islamic law, 'it was a project that has been left incomplete.'[135]

Uṣūl Revisionism

Another stream of 'Islamic modernism' attempted to revise the fundamentals of the Islamic law (*uṣūl al-fiqh*), despite objections of neo-traditionalists to any alteration of the 'fundamentals,'[136] and the harshness of some regimes that claim to be 'Islamic.'[137] However, a number of *uṣūl* revisionists expressed the fact that, 'no significant development in the Islamic law could be carried out without developing the law's fundamental methodology.'[138]

Mohammad Abduh, for example, questioned the notion of 'consensus' in both of its forms – consensus over rulings and consensus over prophetic narrations. He called for a 'rational study' of the rulings and prophetic traditions rather than 'depending on the inheritance of juridical literature.'[139] Abduh's rationality led him to asking serious questions about the validity of many 'isolated narrations' (*ahādīth āḥād*). He wrote:

> What is the worth of a chain of narrators that I myself know nothing about? I know neither those narrators' behavior nor how capable they

> were to understand and memorize. For us, these narrators are merely names that the Shaykhs copied and repeated, and we followed them without having the ability to investigate for ourselves.[140]

Abduh referred to the script of the Qur'an for evaluating the content of prophetic narrations and understanding the practical rulings. He also urged scholars to focus on the Qur'anic message of 'moral education, spirituality, knowledge, and guidance to an excellent social life.'[141] He called Islamic law, according to this fundamental methodology, 'the real law.'[142]

When Abduh applied his rational principles as Mufti and judge, he came up with *fatāwā* that were clearly against the established 'consensus.' For example, he issued *fatāwā* to limit polygamy, give Muslim women divorce rights, legalise sculptures, encourage 'all forms of useful arts,' and to require every Muslim scholar to learn at least one European language.[143]

Ayatollah al-Sadir also introduced some modifications to some basic concepts of *uṣūl al-fiqh*, such as consensus and resolving contradictions (*ḥall al-taᶜāruḍ*). In addition to the traditional Jaᶜfarī definition of the 'consensus of *al-ᶜitrah*,' he approved consensus based on 'the agreement of a large number of jurists and muftis on a certain ruling.'[144] Al-Sadir, again, used the 'theory of probabilities' to prove that the increase in the number of these jurists means the 'conversion' of probability to certainty.[145] Regarding 'resolving contradictions' between two evidences, al-Sadir suggested a method which finds coherence between the direct implication of one evidence with the purpose of the legislator (*maqṣūd al-shāriᶜ*) of the second evidence.[146]

Several contemporary modernists followed Abduh and al-Sadir's ideas in revising 'consensus,'[147] and other *uṣūl*, such as abrogation (*naskh*) of the Qur'anic verses,[148] and authenticating the prophetic traditions based on how much they agree with the principles of the Qur'an.[149] Ibn Ashur, differentiated between prophetic traditions that were meant to be part of the law and other traditions that were merely related to prophetic personal choices and were not meant to be part of the law, as explained before. Several contemporary scholars further developed this view.[150] Ibn Ashur also criticised the classic knowledge of *uṣūl* for 'disregarding the purposes of the law, not including them in the fundamentals, and merely studying them in a partial way within the sections of analogical reasoning, under appropriateness and unrestricted interests, even though they were supposed to be the fundamental of the fundamentals.'[151]

A number of contemporary modernists suggested extensions and re-interpretations of other key notions of *uṣūl* to include the fundamental rule that renders 'rulings changeable according to change in time and place,'[152] or 'to consider the role of time and place in modern ijtihad.'[153] For example, new interpretations of *maṣlaḥah* (interest) argued for extending its individualistic orientation to a societal orientation, i.e., considering what is good for the society as a whole instead of being restricted to individuals.[154] Modernists also have a variety of opinions as to the practical implications of *maṣlaḥah* and its relationship with reason in current time.[155]

Analogical reasoning (*qiyās*) is another 'secondary source of legislation' that was re-interpreted from its traditional deductive structure (considering a single case mentioned in the script as a basis for judgment for a new case) to a form of abduction (considering the largest possible number of cases that are related to the topic and deducing general guidelines for judgement).[156] A number of *uṣūl* revisionists called this new method of *qiyās*, 'wide analogy' (*al-qiyās al-wāsiʿ*).[157]

'Science'-Oriented Re-interpretation

Another stream of Islamic modernism takes another approach to re-interpretation. It is a new school of exegesis that introduces a 'scientific interpretation of the Qur'an and Sunnah.' In this approach, 'rationality' is defined in terms of science, and verses of the Qur'an and prophetic hadith are re-interpreted to fit the latest scientific discoveries.[158] In my view, this approach is apologetic and reformist at the same time. It is reformist in the sense that it opens the script of the Qur'an for new interpretations given what humankind knows today. Meanwhile, it is apologetic when it forces the scripts to mean certain scientific theories, whereas science itself is in a process of evolution.

Generally speaking, modernist approaches to Islamic law overcome a number of shortcomings of both classic and traditionalist approaches and present more realistic answers to everyday questions. However, as western modernism has been increasingly criticised in 'postmodern discourses,' Islamic modernism is also criticised in what I will call 'postmodernist approaches to the Islamic law.' The next section elaborates.

5.5. POSTMODERNIST APPROACHES

Postmodernism is a contemporary and powerful intellectual, political and cultural process/force that aims to disintegrate and reformat a multitude of artistic, cultural, and intellectual traditions. It is a term that has many contradictory definitions ranging from eclecticism and montage to neo-skepticism and anti-rationalism.[159] However, it seems that all postmodernists agree, in various ways, on the failure of modernity, especially in the first half of the twentieth century, due to its own deterministic and universal values.[160] A number of scholars in the field of Islamic studies have internalised a variety of postmodern approaches and applied them to Islamic law.

The common method in all these postmodern approaches is 'deconstruction.' Deconstruction is an idea/process/project proposed by Jacques Derrida in the 1960s as a development of Heidegger's call for the 'destruction' of the western metaphysical tradition.[161]

Deconstruction is a 'tactic of de-centering,'[162] i.e., disrupting repressive and arbitrary hierarchies. Derrida aimed at deconstructing 'logocentrism,' which is a combined term derived from *logos* (God's word) and centrism (being central).[163] Derrida talked about 'logocentrism' as follows:

> [T]o focus attention on what I shall call *logocentrism*: the metaphysics of phonetic writing (for example, of the alphabet) which was fundamentally – for enigmatic yet essential reasons that are inaccessible to simple historical relativism – nothing but the most original and powerful ethnocentrism, in the process of imposing itself upon the world, controlling in one and the same *order:* 1. the *concept of writing* in a world where the phoneticisation of writing must dissimulate its own

history as it is produced; 2. *the history of* (the only) *metaphysics*, which has ... always assigned the origin of truth in general to the *logos*: the history of truth, of the truth of truth, has always been ... the debasement of writing, and its repression outside 'full' speech.[164]

To put the above 'definition' in less obscure terms, I would say that Derrida believed that 'binary and logocentric' terms, (such as, good, man, white, or Europe) are not supposed to be authoritarian and repressive 'centers,' while the 'Other' terms (such as, evil, women, black, or Africa) remain 'marginalised.' He also called for an 'Other logic,' by which the deconstruction of logocentric terms is achieved by shifting the marginalised terms in order to become, 'as feasible as the logocentric term in occupying the center.'[165] The new hierarchy of 'authority' eventually becomes equally unstable; moreover people will wind up surrendering to 'the complete free play of the opposites.'[166] Derrida's theory, or 'project,' as he prefers to call it, prevents any speech (or writing) from being a 'script' or 'text' because, he writes, 'in the absence of a center or origin, everything became discourse.'[167] This theory has an impact on the meaning of 'implication,' because, 'the meaning of meaning (in the general sense of meaning and not in the sense of signalisation) is infinite implication, the indefinite referral of signifier to signified.'[168] With this separation of the signifier from the signified in every 'discourse,' interpretation itself is deconstructed. [169] Thus, a new culture of 'unmaking' is created based on what Hasan described as, 'decreation, disintegration, deconstruction, de-centerment, displacement, difference, discontinuity, disjunction, disappearance, decomposition, de-definition, demystification, de-totalisation, delegitimation.'[170]

Despite the obvious 'binary' logic of the deconstructive 'Other' logic, all postmodern approaches to Islamic law[171] apply deconstruction in order to de-center some sort of binary logocentrism. For the sake of analysis, I will divide these approaches into a number of streams, namely, post-structuralism, historicism, critical legal studies, post-colonialism, neo-rationalism, anti-rationalism, and secularism, as illustrated in Chart 5.12. The differences between these approaches are in what they consider to be their 'logocentric' target, whether it is the Qur'an, the prophetic era, the Islamic schools of thought, discriminatory traditions, or orientalism. Post-structuralists' logocentric terms is the Qur'an itself. Historicists' logocentric term is the prophetic era. Anti-rationalists' logocentric terms are modernist rationality and logic. Critical legal studies scholars' logocentric terms are the traditional schools of thought and discriminatory traditions in the Islamic world, especially against women and non-Muslim minorities in Muslim-majority societies. Finally, post-colonialists' logocentric term is western domination via orientalism. The following will address the above streams, respectively.

Post-Structuralism

Post-structuralism is an analytic tool of postmodernism by which 'texts' are analysed, where text is viewed as the basis of speech,[172] and all human knowledge is considered 'textual.'[173] Several Islamic studies scholars have taken a post-structuralist deconstruction or de-centering approach to the 'text' of the Qur'an, which they view as occupying the 'center of the Islamic culture.'[174] The concept of 'revelation' in the script is re-interpreted/shifted from the traditional position as a divine message to mean that the Prophet received the Qur'an as a 'deciphered message' and delivered it to his people according to his own language and cultural context.[175] The aim of this deconstruction project is to 'free people from the (divine) authority (or sovereignty) of the script,' which is a common theme in the writings of Mohamed Arkoun, Nasr Abū Zaid, Hasan Hanafi, al-Tahir al-Haddad, and also Ebrahim Moosa.[176]

Moreover, semiotic theory entails that 'language does not refer directly to reality,'[177] and metaphysical concepts of that sort are considered, according to postmodernists from Nietzsche to Derrida, a sort of self-projection.[178] In his *al-Turāth wa al-Tajdīd* (that is, Cultural Inheritance and Revitalisation), Hasan Hanafi follows this line of thought, until he concluded that 'scholars of the fundamentals of the religion, when they talk about God, His essence, His attributes and His actions, are actually talking about a perfect human being exaggerated to the maximum possible extent.'[179] He, therefore, calls for the

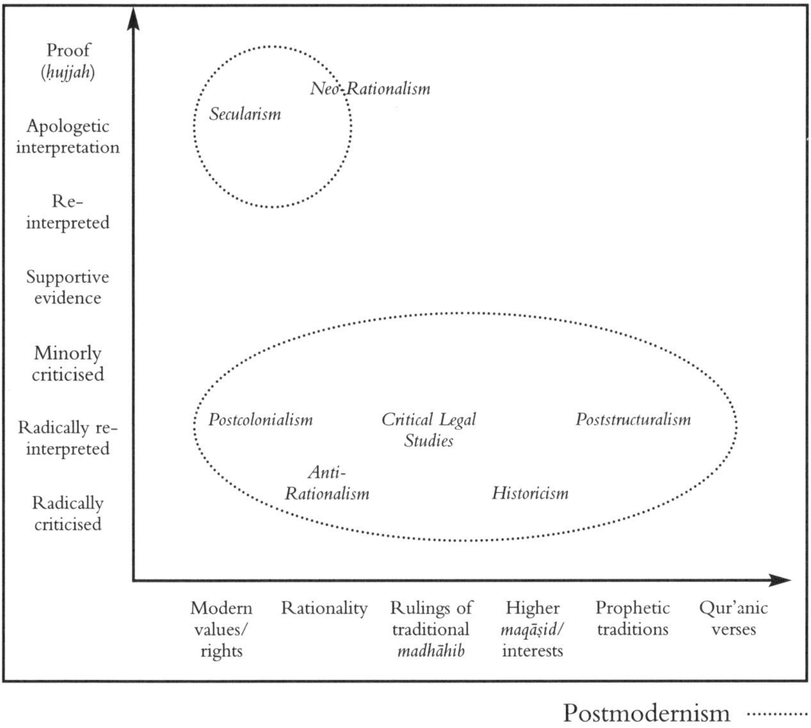

Chart 5.12. Postmodernism tendency in terms of its contributing streams.

replacement of the 'absolute and essentialist' terms of 'God, heaven, hell and hereafter' with the 'non-ambiguous' concepts of 'freedom, democracy, nature and reason.'[180] I fail to understand how these later group of terms are free from ambiguity, and why Hasan Hanafi thought that they are necessarily at odds with the former group of terms! Isn't this way of thinking the very same binary and essentialist thinking that postmodernism is up against?

Deconstruction, in a semiotic sense, might be a good idea/process to finally 'de-center' oppressive social structures and discriminatory laws as will be explained below. However, to put forward a theory for the revitalisation (*tajdīd*) of the Islamic law, as poststructuralists did, one should necessarily build on Muslims' basic established beliefs; otherwise, the theory will be 'non-Islamic' and will certainly never materialise into application.

In this respect, I find Talal Asad's 'postmodern' concept of 'discursive traditions' useful for situating Muslim discourses within their discursive context. Building on Foucault, Asad defines a discursive tradition as a discourse which seeks to instruct practitioners about forms and purposes of their practices.[181] He argues that Islam is a discursive tradition that 'includes and relates itself to the founding texts of the Qur'an and hadith.'[182] Thus, new local developments in Muslims' lives are in an ongoing interaction with the larger framework of Islam to which the core texts belong.

All Muslims, regardless of their differences, believe in God, Prophet Muhammad, and the divine message of the Qur'an. The entire Islamic religion was founded on these three bases and, hence, post-structuralist approaches that end up 'deconstructing' the very concepts of God and divine messages leave no credibility for such proposals of law and creates what I would call an 'epistemological vacuum.'

In terms of the factor of history, we really do not have to say that the Qur'an is a 'coded message' that the Prophet 'deciphered in his own human language' in order to prove that the Qur'anic language and 'signs' are functions of the Arabian seventh century's context. We can simply differentiate between the parts of the Qur'an that deal with specific matters, events, or objects, related to the early Islamic era and other parts that deal with rulings and values that serve human interest at any place and time (despite postmodernism problems with any shape or form of universalism).

Historicity of Means and/or Ends

A historicist postmodern approach suggests that our ideas about texts, cultures and events are determined by their position and function in their original historical context as well as also their later historical developments.[183]

Some deconstructionists have applied the historicism concept to the Qur'an, only to conclude that the Qur'anic script is a 'cultural product' of the culture that produced it.[184] Therefore, they claim, the Qur'an is a 'historic document,' in the sense that it could only be helpful in learning about a specific historic community that existed in the prophetic era.[185] Moghissi claims that 'the shariʿah is not compatible with the principle of equality of human beings.'[186] Ibn Warraq claims that the Islamic human rights scheme shows 'inadequate support for the principle of freedom.'[187] Thus, for Moosa, Islamic jurisprudence could not be evidence for an 'ethical vision,' in the contemporary sense,[188] a position similar to western historicists' position on western jurisprudence, in any case.[189]

Postmodernists also criticise various modernist scholars for 'reinforcing text-fundamentalism' by re-interpreting the scripts to support contemporary ethical norms, although the scripts themselves, historicists believe, are in conflict with these norms.[190] Common examples for this criticism are the modernists' re-interpretation of the scripts to support egalitarianism in the Islamic political model and the status of women in the Islamic law.[191] For Moghissi, 'no amount of twisting and bending can reconcile the Qur'anic injunctions and instructions about women's rights and obligations with the idea of gender equality.'[192] Arkoun called the whole interpretation movement a 'secular movement disguised by religious discourse.'[193]

I would like to say here that the 'historicisation' of Islamic scripts *in toto* and, therefore, rendering their scheme of rights and values 'immoral,' goes against the very belief in the divine source of the Qur'an and the excellence of its value system that Muhammad had applied. Having said that, I also believe that historical events and specific juridical rulings detailed in the Qur'an should be understood within their cultural, geographical, and historical context of the message of Islam. Based on such understanding, Qur'anic specifics could very well apply universally in every place and time. The moral purposes in the Qur'an's various stories and the rulings' purposes and values should guide our ijtihad in order to project these specifics to our changing contexts in the dimensions of space and time, or geography and history. The law that is an outcome of that ijtihad should never contradict with the principle moral values and *maqāṣid* of Islam.

Mentioning the supremacy of moral values in the system of Islamic law, it might be useful to reiterate Ibn al-Qayyim's famous words:

> Islamic Law is based on wisdom and achieving people's welfare in this life and the afterlife. Islamic Law is all about justice, mercy, wisdom,

> and good. Thus, any ruling that replaces justice with injustice, mercy with its opposite, common good with mischief, or wisdom with nonsense, is a ruling that does not belong to the Islamic Law, even if it is claimed to be so according to some interpretation.[194]

The above belief-based position dealing with the Qur'an is a form of interpretation that is on the borderline or overlap area, if you wish, between modernist and postmodernist methods. It is also a position adopted by a number of current scholars. For example, Ayatollah Shamsuddin recommended for today's jurists to take a 'dynamic' approach to *nuṣūs*, and 'not to look at every script as absolute and universal legislation, open their minds to the possibility of "relative" legislation for specific circumstances, and not to judge narrations with missing contexts as absolute in the dimensions of time, space, situations, and people.'[195] He further clarifies that he is 'inclined to this understanding but would not base (any rulings) on it for the time being.' Nevertheless, he stresses the need for this approach for rulings related to women, financial matters, and jihād.[196] Fathi Osman, for another example, 'considered the practical considerations' that rendered a woman's testimony to be less than a man's, as mentioned in verse 2:282. Thus, Osman 're-interpreted' the verse to be a function to these practical considerations.[197] Hasan Turabi holds the same view regarding many rulings related to women and their daily-life practices.[198] Rouget Garoudi's expression of this position was to 'divide the scripts into a section that could be historicised,' such as, again, 'rulings related to women,' and another section that 'represents the eternal value in the revealed message.'[199] Similarly, Abdul-Karim Soroush suggested that the scripts should be 'divided into two parts, essentials and accidentals, accidentals being functions of the cultural, social, and historical environment of the delivery of the main message.'[200] Other similar views regarding the prophetic traditions included Mohammad Shahrur's, who argued that some prophetic traditions are 'not to be considered Islamic law, but rather a civil law, subject to social circumstances, that the Prophet practiced organising society in the area of permissibility, in order to build the Arabic State and Arabic society of the seventh century,' and thus, 'could never be eternal, even if it were true one hundred percent and authentic one hundred percent.'[201]

A similar expression is Mohammad al-Ghazaly's differentiation between 'means' and 'ends.' He allowed the 'expiry' (*intihā'*) of the former and not the latter, which is, in my view, another expression of the above method of interpretation that kept a safe distance from 'historicisation.' Mohammad al-Ghazaly mentioned 'the system of spoils of war,' as an example of these 'changeable means.'[202] More recently, Yusuf al-Qaradawi and Faisal Mawlawi, elaborated on the importance of the 'differentiation between means and ends.' During the deliberations of the European Council for Fatwa and Research, they both applied the same concept to the visual citation of the *hilāl* (Ramadan new moon) being a means for knowing the start of the month rather than an end in its own right. Hence, they concluded that pure calculations shall be today's means of defining the start of the month.[203] Yusuf al-Qaradawi had applied the same concept to Muslim women's garment (*jilbāb*), which he viewed as mere means for achieving the objective of modesty.[204]

In my view, 'differentiating between means and ends' opens a whole lot of possibilities for new and 'radical' ijtihad in the Islamic law. For example, Taha al-Alwani proposed a 'project for reform' in his '*Issues in Contemporary Islamic Thought*,' in which he elaborated on his version of the method of 'differentiation between means and ends.' The following illustrates how al-Alwani applied this approach to the issue of gender equality.

> The Qur'an transported the people of those times to the realm of faith in absolute gender equality. This single article of faith, perhaps more than any other, represented a revolution no less significant than Islam's condemnation of idolatry...In the case of early Muslim society, given the long established customs, attitudes and mores of pre-Islamic Arabia, it was necessary to implement such changes in stages and to make allowances for society's capacity to adjust itself accordingly ... By establishing a role for a woman in the witnessing of transactions, even though at the time of revelation they had little to do with such matters, the Qur'an seeks to give concrete form to the idea of woman as

> participant ... The objective is to end the traditional perception of women by including them, "among such as are acceptable to you as witness" ... the matter of witnessing served merely as a means to an end or as a practical way of establishing the concept of gender equality. In their interpretations of "mistake" and "remind", Qur'anic commentators have approached the issue from a perspective based on the assumption that the division of testimony for women into halves is somehow connected with women's inherent inequality to men. This idea has been shared by classical and modern commentators alike, so that generations of Muslims, guided only by *taqlīd* (imitation), have continued to perpetuate this faulty understanding. Certainly, the attitudes engendered by such a misunderstanding have spread far beyond the legal sphere ...[205]

The above approach is 'postmodern' in the sense of tying the scripts to their historical context. Yet, its referral to the scripts as the divine source for rulings, even in the sense of these rulings being 'means to an end,' is a modernist (albeit radical) re-interpretation.

Neo-Rationalism

Neo-rationalists take a historicist approach to the Islamic law, and refer to the conventional Muʿtazilī/Rational school for a traditional reference for their views.[206] The Muʿtazilī school gave authority to reason (*ʿaql)* as an independent source and as the law's most fundamental evidence, as explained before.[207] However, the difference between neo- and old-rationalists is that the Muʿtazilīs, as explained in the previous chapter, by and large applied the evidences of the Qur'an, hadith, and other secondary sources to the law in a manner that was very similar to other classic schools.[208] Muʿtazilīs acknowledged the 'authority of the Qur'an' as a source of legislation 'based on reason,' because 'according to reason, good and bad could be differentiated and the authority of the Qur'an could be proven, as well as the authority of the prophetic traditions and consensus.'[209] Neo-Rationalists/ Muʿtazilīs, however, gave 'reason' the ability to 'abrogate' scripts.[210] Nevertheless, according to Derrida, and Moosa, 'reason' is one of the concepts that modernity put 'in the center,' and which has to be deconstructed.[211]

Critical Legal Studies

Critical Legal Studies (CLS) is a movement that originated in the United States, which aims to deconstruct accepted legal doctrines in order to support pragmatic policy reform.[212] Its 'deconstruction' is directed towards those in positions of 'power' who structured the law.[213] Philosophers and political activists from diverse roots have subscribed to the CLS movement, such as feminists and anti-racism theorists. A number of scholars of Islamic studies used the CLS methodology to analyse and deconstruct all 'powers' which have affected the Islamic legal system, ranging from 'men' to powerful Arabic tribes.

'Muslim feminists,' for example, challenged the effect that traditional male elitism had on the formation of both the Islamic traditional juridical system and the collection of narrated prophetic traditions that addressed men-women relations.[214] However, it is to be noted that Muslim postmodern feminists take a different approach from other postmodern feminists. While other postmodern feminists deconstruct the 'binary system of gender,' i.e. the very notion of male and female 'difference,'[215] Muslim feminists focus specifically on the historical 'power struggle' between Muslim men and women.

Both modernist and postmodernist Islamic feminism criticise the effect of this power struggle on traditional law authorities, such as Imams, Shaykhs and Ayatollahs.[216] However, postmodern Muslim feminism differs in that it includes in its criticism the authority of the Qur'an and the Prophet himself.[217] Mernissi, for example, challenged every ruling in the Islamic sources that 'puts restrictions on a woman's sexual self-determination,'[218] from the institution of marriage, children's patriarchal lineages, and the veil, to the rulings of divorce, waiting period (*ʿiddah*), and even the 'prohibition of prostitution!'[219] Similarly, some radically 'different' re-interpretation of the Islamic scripts reads 'diversity in sexuality' into the verses and hadith that mention diversity in people's 'colors' as a sign of God's creation.[220]

The Qur'anic description of the 'sin' (*fāḥishah*) of the People of Lot is twisted to have merely meant their 'transgressive behavior with their guests,' rather than any other act.[221] It is obvious that this method stretches the wordings, in the name of interpretation, in order to legalise certain behavior, even when at odds with well-established Islamic principles. Similar to the 'apologetic interpretations' that were mentioned before, 'radical interpretation' is merely a means to justify certain pre-assumptions. My criticism here of such twisted interpretation certainly does not entail any support to systematic violence or discrimination against the interpreters. Judging some act as a 'sin' is one thing, and 'persecuting sinners' is a totally different thing!

Some other scholars took a CLS approach in questioning the political motivations of powerful Arabic tribes, such as Quraysh and Banī-Ummayyah, in relation to some juridical and fundamental rulings. For example, Nasr Abū Zaid relates Imam al-Shāfiʿī's historic piece on the fundamentals of the Islamic law to the desire of Quraysh to 'transform its traditions and culture into a revelation.'[222] Patricia Crone also questioned the effect of the powerful Umayyad caliphs on the formation of the law.[223] Wael Hallaq strongly disagreed,[224] and Abdul-Majeed al-Sagheer wrote a lengthy analysis to prove a view opposite to Crone's. Al-Sagheer proved that al-Shāfiʿī and other jurists proposed the fundamentals of the Islamic law to 'protect the law' from the whims and personal interests of the ruling power, especially the Ummayads, rather than enforce them.[225]

Post-Colonialism

Postcolonial studies were founded to support voices previously marginalised by western colonisation and to 'reject western presumptions of cultural and racial prominence.'[226] Edward Said, following Foucault on the relationship between forms of knowledge and power, was a key contributor to this field.[227] Several scholars took a postmodernist approach to Islamic Studies in a post-colonial sense.[228] Their approach aimed to deconstruct western 'globalising and homogenising forces,'[229] 'project[ing] their own faults onto other people,'[230] 'pre-assuming the west to be the center of the world,'[231] 'coupling westernisation with contemporarisation,'[232] presenting Muslim political and social life as defined by a 'non-rational religion,'[233] and, recently, 'promoting the idea of an "Islamic threat" to the Western civilisation.'[234] Postmodernists call for celebrating the 'Other's' cultural difference.[235] Post-colonialism has also been evident in some scholars' criticism of traditional Orientalist approaches to the Islamic law, which derive 'from essentialist fallacies (prejudices) about Islamic cultures'[236] and pre-assume that the 'Islamic divine is, at best heavily indebted to the juridical traditions of the cultures that gave birth to western civilisation and, at worst, little more than a replica of these traditions.'[237] For classic examples of these traditional Orientalist approaches, which are no longer held by the vast majority of researchers, refer to Goldziher, Schacht, and Gibb's earlier works.[238]

Postmodern approaches to the Islamic law challenged both the traditionalist and modernist approaches by questioning the power/authority that certain concepts, schools, imams, and political leaders had assumed. However, despite their claimed war against 'binary opposites,' postmodern approaches tend to be binary, reductionist, and uni-dimensional. The next chapter will revisit postmodernism, as presented in this section, and will attempt to develop its radical criticism into a more 'multi-dimensional' and 'holistic' approach.

Based on the analysis of classic and contemporary theories of Islamic law that were presented in the previous chapters, the next chapter will propose a systems approach to the theory of Islamic law and present some specific suggestions to enhance its 'openness' and 'purposefulness.' The proposed theory will build on the analysis of sources, implications, and evidences in classic theories, the literature of schools of Islamic law endorsed by traditionalists, new modernist re-interpretations, and the criticism presented by postmodernists.

6

A Systems Approach to Islamic Juridical Theories

Overview

How can *maqāṣid al-sharīʿah* play an actual role in the juridical methods of ijtihad? How does the system feature of 'purposefulness' relate to the *fiqhī* feature of the '*maqāṣid*-isation'? How can we utilize the proposed 'Islamic systems philosophy' in the juridical theory, in order for the Islamic law to stay 'renewable' and 'alive'? How can a systems approach utilise the system features of cognition, holism, multi-dimensionality, and openness in the theory of Islamic law? How can we address the shortcomings of the classic, modernist, and post-modernist theories, which Chapters Three, Four, and Five, respectively outlined?

This chapter attempts to answer the above questions by taking a systems approach to the fundamentals of Islamic law:

- It identifies those specific areas where systems philosophy could contribute to these fundamentals.
- Systems features previously introduced in Chapter Two, purposefulness, cognition, holism, multi-dimensionality, and openness, will be recalled.
- Finally, methods for realising these features in the fundamental methodology of the Islamic law will be proposed.

6.1. TOWARDS VALIDATING ALL 'COGNITIONS'

'Revealed' Ijtihad?

Jurists generally define fiqh as the outcome of human 'understanding' (*fahm*),[1] 'perception' (*taṣawwur*),[2] and 'cognition' (*idrāk*).[3] However, *fiqhī* methods and outcomes are often depicted as 'God's rulings.' Various sections of this book that addressed implications and interpretation show that although the script is heavenly, its interpretation is subject to the exegete's or jurist's worldview. Nonetheless, interpretations are often presented as 'God's commands' in order to be (mis)used for the interests of a powerful few.[4]

In addition, outcome of ijtihad is often included in the category of 'revealed knowledge,' even though the very definition and validity of the methods of ijtihad are subject to wide differences of opinion, as we have seen. A primary example in this regard is consensus (ijmāᶜ). Despite the great many differences over the very definition of consensus, as previously explained, many past and present jurists considered it 'an evidence as certain as the script' (*dalīlun qaṭᶜiyyun kal-naṣṣ*), 'an evidence constructed by The Legislator' (*dalīlun naṣabah al-Shāriᶜ*), and even counted its rejectors amongst 'infidels' (*jāḥid al-ijmāᶜi kāfir*).[5] Readers familiar with traditional fiqh literature know that an ijmāᶜ is often claimed, in rulings of clear difference of opinion, in order to sanction one opinion or the other. Ibn Taymiyah, for example, reviewed Ibn Ḥazm's '*Marātib al-Ijmāᶜ*' (Levels of Consensus) in his '*Naqd Marātib al-Ijmāᶜ*' (that is, Critique of Levels of Consensus). Ibn Taymiyah mentioned numerous examples of inaccurate claims of consensus that Ibn Ḥazm had made regarding a number of *ijtihādī* issues, despite much difference of opinion around them. Examples are 'judging rejecters of ijmāᶜ to be apostates,' 'not allowing women to lead men in collective prayers,' and even 'enforcing the payment of four golden Dinars as *jiziyah* tax.'[6]

I argue, however, that consensus is not a 'S/source of law,' but is merely a mechanism of consultation or, to use systems terminology, multiple-participant decision making. However, ijmāᶜ was (mis-)used by some latter-day scholars in order to monopolise fatwa and restrict it to a specific 'centrist' elite, to use a postmodern concept. I also agree with modernists who suggested that the principle of consensus could be utilised today as a 'mechanism for making collective fatwa,'[7] especially with 'modern technology and instant worldwide communication.'[8] I further agree with other proposals that develop ijmāᶜ to become a form of 'societal participation in the state's affairs.'[9]

On the other hand, some jurists considered the reasoning method of analogy (*qiyās*) to be 'divinely sanctioned.' They suggested that, 'making an analogy between a primary and a secondary case is an analogy carried out by the Legislator Himself' (*tashbīhu farᶜin bi 'aṣlin tashbīh al-Shāriᶜ*).[10] Therefore, even in clear cases of ijtihad via analogical reasoning, some jurists considered themselves to be 'speaking in God's name.'[11] This was a 'disaster,' to quote Garoudi, 'in which the limits between the words of God and the words of humans were erased.'[12]

Separating the Revealed from its 'Cognition'

The position of a group of jurists, known in the literature of Islamic law by '*al-muṣawwibah*' (The Validators), is that rulings are 'assumptions' (*ẓunūn*) on the part of *mujtahidūn* when they reflect upon the scripts. This position makes a clear and much needed distinction between human ideas and the scripts.[13] Furthermore, *al-Muṣawwibah* concluded that different juridical opinions, however contradictory they might be, are all valid expressions of the truth and are all correct (*ṣawāb*).[14] *Al-Muṣawwibah* went further to conclude that, 'there are multiple truths,'[15] an idea that had later influenced medieval 'western philosophy' through Ibn Rushd.[16] Jurists who, often, subscribed to this position were from the jurist/philosopher category, such as Abū al-Hasan al-Ashᶜarī, Abū Bakr ibn al-ᶜArabī, Abū Ḥāmid al-Ghazālī, Ibn Rushd, and a number of Muᶜtazilīs, such as, Abū al-Huzaīl, Abū ᶜAlī, and Abū Hāshim. Al-Ghazālī expressed their view by saying: 'God's judgement, from the jurist's perspective, is what the jurist judges to be most probably true.'[17] However, al-Ghazālī excluded rulings that are 'prescribed according to a *naṣṣ*.'[18] We have demonstrated above how any '*naṣṣ*' could bear a number of interpretations and implications, which would make all judgements be in accordance with what the jurist 'judges to be most probably true.'

A systems approach to the Islamic law, entails viewing it as a 'system,' in the ontological sense of the word. Hence, applying the 'cognitive nature of systems' feature would lead to a conclusion identical to *al-Muṣawwibah's*, i.e., rulings are what the jurist judges to be most probably true, and different juridical opinions are all valid expressions of the truth(s) and are all correct.

In order to systematically separate the 'revealed' from its fiqh or 'cognition,' Chart 6.1 re-draws the relationships between fiqh, sharīᶜah, *ᶜurf*, and *qānūn*, which had been drawn in Chart 3.1. The new relationship-chart reflects the 'cognitive nature' of human systems. Thus, fiqh is shifted from the realm of 'revealed knowledge' to the realm of 'human cognition of that revealed knowledge,' which falls outside the circle of 'revealed knowledge.' Hence, a clear differentiation is suggested between sharīᶜah and fiqh, which implies that no *fiqhī* (practical) opinion is qualified to be a 'matter of belief,' regardless of the considerations of authenticity (*thubūt*), linguistic implications (*dilālah*), consensus, or analogical reasoning.

Moreover, based on the differentiation between types of prophetic actions according to their *maqāṣid*/intents, a section of the prophetic tradition is shifted outside the circle of 'revealed knowledge,' and another section would fall in the 'rough set' on the border of the circle, to borrow a term from systems theory.[19] This 'rough set' is the section of prophetic traditions that were made with specific 'intents,' as al-Qarāfī and Ibn Ashur had suggested, and hence, falls on the 'border' between 'revelation' and 'human decision making.'

Hence, prophetic traditions would fall under one of the following three categories, illustrated on Chart 6.1, from (a) to (c). Category (c) is excluded then from the realm of 'jurisprudence.'

(a) The Prophet's direct conveyance of the message, which al-Qarāfī had called, 'actions in the capacity of conveyance' (*al-taṣarrufu bi al-tablīgh*).

(b) Traditions with specific 'intents,' other than the direct conveyance of the message. Related narrations should be understood and applied in the law in the context of the intent.

(c) Traditions that fall in the realm of human everyday decisions/actions, which Ibn Ashur had referred to as, 'the intent of non-instruction.'

On the other hand, Chart 6.1 suggests that the intersection between *ʿurf* and fiqh should be understood on a level deeper than a 'consideration' in application. An upcoming section elaborated on the relationship between *ʿurf* and fiqh in light of the *maqṣid* of universality of the Islamic law, as Ibn Ashur had proposed in his '*Maqāṣid al-Sharīʿah*.' Thus, fiqh would practically accommodate *ʿurf* that fulfils the requirements of *maqāṣid*, even if this *ʿurf* is different from the 'implication' (*al-dilālah*). This Chapter will also propose an extension of the notion of *ʿurf* in light of the notion of 'worldview.' Finally, both *ʿurf* and fiqh should contribute to *qānūn*, while giving human legislators the freedom to convert *ʿurfī* customs and *fiqhī* rulings into detailed statutes that best suit the society and its needs. One should not copy and paste *fiqhī* rulings or *ʿurfī* stipulations verbatim into the law.

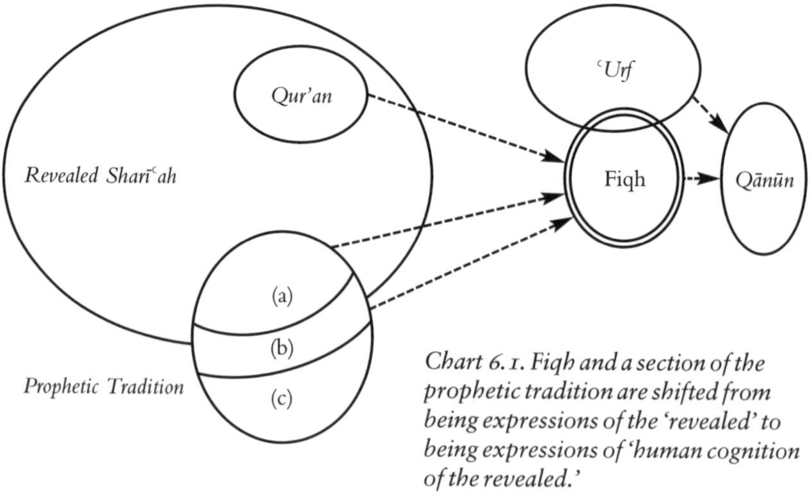

Chart 6.1. Fiqh and a section of the prophetic tradition are shifted from being expressions of the 'revealed' to being expressions of 'human cognition of the revealed.'

6.2. TOWARDS 'HOLISM'

The 'Uncertainty' of Individual Evidence

A few jurists noticed the limitation of the reductionist and atomistic approach that fundamental methodology usually takes. However, their criticism of 'atomism' was based only on its inherent 'uncertainty' as opposed to its binary opposite, 'certainty.' In his book on the fundamentals of law, Fakhr al-Dīn al-Rāzī summarised the different reasons that jurists had mentioned for why any single 'linguistic evidence' (*dalīlu khiṭāb*) of a *naṣṣ* could only be 'probable' (*ẓannī*).[20] Below is a summary of these reasons.

1. There is a possibility that the ruling that we conclude from the single *naṣṣ* has been restricted to certain circumstances, without our knowledge.
2. There is a possibility that the expression of the single *naṣṣ* is metaphoric.
3. Our reference in language is linguists, which are people who could err.
4. Arabic grammar is conveyed to us via ancient Arabic poetry, which was narrated through individuals' narrations (*riwayāt āḥād*). These narrations are not certain and the original poets themselves could have made grammatical mistakes.
5. There is a possibility that one or more of the words of this single *naṣṣ* have multiple meanings.
6. There is a possibility that one or more of the words of the single *naṣṣ* have been altered, over time, in a way that alters the original meaning.
7. There is a possibility that the expression has a hidden (*khafī*) meaning that we do not understand.
8. There is a possibility that the ruling that we conclude from the single *naṣṣ* has been abrogated, without our knowledge.
9. There is a possibility that a ruling that we conclude from a single *naṣṣ* is at odds with 'reason.' In such case (al-Rāzī says), if both reason and narration are confirmed, then one of them is wrong.

Moreover, reason is our means to confirm the validity of narration itself. Therefore, reason has precedence over narrations. Thus, we should follow reason, in such cases, and not the linguistic evidence of the narration.

I would add the following possibilities to the above nine.

1. There is a possibility that a single *naṣṣ* could imply a meaning that 'contradicts' other single *nuṣūṣ*. This did happen in a large proportion of *nuṣūṣ*, and is studied as the standalone subject of 'opposing scripts' (*al-mutaᶜāriḍ*).
2. There is a range of possibilities of error in conveying *āḥād* hadith narrations, which comprise most of the prophetic narrations.
3. There is a range of possibilities for the 'interpretation' of any single *naṣṣ*, which affects the way we conceive its meanings and implications.

Al-Rāzī's 'philosophical background' contributed to his appreciation of how profound it is to claim 'certainty' in single verbal evidences. However, al-Rāzī's concern with the 'uncertainty' of single evidences did not allow him to see the prime problem of single-evidenced approach, which is the partiality and atomism of its 'causation' basis.

Limitation of 'Causation' in Traditionalist and Modernist Theories

It was previously explained how theologians/*kalāmīūn* debated the 'principle of causation' (*al-sababiyyah*) in God's actions. They divided 'God's actions' into creation-related actions (*al-fiᶜl al-khalqī*) and law-related actions (*al-fiᶜl al-tashrīᶜī*).[21] The majority of jurists, who were Ashᶜarites, Salafīs, or Ẓāhirīs, believed that God's 'creation-related' actions are 'above causes.' Yet, some of them assigned 'causes' (*ᶜilal*) to God's 'law-related' actions, with which the rulings were correlated. On the other hand, Muᶜtazilīs, Shia, and Maturidites believed in the causality of all of God's actions. Therefore, a 'causation-based' way of thinking has dominated methodology of Islamic law in all schools and tendencies until today.

Some jurists have stressed the importance of 'holistic evidence' (*al-dalīl al-kullī*). Yet, this evidence had no impact on methodology itself, which remained largely causation-based in, both, theology and law. Al-Juwaynī, for example, considered referring to a 'holistic feature' of the Islamic law for evidence of rulings to be a valid procedure that he called 'holistic analogy' (*qiyās kullī*).[22] Al-Shāṭibī, for another example, considered the fundamentals of the Islamic law (*uṣūl al-fiqh*) to be based on the universal/holistic features of the revealed law (*kulliyyat al-sharīʿah*).[23] He also gave priority to 'holistic/universal fundamentals' (*al-qawāʿid al-kulliyyah*) over 'single and partial rulings' (*āḥād al-juz'iyyāt*). His rationale was that, 'single and partial rulings are there to support holistic fundamentals, which are the purposes of the law that must be maintained.'[24] Again, the implication of these views on the jurists' and theologians' 'causation-based' methodology never materialised.

Islamic modernism pointed to the general difficiency of 'partial and individualistic approaches to Islamic law.'[25] For example as explained earlier, contemporary scholars tried to remedy the 'individuality drawback' (*al-fardiyyah*) in the notion of *maqāṣid*. Such included Ibn Ashur's giving priority to 'societal' over 'individual' *maqāṣid*, Rashid Rida's inclusion of society's 'reform' and 'rights' in his theory of *maqāṣid*, Taha al-Alwani's inclusion of the *maqṣīd* of 'developing civilisation on earth' in his theory, and Yusuf al-Qaradawi's Qur'anic-based 'universal *maqāṣid*' of building good families and nations.[26] However, again, due to its nineteenth-century philosophical 'ceiling' put on modernism, twentieth century Islamic modernism could not break out of the traditional causation-based theological framework.

Islamic modernism, however, recently introduced a significant application of the principle of holism, which is 'thematic exegesis.' Hasan Turabi's '*al-Tafsīr al-Tawḥīdī*' (The Unifying Exegesis) is the clearest example of this approach.[27] Turabi explained that a unifying (*tawḥīdī*) or holistic (*kullī*) approach entails a number of methods on various levels. On the level of language, it entails 'dealing with the Qur'anic language as an integral whole' and 'unifying the language of the Qur'an with the language of the receivers of the message at the time of the revelation.' On the level of human knowledge, it entails a holistic approach to both the unseen and seen worlds with all their multitude of components and rules that govern them. On the level of topics, it entails dealing with themes regardless of the order of verses, in addition to applying them to everyday life. In terms of scope, it has to include people regardless of their space and time. It also entails unifying law with morality and spirituality in one holistic approach.[28]

Towards a 'Holistic' ʿIlm al-Kalām

Contemporary systems philosophy argues a 'synthetic' and 'holistic tendency' that is 'fundamental in nature.'[29] Systems philosophers assert that 'our expanding of the too simple, two-term relation "cause-effect" into a complex series is closer to the structure of this world, as far as we know it.'[30] Thus, in systems philosophy literature, the principle of causation is criticised, along with all theological views that were associated with it, such as, the 'God of Berkeley,' 'divine Substance of Spinoza,' and 'Leibniz's appeal to Pre-established Harmony.'[31] The same systems-based critique could apply to the method of causation in Islamic philosophy of religion (*ʿilm al-kalām*), including the 'causation-based' theological arguments proposed by jurists and philosophers.[32] For the most recent major 'causation-based' argument, this could include theological arguments proposed by Ibn Ḥanbal, Ibn Sīnā, al-Rāzī, al-Ashʿarī, Abdul-Jabbār, al-Ghazālī, al-Māturīdī, al-Āmidī, al-Shāṭibī, Ibn Taymiyah, Ibn Rushd,[33] and Mohammad Abdu.[34]

Systems philosophers mention a number of 'fallacies' that could be counter-arguments for causation thinking based on holistic thinking. In his 'Corpus Errorum,' Korzybski, for example, mentioned a number of these fallacies. These include 'the fallacy of attributing to one cause what is due to many causes,' 'the fallacy of concluding that because one factor plays a role, another does not,' 'the fallacy of drawing negative conclusions from positive observations,' and 'the fallacy that the characteristics of organisms are divisible into two distinct classes; one due to heredity, the other to environment.'[35]

However, in my view, there is no association between theological concepts and the method of 'causation' except in the minds of theologians who used 'the principle of causation' to address the question of the 'existence of God' and other theological questions. Therefore, if 'causation' is to evolve into 'holism' in human science and philosophy, so should theological arguments.

I propose that the 'principle of holism,' as explained in systems philosophy, could play a role in contemporary renewal proposals, not only in Islamic law but in Islamic *ᶜilm al-kalām* (philosophy of religion). Roughly speaking, the 'evidence of creation' (*dalīl al-ikhtirāᶜ*) would rely on the 'impossibility of an action without a purpose,' rather than the 'impossibility of an action without a cause,' as traditionally argued. The 'evidence of sustenance' (*dalīl al-riᶜāyah*) would rely on the balance and 'human-friendliness' of earth's ecosystems and subsystems, rather than classic arguments of direct sustenance. Similarly, the 'evidence of existence' (*dalīl al-wujūd*) would, then, rely on the systematic and integrative design of the universe, as we know it today, rather than the classic 'First Mover' cosmological argument, to use Mohammad Abdu's expression.

6.3. TOWARDS OPENNESS AND SELF-RENEWAL

It was previously explained (in Chapter Two) that a system must maintain a degree of openness and self-renewal in order to 'stay alive.' This section proposes two mechanisms towards a desired openness and self-renewal in the Islamic law, respectively. First, change of rulings with the change of the jurist's 'worldview' or 'cognitive culture' is proposed as a mechanism of openness in the system of Islamic law. Second, 'philosophical openness' is proposed as a mechanism of self-renewal in the system of Islamic law.

Change of Rulings with 'Cognitive Culture'

'Worldview' is the translation of the German term 'Weltanschauung,' a hundred year old term literally meaning 'world outlook.'[36] A worldview is 'a set of pre-suppositions which we hold about the basic makeup of the world,'[37] 'a frame of reference for human experience,'[38] and 'a system of belief.'[39] Thus, a worldview is the product of a number of factors that shape human 'cognition' of the world. The following are examples of 'theories' that make up a human worldview.

1. God, the world, human beings, afterlife, knowledge, morality, and history.[40]
2. Myth, doctrine, ethics, rituals, and society.[41]
3. Beliefs, concepts, sense of order, social constructs, role-models, and moral precepts.[42]
4. The natural world, ethics, politics, biology, psychology, methods of scientific investigation, and many other factors.[43]
5. God, oneself, nature, space, and time.[44]

All of the above theories show that a worldview is shaped by everything around us, from religion, self-portrayal, geography, and the environment, to politics, society, economy, and language. Using the word 'culture' in a broad sense, worldview represents 'cognitive culture.'[45] Cognitive culture is the mental framework and sense of reality through which people view and interact with the outside world.

Traditionally, the fundamental of *al-ʿurf* (customs) in the theory of Islamic law deals with the 'interaction with the outside world.' A Ḥanafī fundamental rule states that 'an implicit condition according to custom is similar to an explicit condition according to scripts' (*al-maʿrūfu ʿurfan kal-mashrūṭi naṣṣan*).[46] Various schools of law agree to this rule on the application level, 'when there is no specific *naṣṣ* to refer to.'[47] The purpose behind *al-ʿurf* consideration is to accommodate the circumstances of some people that are different from Arabic customs, which are the jurists's 'default' customs.[48] However, the practical implication of *al-ʿurf* on fiqh itself is quite limited. Standard examples mentioned in the book of *uṣūl* of what is subject to *ʿurf* in the Islamic law is the value of a dowry, the currency used in trade transactions, covering or uncovering a (man's) head, and common usage of some Arabic words.[49] It is clear that these standard examples do not reflect, in any significant way, variations in human life other than the 'default' medieval Arabic world.

Thus, many Islamic rulings remained coupled with Arabic customs of the first two or three Islamic centuries and that era's political borders, geography, food, economic resources, and social system, i.e., worldview. For example, the forms of charity one pays to the poor at the end of Ramadan (*ṣadaqah al-fiṭr*) is still stipulated according to common foodstuffs of the seventh century CE mentioned in the related hadith, i.e., dates, raisins, and barley.[50] According to many scholars even today, a number of Islamic rulings continue to be based on the 'political borders' between 'the land of Islam' and 'the land of war.'[51] According to all written legal systems driven from the Islamic schools of law, a Muslim girl cannot get married unless she delegates her father (or a close male) to pronounce the marriage vows on her behalf, as was the Arabic tradition. Usually, marriage vows themselves could only be in Arabic. A compensation paid for unintentional killing is still the responsibility of one's 'tribe' (*al-ʿāqilah*) even in non-tribal social systems.[52] Similarly, in some remote areas, liability for murder for an unknown perpetrator is determined according to *qasāmah* (which is a form of 'territorial liability,' according to Ḥanafīs and Zaydīs, and a 'next of kin liability,' according to the rest of classic schools).[53]

The clearest example that I came across demonstrating 'closeness' within an Arabic 'worldview' is Ibn Taymiyah's *Iqtiḍā' al-Ṣirāṭ al-Mustaqīm* (Requirements for the Straight Path). He claims that, 'the People of the Tradition (*ahl al-sunnah*) believe that the Arabic race (*jins al-ʿarab*) is better than other non-Arab races (*jins al-ʿajam*).' He, then, described people who disagree with that as 'nationalists' (*shuʿūbiyyūn*), since they 'prefer some other nations over Arabs.'[54] Similar prejudices exist in almost every nation and ethnic group. However, they led Ibn Taymiyah to issue rulings that were 'discriminatory,' despite the well-known principle (*aṣl*) of equality of races in numerous Qur'anic verses and prophetic narrations. He disapproved of non-Arabs leading Arabs in governments or even collective prayers, prescribed Arabic attires for all Muslims and made non-Arabic styles 'detested,' favored Arabs in government allowances (*al-ʿaṭā'*),[55] and rendered non-Arab men 'incompetent' (*aqallu kafā'ah*) to marry Arab women.[56] These views are obviously contrary to the *maqāṣid* of equality of human beings expressed in numerous scripts.

Based on the 'cognitive nature of the law' proposed above, *al-ʿurf* is what the jurist views as *ʿurf*, according to his/her worldview, as long as it does not contradict the basic principles of *maqāṣid al-sharīʿah*. Hence, the 'jurist's worldview' is proposed here as an expansion to *al-ʿurf* method for accommodating changes from the 'default Arabic customs' (of the first few Islamic centuries).

Chart 6.2 shows the place that the 'jurist's worldview' takes in the system of Islamic law. This chart illustrates the centrality of the role of the jurist, which is a result of the inclusion of 'worldview' in the system of Islamic law. The Qur'an and the sections of the prophetic traditions that are law-related are the jurist's 'sources' and part of his/her 'worldview' too. The other components of a jurist's worldview are combined with 'sources' in order to produce fiqh. A 'worldview,' however, has to be 'competent,' i.e., built on a 'scientific' basis, as explained below. A jurist without a 'competent worldview' is not 'competent' enough to make accurate *fiqhī* judgements. This competence is another expansion to the skills of '*fiqh al-wāqi*ᶜ' (understanding the status quo), which Ibn al-Qayyim set as a condition for competence in ijtihad.[57] This proposal has the following two impacts on the law.

First, considering changes in the jurist's 'worldview' will decrease literalism in the Islamic law. A literal following of a ruling turns it into some sort of 'ritual.' I argue that it is necessary to maintain constancy in the area of rituals (*ᶜibādāt*) in the Islamic law, such as prayers, fasting, and pilgrimage. However, exaggerating the area of *ᶜibādāt* always happens at the expense of the *maqāṣid*. A balance between these two ends is required.

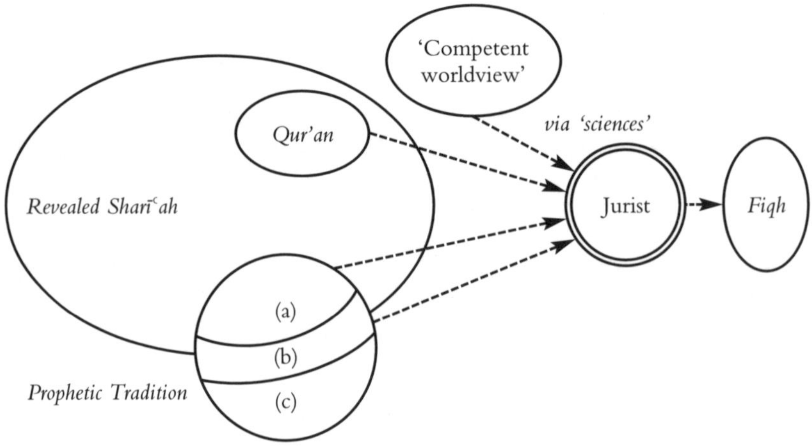

Chart 6.2. The jurist's 'worldview' is a prime factor in shaping fiqh.

The following examples illustrate this point. The purpose behind the end-of-Ramadan charity (*ṣadaqah al-fiṭr*) is to help the poor. It is reported that the Prophet had said, 'on that day, give the poor enough so they do not have to beg.'[58] However, this charity was placed under the category of '*ʿibādāt*' and, therefore, applied in every place and time to the letter. When geography and society change to the extent that dates, raisins, and barley become of no use to the poor (and '*aqiṭ*' no longer exists), a literal and 'ritualistic' application of this charity would defeat the purpose behind it.

Similarly, in some developing countries with a majority of Muslims, one's relatives are held responsible for paying the compensation for unintentional killing (*diyyah*) because they are supposed to be of his or her 'tribe' (*ʿāqilah*), as mentioned above.[59] But if little significance is accrued to one's tribe or ethnic group, due to a different 'worldview' of social structures, then a literal application of *al-ʿāqilah* goes against the purpose of justice itself.

Finally, (Arabic) marriage vows and Friday sermons are generally not understood in non-Arab speaking communities.[60] Conducting these in the Arabic language is due to the rulings that decreed that vows and sermons are rituals (*ʿibādāh*) in their own right. Thus, the sentimental meaning of the vows and the social meaning of the sermons are compromised. This analysis is not suggesting that acts of worship (*ʿibādāt*) and purposes of the law (*al-maqāṣid*) are in contradiction. 'Worship' is a purpose of the Islamic law in its own right. However, it has to be balanced with other social purposes.

The second impact of the proposed condition of a 'competent worldview' is 'opening' the system of Islamic law to advances in natural and social sciences. Judgements about some status quo or 'reality' can no longer be claimed without proper research that is based on sound and 'competent' physical or social sciences methodology. We have seen how issues related to legal capacity, such as 'the sign of death,' 'maximum pregnancy period,' 'age of differentiation,' or 'age of puberty,' were traditionally judged based on 'asking people.' Since 'methods of scientific investigation' are part of one's worldview,' as Richard DeWitt argued,[61] I would say that 'asking people' cannot be claimed today without some statistical proof! This takes us to the realm of science (natural and social), and defines a mechanism of interaction between the Islamic law and other branches of knowledge. Therefore, a jurist should consult specialists in medical fields and ask them to determine the signs of death and the minimum and maximum periods of pregnancy, etc. Empirical data should have 'authority' (*ḥujjah*) in this area, even if it were 'uncertain' according to traditional logic. Similarly, specialists in the field of psychology should define the concept and age of 'differentiation.' And so on.

It is true that 'science' evolves with time, and this will entail regular updating of our scientific decisions and answers. Nevertheless, the evolution of science is part of the natural evolution of the jurist's 'world view,' and accordingly must be reflected in the law. This maintains 'openness' in the system of Islamic law.

Self-Renewal via Philosophical Openness

Islamic law could achieve self-renewal through openness to another component of a competent jurist's 'worldview,' which is philosophy. Since the 'fundamentals of the Islamic law' is, more or less, the philosophy of Islamic law, it is necessary that the 'fundamentals' maintain a degree of openness to philosophical investigation, which evolves with the evolution of human knowledge, in general.

However, historically, the vast majority of Islamic scholars, in traditional schools of law, rejected any attempt to utilise philosophy in developing Islamic law or Islamic knowledge, in general. Usually citing examples of some Greek metaphysical theories that go against popular Muslim beliefs,[62] some scholars issued *fatāwā* to ban studying and teaching philosophy in educational institutes because it was based on 'non-Islamic metaphysics.'[63] Based on these *fatāwā* forcing a choice between philosophy and 'following the path of the Qur'an,' philosophers are accused of apostasy, and philosophy books are not to be owned, sold, or honored. The issuers of such *fatāwā* have been amongst the key jurists in Islamic schools of law, such as Ibn ʿAqīl (d. 1119 CE), al-Nawawī (d. 1277 CE), al-Suyūṭī (d. 1505 CE), al-Qushaīrī (d. 1127 CE), Ibn Raslān (d. 1595 CE), al-Shirbīnī (d. 1579 CE), and Ibn al-Ṣalāḥ (d. 1246 CE).[64] Ibn al-Ṣalāḥ's fatwa is the most cited on the topic in the literature of Islamic law. In his fatwa, Ibn al-Ṣalāḥ declared philosophy to be 'the root of foolishness and promiscuity,' and 'the sword' to be the best way to deal with teachers of philosophy.[65] This violent reaction had suppressed interest in philosophy in most Islamic circles.[66] Scholars would have to study philosophy or logic in secret, would inform only their closest students, and would never disclose such activities in their writings.[67] Ibn Rushd (Averröes, d. 584 AH/1189 CE) was an example of jurists/philosophers who was persecuted and whose books were burnt because he violated the above *fatāwā*.[68]

Simultaneously, a few scholars announced their dislike to Greek philosophy and its 'non-Islamic methods,' and put an effort in formally criticising it and even suggesting alternative ideas, especially in logic, from their own viewpoints. This was the position taken by Ibn Ḥazm[69] and Ibn Taymiyah.[70] Ibn Ḥazm did not denounce logic as other scholars did. In fact, he believed that logic is the criterion by which 'one could evaluate any knowledge (*miʿyāru kulli ʿilm*).'[71] Ibn Ḥazm explained how modal logic could correspond to logic of duties in the Islamic law, an idea he perhaps owes to al-Ghazālī's *Mustaṣfā*.[72] Nevertheless, Ibn Ḥazm's *Taqrīb al-Manṭiq* (Facilitating Logic) was, to my knowledge, the first attempt to elaborate on the correspondence between possibility and permissibility, implication and obligation, and impossibility and prohibition,[73] eight centuries before contemporary 'deontic logic.'[74] Ibn Ḥazm presented a controversial reconstruction of Aristotle's syllogism itself to fit his own philosophy, which is the school of Islamic law known as literalism (*al-ẓāhiriyyah*).[75] For example, he supported 'causation' in natural phenomena but not in 'revealed law' and, hence, he rejected all forms of analogical reasoning and criticised others who endorsed it.[76]

On the other hand, Ibn Taymiyah's critique of Aristotle was detailed and everlasting.[77] He rejected Aristotle's distinction between essence and accident as arbitrary and, therefore, rejected any truth 'by definition' in universal propositions[78]. According to Ibn Taymiyah, the differences between *busr* (unripe dates), *ruṭab* (somewhat ripe dates), and *tamr* (mature dates) do not reflect three different 'essences,' as Aristotelians suggest.[79] These would be three 'mental universals' (*kulliyyātun fī al-dhihn*), to use Ibn Taymiyah's words.[80] Hence, Ibn Taymiyah criticised the restriction of legal reasoning to syllogistic reasoning, which proceeds from 'universal propositions.' He gave 'analogy by resemblance' (*qiyās al-shabah*) as a counter-example.[81] Like Ibn Ḥazm, Ibn Taymiyah also used his critical analysis in support of his own 'philosophical project,' which was nominal at heart.[82] He further criticised al-Ghazālī and other scholars, who claimed to have endorsed Greek philosophy as a mere logical tool without endorsing its metaphysical basis.[83]

Yet, a few jurists decided to reject Greek metaphysics and accept Greek logic. Al-Ghazālī (d. 504 AH/1111 CE) harshly criticised Greek philosophy for its 'paganism' and accused Muslim philosophers of apostasy, on one hand.[84] On the other hand, al-Ghazālī accepted Aristotle's logical 'tool' (Greek: Organon, Arabic: *ālah*), and even judged it to be a 'necessary introduction to all branches of knowledge,' without which there is 'no confidence in a scholar in any field of knowledge.'[85] Al-Ghazālī 'internalised' Greek logic as a way of thinking and, thus, eventually was able to introduce a way of merging logic of reasoning/ijtihad into Islamic law. In *al-Qisṭās* (The Scale), al-Ghazālī 'proved' several of Aristotle's inferences, such as Modus Ponens and Modus Tollens, via referring to the Qur'anic 'logical arguments.'[86] For example, after citing the verse, 'If there were other gods in either heavens or earth besides God alone, they would both dissolve in chaos,'[87] al-Ghazālī made the following Modus Tollens reasoning: 'More than one god[88] implies disorder. And since there is no disorder, there is no more than one god.' Thereafter, al-Ghazālī used Arabic roots derived directly from the Qur'an, or familiar Islamic law terminology, instead of the usual philosophical terminology. For example, he developed *al-maḥmūl* (attribute predicate) into *al-ḥukm* (ruling), *al-ḥadd al-awsaṭ* (middle term) into *al-ᶜillah* (cause), *al-muqaddimah* (premise) into *al-aṣl* (fundamental rule), *al-natījah* (conclusion) into *al-farᶜ* (detailed ruling), and *al-mumkin* (possible) into *al-mubāḥ* (permissible).[89] The most creative idea that al-Ghazālī developed was incorporating syllogistic deduction in the methodology of *qiyās*.[90] To 'formalise' *tanqīḥ al-manaṭ* (the search for the ᶜ*illah* of the ruling), al-Ghazālī applied a series of disjunctive syllogisms to the first situation.[91] For example, he made the following reasoning: 'One value compared to another has to be greater, equal, or less. If we prove one of them, then the other two are necessarily false.'[92] Then, al-Ghazālī used hypothetical syllogism, considering the middle term of the two propositions to be the ʿ*illah* itself, in order to pass the judgment of the first situation to the second.[93] For example, he wrote: 'Every wine intoxicates. Everything that intoxicates is forbidden. Therefore, wine is forbidden.'[94] Note here that he considered intoxication to be the 'middle term,' or, in his 'Islamic' expression, the 'ʿ*illah*.'

Thus, despite al-Ghazālī's harsh attack on Greek philosophy, his incorporation of Aristotle's logic in his Islamic juridical reasoning process was faithful and creative, even though it brought upon him the harsh criticism of, both, nominalists and literalists.[95] Al-Āmidī (d. 1236 CE), al-Subkī (d. 1374 CE), and a few other scholars, especially from the Ashʿarite and Shāfiʿī schools, to which al-Ghazālī belonged, concurred with al-Ghazālī in differentiating between 'abstract tools' that Muslims could borrow from non-Muslims and other ideas and concepts, which could not be borrowed.[96] This opinion is similar to some present-day 'neo-literalist' *fatāwā*, which permits imitating knowledge only related to 'technology from the West,' rather than knowledge related to humanities and social sciences.

Despite al-Ghazālī's popularity, the general ban on philosophy contributed to stagnation in the theory and reasoning methodology of the Islamic law across the board. *Uṣūl* continued to focus on direct linguistic implications and superficial logical derivations. The *fiqhī* system of reasoning continued to be more or less a 'mechanical propositional system' that deals with duties and prohibitions.

The closest analogy to the traditional *fiqhī* reasoning system in modern times is deontic logic. Although 'deontic logic' is a term coined by von Wright in the middle of the twentieth century,[97] one notices that von Wright's standard system, its relation to modal logic, and its main axioms are actually quite similar to traditional *fiqhī* reasoning. For instance, von Wright's 'law of commitment' that states: 'if doing what we ought to do commits us to do something else, then this new act is also something that we ought to do,'[98] is the same fundamental rule, '*mā lā yatimmu al-wājibu illā bihi fahuwa wājib*.'[99] Contemporary philosophy of law does not accept deontic logic as a valid legal reasoning system.[100] The main reasons are deontic logic's strict binary classification of duties, its insensitivity to the factor of time, and its monotonic exclusion of exceptional cases.[101]

On the other hand, the theory of Islamic law did not benefit from original contributions that Islamic philosophers made to Greek philosophy and, especially, logic as a science. For example, Avicenna (Ibn Sīnā, d. 1037 CE) made an original contribution to logic by carefully reconstructing Aristotle's theory of modal syllogism after distinguishing various temporal (time dependant) cases.[102] This contribution could have been useful in adding a temporal dimension to standard syllogistic derivations and, potentially, adding a much-needed time dimension to the logic of the Islamic law. Another original contribution, made by Islamic philosophers and not utilised by Islamic jurists, was al-Fārābī's (d. 338 AH/950 CE) syllogistic theory of inductive argumentation,[103] which could have added an also much needed inductive dimension to reasoning in the Islamic law. Similarly, Ibn Ḥazm and Ibn Taymiyah's critiques of Aristotelian logic 'set the stage for the rise of the inductive logic of J.S. Mill,'[104] of which Islamic law itself did not make use.

Contrary to most jurists, Averröes (al-Walīd ibn Rushd) articulated a stand that was most open to human knowledge. Out of a Qur'anic obligation on Muslims to reason and reflect upon God's creation, Averröes endorsed all sound philosophical reasoning, 'regardless of the religion of its conveyer.'[105] Averröes's solution for any apparent contradiction between reason and the scripts is to 'reinterpret' the scripts, as much as language permits, in order to 'fit the conclusions of reason.'[106] He also blamed al-Ghazālī and other jurists for hastily accusing philosophers of heresy without attempting to understand their positions. Averröes's method in matching reason and scriptures, openness to the 'Other,' refusal of hasty accusations of heresy, and his calls for the utilisation of philosophy in realistic reform, had a clear impact on the modern Islamic reformist movement of the past century.[107] Nevertheless, according to the manuscripts that we now know about,[108] Averröes did not discuss the relationship between his views in philosophy and his views in Islamic law. Hence, contrary to some researchers' views,[109] I think that there is a gap between Averröes, the 'Commentator' and 'Second Teacher,' who defended philosophical reasoning in his '*Faṣl al-Maqāl*' and his renowned commentary on Aristotle's works,[110] and Averröes, the judge and jurist, who mostly supported his traditional Mālikī *madhhab* in his comprehensive encyclopaedia on Islamic fiqh which he called *Bidāyah al-Mujtahid*. Therefore, for the system of Islamic law to maintain its self-renewal, it is necessary to adopt Averröes's openness to all philosophical investigation and to extend this openness to the theories of the fundamentals/*uṣūl* themselves.

6.4. TOWARDS MULTI-DIMENSIONALITY

Chapter Two explained, in abstract terms, the limitations of binary categorisations, and also the importance of multi-dimensionality as a principle systems feature and a more realistic, i.e., everyday, way of thinking. Multi-dimensionality, as explained before, entails a spectrum of levels between binary opposites. Chapter Five applied this concept to '*hujjiyyah*,' which varies from 'authority' to 'radically criticised,' and to sources of legislation, which varies from rational to heavenly. This section will take the system of Islamic law further steps towards multi-dimensionality by applying it to two 'fundamental' concepts, namely, certainty (*al-qaṭ*ᶜ) and opposition (*al-ta*ᶜ*āruḍ*).

Spectrum of Certainty

The treatment of every topic in the *uṣūlī* literature had to start with a 'definition' (*ta*ᶜ*rīf*) of concepts. Typically, and obviously under the effect of Aristotlean logic, a definition is either by 'essence' (*al-ḥadd*) or by 'description' (*al-rasm*). An essence-based definition typically includes an etymological analysis of the word, in order to define the 'whatness' of its related concept.[111] The *Mashshā'ūn* (Peripatetics) 'description' defined concepts/terms in terms of attributes that 'discriminates' them from other concepts/terms.[112] However, in his critique of (Greek) philosophy, Ibn Taymiyah elaborated on the discriminative role of definitions and criticised the Ashᶜarites, Muᶜtazilīs, and the Jaᶜfarīs who followed al-Ghazālī in his 'essence-oriented' approach.[113] Ibn Taymiyah criticised al-Ghazālī's 'logical introduction' of his *Mustaṣfā*, and argued that the purpose of an essence-based definition is 'discrimination' (that is, *al-tamyīz*) between concepts, in any case.[114]

Thus, the jurists' method of *tamyīz* between concepts, whether essence- or description-based always resulted in defining every concept in relation to a 'binary opposite.' The popular Arabic saying goes: 'Things are distinguished based on their opposites' (*biḍiddihā tatamayyaz al-ashyā'*).

Chart 6.3. Traditionally, juridical evidences are divided between 'certain', and 'uncertain' categories.

certain	*uncertain*

'Certainty' (*al-qaṭʿ*) versus 'uncertainty' (*al-ẓann*) is a powerful and dominant dichotomy in various methodologies and schools of Islamic law (Chart 6.3).[115] Al-Ghazālī defined logic itself as the 'law that identifies definitions and analogies, and differentiates certain (*yaqīnī*) knowledge from other knowledge.'[116] Some fundamental 'evidences' were legitimised for a sole goal of 'expanding the area of certainty' in Islamic law. For example, Ali Juma argues for the necessity of ijmāʿ (consensus) since, 'restricting fundamental tools to understanding the implications of scripts made the area of certainty less than adequate, and created a real problem that required giving legitimacy to ijmāʿ as an evidence that expands the area of certainty and transfers doubtful implications to the circle of absoluteness.'[117] Always sought after and often claimed, 'certainty' contributed an attitude of absolutism that had generated a range of problems. Certainty was claimed in various forms, including linguistic implication (*qaṭʿiyyah al-dilālah*), historical authenticity (*qaṭʿiyyah al-thubūt*), and logical implication (*al-qaṭʿ al-manṭiqī*). These forms are introduced and their negative implications outlined below.

First, 'clear' instructions of the Qur'an and hadith were claimed to be 'certain' in their linguistic implication (*qaṭʿī al-dilālah*). Consider the following four narrations, as they appear in collections of hadith.

1. The Prophet heard that two men had a fight (over renting a farm). Thus, he said: 'If this is going to be your attitude, then do not rent farms.'[118]
2. A woman said: 'O Messenger of God. This is my son whom I carried in my belly, fed from my breast, and laid on my lap. His father divorced me and now wants to take him from me.' The Messenger of God, peace be upon him, told her: 'You have priority to his custody unless you get married.'[119]
3. The Prophet said: 'A Muslim does not pay charity for his horse.'[120]
4. The Prophet said: '... And blood money for a soul is one hundred camels ...'[121]

Therefore, according to the linguistic *dilālah* of the above four narrations and their implied certainties:

1. Renting farms is forbidden.[122]
2. A divorcee loses custody of her child if she gets married.[123]
3. There is no zakah charity due on horses.[124]
4. Blood money is one hundred camels.[125]

The method of extracting rulings from 'clear,' and thus, 'certain' scripts actually does take into consideration the fact that 'another narration' might imply a change of status in what is thought to be an obligation. Nevertheless, scholars maintained that this other factor has to be at the same level of certainty (*daraja al-qaṭᶜiyyah*) as the first narration;[126] otherwise, the obligation remains in effect. Because the first order was given by God or the Prophet, any other statement that could have have influence in the matter should come from the same source, even if it is a prophetic approval (*iqrār*) and not a clear command. Let us assume that one interpretation of a prophetic command suggests that it was not meant to be certain and definite, but had a specific context that necessitates issuing such a command (for example, an economical, political, or environmental context). The following are examples of such interpretations or specifications for the above four examples:

1. The Prophet forbade the companions from renting farms only because of the fight that had happened and, therefore, this order applies only when there is a possibility of disputes.[127]
2. The Prophet knew that this custody arrangement is best for the specific social case he was dealing with. The Prophet was not issuing a general command. In other words, he was acting with an 'intent of judgeship' and not with an 'intent of conveyance' in this case.[128]
3. If horses amount to a significant fortune, then zakah applies to them.[129]
4. The conditions of blood money and the one hundred camels are dependent upon the dominant culture in Arabia.[130]

In traditional schools of law, none of the above four arguments is generally accepted, except for the first. However, the reason behind accepting the first argument is that there are 'equally authentic' narrations that imply that the Prophet approved some other farm rentals. The other three interpretations, which were not supported by other 'certain' evidences, are rejected. The implications of the commands are certain (*qaṭᶜiyyah*) while the hypothesised circumstances that were not clearly stated in any narration do not have the same status of certainty (*darajah al-qaṭᶜiyyah*) and are, therefore, speculative (*maẓnūn*). After all, another fundamental rule states: 'Certainty cannot be removed by doubt' (*al-yaqīnu la yazūlu bi al-shak*). So therefore, since stated commands are usually mentioned in the Qur'an or collections of hadith without necessarily elaborating on all underlying circumstances, as explained before, the binary concept of 'certainty' in linguistic implication (*qaṭᶜiyyah al-dilālah*) creates a problem of narrow, out of context, and partial views in many *fiqhī* rulings.

Certainty in historical authenticity (*qaṭᶜī al-thubūt*) is also claimed on various levels, ranging from the 'most well-known' level (*al-mutawātir*, frequently recurring narrations) to the individual narrations (*khabar al-wāḥid*). *Al-mutawātir* level of authenticity is reached when a narration is conveyed through a 'large number of people who could not possibly agree to lie' (*jamᶜun yastaḥīlu tawāṭu'uhum ᶜalā al-kadhib*).[131] The Qur'an as a whole and a few prophetic traditions fall under this category.[132] In addition, most scholars believe that an *āḥād* narration that the 'Muslim nation approves' (*khabar al-āḥād al-ladhī talaqqathu al-ummatu bi al-qabūl*) is also 'certain.' In his authoritative Introduction to the Terminology of Narrations, Ibn al-Ṣalāḥ states that narrations that both Imam Bukhārī and Imam Muslim agree upon are authentic with 'certainty' (*maqṭūᶜun bi-ṣiḥḥatih*). Ibn al-Ṣalāḥ claims that these two scholars's approval of a narration 'logically entails' (*lāzimun min dhālik*) the whole ummah's approval. Then, since the ummah is 'infallible' (*maᶜṣūmah*), he proceeds, these narrations entail 'absolute theoretical knowledge' (*al-ᶜilm al-yaqīnī al-naẓarī*).[133] Most scholars agree with Ibn al-Ṣalāḥ.

Ibn Taymiyah, for example, uses the same argument for *āḥād* narrations, which 'the ummah approves,' for proving the 'fundamentals of creeds' (*ithbātu uṣūl al-diyānāt*).[134] In matters of belief (*iᶜtiqād*), he, therefore, includes issues, such as 'ascribing to God attributes' (*ṣifāt*), 'showing patience with sultans from Quraish,' 'wiping one's shoes during ablution,' and rendering Sufi songs (*qaṣā'id*) 'an innovation in the faith.'[135] The danger in these claims manifests when these *āḥād* narrations, such as the ones that Ibn Taymiyah is referring to, undergo formal authentication procedures (*al-ḥukmu ᶜalā al-hadīth*). These procedures, and the credibility of many of the narrators from various generations, are widely disputed even within each traditional school. Hence, irreconcilable differences in the 'fundamentals of faith' occur, which might lead to serious conflicts and wars, as had happened recurrently in the Islamic history. Therefore, it is pertinent to foster a culture of tolerance and mutual co-existence to, at the very least, separate *āḥād* narrations from fundamentals of faith. 'What remains,' Khaled Abou El Fadl writes, 'is the empirical claim – what remains is sociology.'[136]

Jurists created a new category for the intersection of the two categories of certainty mentioned above (Chart 6.4), historically authentic and linguistically implied (*qaṭᶜī al-thubūti qaṭᶜī al-dilālah*). It is a category of highest certainty, 'integral part of the religion' (*maᶜlūmun min al-dīni bi al-ḍarūrah*), which are 'absolute matters of the faith' (*qaṭᶜiyyāh al-iᶜtiqād*). Consequently, most scholars agree that the definition of an 'apostate' is the person who rejects any of these 'highly certain' matters.[137] Now, 'consensus of scholars' (*ijmāᶜ al-ᶜulamā'*) started to undergo a process of historical authentication (*al-taḥaqququ min wuqūᶜ al-ijmāᶜ*) as well. Then, despite the great many differences over the very definition of ijmāᶜ, it was used to add many controversial issues to the 'highly certain' category. Historically, this resulted in a number of dramatic conflicts based on accusations and counter-accusations of 'apostasy' amongst followers of different schools of law, as mentioned before. These conflicts were over rulings that were included in *al-maᶜlūmu min al-dīni bi al-ḍarūrah*.

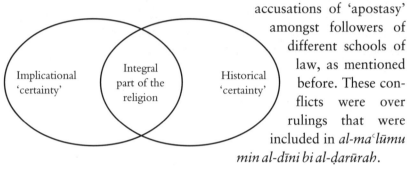

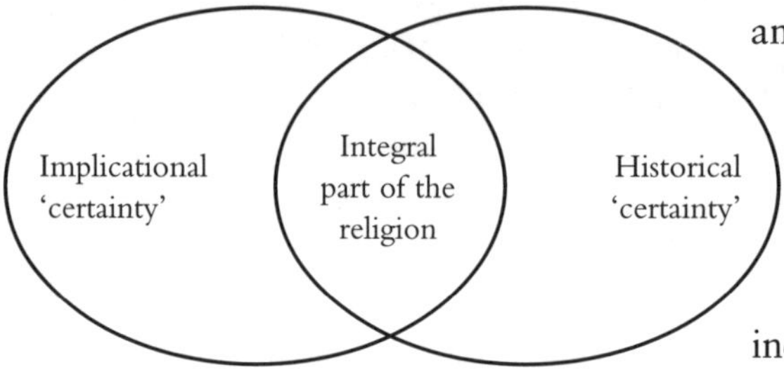

Chart 6.4. An evidence that is historically 'authentic' and linguistically 'implied' entails being an 'integral part of the religion.'

Finally, certain logical implication (*al-qaṭᶜ al-manṭiqī, al-luzūm al-manṭiqī*, or *al-yaqīn al-manṭiqī*) is another binary claim of 'certainty.' In the methodology of Islamic law, logical implication is used in the area of analogical reasoning (*qiyās*), which is based on similar 'causes' (*ᶜilal*), as explained before. However, in addition to the Shia, Zaydīs, Literalists, and some Muᶜtazilīs, who do not approve analogical reasoning in the Islamic law to start with,[138] some Sunni scholars expressed unease about the 'certainty' of *ᶜilal*. Al-Ghazālī, for example, wrote that there are six reasons for 'probability' (*iḥtimāl*) in an *ᶜillah* of a certain ruling:[139]

1. We assume a certain cause for a ruling that does not have a cause, according to God.[140]
2. The ruling has a cause, according to God, but we make a mistake in concluding it.
3. The ruling has more than one cause, according to God, but we make a mistake in restricting it to one cause.
4. The ruling has one cause, according to God, but we make a mistake in adding invalid causes to it.

5. We succeed in defining the cause of one ruling precisely, but make a mistake in considering this ruling analogous to another, which is not, according to God.
6. We make the mistake of claiming a certain cause behind a ruling by pure speculation, without putting the right amount of effort (ijtihad).

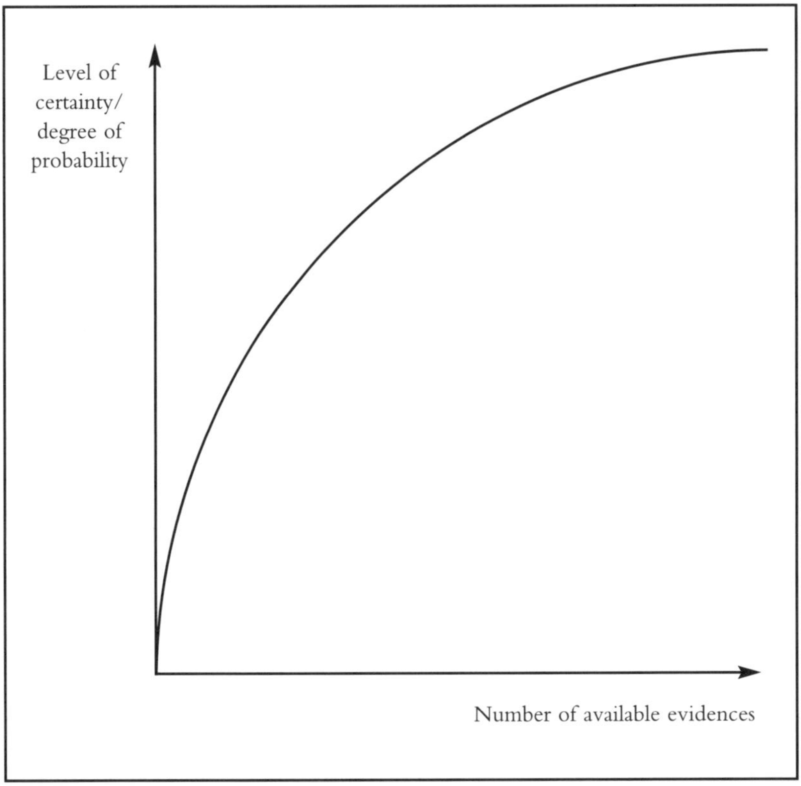

Chart 6.5. Certainty/Probability increases (non-linearly) with the number of available evidences

Finally al-Ghazālī actually added *al-muṣawwibah's* opinion as another possibility, which is that God did not assign a single correct cause for every ruling and that the correct cause is what every *mujtahid* perceives to be a correct cause. Al-Ghazālī's separation between correctness 'according to God' (*ᶜind Allāh*) and according to the *mujtahid*, in the above analysis of the *ᶜillah*, supports the human cognitive nature of reasoning and fiqh, in general, as Section 6.1 had proposed. Thus, it places reasoning by analogy amongst 'uncertain,' rather than 'certain,' evidences.

The above binary approach to the concept of certainty is history! Today's basic mathematics assigns probability for any parameter based on the number of evidences supporting it. Therefore, there is a 'spectrum' of certainties for any evidence, rather than a binary dichotomy. Certainty (or probability, if you wish) increases in a non-linear mode with the number of available evidences (Chart 6.5). I would argue that the Qur'anic logic for proving the existence of God takes a 'continuous,' rather than 'binary,' approach to certainty; the more evidence humans find, the greater certainty (*yaqīn*) they acquire. Accounting for the amount of 'uncertainty' inherent in legal reasoning allows flexibility in the produced rulings.

Resolving 'Opposition' Through Multi-Dimensionality

In Islamic juridical theory, there is a differentiation between opposition or disagreement (*taᶜāruḍ or ikhtilāf*) and contradiction (*tanāquḍ* or *taᶜānud*) of evidences (verses or narrations).[141] Contradiction is defined as 'a clear logical conclusion of truth and falsehood in the same aspect' (*taqāsum al-ṣidqi wa al-kadhib*).[142] On the other hand, conflict or disagreement between evidences is defined as an 'apparent contradiction between evidences in the mind of the scholar' (*taᶜāruḍun fī dhihn al-mujtahid*).[143] This means that two seemingly disagreeing (*mutaᶜāriḍ*) evidences are not necessarily in contradiction. It is the perception of the jurist that they are in contradiction which can occur as a result of some missing information regarding the evidence's timing, place, circumstances, or other conditions.[144]

On the other hand, true contradiction takes the form of a single episode narrated in truly contradicting ways by the same or different narrators.[145] This kind of discrepancy is obviously due to errors in narration related to the memory and/or intentions of one or more of the narrators.[146] The 'logical' conclusion in cases of contradiction is that one of the narrations is inaccurate and should be rejected (perhaps both narrations, if one could prove that). For example, Abū Hurayrah narrated, according to Bukhārī: 'Bad omens are in women, animals, and houses.'[147] However, (also according to Bukhārī) ʿĀ'ishah narrated that the Prophet had said: 'People during the Days of Ignorance (*jāhiliyyah*) used to say that bad omens are in women, animals, and houses.'[148] These two 'authentic' narrations are at odds and one of them should be rejected. It is telling that most commentators rejected ʿĀ'ishah's narration, even though other 'authentic' narrations support it.[149] Ibn al-ʿArabī, for example, commented on ʿĀ'ishah's rejection of the above hadith as follows: 'This is nonsense (*qawlun sāqiṭ*). This is rejection of a clear and authentic narration that is narrated through trusted narrators!'[150]

According to various traditional and contemporary studies on the issue of *taʿāruḍ* contradiction in the above sense, is rare.[151] Most cases of *taʿāruḍ* are disagreements between narrations because of, apparently, a missing context, not because of logically contradicting accounts of the same episode.[152] There are six strategies that jurists defined to deal with these types of disagreements in traditional schools of law:

1. Conciliation (*al-jamʿ*): This method is based on a fundamental rule that states that, 'applying the script is better than disregarding it (*iʿmāl al-naṣṣi awlā min ihmālih*).'[153] Therefore, a jurist facing two disagreeing narrations should search for a missing condition or context, and attempt to interpret both narrations based on it.[154]
2. Abrogation (*al-naskh*): This method suggests that the later evidence, chronologically speaking, should 'abrogate' (juridically annul) the former. This means that when verses disagree, the verse that is (narrated to be) revealed last is considered to be an abrogating evidence (*nāsikh*) and others to be abrogated (*mansūkh*). Similarly, when prophetic narrations disagree, the narration that has a later date, if dates are known or could be concluded, should abrogate all other narrations. Most scholars do not accept that a hadith abrogates a verse of the Qur'an, even if the hadith were to be chronologically subsequent. This is related to comparing 'degrees of certainty.'

The concept of abrogation, in any of the above senses, does not have supporting evidence from the words attributed to the Prophet in traditional collections of hadith. Etimologically, abrogation (*naskh*) is derived from the root *na sa kha*. I carried out a survey on this root and all its possible derivations in a large number of today's popular collections of hadith, including al-Bukhārī, Muslim, al-Tirmithī, al-Nasā'ī, Abū Dawūd, Ibn Mājah, Aḥmad, Mālik, al-Dāramī, al-Mustadrak, Ibn Ḥibbān, Ibn Khuzaymah, al-Bayhaqī, al-Dārquṭnī, Ibn Abī Shaybah, and ʿAbd al-Razzāq. I found no valid hadith attributed to the Prophet that contains any of these derivations of the root *na sa kha*. I found about 40 instances of 'abrogations' mentioned in the above collections, which were all based on one of the narrators' opinions or commentaries, rather than any of the texts of the hadith. The concept of abrogation always appears within the commentaries given by companions or other narrators, commenting on what appears to be in disagreement with their own understanding of the related issues. According to traditional exegeses, the principle of abrogation does have evidence from the Qur'an, although the interpretations of the related verses are subject to a difference of opinion.[155]

3. Elimination (*al-tarjīh*): This method suggests endorsing the narration that is 'most authentic' and dropping or eliminating other narrations. The 'eliminating' narration is called *al-riwāyah al-rājiḥah*, which literally means the narration that is 'heavier in the scale.' According to scholars of hadith, an eliminating (*rājiḥah*) narration must have, as compared to the other narration, one or more of the following characteristics: a larger number of other supporting narrations, a shorter chain of narrators, more knowledgeable narrators, narrators more capable of memorisation, more trustworthy narrators, first-hand account versus indirect accounts, shorter time between the narration and the narrated incident, narrators able to remember and mention the date of the incident versus others, less ambiguity, less rhetoric, and a number of other factors.[156]
4. Waiting (*al-tawaqquf*): This method recommends that the scholar is not to make any decision until one of the above three methods is evident.

5. Cancellation (*al-tasāquṭ*): This method recommends that the scholar is to disregard both narrations because of the uncertainty in both.
6. Choice (*al-takhyīr*): This method allows the scholar to choose whatever is rendered suitable for the situation at hand.

Ḥanafīs apply abrogation before any other method, followed by the method of elimination.[157] All other schools of law give priority, theoretically, to the method of conciliation (*al-jam*ᶜ). Although most schools of law agree that applying all scripts is better than disregarding any of them, most scholars do not seem to give priority, on a practical level, to the method of conciliation. The methods that are used in most cases of *ta*ᶜ*āruḍ* are abrogation and elimination.[158] Therefore, a large number of evidences are cancelled, one way or the other, for no good reason other than that the jurists' failing to understand how they could fit them in a unified perceptual framework. Thus, invalidating these evidences is more or less arbitrary. For example, narrations are invalidated (outweighed) if narrators did not happen to 'mention the date of the incident,' the wording related to the Prophet happened to be more 'metaphoric,' or a narrator happened to be female – in which case the male's 'opposing' narration takes precedence.[159] Therefore, *al-naskh* and *al-tarjīḥ* reflect the general feature of binary thinking in fundamental methodology. It is essential that the method of conciliation make use of the concept of multi-dimensionality in overcoming this drawback.

One practical consequence of cancelling a large number of verses and prophetic narrations in the name of *naskh* and *tarjīḥ* is a great deal of 'inflexibility' in the Islamic law, i.e., inability to address various situations adequately. Reflection upon pairs of *muta*ᶜ*āriḍ* narrations show that their disagreement could be due to a difference in surrounding circumstances, such as war and peace, poverty and wealth, urban and rural life, summer and winter, sickness and health, or young and old. Therefore, the Qur'anic instructions or the Prophet's actions and decisions, as narrated by his observers, are supposed to have differed accordingly. Lack of contextualisation limits flexibility. For example, eliminating the evidences that occurred in the context of peace for the sake of evidences that occurred in the context of war, combined with literal methods, limits the jurist's ability to address both contexts. When this is combined with a strict binary methodology, the outcomes result in specific rulings for specific circumstances that are made universal and eternal.

One revealing example is verse 9:5 of the Qur'an, which has come to be named, 'The Verse of the Sword' (*āyah al-saīf*). It states: 'But when the forbidden months are past, then slay the pagans wherever you find them, and seize them.'[160] The historical context of the verse, in the ninth year of *hijrah*, is that of a war between Muslims and the pagans of Makkah. The thematic context of the verse in chapter nine is also the context of the same war, which the chapter is addressing. However, the verse was taken out of its thematic and historical contexts and claimed to have defined the ruling between Muslims and non-Muslims in every place, time, and circumstance. Hence, it was perceived to be in disagreement with more than two hundred other verses of the Qur'an, all calling for dialogue, freedom of belief, forgiveness, peace, and even patience. Conciliation between these different evidences, somehow, was not an option. To solve the disagreement, based on the method of abrogation, most exegetes concluded that this verse (9:5), which was revealed towards the end of the Prophet's life, abrogated each and every '*mutaʿāriḍ*' verse that was revealed before it.

Therefore, the following verses were considered abrogated: 'no compulsion in the religion;' 'forgive them, for God loves those who do good to people;' 'repel evil with that which is best;' 'so patiently persevere;' 'do not argue with the People of the Book except with means that are best;' and '(say:) You have your religion and I have my religion.'[161] In addition, a large number of prophetic traditions that legitimise peace treaties and multi-cultural co-existence, to use contemporary terms, were also abrogated.

One such tradition is 'The Scroll of Madinah' (*ṣaḥīfah al-madīnah*), in which the Prophet and the Jews of Madinah wrote a 'covenant' that defined the relationship between Muslims and Jews living in Madinah. The scroll stated that, 'Muslims and Jews are one nation (ummah), with Muslims having their own religion and Jews having their own religion.'[162] Classic and neo-traditional commentators on the *ṣaḥīfah* render it 'abrogated,' based on the Verse of the Sword and other similar verses.[163] Seeing all the above scripts and narrations in terms of the single dimension of peace versus war might imply a contradiction, in which the 'final truth' has to 'belong' to either peace or war. The result will have to be an unreasonable fixed choice between peace and war, for every place, time, and circumstance.

What added to the problem is that the number of cases of abrogation claimed by the students of the companions (*al-tābiʿīn*) is higher than the cases claimed by the companions themselves.[164] After the first Islamic century, one could furthermore notice that jurists from the developing schools of thought began claiming many new cases of abrogation, which were never claimed by the *tābiʿīn*. Thus, abrogation

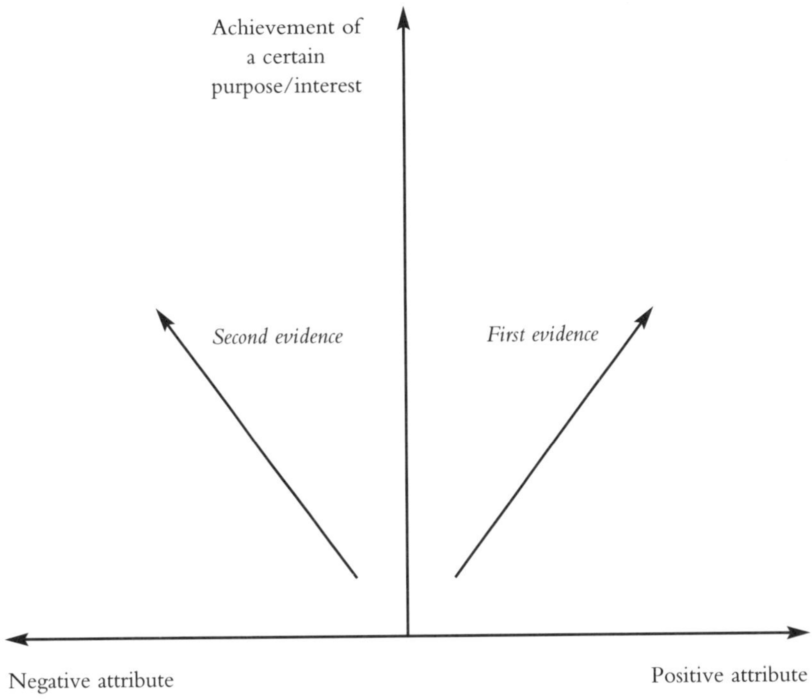

Chart 6.6. Seemingly contradicting 'attributes' in one dimension could be positively contributing to a different dimension related to purposes.

became a method of invalidating opinions or narrations endorsed by rival schools of law. Abū al-Ḥasan al-Karkhī (d. 951 CE), for one example, writes: 'The fundamental rule is: Every Qur'anic verse that is different from the opinion of the jurists in our school is either taken out of context or abrogated.'[165] Therefore, it is not unusual in the *fiqhī* literature to find a certain ruling to be abrogating (*nāsikh*) according to one school and abrogated (*mansūkh*) according to another. This arbitrary use of the method of abrogation has exacerbated the problem of lack of multi-dimensional interpretations of the evidences.

Multi-dimensionality, combined with a *maqāṣidī* approach, could offer a solution for the dilemmas of opposing evidences. Consider, for example, one attribute, with a positive and negative dimension (Chart 6.6). Two evidences might be 'in opposition,' in terms of this one attribute, such as war and peace, order and forbiddance, standing and sitting, men and women, and so on. If we restrict our view to one dimension, we will find no way to reconcile the evidences. However, if we expand the one-dimensional space into two dimensions, the second of which is a *maqṣid* to which both evidences contribute, then we will be able to 'resolve' the opposition and understand/interpret the evidences in a unified context.

The following are typical examples from the classic literature on *ikhtilāf al-adillah* (opposition of evidences), which also represent some traditionalist and modernist views today. However, it will be shown that the 'opposition' claimed could be resolved via the multi-dimensional and purposeful method proposed above.

1. There is a large number of opposing evidences related to different ways of performing 'acts of worship' (*ʿibādāt*), all attributed to the Prophet. These opposing narrations have frequently caused heated debates and rifts within Muslim communities. However, understanding these narrations within a *maqṣid* of magnanimity (*taīsīr*) entails that the Prophet did carry out these rituals in various ways, suggesting flexibility in such matters.[166] Examples of these acts of worship are the different ways of standing and moving during prayers,[167] concluding prayers (*tashahhud*),[168] compensating prostration (*sujūd al-sahū*),[169] reciting 'God is Great' (*takbīr*)

during ᶜĪd prayers,[170] making up for breaking one's fasting in Ramadan,[171] details of pilgrimage, and so on.

2. There is a number of opposing narrations that address matters related to customs (*al-ᶜurf*), which were also classified as 'in opposition.' However, these narrations could all be interpreted through the *maqṣid* of 'universality of the law,' as Ibn Ashur had suggested.[172] In other words, differences between these narrations should be understood as differences in the customs for which the various narrations attempted to show consideration, rather than 'contradiction.' One example is the two narrations, both attributed to ᶜĀ'ishah, one of which forbids 'any woman' from marriage without the consent of her guardian, while the other allows previously married women to make their own independent choices on marriage.[173] It is also narrated that ᶜĀ'ishah, the narrator of the two narrations herself, did not apply the 'condition' of consent in some cases.[174] Ḥanafīs explained that, 'the (Arabic) custom goes that a woman who marries without her guardian's consent is shameless.'[175] Understanding both narrations in the context of considering customs based on the law's 'universality' resolves the contradiction and provides flexibility in carrying out marriage ceremonies according to different customs in different places and times.
3. A number of narrations were classified under cases of abrogation, even though they were, according to some jurists, cases of gradual application of rulings. The purpose behind the gradual applications of rulings on a large scale is, 'facilitating the change that the law is bringing to society's deep-rooted habits.'[176] Thus, 'opposing narrations' regarding the prohibition of liquor and usury, and the performance of prayers and fasting, should be understood in terms of the prophetic 'tradition' of gradual application of high ideals in any given society.
4. A number of opposing narrations are considered 'contradictory' because their statements entail different rulings for similar cases. However, taking into account that these prophetic statements addressed different people (companions) could 'resolve the opposition.' In these cases, the juridical *maqṣid* of 'fulfilling the best

interest of people' would be the key to interpreting these narrations based on the differences between these companions. For example, a few narrations reported that the Prophet told a divorcee that she loses her custody of her children if she gets married.[177] Yet, a number of other 'opposing' narrations entail that divorcees could keep their children in their custody after they get married. The opposing narrations included Umm Salamah's case; Umm Salamah kept custody of her children after she married the Prophet.[178] Thus, relying on the first group of narrations, most schools of law concluded that custody is automatically transferred to the father if the mother gets married. They based their elimination of the second group of narrations on the fact that the first group was 'more authentic,' being narrated by Bukhārī and Ibn Ḥanbal.[179] Ibn Ḥazm, on the other hand, accepted the second group of narrations and rejected the first group based on his suspicion of one of the narrator's capability of memorisation.[180] However, after citing both opinions, al-Ṣanaʿānī commented: 'The children should stay with the parent who fulfils their best interest. If the mother is the better caregiver and will follow up on the children diligently, then she should have priority over them ... The children have to be in the custody of the more capable parent, and the Law cannot possibly judge otherwise.'[181]

Multi-dimensionality also entails considering more than one *maqṣid*, if applicable. In this case, the way of 'resolving oppositions' that fulfils these *maqāṣid* in the highest order should be given priority.

Multi-dimensionality and Postmodernism

Multi-dimensionality is also an important feature that resolves one of postmodernism's primary contradictions. Despite the goal of 'deconstructing binary opposites' in all streams of postmodernism, postmodern approaches themselves tend to be binary, reductionist, and uni-dimensional. It is true that postmodern approaches to the Islamic law have raised important questions about the ill-deserved 'centricity' of some juridical concepts, schools, and powerful characters and groups. They have also strived to uncover the cultural and historical dimensions of juridical theories and rulings, and the 'discursive traditions' that evolved over the course of the history of the Islamic law.

However, postmodernists tend to focus on one dimension/approach to the whole theory of Islamic law, whether it is linguistic, logical, historical, or cultural, and ignore all other dimensions. An 'Islamic feminist' approach, for example, raises essential questions that beg for fundamental answers. However, the he-she struggle is not the only dimension or force that shaped the Islamic law over its long history, as appears in some of their writings. Thus, a number of other essential dimensions and forces, as for example, political and economic, etc., which has shaped the law are overlooked in much of their discourse.

Similarly, post-colonial critiques tend to restrict their assessment of western scholarship in Islamic Studies to 'classic' essentialist Orientalism. They often overlook a large number of serious research projects and useful contributions to Islamic scholarship that also originated from western scholarship.

This book calls for a critical and multi-dimensional approach to the theory of Islamic law, in order to avoid reductionist views and binary thinking. As such, I have attempted to account for a number of dimensions of the Islamic schools/theories of law, including sources, linguistic derivations, reasoning methods, and schools/streams of thought, in addition to the dimensions of culture and history, or space and time. Disconnected and 'deconstructed' segments cannot form a whole picture, unless we account for the systemic inter-relations and structural connections between them.

Thus, despite the postmodernist war on macro-theories, I believe that a critical, multi-dimensional, systems-based, and purpose-oriented approach offers an adequate framework for analysis and development of the theory of Islamic law.

6.5. TOWARDS 'PURPOSEFULNESS'

Chapter Two explained how this research considers 'purposefulness' to be the principle feature of its systems approach. It was also shown how 'purposefulness' is a common link amongst all other basic system features, such as cognition, holism, openness, hierarchy, interrelationship, and multi-dimensionality. On the other hand, Chapter One introduced the theory of 'purposes,' or *maqāṣid*, of the Islamic law, as a contemporary project for development and reform in the Islamic law. Chapter One, furthermore, demonstrated how *al-maqāṣid* theory meets the basic methodological criteria of rationality, utility, justice, and morality. Based on the survey of traditional and contemporary theories of Islamic law presented previously this section will show how the 'purposefulness' feature, or a purpose/*maqāṣid*-based approach could contribute to the development of the fundamentals of Islamic law and current attempts to address some of its inadequacies. Each subsection will deal with one area within the fundamental *uṣūl*.

The 'Implication of the Purpose'

Perhaps under the influence of 'the principle of causation' in Greek philosophy, traditional 'implications' of terms and expressions from the scripts did not include a purpose, or *maqṣid*, implication. A 'clear expression' (the Ḥanafī '*ʿibārah*' or the Shāfiʿī '*ṣarīḥ*'), which was given priority over all other expressions, is a direct reading of the script. This reading applies the literal meaning in the name of being *muḥkam*, *naṣṣ*, or *ẓāhir*. The 'purpose' of the expression would probably fall under one of the 'non-clear' categories: 'in need of explanation' (*mufassar*), 'indirect implication' (*ishārah*); 'omitted expression' (*iqtiḍa'*); or 'alluding (to the appropriateness factor)' (*īmā'*). These types of terms, as explained before, lack juridical authority (*ḥujjiyyah*) because of their 'uncertainty' (*ẓanniyyah*).

Moreover, contrary implications, applied by all schools except for the Ḥanafīs, were restricted to the categories of title (*al-laqab*), attribute (*al-waṣf*), condition (*al-sharṭ*), limit (*al-ghāyah*), and number (*al-ʿadad*). This means that if one of these expressions is used in a script, the 'contrary' expression is excluded, regardless of the 'purpose' consideration. Thus, any 'title,' 'attribute,' 'condition,' 'limit,' or 'number,' that is different from what is mentioned in the script, is unacceptable, even if it happens to achieve the 'purpose' of the same script in a similar or better way. The purpose is, again, too 'uncertain' to 'oppose' the 'logical' contrary evidence. This added to the general literal character of linguistic evidences, which were also given priority over all other rational evidences. Thus, as Ibn Ashur writes, 'jurists gave themselves unnecessary trouble by seeking to clarify the ambiguous and qualify the unrestricted ... even though ... scripts covering the particulars of individual cases are equally open to generalisation and particularisation.' [182]

Lack of an 'implication of purposes' is a general drawback in dealing with 'legal texts,' even in contemporary schools of philosophy of law.[183] The German school, especially Jhering,[184] and French school, especially Gény,[185] called for greater 'purposefulness' in the law. Both schools called for a 'reconstruction' of the law based on 'interests' and the 'purpose of justice.'[186] Jhering called for the replacement of the 'mechanical law of causality' with the 'law of purpose.' He articulated his view as follows:

> In 'Cause,' the object upon which the effect is produced is passive. The object appears simply as a single point in the universe at which the law of causality is carried out in that moment. In 'purpose,' on the other hand, the thing which is set in motion by it appears as self-active; it acts. Cause belongs to the past, purpose to the future. External nature, when questioned regarding the reason of its processes, directs the questioner to look back; whilst the will directs him forward ... But however the purpose may be combined with the act, and whatever the nature of the purpose may be, without a purpose action is unthinkable. *Acting, and acting with a purpose, are synonymous.* An act without a purpose is just as much an impossibility as is an effect without a cause.[187]

Moreover, Gény called for a method that gives more significance to 'legislative intent,' which is 'derived from the text' and, thus, 'dictates the interpreter's decision.'[188] However, these calls did not materialise into major changes in the general methodology of today's positive law.[189] Thus, the enhancing of 'purposefulness' is a much needed component for philosophy of law, in general.

In Islamic jurisprudence, '*dilālah al-maqṣid*' (The implication of the purpose) is a new expression that has recently appeared in Islamic modernist expressions of *uṣūl al-fiqh*.[190] So far, however, this implication is generally not considered 'certain' (*qaṭʿiyyah*) enough to be given specific juridical authority (*ḥujjiyyah*). Chapter Five showed that many 'modernists' criticise contemporary 'literalism' in Islamic law, and even define themselves as a center between the 'extremes of literalism and secularism.' Nonetheless, literalism remains a general feature in modernist trends, including its reformist stream, as long as it gives ultimate theoretical authority (*ḥujjiyyah*) to the category of 'clear' linguistic evidence over 'unclear and uncertain' expressions of *maqāṣid* and higher values.

Moreover, Islamic modernism did not take a clear position on the issue of 'uncertainty' of *maqāṣid* and *maṣāliḥ*. Al-Shāṭibī's position was more supportive of *al-maqāṣid* when he described them as the 'fundamentals of religion, basic rules of the revealed law, and universals of belief' (*uṣūl al-dīn wa qawāʿid al-sharīʿah wa kullīiyyah al-millah*).[191] Ibn Ashur, the leading modernist '*maqāṣidī*,' described *al-maqāṣid* as 'certain or uncertain close to certain' (*qaṭʿī aw ẓannī qarīb min al-qaṭʿī*).[192] Yet, so far, 'purposefulness' is proscribed, theoretically speaking, from playing a primary role in the derivation of rulings from related scripts.

On the other hand, Islamic postmodernism 'deconstructed' *al-maqāṣid* of the scripts, much as it deconstructed the scripts themselves. Chapter Five explained how 'Islamic postmodernists' call a modernist

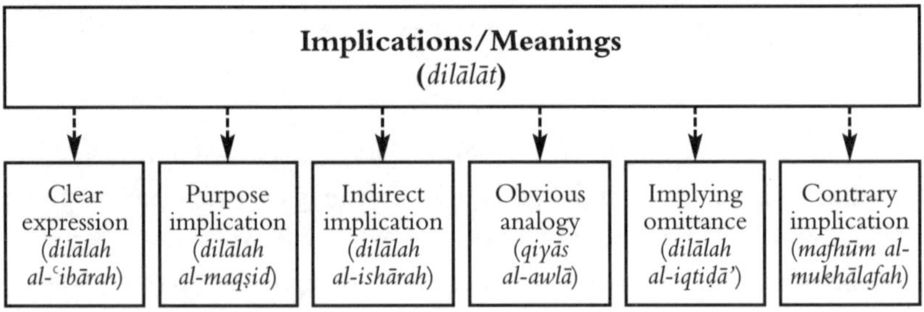

Chart 6.7. Adding the implications of the purpose (dilālah al-maqṣid) to valid implications/meanings. Its priority should depend on the importance of the implied purpose.

interpretation based on *maṣlaḥah* or *maqāṣid* 'twisting and bending,'[193] 'a secular movement disguised by religious discourse,'[194] and a 'justification for oppressive rulers.'[195] Postmodernists accuse modernists of encouraging 'fundamentalism' via such interpretations.[196]

Nevertheless, the sub-system of linguistic evidences in the fundamentals of Islamic law could achieve more 'purposefulness' through the following specific suggestions:

1. The 'implication of the purpose' (*dilālah al-maqṣid*) should be added to the types of linguistic implications of the scripts (Chart 6.7). However, its 'priority,' relative to the other implications, should not be pre-set. It should be subject to the situation at hand and the importance of the *maqṣid* itself.
2. The possibility of specification (*takhṣīṣ*), interpretation (*ta'wīl*), and abrogation (*naskh*) were the three criteria that differentiated types of 'clear expressions,' namely, 'firmly constructed' (*muḥkam*), 'text' (*naṣṣ*), 'apparent' (*ẓāhir*), and 'explained' (*mufassar*). In addition to the above levels of clarity being 'arbitrary,' as I had argued in Chapter Four, *al-maqāṣid* themselves could be bases for specification and interpretation. An expression could be specified, or interpreted, via its purpose or purposes of other 'opposing' expressions. On the other hand, 'abrogation' is a form of gradual application of the rulings that should be understood in line with the purpose of 'magnanimity' of the Islamic law.
3. The purpose of the expression should also decide the validity of its 'contrary implication,' as opposed to the way this validity is decided via a 'logical' debate over whether or not 'one ratio legis could imply two opposite rulings simultaneously.'[197] Thus, if 'contrary' expressions are implied by other scripts, then all 'opposing' implications should be considered within a higher purpose or *maqṣid*.
4. A scriptural expression of a higher purpose of the law, which is usually a 'general' and 'unqualified' expression, should not be, as a general rule, 'specified' or 'qualified' by individual scripts. Nor should individual scripts be ignored for the sake of 'general' and 'unqualified' scripts. All expressions should be considered within a general framework of their purposes.

5. The relationship between 'qualified' and 'non-qualified' terms addressing the same ruling in different cases, which is a matter of difference of opinion, should be defined based on the achievement of *maqāṣid*, rather than on a general linguistic or logical rule.

Purposeful Interpretations of Primary Sources

The 'thematic exegesis school' took steps towards a more 'purposeful/*maqāṣidī*' Qur'anic exegesis. The method of reading the Qur'anic text in terms of themes, principles, and higher values, is based on a perception of the Qur'an as a 'unified whole.'[198] Based on this holistic approach, the small number of verses related to rulings, which are traditionally called the 'verses of the rulings' (*āyāt al-aḥkām*), will extend from a few hundred verses to the entire text of the Qur'an. Chapters and verses addressing faith, prophets' stories, the hereafter, and nature, will then all comprise parts of a holistic picture and, thus, play a role in shaping juridical rulings. This approach will also allow principles and moral values, which are the main themes behind the Qur'anic stories and sections on the hereafter, to become ratio legis (*ʿilal*) for the rulings, in addition to the literal 'causes' that are 'extracted' via traditional methods of extraction of the grounds (*takhrīj al-manāṭ*). This would aid in eliminating the alternatives (*tanqīḥ al-manāṭ*), and asserting the realisation of the ratio legis (*taḥqīq al-manāṭ*), as explained earlier.

A purpose-oriented approach to the narrations of hadith proceeds from a similar holistic perception of the Prophet's life and sayings. This method also attempts to draw a holistic picture of the prophetic tradition (Sunnah). The authenticity of individual narrations that are incoherent with obvious Islamic values would be put into question. This type of 'systematic incoherence' is different from the 'content incoherence' (*shudhūdh al-matn*) criterion in the traditional 'invalidating the content' (*taḍʿīf al-matn*) process. 'Content incoherence' means that a narration is in 'opposition' (*taʿāruḍ*) with some other narration (by the same or a different narrator). If jurists are not able to reconcile the (linguistic) implication of the two narrations (or the implication of their 'causes'/*ʿilal*), then the 'less certain' narration is considered incoherent. However, 'systematic incoherence' is inconsistency with the general principles of 'Islam,' as concluded via a holistic understanding of its scripts. Hence, 'systematic coherence' could be a name given to the method suggested by many modern reformists, which would then authenticate prophetic narrations, 'based on how much they agree with the principles of the Qur'an.'[199] Thus, 'systematic coherence' should be added to the conditions of authenticating the *matn* of prophetic narrations (which were previously summarised in Chart 4.6).

Finally, a *maqāṣid* approach could fill a crucial gap in the narration of hadith, in general, which is the gap of missing contexts. The vast majority of prophetic narrations, in all schools, are composed of one or two sentences or the answer of one or two questions, without elaborating on the historical, political, social, economical, or environmental context of the narration. In some cases, the companion or narrator ends his/her narration by saying: 'I am not sure whether or not the Prophet said ... because (we were in the context) of ....' Usually, however, the context and its impact on how the narration is understood and applied are left to the speculation of the narrator or jurist. The 'holistic picture' that was mentioned above helps in overcoming this lack of information through understanding the general purposes of the law.

Prophetic Purposes and Intents

Moreover, *al-maqāṣid*, in the sense of the intents of the Prophet, could also be utilised in contextualising narrations. It was explained, in Chapter Four, how al-Qarāfī differentiated between the Prophet's actions 'as a conveyer of the divine message, a judge, and a leader,' and suggested that each of these intents has a different 'implication in the law.' Ibn Ashur added other types of 'prophetic intents,' which is a significant expansion of the scope of *dilālāt* via *maqāṣid*. Ibn Ashur demonstrated the prophetic intents that he proposed via a number of hadith narrations.[200] The following are some examples, according to Ibn Ashur.[201]

1. The intent of legislation. One example is the Prophet's sermon at the farewell pilgrimage, during which he, reportedly, said: 'Learn your rituals from me [by seeing me performing them], for I do not know whether I will be performing pilgrimage after this pilgrimage of mine.' He also said after concluding the same sermon: 'Let those present inform those who are absent.'
2. The intent of issuing edicts/fatwa. One example is the Prophet's edicts during his 'farewell pilgrimage,' when a man came to him and said: 'I sacrificed before throwing the pebbles.' The Prophet advised: 'Throw, and don't worry.' Then another man came and said: 'I shaved before sacrificing,' and the Prophet answered: 'Sacrifice, and don't worry.' The narrator said that he was not asked about anything that one would do after or before without his saying, 'Do it, and don't worry.'
3. The intent of judgeship. Examples are: (1) the Prophet's settlement of the dispute between a man from Hadramawt and a man from Kindah regarding a piece of land; (2) the Prophet's settlement between the Bedouin and his adversary, when the Bedouin said: 'O Messenger of God, judge between us;' and (3) the Prophet's settlement between Ḥabībah and Thābit. Ḥabībah bint Ṣahl, Thābit's wife, complained to the Prophet that she did not love her husband and that she wanted to divorce him. The Prophet said: 'Will you give him back his walled garden?' She said: 'I have all that he has given to me.' Then, the Prophet said to Thabit: 'Take it from her.' And so he took his walled garden and divorced her.
4. The intent of leadership. Examples are the prohibition of eating donkey meat in the battle of Khaybar, the permission to cultivate barren lands, and the Prophet's statement at the battle of Ḥunayn: 'Whoever has killed an enemy and has evidence of his actions can claim the enemy's property.'
5. The intent of guidance (which is more general than that of legislation). An example is found in Ibn Suwayd's narration, in which he said: 'I met Abū Dharr, who was wearing a cloak, and his slave, too, was wearing a similar one. I asked the reason for it. He replied, "I scolded a slave by calling his mother bad names." The Prophet said to me, "O Abū Dharr! Did you abuse him by calling

his mother bad names? You still have some characteristics of the age of pagan ignorance. Your slaves are your brethren."'

6. The intent of conciliation. One example is when the Prophet requested Barīrah to return to her husband after she divorced him. Barīrah said: 'O God's Apostle! Do you order me to do so?' He said, 'No, I only intercede for him.' She said, 'I do not need him.' Also, Bukhārī reported that when Jābir's father died, Jābir asked the Prophet to speak with his father's creditors so that they might waive some of his debt. The Prophet then accepted their refusal to do so. Another example of conciliation is when Kaᶜab ibn Mālik demanded repayment of a debt from ᶜAbdullāh ibn Abū Ḥadrad, the Prophet requested Kaᶜab to deduct half of the debt, and Kaᶜab agreed.
7. The intent of giving advice. One example is when ᶜUmar ibn al-Khaṭṭāb gave someone a horse as charity and the man neglected it. ᶜUmar wished to buy the horse from the man, thinking that he would sell it cheaply. When he asked the Prophet about it, he told him: 'Do not buy it, even if he gives it to you for one dirham, for someone who takes back his charity is like a dog swallowing its own vomit.' Also, Zayd narrated that the Prophet said: 'Do not sell the fruits before their benefit is evident,' but Zayd commented that this was, 'only by way of advice, for some people had quarreled too much over that matter.'
8. The intent of counseling. For example Bashīr informed the Prophet that he had given one of his sons a special gift. The Prophet asked him: 'Have you done the same with all your sons?' He said: 'No.' The Prophet said: 'Do not call me as a witness to injustice.'
9. The intent of teaching high ideals. For example, the Prophet asked Abū Dharr: 'Do you see (the mountain of) Uḥud?' Abū Dharr replied: 'I do!' The Prophet said: 'If I had gold equal to the mountain of Uḥud, I would love that, before three days had passed, not a single Dinar thereof remained with me if I found somebody to accept it, excluding some amount that I would keep for the payment of my debts.' Similarly, al-Barā' ibn ᶜĀzib said: 'God's Messenger commanded us to practice seven things and prohibited us from practicing seven. He commanded us to visit the sick, to

walk behind funeral processions, to pray for someone upon sneezing, to approve of someone's oath, to help the oppressed person, to spread the greeting of peace, and to accept the invitation of the invitee. On the other hand, he prohibited us from wearing gold rings, using silver utensils, using red saddlecloth made of cotton, wearing Egyptian clothes with silky extensions, clothes made of thick silk, thin silk, or normal silk.' Similarly, ʿAlī ibn Abī Ṭālib narrates: 'God's Apostle forbade me to use gold rings, to wear silk clothes and clothes dyed with saffron, and to recite the Qur'an while bowing and prostrating in prayer. I am not saying he forbade you these things.' Likewise, with the same educational intent, the Prophet told Rafiʿ ibn Khadīj: 'Do not rent your farm, but cultivate the land yourself.'

10. The intent of disciplining his companions. For example, the hadith: 'By God! He does not believe! By God! He does not believe!' It was said, 'Who is that, O Messenger of God?' He said: 'The person whose neighbor does not feel safe from his evil.'
11. Intent of non-instruction. This includes the hadith that described the way the Prophet ate, wore his clothes, laid down, walked, mounted his animal, and placed his hands when prostrating in prayer. Another example is the report that the Prophet stopped on the farewell pilgrimage at a hill overlooking a watercourse in Banī Kinānah, on which ʿĀ'ishah commented: 'Camping at al-Abṭaḥ is not one of the ceremonies of hajj, but was simply a place where the Prophet used to camp so that it might be easier for him to leave for Madinah.'

Ibn Ashur's extension of the *dilālāt* of the hadith, as shown in the above examples, raises the level of 'purposefulness' in traditional methods and allows much flexibility in interpreting and applying the narrations.

Analogy via Purposes

The majority of schools and jurists allow analogy based on the *ʿillah* (cause) of the ruling and not the 'wisdom' (*ḥikmah*) behind the ruling, as previously explained. Their rationale is to preserve '*inḍibāt*' (that is exactness) of the ratio legis, which is its 'constancy with the change of time and place.' In other words, in order to preserve formality on a procedural level, jurists decide that the ratio legis behind a ruling should never change with circumstances. Even those who allow *al-ḥikmah* to become a ratio legis for rulings, made a condition that it should be 'exact.'[202]

However, a careful analysis of the 'exactness' of the *ʿillah* reveals that it is usually changeable and cannot be precisely defined, as Ibn Qudāmah, a key Ḥanbalī jurist, argued.[203] Ibn Qudāmah referred to the classic example of allowing an ill person to break his/her fasting based on the 'exactness' of the *ʿillah* of 'sickness,' and commented: 'But sickness is not "exact," because diseases vary. Some diseases harm a fasting person and some others are unrelated to fasting, such as toothaches, small wounds, blisters, minor ulcers, etc. Thus, "sickness" cannot be a valid criterion in its own right, and the wisdom, which is avoiding possible harm, should be endorsed as the criterion.'[204] Ibn Qudāmah's argument actually applies to all kinds of *ʿilal*. In addition, the 'wisdom' that he referred to in the above example is what jurists called *al-munāsabah*, or 'appropriateness,' of the *ʿillah*, or the 'fulfilment of the interest' (*taḥqīq al-maṣlaḥah*). As explained earlier in Chapter One, jurists began defining *maṣāliḥ* in terms of *maqāṣid* from the fifth Islamic century, and hence, they identified 'appropriateness' with 'purposefulness.'

However, once more, the 'uncertainty' of purposes prevented them from their approval as *ʿilal*, in their own right. Perhaps under the effect of Greek logic, especially Aristotle (through Ibn Sīnā), most jurists agreed to prefer deduction (*al-istinbāṭ*) over induction (*al-istiqrā'*) as their means for 'logic certainty' (*al-yaqīn al-manṭiqī*). Aristotle had argued that induction could be either complete (covering every related incident) or incomplete (not covering every related incident). Thus, he argued that given the 'uselessness of complete induction' and the 'uncertainty of incomplete induction,' induction is not a feasible tool for logical certainty.[205] This is the same argument, word for word, which jurists in various schools have used, from al-Rāzī and al-Ghazālī to al-Suyuṭī and al-Āmidī.[206] Thus, formal partial analogy, which is based on one evidence, has been given precedence over holistic purpose-based concepts, which are based on (incomplete) inductive surveys. The multi-dimensional view of 'certainty' which was presented in a previous section aims to support 'purposefulness' in the reasoning-by-analogy subsystem of the Islamic fundamentals of law.

Interests Coherent with Purposes

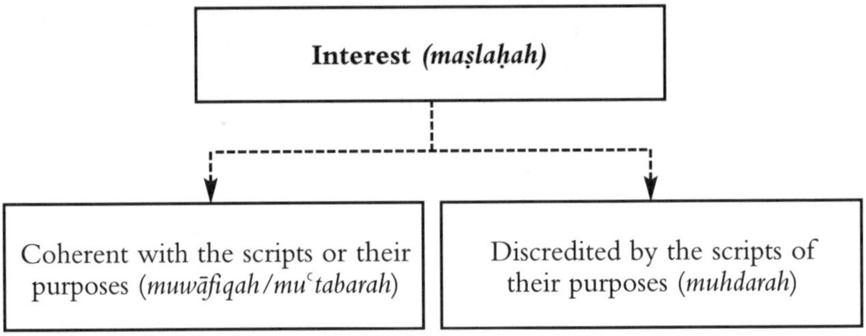

Chart 6.8. Classification of interests based on their coherence with the scripts or their purposes.

Many jurists were concerned that giving independent legitimacy to 'interests' might contradict with the scripts.[207] The same concern is expressed in philosophy of law regarding the relationship between claimed 'intents' and statutes. As such, the United States Supreme Court, and several British jurists, made a condition to the claiming of any intent. They maintain that, 'the only admissible source of evidence as to the legislator's specific intent is the text of the statute.'[208] I argue that this condition could also resolve the controversy over the independent legitimacy of '*maṣāliḥ*' in Islamic law. Since *maqāṣid* is 'induced' from the scripts, *maṣlaḥah* would have juridical legitimacy if it were identified with *maqāṣid*, as many jurists have suggested.[209] Hence, supported (*muʿtabarah*) and unrestricted (*mursalah*) interests will merge into one category of interests that are mentioned either explicitly or implicitly in the scripts, as long as they achieve 'purposefulness' in the system of law. Chart 6.8 represents this re-classification of interests.

Juridical Preference Based on Purposes

Schools of Islamic law that endorsed juridical preference (*istiḥsān*) claimed that they were trying to mend a gap in formal (syllogistic) analogy/*qiyās*.[210] In my view, the gap is not in the process of formal analogy, but rather in the literal definition of the cause/*ᶜillah*, which frequently misses the 'point' or the 'purpose' behind the ruling. Hence, *istiḥsān* simply meant to overlook the formalities of 'implications' and apply the purpose directly. The following are illustrative cases from Ibn al-Ḥasan al-Shaybānī's '*al-Mabsūt*.' Note the 'historicity' of many of these cases, which are recalled here only for illustrative purposes.

1. Abū Ḥanīfa applied *istiḥsān* in pardoning criminals, such as looters, after a long period of time, in which a looter, 'moved away, proved to have changed, and repented.' He decided not to apply a punishment in this case, despite the existence of its *ᶜillah* (cause), because, 'the purpose of punishment is to deter people from crime, which no longer applies to such cases.'[211]
2. Trade transactions with payments postponed until certain events take place (at an undefined time) are 'void,' according to Ḥanafīs. However, for people's best interest, Ibn al-Ḥasan al-Shaybānī applied *istiḥsān* to legalise this transaction on condition that the buyer pays the due amount immediately.[212]
3. Abū Ḥanīfa allowed 'ambiguities' in contracts that 'do not lead to disputes according to local customs,' such as, 'the ambiguity in the width or height of a building.' A literal application of the narrations that 'did not allow ambiguities in contracts' goes against Abū Ḥanīfa's opinion. However, Abū Ḥanīfa applied *istiḥsān* by considering the 'purpose' of the narrations, which is to 'prevent disputes.'[213]
4. Similarly, Abū Ḥanīfa allowed rental contracts that were timed with 'inexact' timings, for instance, 'the time when the pilgrimage caravan leaves from Kufa to Makkah.' Unknown elements in a contract make it void, according to direct analogies with related hadith, but *istiḥsān* allows ambiguity in timing for the purpose of facilitation.[214]

5. Abū Ḥanīfa applied *istiḥsān* in allowing Arabic words of 'engagement' (*khiṭbah*) to be used as marriage vows, 'if these are the words that people use in a particular dialect with an "intent" (*murād*) to get married.'[215] Again, consideration is given to the 'purpose' or 'intent' here.
6. If the buyer of an animal rides it after buying it, then he/she is declaring it 'acceptable,' as Ḥanafīs judge. However, if he/she rides this animal with an 'intent' of leading it where it is supposed to eat or drink, then this is not a 'declaration of acceptance,' based on an *istiḥsān* which considered the intent of the action.[216]
7. If a cat drinks from a cup, then its saliva makes that cup 'unclean' (*najis*), according to Ḥanafīs, 'based on an analogy between its saliva and its meat, which is forbidden.' However, because of the 'difficulty of applying this ruling to domestic cats,' Abū Ḥanīfa decided to judge this cup as 'clean but detested.' Thus, the purpose of 'facilitation' was the criterion for deciding on this matter.[217]
8. Abū Ḥanīfa applied *istiḥsān* in allowing the payment of zakah on camels in terms of sheep, as the hadith states, or in terms of camels, contrary to the literal wordings of the hadith, 'because this is going to be more beneficial for the owner of the herd.' Thus, the purpose of benefit was the criterion for deciding on this matter.[218]

Most repugnant ends: Forbidden means	Ends 'in between': Lawful means	Best ends: Obligatory means

Chart 6.9. Levels of ends and alternative levels of means, according to al-Qarāfī.

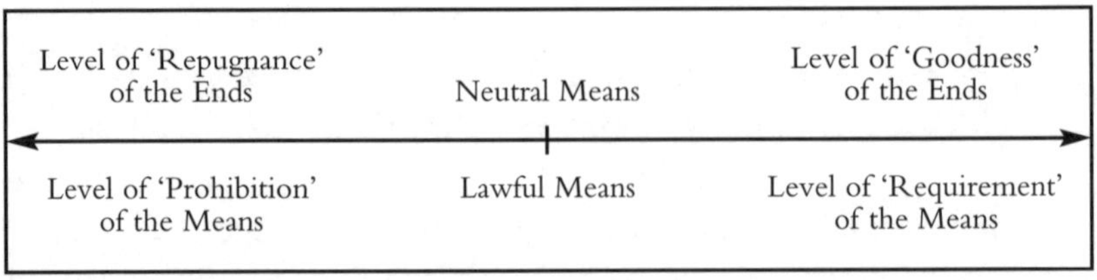

Chart 6.10. A spectrum of levels between good ends/required means and repugnant ends/prohibited means.

Therefore, as the above examples clearly show, *istiḥsān* is basically a form of adding 'purposefulness' to juridical reasoning. Nevertheless, schools of law that did not endorse *istiḥsān* had attempted to realise 'purposefulness' via other methods.

'Opening the Means' to Achieve Good Ends and Maqāṣid

Some Mālikīs proposed 'opening the means' (*fatḥ al-dharā'iᶜ*) in addition to 'blocking' them (*sadd al-dharā'iᶜ*).[219] Al-Qarāfī divided rulings into means (*wasā'il*) and ends/purposes (*maqāṣid*). He suggested that means that lead to prohibited ends should be blocked, and means that lead to lawful ends should be opened.[220] Thus, al-Qarāfī linked the ranking of means to the ranking of their ends, and he suggested three levels for ends, namely, 'most repugnant' (*aqbaḥ*), best (*afḍal*), and 'in between' (*mutawassiṭah*), as Chart 6.9 illustrates. Ibn Farḥūn (d. 769 AH), also from the Mālikī school, applied al-Qarāfī's 'opening the means' to a number of rulings.[221]

Thus, Mālikīs do not restrict themselves to the negative side of 'consequentialist' thinking, to borrow a term from moral philosophy. They expand this method of thinking to the positive side of it, which entails opening means to achieving good ends, even if these ends were not mentioned in specific scripts. And in order to give al-Qarāfi's *maqāṣid*-based expansion of blocking the means more flexibility, Chart 6.10 suggests a 'continuous' measure of 'goodness' and 'repugnance' of ends, to use al-Qarafi's expressions. 'Neutral' ends, then, would entail 'lawful' means.

Customs and the Purpose of 'Universality'

Al-Tahir ibn Ashur proposed a novel view of the fundamental of 'custom' (*al-ᶜurf*) based on the purposes of Islamic law. He wrote a chapter in his '*Maqāṣid al-Sharīᶜah*' on *al-ᶜurf*, which was entitled with a *maqṣid* that he called, 'The Universality of the Islamic Law.'[222] In this chapter, Ibn Ashur did not consider the effect of custom on the application of narrations, as is the traditional view. Instead, he considered the effect of (Arabic) customs on narrations themselves. The following is a summary of Ibn Ashur's argument.

First, Ibn Ashur explained that it is necessary for the Islamic law to be a universal law, since it claims to be 'applicable to all humankind everywhere on earth at all times,' as per a number of Qur'anic verses and hadith that he cited.[223] Then, Ibn Ashur elaborated on the wisdoms behind choosing the Prophet from amongst Arabs, such as the Arabs' isolation from civilisation, which prepared them, 'to mix and associate openly with other nations with whom they had no hostilities, in contrast to Persians, Byzantines, and Copts.' Yet, for the Islamic law to be universal, 'its rules and commands should apply equally to all human beings as much as possible,' as Ibn Ashur confirmed. That is why, he wrote, 'God had based the Islamic law on wisdoms and reasons that can be perceived by the mind and which do not change according to nations and custom.' Thus, Ibn Ashur provided explanation as to why the Prophet forbade his companions to write down what he says, 'lest particular cases be taken as universal rules.' Ibn Ashur began applying his ideas to a number of narrations, in an attempt to filter out Arabic customs from popular traditional rulings. He wrote:[224]

> Therefore, Islamic law does not concern itself with determining what kind of dress, house, or mount people should use ... Accordingly, we can establish that the customs and mores of a particular people have no right, as such, to be imposed on other people as legislation, not even the people who originated them ... This method of interpretation has removed much confusion that faced scholars in understanding the reasons why the law prohibited certain practices ... such as the prohibition for women to add hair extensions, to cleave their teeth, or to tattoo themselves ... The correct meaning of this, in my view ... is that these practices mentioned in hadith were, according to Arabs, signs of a woman's lack of chastity. Therefore, prohibiting these practices was actually aimed at certain evil motives ... Similarly, we read: ... 'believing women should draw over themselves some of their outer garments' (*Surat al-Aḥzāb*) ... This is a legislation that took into consideration an Arab tradition, and therefore does not necessarily apply to women who do not wear this style of dress ...

Therefore, based on the purpose of 'universality' of the Islamic law, Ibn Ashur suggested a method of interpreting narrations through understanding their underlying Arabic cultural context, rather than treating them as absolute and unqualified rules. Thus, he read the above narrations in terms of their higher moral purposes, rather than norms in their own right. This method of dealing with customs enhances 'purposefulness' in the system of Islamic law.

Presumption of Continuity

The principle of 'presumption of continuity' (*istiṣḥāb*) is a 'logical evidence' (*dalīl ʿaqlī*), as jurists say. However, the application of this principle could be viewed as an implementation of the higher purposes of Islamic law. For example, the 'presumption of innocence until proven guilty' is aimed to maintain the purpose of justice,[225] the presumption of permissibility until proven forbidden is aimed to maintain the purposes of magnanimity and freedom of choice,[226] and the presumption of continuity of certain attributes, such as, limited financial ability,[227] and intention for worship (*niyyah al-ʿibādah*),[228] are aimed to maintain the purpose of facilitation.

In addition, al-Turabi suggested an expansion of the traditional presumption of continuity to a 'wide presumption of continuity,' where 'all values, such as justice, family, and even rituals, as they were known and practiced by people according to their sincere disposition,' are to be 'presumed as default.' The only exception from this rule of 'presumption of continuity,' is what the revealed law had corrected and amended.[229] Thus, the principle of 'presumption of continuity,' in its classic and modernist forms, is a form of realisation of the purposes of Islamic law.

'Purposefulness' as Common Grounds for Schools of Law

Today, in the beginning of the twenty-first century, sharp 'scholastic' divisions take the shape of a Sunni-Shia division, which many like to perceive as a 'sectarian' division, for various motives. The juridical and 'narrational' differences between various Sunni and Shia schools, as outlined in the previous chapters, boil down to their 'politics' rather than their 'faith.' However, today, deep divisions between Sunni and Shia are constructed through courts, mosques, and social dealings in most countries, causing these divisions to develop into violent conflict in a number of countries. These divisions have added to a wide-spreading culture of civil intolerance and inability of coexistence with the 'Other.'

I carried out a survey on the latest studies on *al-maqāṣid*, which were written by key Sunni and Shia scholars. The survey revealed to me an interesting identicalness between both approaches to *maqāṣid*.[230] Both approaches address the same topics (ijtihad, *qiyās, ḥuqūq, qiyam, akhlāq*, and so on), refer to the same jurists and books (al-Juwaynī's *Burhān*, Ibn Bābawayh's *ᶜIlal al-Sharā'iᶜ*, al-Ghazālī's *Mustaṣfā*, al-Shāṭibī's *Muwāfaqāt*, and Ibn Ashur's *Maqāṣid*), and use the same theoretical classifications (*maṣāliḥ, ḍarūrāt, ḥājiyyāt, taḥsīniyyat, maqāṣid ᶜāmmah, maqāṣid khāṣṣah*, and so on). Most of the juridical differences between Sunni and Shia *fiqhī* schools are due to differences over *āḥād* narrations and detailed rulings. A *maqāṣidī* approach to fiqh is a holistic approach that does not restrict itself to one narration or partial ruling, but rather refers to general principles and common ground. Implementing the 'higher' purposes of unity and reconciliation of Muslims has a higher priority over implementing *fiqhī* details. Accordingly, Ayatullah Mahdi Shamsuddin prohibited aggression along Shia-Sunni lines based on 'the higher and fundamental purposes of reconciliation, unity, and justice.'[231] A *maqāṣidī* approach takes the issues to a higher philosophical ground and, hence, overcomes differences over the political history of Muslims and encourages a much-needed culture of conciliation and peaceful co-existence.

Purposefulness as the Fundamental Criteria for Ijtihad

Based on the above analysis of 'purposefulness' in various fundamental linguistic and rational evidences/methods, it is clear that the realisation of purposes is not specific to a few *uṣūl* methods, such as analogy or interest, the latter of which many traditional and contemporary theories suggested. I argue that the realisation of the purposes/*maqāṣid* of the Islamic law is the core objective of all fundamental linguistic and rational methodologies of ijtihad, irrespective of their various names and approaches. Moreover, the realisation of *maqāṣid*, from a systems point of view, maintains openness, renewal, realism, and flexibility in the system of Islamic law.

Therefore, the validity of any ijtihad should be determined based on its level of 'purposefulness,' i.e., the level of its realisation of *maqāṣid al-sharīʿah*. Likewise, the validity of a ruling should be determined based on its level of the realisation of *maqāṣid*. A choice between alternative rulings, or outcomes of ijtihad, is traditionally carried out through a fixed ranking of the fundamental methods involved in that ijtihad, such as, consensus, analogy, companion's opinion, or the tradition of the People of Madinah. Schools of law differed over the ranking of fundamental methods. However, based on the above analysis of 'purposefulness' in fundamental methods, a choice between alternative outcomes of ijtihad should be carried out based on the fulfilment of *maqāṣid*, regardless of the jurist's school or tendency. The outcome that achieves its *maqṣid* should be validated. Thus, if the implication of one *maqṣid* goes against the implication of another, the *maqṣid* that is deemed higher, based on the hierarchies previously explained in Chapter One, should be given precedence. In conclusion, hence the process of ijtihad becomes, effectively, a process of realising 'purposefulness' in Islamic law.

7

Conclusions

This book presented research in a number of areas related to the proposed systems approach to the philosophy and fundamentals of Islamic law. The following is a summary of my own research findings in this work, which range from theoretical conclusions to *fiqhī* opinions. I decided to divide these findings according to the various themes they fell under.

Classic Conceptions and Classifications of Maqāṣid

Traditional and contemporary definitions and classifications of *maqāṣid* were given a special attention in this book. Jurists used the term '*maqāṣid*' to refer to purposes, objectives, principles, intents, goals, ends, and telos. Also, *maqāṣid* was often used as alternative expressions to 'interests' (*maṣāliḥ*). *Maqāṣid* were previously classified in various ways, according to a number of dimensions, namely, levels of necessity, scope of the rulings aiming to achieve purposes, scope of people included in purposes, and levels of universality of objectives, which I found quite similar to the twentieth century's Abraham Maslow's hierarchy of human objectives.

On the other hand, contemporary legal theorists criticised traditional classification of necessities (*ḍarūrāt*) for a number of reasons, including their individualistic scope, not including universal norms/values, and being based exclusively on surveys of *fiqhī* literature rather than original scripts. Thus, contemporary scholarship introduced new classifications of *al-maqāṣid* based on avoiding the above limitations. These new *maqāṣid* were representations of each scholar's own viewpoint for reform and 'modernisation' in the Islamic law. Thus, the 'structure' of *al-maqāṣid* is best described as a multi-dimensional structure, in which levels of necessity, scope of rulings, scope of people, and levels of universality are all valid dimensions that represent valid viewpoints and classifications.

Moreover, I agree with al-Tahir ibn Ashur that the *maqṣid* of 'freedom' (*ḥurriyyah*), which was proposed by a number of contemporary writers and jurists, is different from the purpose of 'freedom' (*ḥurriyyah* or *ᶜitq*), mentioned in traditional schools, which only meant freedom from slavery (defined in the historic sense), rather than freedom (or liberty) in the contemporary sense. However, the basic meaning of freedom is part and parcel of a number of Islamic concepts that were expressed in different terms.

This book also presented a historical survey of the theory of *maqāṣid al-sharīᶜah*, starting with the post-prophetic era and until modern times. The following is a summary of this survey, starting with the companions' ijtihad, especially Omar's, until al-Shāṭibī, who developed the theory to its classic form.

'ᶜUmar's ijtihad' is proof that the companions did not always apply what *uṣulīs* later called *dilālah al-lafẓ* (the implication of the term), and that they frequently applied what this book called '*dilālah al-maqṣid*.' However, the idea of *maqāṣid* was not the subject of separate monographs or special attention until the end of the third Islamic century, when the first known volume, in which the term '*al-maqāṣid*' was used in the title of a monograph on prayers written by al-Tirmidhī al-Ḥakīm. On the other hand, the first known book on the *maqāṣid* of worldly dealings (*muᶜāmalāt*) is Abū Zayd al-Balkhī's *al-Ibānah ᶜan ᶜilal al-diyanah* (Revealing Purposes in Religious Practices). The oldest manuscript that I found in the Egyptian Dār al-Kutub on the topic of *al-maqāṣid* was al-Qaffāl's *Maḥāsin al-Sharā'iᶜ* (The Beauties of the Laws). This book calls for more attention to be given to this manuscript being an important step in the development of *al-maqāṣid* theory. Finally, contrary to the view that research on *maqāṣid al-sharīᶜah* was restricted to the Sunni schools of law until the twentieth century, Ibn Babaweah al-Sadouk al-Qummi's "*ᶜilal al-Sharā'iᶜ*" (The Reasons behind the Rulings) is the earliest Shia book on *maqāṣid*.

Regarding the history of the *ḍarūrāt* terminology, the earliest known theoretical classification was introduced by al-ᶜĀmirī al-Faylasūf in his, *al-Iᶜlām bi-Manāqib al-Islām* (Awareness of the Traits of Islam). Then, Al-Juwaynī coined the various terms of 'necessities' that are used until today. Al-Juwaynī's '*Ghiāth al-Umam*' (The Salvage of the Nations) is another important contribution to *al-maqāṣid* theory and an early project for the 're-construction' of the whole Islamic law based on its *maqāṣid*. Abū Ḥāmid al-Ghazālī, al-Juwaynī's student, did not give independent legitimacy (that is, *ḥujjiyyah*) to any of his proposed *maqāṣid/maṣāliḥ*, perhaps, under the influence of his Shāfiᶜī school. Yet, al-Ghazālī made an important contribution by using the *maqṣid* as ratio legis (*ᶜillah*), despite its alleged 'non-exactness.' Finally, the most significant development of the *maqāṣid* theory was al-Shāṭibī's '*al-Muwāfaqāt fī Uṣūl al-Sharīᶜah*' (Congruences in the Fundamentals of the Revealed Law). I accounted for three ways in which al-Shāṭibī developed the theory of *maqāṣid*, namely, from 'unrestricted interests' to 'fundamental of law,' from 'wisdoms behind the ruling' to 'bases for the ruling,' and lastly, from 'uncertainty' (*ẓanniyyah*) to 'certainty' (*qaṭᶜiyyah*).

Contemporary Conceptions of Maqāṣid and Their Significance

This book surveyed the evolution of *al-maqāṣid* theories and conceptions, and argued that current conceptions are closer to addressing current issues than classic conceptions. It was shown how the 'preservation of offspring' evolved into 'care for the family' and proposals for a civil 'Islamic social system,' how the 'preservation of mind' evolved into 'propagation of scientific thinking,' 'travelling for the pursuit of knowledge,' 'suppressing the herd mentality,' and even 'avoiding brain drain,' and how the 'preservation of honor' evolved into 'preservation of human dignity' and 'protection of human rights.' I suggested that a *maqāṣid*-based approach to the issue of human rights could support the Universal Islamic Declaration of Human Rights and the view that Islam could add 'new positive dimensions to human rights.'

On the other hand, the 'preservation of religion' was shown to have evolved to 'freedom of belief' in contemporary expressions, and the 'preservation of wealth' was shown to have evolved to 'economic development' and 'diminishing the difference between economic levels.' This book suggested 'human development' as a contemporary expression of *maṣlaḥah*, which could be measured empirically via the UN 'human development targets.'

Multi-Disciplinarity

The multi-disciplinary research experience of this work lead me to conclude that 'disciplinisation' should not be an obstacle in the way of using relevant concepts from 'different' fields in research endeavors. Nor should it be a way of monopolising sources of reference in any discipline in order to restrain creativity and control new ideas. In terms of developing the discipline of the theory/fundamentals of Islamic law, it is necessary to be open to relevant ideas from other disciplines. Otherwise, the Islamic legal theory will remain strictly within the boundaries of traditional literature and its manuscripts, and the outcome rulings of Islamic law will remain largely 'outdated.'

Systems Analysis

Historically, the general orientation of philosophical analysis was partial rather than holistic and mainly focused on static relationships between decomposed elements, unlike systems analysis which is a holistic and dynamic approach. Systems analysis is based on the definition of systems, i.e., the analyst assumes that the analysed entity is 'a system,' and proceeds to identify its features, as defined in systems theory. However, current systems-based methods are still based on the simple definition of systems as 'sets of interacting units,' and, hence, is missing a variety of system features that could be of use to analysis. Moreover, many hierarchy-based theories are primarily oriented to the physical world of matter and, hence, not applicable to investigation in the realm of ideas and law. Also, many systems-based classifications are still binary and one-dimensional, contrary to the multidimensional feature of systems that was proposed by systems theorists.

To remedy the above limitations, this book suggested a number of basic systems features and utilised them in the analysis of the 'system' of Islamic law, namely, the cognitive nature of systems, wholeness, openness, interrelated hierarchy, multi-dimensionality, and purposefulness, the latter being the core system feature in this work.

Classifying Theological Schools Regarding 'Causation'

This book also surveyed the various positions that schools of Islamic theology (*al-madhāhib al-kalāmiyyah*) took regarding the applicability of the 'principle of causation' (*al-sababiyyah*) to God. Muᶜtazilīs and Shia judged that divine actions 'must' have causes/purposes, based on the principle of embellishment and repugnance (*al-taḥsīn wa al-taqbīḥ*). Ashᶜarites and Salafīs judged that divine actions are above causes and purposes, and that without the sharīᶜah, actions are equally 'embellished' and 'repugnant.' Finally, Maturidites attempted to strike a middle ground between the above two opinions by judging that divine actions have causes/purposes out of God's grace, not out of the principle of *al-taḥsīn wa al-taqbīḥ*.

Criticising 'causation,' however, does not entail the deconstruction of theology, as many systems theorists claimed. This book argues that there is no association between the concept of God and the idea of 'causation' except in the minds of theologians who used 'the principle of causation' to prove the existence of God. Thus, the 'principle of holism' could provide an alternative and updated argument for the existence of God and other classic theological proofs. Therefore, a systems approach is useful for contemporary renewal proposals in theology as well.

What is 'Islamic Law'?

This book called for a clear distinction between a number of terms, all of which have been used synonymously with 'Islamic law' in literature written in the English language, namely, fiqh, shariᶜah, *qanūn*, and *ᶜurf*. The term 'fiqh' is understood to represent the 'cognitive' part of the Islamic law, while the term 'shariᶜah' represents the 'heavenly' part of this law (from the believers's perspective). Blurring the line between fiqh and sharīᶜah gives way to claims of 'divinity' and 'sanctity' in human juridical ijtihad, and contributes to violence based on mutual accusations of heresy and resistance of renewal in the Islamic law. On the other hand, *qanūn* and *ʿurf* represent specific legal systems and customs, respectively.

The Evolution of Traditional Schools of Islamic Law

This book summarised the factors that led to the formation of 'supporters of opinion' (*ahl al-ra'ī*) and the 'supporters of narration' (*ahl al-athar*) tendencies as follows: political/sectarian conflicts, migration of the companions, and personalities of the imams of the time. *Ahl al-ra'ī* tendency was not restricted to Iraq because the Ḥijāzī school, especially in Madinah, also practiced *al-ra'ī* through the method of interest/*maṣlaḥah*, especially in the fiqh of Mālik and his students. Nor was the difference between *ahl al-ra'ī* and *ahl al-athar* a matter of 'traditionists' versus 'liberals,' because both schools represented alternative methodologies of authenticating and applying the scripts.

I also criticised the traditional 'feature-based' classification of schools of Islamic law, which misses the similarity between 'evidences' that have different names in different schools and the differences between 'evidences' that have similar names. Traditional classifications also did not account for other non-binary features, such as historical and geographical factors.

Then, tracing 'chains of studentship' proves that, generation after generation, schools of law grew more isolated, and that the 'era of declination' started when jurists started to be trained in one *madhhab* only and call the imam and his students's opinions 'scripts,' and when their books become exceedingly abstract and complex.

Fundamental Sources/Scripts

There is a general agreement in all existing schools of Islamic law over the contents of the Qur'an, as it exists today. ʿAbdullāh ibn Masʿūd's version, which is endorsed by the Ḥanafī School for the purposes of the law, did not produce significantly different opinions from the rest of the schools of law. Significant differences, especially between Sunni and Shia schools, remain in the area of *kalām* and political positions over the companions' civil war, rather than sources and rulings in the Islamic law.

Schools of law differed over what to be included in the Prophet's 'conveying of the divine message.' This book argues that narrations such as 'pollenating of the palm trees' and '*al-ghīlah*' keep what is to be included in the category of the 'worldly affairs of the Prophet,' an open question. Similarly, the view that classifies the Prophet's worldly actions contrary to his 'acts of worship' (*ibādāt*), which are defined as actions that 'cannot be rationalised,' also keeps the question on how to define *ibādāt* open.

Linguistic Evidences

Classifications of levels of clarity, such as *muḥkam*, *naṣṣ*, and *ẓāhir* proved to be largely 'arbitrary,' given all the differences over what entails specification, interpretation, and abrogation for the vast majority of scripts and narrations. The method of 'contrary implication' is also criticised being equivalent to a strict 'exclusive-OR' logical tool that does not allow variations in rulings based on the situation. Thus, the method of 'contrary implication' contributes to an increase in the number of 'opposition' (*taᶜāruḍ*) cases and related cancellation and abrogation decisions. The analysis also showed that due to the priority given to linguistic implications, jurists resorted to the fundamentals of 'specifity' and 'qualification' more than the fundamentals of 'social justice' and 'common good.'

Rational Evidences

The rest of the *uṣūlī* evidences were analysed in terms of the differences of opinion over their legitimacy, as well as their similarities and agreement with *al-maqāṣid*. The following are my main findings in this area in a point form.

1. There is no 'consensus' over any definition of 'consensus' (ijmāᶜ).
2. There is a difference between *ᶜillah*, *ḥikmah*, and *maqṣid* in analogical reasoning.
3. Every school of law that rejected the fundamental method of '*maṣlaḥah*' replaced it with some alternative evidence, except for the Ẓāhirī school.

4. 'Blocking the means' is a consequentialist approach that could be misused by some pessimistic jurists or politically-motivated authorities.
5. Presumption of continuity (*istiṣḥāb*) is a reasoning principle, rather than a 'source of legislation' in its own right.

Contemporary Theories in Islamic Law

After a survey of current classifications of Islamic 'tendencies' and 'ideologies,' this book concluded that these classifications still, for the most part, revolve around the 'classic' three-class typology of fundamentalism, modernism, and secularism. RAND's recent classification of 'tendencies' is an extensive study that deserves a special analysis. However, it is by and large based on positions from the United States foreign policies, does not capture basic theoretical differences over fundamentals of Islamic law, inaccurately includes 'secular philosophers' in traditionalism's 'sources of Islamic law,' misclassifies 'historicity' as a 'modernist' trend, and does not differentiate between various streams of 'Islamic modernism.'

The popular three-fold literalism-reformism-westernisation classifications, usually proposed by centrist reformists are pigeon-hole classifications that assume consistency in their ideal types, classify scholars rather than methods, inaccurately use 'westernisation' and 'modernisation' as synonyms, and inaccurately label some rational views of the Islamic law as secular.

A Proposed Classification for Theories of Islamic Law

This book proposed a shift in the 'levels of authority' from the usual binary categorisation of valid/invalid evidences into a multi-level 'spectrum' of validity of evidences and sources. Current sources in theories of Islamic law are identified as Qur'anic verses, prophetic narrations, traditional schools of Islamic law, *maṣāliḥ*, rational arguments, and modern international declarations of rights. The current major 'tendencies' in various contemporary theories of Islamic law are identified as traditionalism, modernism, and postmodernism. Each of the above 'tendencies,' the book illustrates, is the result of a number of theoretical 'streams' that contributed to it, which could also overlap on specific issues.

Traditionalism includes the streams of scholastic traditionalism, scholastic neo-traditionalism, neo-literalism, and ideology-oriented theories. Scholastic traditionalism holds one of the traditional schools of Islamic law as the ultimate source of law and allows ijtihad only if there is no previous ruling in the chosen *madhhab*. Scholastic neo-traditionalism is open to more than one school of law for reference on valid rulings, and not restricted to one school. There are various degrees of this openness, from openness to all schools of law to openness to one circle of either Sunni or Shia schools. Neo-literalism is both a Sunni and Shia phenomenon, which differs from classic literalism in its complete dependence on the hadith collections approved only in one school of law. However, neo-literalism agrees with classic literalism in being against the idea of the purposes/*maqāṣid* as legitimate source of jurisprudence. Finally, ideology-oriented theories criticises modern 'rationality' and values for their biased 'western-centricity.'

Then, Islamic modernism includes the 'streams' of apologetic reinterpretation, reformist reinterpretation, dialogue-oriented reinterpretation, interest-oriented theories, and *uṣūl* revision. Key contributors to Islamic modernism integrated their Islamic and western education into new proposals for Islamic reform and 're-interpretation.'

Mohammad Abduh and his main students, Rashid Rida and al-Tahir ibn Ashur, contributed to a new school of Qur'anic exegesis that is 'coherent with modern science and rationality.' This school, which is referred to here as 'reformist re-interpretation,' introduced 'contextual interpretation' as a new methodology of exegesis. On the other hand, an apologetic re-interpretation school merely justified specific status quo, usually based on some political orientation. However, I argued that worldly matters should not be given a sacred halo by forcefully reading them into the Qur'an or hadith.

Finally, *uṣūl* revisionism attempted to revise *uṣūl al-fiqh*, through questioning the notions of 'consensus,' 'authenticity,' and 'abrogation,' and introducing new interpretations of *maṣlaḥah* (interest).

Islamic postmodernism included streams of post-structuralism, historicism, critical legal studies, post-colonialism, neo-rationalism, anti-rationalism, and secularism. The common method in all these postmodern approaches is 'deconstruction,' in a Derridean style. The post-structuralist stream aims to 'free people from the authority of the script,' and applies semiotic theory to the text of the Qur'an in order to 'separate the implication form the implied.' The historicist postmodern stream views the Qur'an and hadith as 'cultural products,' and suggests modern declarations of rights as sources for ethics and legislation. Neo-rationalists take a historicist approach to the Islamic law, and they refer to the conventional Muᶜtazilī/Rational school for a traditional reference for their views.

An Islamic version of Critical Legal Studies (CLS) aims to 'deconstruct' positions of 'power' that influenced the Islamic law, such as powerful Arabic tribes and 'male elitism.' There is a scholarly debate on whether jurists had 'served the interests of rulers' or 'protected the law from the rulers.' Islamic post-colonialism criticised classic orientalist approaches to the Islamic law, and called for approaches that are not based on 'essentialist fallacies (prejudices) about Islamic cultures.'

A Systems Approach to Theories of Islamic Law

Finally, this work presented a systems approach to the theories of Islamic law, in which the proposed systems features (cognitive nature of systems, wholeness, openness, interrelated hierarchy, multi-dimensionality, and purposefulness) are realised via specific theoretical suggestions. First, towards validating all 'cognitions,' this book argues that ijtihad should not be viewed as embodying 'God's commands,' even it were based on 'consensus' (ijmāᶜ) or analogical reasoning (*qiyās*). This position is similar to *al-muṣawwibah's* view, which is based on recognising the 'cognitive nature' of the Islamic law. Then, considering the Prophet's 'cognition' or 'intent' in his sayings and actions, this work utilised al-Qarāfī and Ibn Ashur's consideration of prophetic intents in order to expand the traditional messenger/human categorisation of prophetic actions. The additional category includes prophetic traditions with specific 'intents.'

Towards realising the feature of encouraging holistic views of the system of Islamic law, the book traced the impact of juridical thinking that is based on the 'principle of causation.' Al-Rāzī's concerns with claiming 'certainty' in single evidences were useful. However, al-Rāzī did not address the prime problem of atomistic approaches, which is their lack of comprehensiveness in their causation basis. Therefore, a systems approach is useful for contemporary renewal proposals in theology as well.

Towards realising the features of openness and self-renewal in the system of Islamic law, this book suggests the change of rulings with the change of the jurist's worldview or cognitive culture as a mechanism of openness in the system of Islamic law, and philosophical openness, as a mechanism of self-renewal in the system of Islamic law. Traditionally, the practical implication of the evidence of *al-ᶜurf* is quite limited, and Islamic rulings continue to be based on Arabic customs. Thus, a 'jurist's worldview' is proposed as an expansion to *al-ᶜurf* consideration, in order to achieve the 'universality' purpose of the law. The necessary skill for ijtihad, which jurists called '*fiqh al-wāqiᶜ*' (understanding the status quo), was developed to mean a jurist's 'competent worldview,' hence, 'opening' the system of Islamic law to advances in natural and social sciences.

Regarding 'philosophical openness,' the book finds that the theory of Islamic law did not benefit from original contributions that Islamic medieval philosophers made to philosophy and logic, for example, Avicenna's 'time dependant' syllogism, al-Fārābī's theory of inductive argumentation, Ibn Rushd's openness to all philosophical investigation, and Ibn Ḥazm and Ibn Taymiyah's critiques of Aristotelian logic. Islamic law could achieve self-renewal through openness to (renewable) philosophical investigation.

Towards achieving the feature of multi-dimensionality in the system of Islamic law, the roots of binary thinking that dominated schools of Islamic law were traced. First, the jurists' methods of '*tamyīz*' between concepts, whether essence- or description-based, always resulted in defining every concept in relation to some 'binary opposite.' For example, the quest for 'absolute certainty' (*yaqīn*) in juridical thinking, whether it takes the form of linguistic implication, historical authenticity, or logical implication, is unsubstantiated, and should be dealt with, theoretically speaking, according to a continuous (probability) spectrum, rather than the binary certain/uncertain classification. The evidence for this from Islamic sources is that the Qur'anic logic for proving the existence of God also takes a 'continuous,' rather than 'binary,' approach to certainty. On the other hand, multi-dimensionality combined with a *maqāṣidī* approach, could offer a theoretical solution to the dilemmas of opposing evidences. Then, although post-modern approaches to the Islamic law raise important questions about binary 'centricity,' they themselves tend to use binary and uni-dimensional approaches. A multi-dimensional approach to the theory of the Islamic law avoids such reductionist methodologies.

Finally, a number of specific *uṣūlī* proposals were made towards supporting the feature of 'purposefulness' in the system of Islamic law, which is the most fundamental feature for systems thinking, as this book had argued. The following is a summary of these proposals in a point form:

1. Juridical authority (*ḥujjiyyah*) is given to *dilālah al-maqṣid* (the implication of the purpose).
2. The priority of *dilālah al-maqṣid*, relative to other implications, should be subject to the situation at hand and the importance of the *maqṣid* itself.
3. The purpose of an expression should decide the validity of its 'contrary implication.'
4. A scriptural expression of a higher purpose of the law, which is usually a 'general' and 'unqualified' expression, should not be 'specified' or 'qualified' by individual scripts.
5. Moral values should have the status of ratio legis for related rulings, in addition to the literal 'causes' that are 'extracted' via traditional methods.
6. 'Systematic coherence' is a proposed expansion of the classic 'content coherence' (*ʿadam shudhūdh al-matn*).
7. A *maqāṣid* approach could fill the gap of missing contexts in the narration of hadith.
8. *Al-maqāṣid*, in the sense of the 'intents' of the Prophet, could also be utilised in 'contextualising' narrations, based on Ibn Ashur's proposed prophetic 'intents,' namely, legislation, issuing edicts,

judgeship, leadership, guidance, conciliation, advice, counseling, and non-instruction.

9. A careful analysis of the 'exactness' of the *ʿillah* reveals that it is usually changeable and cannot be 'precisely defined,' as traditionally claimed.
10. The controversy over the independent legitimacy of '*maṣāliḥ*' would cease to exist if they are related to 'purposefulness,' i.e., identified with '*maqāṣid*.'
11. *Istiḥsān* is a form of adding 'purposefulness' to juridical reasoning. Nevertheless, schools of law that did not endorse *istiḥsān* had attempted to realise 'purposefulness' via other methods.
12. 'Considering the means' should not be restricted to the negative side of the 'consequentialist' approach.
13. Al-Qarāfī's expansion of 'blocking the means' to also include 'opening the means' is further expanded via a suggested 'continuous' measure of 'goodness' and 'repugnance' of ends.
14. Ibn Ashur's analysis of the effect of (Arabic) customs on narrations themselves enhances the purpose of universality in the Islamic law.
15. The principle of 'presumption of continuity' (*istiṣḥāb*) is presented as an implementation of higher purposes of Islamic law, such as justice, facilitation, and freedom of choice.

Thus, a *maqāṣidī* approach takes the juridical issues to a higher philosophical ground, and hence, overcomes (historical) differences over politics between Islamic schools of law, and encourages a much-needed culture of conciliation and peaceful coexistence. Moreover, the realisation of purposes should be the core objective of all fundamental linguistic and rational methodologies of ijtihad, regardless of their various names and approaches. Therefore, the validity of any ijtihad should be determined based on its level of achieving 'purposefulness,' or realising *maqāṣid al-sharīʿah*.

NOTES

INTRODUCTION

1. Shams al-Dīn ibn al-Qayyim, *Iʿlām al-Muwaqqiʿīn*, ed. Taha Abdul Rauf Saad (Beirut: Dar al-Jīl, 1973), vol.3, p.3.
2. Based on: CIA, *The World Factbook*; available from http://www.cia.gov/cia/publications/factbook.
3. John L. Esposito, ed., *The Oxford History of Islam* (Oxford: University Press, 1999), p.690.
4. United Nation Development Programme UNDP, Annual Report (2005 [cited Jan. 2006]); available from http://www.undp.org/annualreports/.
5. (ṢAAS) – *Ṣallā Allāhu ʿalayhi wa sallam*. May the peace and blessings of God be upon him. Said whenever the name of Prophet Muhammad is mentioned.
6. Stephen Reed, *Cognition: Theory and Applications*, 4th ed. (USA: Brooks/Cole, 1996), p.220.
7. Al-Tahir ibn Ashur, *Maqāṣid al-Sharīʿah al-Islāmiyyah*, ed. el-Tahir el-Mesawi (Kuala Lumpur: al-Fajr, 1999), p.2.
8. Refer to Section 2.5.
9. This was a theme in: Conference: Purposes of Islamic Law and Means of Achieving them in Muslim Societies, International Islamic University of Malaysia: Malaysia, August, 2006.

CHAPTER ONE

1. Mohammad al-Tahir ibn Ashur, *Ibn Ashur, Treatise on Maqāṣid al-Shariʿah*, trans. Muhammad el-Tahir el-Mesawi (London, Washington: International Institute of Islamic Thought (IIIT), 2006), p.2.
2. Rudolf von Jhering, *Law as a Means to an End* (Der Zweck im Recht), trans. Isaac Husik, 2nd reprint ed. (New Jersey: The Lawbook Exchange (Originally published 1913 by Boston Book Co.), 2001) p.35.
3. Ibn Ashur, *Maqāṣid al-Sharīʿah al-Islāmiyyah*, p 183.
4. Abdul-Malik al-Juwaynī, *Ghīath al-Umam fī Iltiyāth al-Ẓulam*, ed. Abdul-Azim al-Deeb (Qatar: Wazarah al-Shu'ūn al-Dīniyyah, 1400 AH) p.253.
5. Al-Ghazālī, *al-Mustaṣfā*, vol. 1, p.172.
6. Abū Bakr al-Mālikī ibn al-ʿArabī, *Al-Maḥṣūl fī Uṣūl al-Fiqh*, ed. Hussain Ali

Alyadri and Saeed Foda, 1st ed. (Amman: Dār al-Bayāriq, 1999), vol. 5, p.222. Al-Āmidī, *al-Iḥkām,* vol. 4, p.286.

7. Najm al-Dīn al-Ṭūfī, *al-Taʿyīn fī Sharḥ al-Arbaʿīn* (Beirut: al-Rayyān, 1419 AH), p.239.
8. Shihāb al-Dīn al-Qarāfī, *al-Dhakhīrah* (Beirut: Dār al-ʿArab, 1994), vol. 5, p.478.
9. Al-Ghazālī, *al-Mustaṣfā*, vol. 1, p.172, Ibn al-ʿArabī, *al-Maḥṣūl fī Uṣūl al-Fiqh,* vol. 5, p.222, al-Āmidī, *al-Iḥkām*, vol. 4, p.287.
10. Al-Ghazālī, *al-Mustaṣfā*, vol. 1, p.172, al-Shāṭibṭī, *al-Muwāfaqāt*, vol. 3, p.47.
11. Al-Shāṭibṭī, *al-Muwāfaqāt*, vol. 3, p.5.
12. Ibid., vol. 3, p.17.
13. Ibid., vol. 1, p.151.
14. Gamal Attia, *Naḥwa Tafʿīl Maqāṣid al-Sharīʿah* (Amman: al-Maʿhad al-ʿĀlamī li al-Fikr al-Islāmī, 2001) p.45.
15. A. H. Maslow, "A Theory of Human Motivation," *Psychological Review*, no. 50 (1943): 50, p.370–96.
16. A. H. Maslow, *Motivation and Personality*, 2nd ed. (New York: Harper and Row, 1970), Maslow, "*A Theory of Human Motivation.*"
17. According to a discussion with Shaykh Hasan al-Turabi (Oral Discussion, Khartoum, Sudan, August 2006).
18. Numan Jughaim, *Ṭuruq al-Kashf ʿan Maqāṣid al-Shāriʿ* (International Islamic University, Malaysia. Published by Dār al-Nafā'is, 2002), p.26–35.
19. Mohammad Rashid Rida, *al-Waḥī al-Moḥammadī: Thubūt al-Nubuwwah bi al-Qur'ān* (Cairo: Mu'asasah ʿIzz al-dīn, no date) p.100.
20. Ibn Ashur, *Maqāṣid al-Sharīʿah al-Islāmiyyah*, p.183.
21. As in, for example, Kamāl al-Dīn al-Siwāsī, *Sharḥ Fatḥ al-Qādir*, 2nd ed. (Beirut: Dar al-Fikr, no date), vol.4, p.513.
22. For example, Surah *al-Kahf*, 18:29.
23. Mohammad al-Tahir ibn Ashur, *Uṣūl Al-Niẓām Al-Ijtimāʿī fī al-Islām*, ed. Mohammad el-Tahir el-Mesawi (Amman: Dār al-Nafā'is, 2001) p.256, 268.
24. Ibid, p.270–281.
25. Gamal Attia, *Naḥwa Tafʿīl Maqāṣid al-Sharīʿah*, p.49.
26. Yusuf al-Qaradawi, *Kayf Nataʿāmal Maʿa al-Qur'ān al-ʿAẓīm?*, 1st ed. (Cairo: Dār al-Shorūq, 1999).
27. Oral Discussions, London, UK, March, 2005, and Sarajevo, Bosnia, May, 2007.
28. Taha Jabir al-Alwani, *Maqāṣid Al-Sharīʿah*, 1st ed. (Beirut: IIIT and Dār al-Hādī, 2001), p.25.
29. Oral Discussion, Cairo, Egypt, April, 2007.

30. Around the seventh Islamic year AH. The location was a few miles away from Madinah.
31. Moḥammad al-Bukhārī, *al-Ṣaḥīh*, ed. Mustafa al-Bagha, 3rd ed. (Beirut: Dār ibn Kathīr, 1986) vol. 1, p.321, Abū al-Ḥussain Muslim, *Ṣaḥīh Muslim*, ed. Mohammad Fouad Abdul-Baqi (Beirut: Dār Iḥyā' al-Turāth al-ᶜArabī, no date) vol. 3, p.1391.
32. Narrated by Abdullāh ibn ᶜUmar, according to al-Bukhārī, vol. 1, p.321, and Muslim, vol. 3, p.1391.
33. ᶜAlī ibn Ḥazm, *al-Muḥallā*, ed. Lajnah Iḥyā' al-Turāth al-ᶜArabī, 1st ed. (Beirut: Dār al-Āfāq, no date), *al-Muḥallā*, vol. 3, p.291.
34. Yaᶜqub Abū Yūsuf, *al-Kharāj* (Cairo: al-Maṭbaṭᶜah al-Amīriyyah, 1303 AH) p.14, 81, Yaḥyā ibn Ādam, *al-Kharāj* (Lahore, Pakistan: al-Maktabah al-ᶜIlmiyyah, 1974) p.110.
35. The Qur'an, Surah *al-Ḥashr*, 59:7. I preferred 'domination of wealth' to express '*dūlatan bayn al-ghaniyyā'i minkom*,' rather than 'a circuit between the wealthy' (as in Yusuf Ali's translation) or 'commodity between the rich' (as in Picktall's translation).
36. Mohammad Biltaji, *Manhaj ᶜUmar Ibn al-Khaṭṭāb fī al-Tashrīᶜ*, 1st ed. (Cairo: Dār al-Salām, 2002) p.190.
37. Al-Walīd ibn Rushd (Averröes), *Bidāyah al-Mujtahid wa Nihāyah al-Muqtaṣid* (Beirut: Dār al-Fikr, no date), vol. 1, p.291.
38. Al-Siwāsī, *Sharḥ Fatḥ al-Qādir*, vol. 2, p.192, Abū ᶜUmar ibn ᶜAbd al-Barr, *al-Tamhīd*, ed. Mohammad al-Alawi and Mohammad al-Bakri (Morrocco: Wazārah ᶜUmūm al-Awqāf, 1387 AH), vol. 4, p.216.
39. Yusuf al-Qaradawi, "Fiqh al-Zakah" (Ph.D. diss, al-Azhar University, Egypt, Published by *al-Risālah*, 15th ed, 1985), vol. 1, p.229.
40. Opinion strongly expressed in: ᶜAlī ibn Ḥazm, *al-Muḥallā*, ed. Lajnah Iḥiyā' al-Turāth al-ᶜArabī, 1st ed. (Beirut: Dār al-Āfāq, no date) *al-Muḥallā*, p.209.
41. Al-Qaradawi, "Fiqh Al-Zakah", vol. 1, p.146–148.
42. Al-Bukhārī, *al-Ṣaḥīḥ*, Kitāb al-Ḥajj, Bāb al-Raml.
43. Al-Shāṭibī, *al-Muwāfaqāt*, vol. 2, p.6.
44. A proposed classification of the contemporary schools of Islamic law is provided in Chapter 5.
45. M. Said Ramadan al-Bouti, *Ḍawābiṭ al-Maṣlaḥah fī al-Sharīᶜah al-Islāmiyyah*, 6th ed. (Damascus: al-Risālah Foundation, 2001) p.129–43.
46. Ibid., p.143.
47. This is Mālik's opinion, but all other schools disagreed with ᶜUmar on this issue. Refer to: Ibn Rushd, *Bidāyah al-Mujtahid*, p.290–91.
48. According to: Ahmad al-Raysuni, *Naẓariyyat al-Maqāṣid ᶜind al-Imām al-Shāṭibī*, 1st ed. (Herndon, VA: IIIT, 1992).

49. Also according to Ahmad al-Raysuni, in: Mohamed Saleem el-Awa, ed., *Maqāṣid al-Sharīʿah Al-Islāmiyyah: Dirāsāt fī Qaḍāyā Al-Manhaj wa Qaḍāyā al-Taṭbīq* (Cairo: al-Furqān Islamic Heritage Foundation, al-Maqāṣid Research Centre, 2006), p.181.
50. Mohammad Kamal Imam, *al-Dalīl al-Irshādī Ilā Maqāṣid al-Sharīʿah al-Islāmiyyah* (London: al-Maqāṣid Research Centre, 2007), Introduction, p.3.
51. I learnt about the book from Professor Ahmad al-Raysuni of the Organization of Islamic Conference (OIC), Fiqh Council, in Jeddah (Oral Conversation, Jeddah, Saudi Arabia, April 2006). I obtained a microfilm of the manuscript with the help of Professor Ayman Fouad, who edits manuscripts for Al-Furqan Islamic Heritage Foundation, London, UK (Cairo, July 2006). Al-Qaffāl al-Shāshī, "Maḥāsin al-Sharā'iʿ," in *Fiqh Shāfiʿī*, Manuscript No. 263 (Cairo, Dār al-Kutub: 358 AH/ 969 CE).
52. Hasan Jabir, "al-Maqāṣid fī al-Madrasah al-Shīʿiyyah", in: El-Awa, Mohamed Saleem, ed. *Maqāṣid al-Sharīʿah al-Islāmiyyah: Dirāsāt fī Qaḍāyā al-Manhaj wa Qaḍāyā al-Taṭbīq* (Studies in the Philosophy of Islamic Law: Theory and Applications). 1st ed. (Cairo: al-Furqan Islamic Heritage Foundation, Al-Maqāṣid Research Centre, 2006) p.325. Also: Oral Discussion over the issue in Alexandria, Egypt, August, 2006.
53. According to Prof. Mohammad Kamal Imam of Alexandria University's Faculty of Law (Oral Discussion, Cairo, Egypt, August, 2006).
54. Ibn Bābawayh al-Ṣadūq al-Qummī, *ʿIlal Al-Sharā'iʿ*, ed. Mohammad Sadiq Bahr al-Ulum (Najaf: Dār al-Balāghah, 1966).
55. According to Prof. Ahmad al-Raysuni, Oral Discussion, Jeddah, November 2006. He referred me to: Abū al-Ḥasan al-Faylasūf al-ʿĀmirī, *al-Iʿlām bi-Manāqib al-Islām*, ed. Ahmad Ghurab (Cairo: Dār al-Kitāb al-ʿArabī, 1967).
56. Oral discussion with Shaykh Bin Bayyah in Makkah, Saudi Arabia, April 2006.
57. Gasser Auda, "Dawarān al-Aḥkām al-Sharʿiyyah Maʿa Maqāṣidihā Wujūdan wa ʿAdaman: Dirāsah 'Uṣūliyyah Nāqdiah Taṭbṭīqiyyah (Change of Statutes According to Their Purposes: A Methodological, Critical and Applied Study)" (Master of Jurisprudence diss., Islamic American University, 2004).
58. Al-Juwaynī, *al-Burhān,* 4th ed, vol. 2, p.621, 22, 747.
59. Ibid.
60. Al-Juwaynī, *al-Ghayyathī*, p.434.
61. Ibid., p.490.
62. Ibid., p.446, 73, 94.
63. Refer to the introduction of *Giath al-Umam,* written by Abdul-Azim al-Deeb, which outlines the historical and political context of the book.

64. Al-Ghazālī, *Al-Mustaṣfā* p.258.
65. Ibid., p.172.
66. Ibid., p.174.
67. Ibid., p.265.
68. Al-ʿIzz ibn ʿAbd al-Salām, *Maqāṣid al-Ṣawm*, ed. Iyad al-Tabba, 2nd ed. (Beirut: Dār al-Fikr, 1995),
69. Al-ʿIzz ibn ʿAbd al-Salām, *Qawāʿid al-Aḥkām fī Maṣāliḥ al-Anām* (Beirut: Dār al-Nashr, no date), vol. 2, p.221.
70. Ibid., vol. 2, p.160.
71. Imam, *al-Dalīl al-Irshādī*, p.54–60.
72. Shihāb al Dīn al-Qarāfī, *al-Furūq* (Maʿa Hawāmishihi), ed. Khalil Mansour (Beirut: Dār al-Kutub al-ʿIlmiyyah, 1998), vol. 1, p.357.
73. Ibn Ashur, *Maqāṣid al-Sharīʿah al-Islāmiyyah*, p.100.
74. Al-Qarāfī, *al-Dhakhīrah*, vol. 1, p.153. Al-Qarāfī, *al-Furūq* (Maʿa Hawāmishihi), vol. 2, p.60.
75. Shams al-Dīn ibn al-Qayyim, *Iʿlām al-Muwaqqiʿīn*, ed. Taha Abdul Rauf Saad (Beirut: Dār al-Jīl, 1973), vol. 1, p.333.
76. Al-Shāṭibī, *al-Muwāfaqāt,* vol. 2, p.6.
77. Ibid., vol. 2, p.25.
78. Ibid., vol. 2, p.61.
79. Al-Raysuni, *Naẓariyyah al-Maqāṣid*, p.169.
80. Al-Shāṭibī, *al-Muwāfaqāt,* vol. 4, p.229.
81. Ibid., vol. 2, p.6.
82. For example, Shaykh Ali Jumah, Mufti of Egypt (Oral Discussion, Cairo, Egypt, December 2005).
83. Al-ʿĀmirī, *al-Iʿlām*, p.125.
84. Al-Juwaynī, *al-Burhān*, vol. 2, p.747.
85. Al-Ghazālī, *al-Mustaṣfā*, p.258.
86. Ibn Ashur, *'Uṣūl al-Niẓām al-'Ijtimāʿī fī al-Islām*, p.206.
87. For example, Shaykh Ali Jumah, Mufti of Egypt (Oral Discussion, Cairo, Egypt, December 2005).
88. Auda, *Fiqh al-Maqāṣid*, p.20.
89. Al-Bukhārī, *al-Ṣaḥīḥ*, vol. 1, p.37.
90. Yusuf al-Qaradawi, *Madkhal li-Dirāsah al-Sharīʿah al-Islāmiyyah* (Cairo: Wahba, 1997) p.101, Attia, *Naḥwa Tafʿīl Maqāṣid al-Sharīʿah*, p.170, Ahmad al-Raysuni, Mohammad al-Zuhaili, and Mohammad O. Shabeer, "Ḥuqūq al-Insān Miḥwar Maqāṣid al-Sharīʿah," Kitāb al-Ummah, no. 87 (2002), Mohamed el-Awa, *al-Fiqh al-Islāmī fī Ṭarīq al-Tajdīd* (Cairo: al-Maktab al-Islāmī, 1998) p.195.
91. Mohammed Osman Salih, "al-Islām Huwa Niẓām Shāmil Liḥimāyah wa

Taᶜzīz Ḥuqūq al-Insān" (paper presented at the International Conference on Islam and Human Rights, Khartoum, 2006).

92. University of Toronto Bora Laskin Law Library, *International Protection of Human Rights* (2004 [cited Jan. 15th, 2005]); available from http://www.law-lib.utoronto.ca/resguide/humrtsgu.htm.
93. United Nations High Commission for Human Rights UNHCHR, *Specific Human Rights Issues* (July, 2003 [cited Feb. 1st, 2005]); available from http://www.unhchr.cah/Huridocda/Huridoca.nsf/(Symbol)/E.CN.4.Sub.2.2003.NGO.15.En.
94. Ibid.
95. Salih, "al-Islām Huwa Niẓām Shāmil Liḥimāyat wa Taᶜzīz Ḥuqūq al-Insān." Murad Hoffman, *al-Islām ᶜĀm Alfayn* (Islam in the Year Two Thousand), 1st ed. (Cairo: Maktabah al-Shurūq, 1995) p.56.
96. Al-ᶜĀmirī, *al-Iᶜlām*, p.125.
97. Ibn Ashur, *Maqāṣid al-Sharīᶜah al-Islāmiyyah*, p.292.
98. Attia, *Naḥwa Tafᶜīl Maqāṣid al-Sharīᶜah*, p.171, al-Raysuni, al-Zuhaili, and Shabeer, "*Ḥuqūq al-Insān Miḥwar Maqāṣid al-Sharīᶜah*."
99. The Qur'an, Surah *al-Baqarah*, 2:256. This is my translation for '*lā ikrāha fī al-dīn*.' I understand that it means that there is no compulsion in any matter of the religion, rather than merely 'in religion,' as in other translations (for example, Yusuf Ali's and Picktall's).
100. Quttub Sano, *Qirā'ah Maᶜrifiyyah fī al-Fikr al-'Uṣūlī*, 1st ed. (Kuala Lumpur: Dār al-Tajdīd, 2005) p.157.
101. United Nation Development Programme UNDP, *Annual Report 2004* (2004 [cited Feb. 5th, 2005]); available from http://www.undp.org/annualreports/2004/english.
102. Mohammad Shakir al-Sharif, *Ḥaqīqah al-Dīmuqrāṭiyyah* (Riyadh: Dār al-Waṭan, 1992), p.3, Mohammad Ali Mufti, *Naqd al-Judhūr al-Fikriyyah li al-Dīmuqrāṭiyyah al-Gharbiyyah* (Riyadh: al-Muntadā al-Islāmī and Majallah al-Bayān, 2002), p.91.

CHAPTER TWO

1. Robert Flood and Ewart Carson, *Dealing with Complexity: An Introduction to the Theory and Application of Systems Science*, vol. 2 (New York and London: Plenum Press, 1993), 2nd ed. p.247.
2. E. Laszlo, *The World System* (New York: George Braziller Inc, 1972), p.151.
3. Ibid.
4. E. von Glaserfeld, *The Construction of Knowledge: Contributions to Conceptual Semantics* (California: Intersystems Seaside, 1987).
5. Konrad Z. Lorenz, "The Fashionable Fallacy of Dispensing with

Description" (paper presented at the 25th International Congress of Physiological Sciences, Munich, July 25–31, 1971).

6. Lars Skyttner, *General Systems Theory: Ideas and Applications* (Singapore: World Scientific, 2002), p.7.
7. John Laszlo, *The Systems View of the World: A Holistic Vision for Our Time* (Hampton Press, 1996), p.197.
8. Michael Beany, "Analysis", *Stanford Encyclopedia of Philosophy* (2003 [cited Jan. 5th, 2007]); available from http://plato.stanford.edu/ entries/ analysis/.
9. Refer, for example, to the entries on 'analysis' in: *The Routledge Encyclopedia of Philosophy*, ed. Edward Craig (London: Routledge, 1998), Robert Audi, *The Cambridge Dictionary of Philosophy*, 2nd ed., vol. 1 (Cambridge: Cambridge University Press, 1999), Simon Blackburn, *The Oxford Dictionary of Philosophy* (Oxford: Oxford University Press, 1996).
10. Beany, "Analysis", *Stanford Encyclopedia of Philosophy.*
11. John Ongley, "What Is Analysis? Review of Michael Beany's 'Analysis'," *Bertrand Russell Society Quarterly*, no. 127 (2005): No.27.
12. This is the translators' depiction of the Greek word 'akolouthôn.' According to *The American Heritage Dictionary of the English Language*, Fourth Edition, it is, 'one that occurs or exists concurrently with another.'
13. Jaakko and Remes Hintikka, *The Method of Analysis*, ed. D. Reidel (Dordrecht: 1974), p.9–10.
14. Eileen C Sweeney, "Three Notions of Resolution and the Structure of Reasoning in Aquinas," *The Thomist* 58 (1994): vol. 58, p.197–243.
15. Al-Walīd ibn Rushd (Averröes), *Mukhtaṣar Manṭiq Arisṭo*, ed. Jirar Jahami (Beirut: Dār al-Fikr al-Lubnānī, 1992), p.5.
16. Aristotle, *The Works of Aristotle*, vol. 1, Great Books of the Western World (London: Encyclopaedia Britannica INC, 1990), vol. 1.
17. Ibn Rushd. *Mukhtaṣar Manṭiq Arisṭo*, p.5.
18. Sweeney, "Three Notions of Resolution", p.197.
19. René Descartes, *Rules for the Direction of the Mind: The Philosophical Writings of Descartes*, ed. J. Cottingham et al. (Cambridge: Cambridge University Press, 1684).
20. John Locke, *An Essay Concerning Human Understanding*, ed. P. H. Nidditch, 4 ed. (Oxford: Oxford University Press, 1975), 4th ed.
21. Ongley, "What Is Analysis?"
22. Beany, "Analysis", *Stanford Encyclopedia of Philosophy.*
23. Skyttner, *General Systems Theory.*
24. Beany, "Analysis", *Stanford Encyclopedia of Philosophy.*
25. Peter A. Corning, "Synergy: Another Idea Whose Time Has Come?" *Journal*

of Social and Evolutionary Systems, vol. 1, no. 21 (1998): 21.

26. Skyttner, *General Systems Theory*.
27. Kenneth E. Kendall and Julie E. Kendall, *Systems Analysis and Design*, 4th ed. (New Jersey: Prentice-Hall, 1999), p.27.
28. Skyttner, *General Systems Theory*, p.5.
29. Kendall, *Systems Analysis and Design*, 4th ed, p.27.
30. Hugh R. King, "A. N. Whitehead and the Concept of Metaphysics," *Philosophy of Science* (1947): vol. 14, no. 2, p.132.
31. Beany, "Analysis," *Stanford Encyclopedia of Philosophy*.
32. Skyttner, *General Systems Theory*, p.5.
33. G. Auda, "Cooperative Modular Neural Network Classifiers," Ph. D. Thesis (University of Waterloo, 1996), pp.32, 34, 91, 105, 111.
34. Von Bertalanffy, "General Systems Theory: Foundations, Development, Applications" (New York: George Braziller, 1969).
35. J. Smuts, *Holism and Evolution*, reprint ed. (Westport, Connecticut: Greenwood Press, 1973).
36. J. Litterer, *Organizations: Systems, Control and Adaptation* (New York: John Wiley, 1969).
37. Skyttner, *General Systems Theory*.
38. D. Hitchins, *Putting Systems to Work* (New York: John Wiley, 1992).
39. D. Katz and L. Kahn, *The Social Psychology of Organizations* (London: John Wiley, 1966).
40. R. Ackoff, *Creating the Corporate Future* (New York: John Wiley, 1981).
41. W. Churchman, *The Design of Inquiring Systems: Basic Concepts of Systems and Organizations* (New York: Basic Books, 1979).
42. K. Boulding, "General Systems as a Point of View," in *Views on General Systems Theory*, ed. A. Mesarovic (New York: John Wiley, 1964).
43. D. Bowler, *General Systems Thinking* (New York: North Holland, 1981).
44. H. Maturana and V. Varela, *The Tree of Knowledge* (London: Shambala, 1992).
45. Niklas Luhmann, *Law as a Social System*, trans. Klaus Ziegert. Introduction by Richard Nobles and David Schiff (Oxford: Oxford University Press, 2004) p.10.
46. Jamshid Gharajedaghi, *Systems Thinking: Managing Chaos and Complexity. A Platform for Designing Business Architecture* (Boston: Butterworth-Heinemann, 1999).
47. D.K. Hitchins, *Advanced Systems, Thinking and Management* (Norwood, MA: Artech House, 2003).

48 A. Koestler, *The Ghost in the Machine* (London: Arkana, 1967).

49. G. Auda, Ph.D. Thesis (University of Waterloo, 1996), p.60.

50. W. Weaver, "Science and Complexity," *American Scientist* 36, no. 194 (1948).
51 H. Simon, *The Sciences of the Artificial* (London: MIT Press, 1969).
52. R. Ackoff, "Towards a System of Systems Concepts," *Management Science* 17, no. 11 (1971).
53. J. Jordan, *Themes in Speculative Psychology* (London: Tavistock Publications, 1968).
54. S. Beer, *Brain of the Firm* (London: Penguin Press, 1972).
55. Skyttner, *General Systems Theory*. In this book, Skyttner also presented a survey and bibliography on systems theory, which I found helpful.
56. R. Fivaz, *L'ordre Et La Volupte* (Lausanne: Presses Politechniques Romandes, 1989).
57. K. Boulding, *Ecodynamics* (London: Sage Publications, 1978).
58. J. Miller, *Living Systems* (New York: McGraw-Hill, 1978).
59. Ibid.
60. J. Lovelock, *The Ages of Gaia* (New York: Norton and Co, 1988).
61. J.W. Kirchner, "The Gaia Hypothesis: Are They Testable? Are They Useful?" in *Scientists on Gaia*, ed. S. Schneider (Cambridge, New York: MIT Press, 1991).
62. T. de Chardin, *The Phenomenon of Man* (no date).
63. Ervin Laszlo, *Introduction to Systems Philosophy – Towards a New Paradigm of Contemporary Thought* (New York: Gordon and Breach, Science Publishers, 1972).
64. J. E. Salk, *Anatomy of Reality* (Westport, Connecticut: Greenwood Publishing Group Inc, 1983).
65. G. Klir, *Architecture of Systems Problem Solving* (New York: Plenum Publishing Corp, 1985).
66. N. Cook, *Stability and Flexibility: An Analysis of Natural Systems*. (New York: Pergamon Press, 1980).
67. Peter Checkland, *Systems Thinking, Systems Practice* (New York: Wiley, 1999).
68. W.T. Powers, *Behaviour: The Control of Perception* (New York: Aldine de Gruyter, 1973).
69. Aḥmad ibn Taymiyah, *Kutub wa Rasā'il wa Fatwā*, ed. Abdul-Rahman al-Najdi, 2nd ed. (Riyadh: Maktabah ibn Taymiyah, no date), vol.19, p.131.
70. Abd al-Rahman Shaikhi-Zadah, *Majmaʿ al-Anhur* (Beirut: Dār al-Kutub al-ʿIlmiyyah, 1998), vol. 1, p.11.
71. Ibn Amir al-Haj, *Al-Taqrīr wa al-Taḥbīr fī ʿIlm Uṣūl al-Fiqh* (Beirut: Dār al-Fikr, 1996), vol. 1, p.26.
72. Ibn Taymiyah, *Kutub wa Rasā'il wa Fatwā*, vol. 13, p.113.

73. Bar al-Din Al-Eini, *ᶜUmdah al-Qārī Sharḥ Ṣaḥīḥ al-Bukhārī* (Beirut: Dār Iḥyā' al-Turāth al-ᶜArabī, no date), vol. 2, p.52.
74. ᶜAlī al-Subkī, *Al-'Ibhāj fī Sharḥ al-Minhāj* (Beirut: Dār al-Nashr, 1983), vol. 1, p.39.
75. Laszlo, *The Systems View of the World: A Holistic Vision for Our Time*, p.4. Smuts, *Holism and Evolution*, pp.1–3.
76. Alfred Korzybski, *An Introduction to Non-Aristotelian Systems and General Semantics*, Fourth ed. (Lakeville, Connecticut: The International Non-Aristotelian Library Publishing Company, 1958) p.xxxviii.
77. Refer, for example, to: Abd al-Malik al-Juwaynī, *Al-Burhān fī 'Uṣūl al-Fiqh*, ed. Abdul-Azim al-Deeb, 4th ed. (Manṣūrah: al-Wafā', 1418 AH/1998 CE), vol. 2, p.590, Ibrāhīm al-Ghirnāṭī al-Shāṭibī, *Al-Muwāfaqāt fī 'Uṣūl al Sharīᶜah*, ed. Abdullah Diraz (Beirut: Dār al-Maᶜrifah, no date), vol. 1, p.29.
78 Al-Shāṭibī, *Al-Muwāfaqāt,* vol.2, p.61.
79 Maturana, *The Tree of Knowledge*, p.v.
80. Von Bertalanffy, "General Systems Theory."
81. Jamᶜiyyah al-Majalah, *Majallah al-Aḥkām al-ᶜAdliyyah*, ed. Najib Hawawini (Karkhaneh Tijarah Kutub, no date), p.100.
82. Abū Muzafar al-Samaani, *Qawāṭiᶜ al-'Adillah fī al-'Uṣūl*, ed. Ismail al-Shafie (Beirut: Dār al-Kutub al-ᶜIilmiyyah, 1997), vol. 2, p.84, Abū Ḥāmid al-Ghazālī, *Al-Mustaṣfā fī ᶜIlm al-'Uṣūl*, ed. Mohammed Abdul-Salam Abdul Shafi, 1st ed. (Beirut: Dār al-Kutub al-ᶜIlmiyyah, 1413 AH), vol. 1, p.296, Shams al-Dīn ibn al-Qayyim, *Iᶜlām al-Muwaqqiᶜīn*, ed. Taha Abdul Rauf Saad (Beirut: Dār al-Jīl, 1973), vol. 1, p.333.
83. Gasser Auda, Ph. D Thesis (University of Waterloo, 1996), p.19.
84. Ibid., p.6.
85. Robert A. Wilson and Frank C. Keil, ed., *The MIT Encyclopedia of the Cognitive Sciences* (London: The MIT Press, 1999), pp.104–05.
86. Auda, Ph.D. Thesis, p.32.
87. Features could be visual, functional, numerical, or a combination of factors. For example, a few objects could be categorised according to the features of color, weight, volume, price, shape, and so on. Each of these characteristics could produce a number of categorisations. For example, color categorisation, which is how humans define color sensations in terms of words, varies across languages and cultures and is affected by a number of psychophysical and neurophysiological factors.
88. G. Auda and M. Kamel. "A Modular Neural Network for Vague Classification." Lecture notes in *Computer Science* vol. 2005: *Lecture notes in Artificial Intelligence* (2000), p.584.
89. In the example given above, the same objects could be categorised in terms of a

concept, such as 'utility.' 'Utility' of an object is not a simple true-or-false feature, i.e, an object 'has utility' or 'has no utility.' Utility could be a complex combination of the object's price, aesthetic value, historic value, usefulness to a certain society, and other dimensions. The 'vague' line between the categories of, for example, high, medium, and low utility, is not a clear number or measure.

90. Jamshid Gharajedaghi, "Systems Methodology: A Holistic Language of Interaction and Design. Seeing through Chaos and Understanding Complexities," in systemsthinkingpress.com (2004), p.38.
91. Ibid., p.12.
92. Refer, for example, to: al-Shāṭibī, *Al-Muwāfaqāt*, vol. 1, p.173, vol. 3, p.1.
93. Gasser Auda, *Fiqh al-Maqāṣid: Ināṭah al-Aḥkām al-Sharᶜiyyah bi-Maqāṣidihā* (Virginia, IIIT: al-Maᶜhad al-ᶜĀlamī li al-Fikr al-Islāmī, 2006), p.51.
94. Aḥmad ibn Taymiyah, *Daqā'iq al-Tafsīr*, ed. Mohammad al-Julainid (Damascus: Mu'asasah ᶜUlūm al-Qur'ān, 1404 AH), vol. 2, p.110.
95. Moḥammad al-Ṭayyib al-Baṣrī, *Al-Muᶜtamad fī 'Uṣūl al-Fiqh*, ed. Khalil al-Mees, 1st ed. (Beirut: Dār al-Kutub al-ᶜIlmiyyah, 1983 CE/1403AH), vol. 2, p.184. Also, refer to: Ahmad al-Tayyib, "Naẓariyyah al-Maqāṣid ᶜInd al-Shāṭibī wa Madā Irtibāṭihā bi al-'Uṣūl al-Kalāmiyyah," *Al-Muslim al-Muᶜāṣir*, no. 103 (2002), p.39, Taha Jabir al-Alwani, "Maqāṣid al-Sharīᶜah," in *Maqāṣid al-Sharīᶜah*, ed. Abdul-Jabbar al-Rifaie (Damascus: Dār al-Fikr, 2001), p.75, Hasan al-Shafie, *Al-Āmidī wa Ārā'uhu al-Kalāmiyyah*, 1st ed. (Cairo: Dār al-Salām, 1998), p.441.
96. Al-Tayyib, "Naẓariyyah al-Maqāṣid."
97 Ibid.
98. Taha Jabir al-Alwani, *Maqāṣid al-Sharīᶜah*, 1st. ed. (Beirut: IIIT and Dār al-Hādī, 2001), p.75.
99. Abū Ḥāmid al-Ghazālī, *Tahāfut al-Falāsifah* (Incoherence of the Philosophers). Translated by M. S. Kamali (Pakistan Philosophical Congress, 1963 [cited January 18th 2005]); available from http://www.muslimphilosophy.com.
100. Shihāb al-Dīn al-Ālūsī, *Rūḥ al-Maᶜānī fī Tafsīr al-Qur'ān al-ᶜAẓīm* (Beirut: Dār Iḥyā' al-Turāth al-ᶜArabī, no date), vol. 15, p.39.
101. ᶜAlī abū al-Ḥasan al-Āmidī, *Al-Iḥkām fī 'Uṣūl al-Aḥkām*, ed. Sayid al-Jumaili, 1st ed. (Beirut: Dār al-kitāb al-ᶜArabī, 1404 AH), vol. 3, p.249.
102. Al-Shāṭibī, *Al-Muwāfaqāt,* vol. 2, p.6.
103. Al-Tayyib, "Naẓariyyah Al-Maqāṣid."
104. Ibn al-Qayyim, *Iᶜlām Al-Muwaqqiᶜīn*, vol. 3, p.3.
105. Al-Ghazālī, *Tahafut.*

106. Ibid.
107. Al-Shāṭibī, *Al-Muwāfaqāt*, vol. 2, p.25.

CHAPTER THREE

1. For example: Mohammad Abdul-Khaliq Omar, *Reasoning in Islamic Law*, 3rd ed. (Cairo: M. Omar, 1999), Tariq Ramadan, "Stop in the Name of Humanity," *Globe and Mail* (London) Wednesday, March 30, 2005, p.28, WLUML, Women Living under Muslim Laws [cited Jan 5th, 2006]; available from http://www.wluml.org/english, Haideh Moghissi, *Feminism and Islamic Fundamentalism: The Limits of Postmodern Analysis* (New York: Zed Books, 1999), p.141, Aharon Layish, "Interplay between Tribal and Shari Law: A Case of Tibbawi Blood Money in the Sharia Court of Kufra," *Islamic Law and Society* 13, no. 1 (2006): p.63.
2. For example, The Qur'an Surah *al-Nisā'*, 4:78, Surah *al-Anᶜām*, 6:25, Surah *al-Tawbah*, 9:122, respectively (as trans. by Yusuf Ali, Picktall, and Irving).
3. For example: Mohammad Abū Zahra, *'Uṣūl Al-Fiqh* (Cairo: Dār al-Fikr al-ᶜArabī, 1958), p.5.
4. Ramadan, "Stop in the Name of Humanity."
5. Tariq Ramadan, *To Be a European Muslim* (Leicester: Islamic Foundation, 1999), p.28. The verses are: The Quran, Surah *al-Māi'dah*, 5:48, and Surah *al-Jāthiyah*, 45:18.
6. Ibn Taymiyah, *Kutub wa Rasā'il wa Fatwā (Books, Letters and Legal Opinions)*, vol. 13, p.113.
7. Al-Subkī, *Al-Ibhāj fī Sharḥ al-Minhāj*, vol. 1, p.39.
8. Al-Haj, *Al-Taqrīr*, vol. 1, p.26.
9. For example, Shaikhi-Zadah, *Majmaᶜ Al-Anhur*, vol. 1, p.11.
10. For example, Ibid.
11. Ibn Ashur, *Maqāṣid al-Sharīᶜah al-Islāmiyyah*, Chapter 6.
12. Moḥammad ibn Manẓūr, *Lisān al-ᶜArab* (Beirut: Dār Ṣādir, no date), vol. 13, p.350.
13. Rashid Rida, "Mujmal al-Aḥwāl al-Siyāsiyyah," Al-ᶜUrwah al-Wuthqā, Feb. 29th, 1898 CE.
14. al-Sayed Sabiq, *Fiqh al-Sunnah* (Cairo: Dār al-Fatḥ li al-Iᶜlām al-ᶜArabī, 1994), vol. 2, p.227.
15. Ibid.
16. Al-Mubarak al-Jazri, *Al-Nihāyah fī Gharīb al-Ḥadīth wa al-Athar* (Beirut: Al-Maktabah al-ᶜIlmiyyah, 1979), vol. 3, p.216.
17. Aharon Layish, "Interplay between Tribal and Shari Law", p.63.
18. Refer to *Women Living under Muslim Laws* website, www.wluml.org.
19. Salah al-Din Sultan, "Ḥujiyyah al-'Adillah al-Mukhtalaf ᶜAlayhā fī al-

Sharīʿah al-Islāmiyyah" (Ph.D. diss, Cairo University, 1992), p.620.

20. Refer to: Ismāʿīl ibn Kathīr, *Al-Bidāyah wa al-Nihāyah,* (no date), vols. 11 and 12, Ali al-Shaybani, *Al-Kāmil fī al-Tārīkh*, 2nd ed. (Beirut: Dār al-Nashr, 1994), vols. 2, 8, 10.
21. For details, refer to Bukhārī's collection: al-Bukhārī, *Al-Ṣaḥīḥ*, vol.4, p.1638, vol. 6, p.2666, and to Mohammad ibn ʿUmar al-Rāzī, *Al-Maḥsūl fī ʿIlm al-'Uṣūl*, ed. Taha Jabir al-Alwani, 1st ed. (Riyadh: Mohammad ibn Saud Islamic University, 1400 AH), vol. 5, p.529.
22. Abd al-Raḥmān ibn Khaldūn, *Muqaddimah ibn Khaldūn*, 5th ed. (Dār al-Qalam, 1984), vol.2, p.608.
23. Moḥammad Abu Zahrah, *Tārīkh al-Mathāhib al-Islāmiyyah* (Cairo: Dār al-Fikr al-ʿArabī, no date), p.48.
24. Abu Zahrah, *'Uṣūl Al-Fiqh*, p 42.
25. Ibn Khaldūn, *Al-Muqaddimah,* vol. 7, p.683.
26. Badr al-Dīn al-Zarkashī, *Al-Ijābah li 'īrād mā Istadrakathu ʿĀ'isha ʿAlā al-Ṣaḥabah*, ed. Said Al-Afghani, 2nd ed. (Beirut: Al-Maktab al-Islāmī, 1970).
27. Refer, for some *fiqhī* examples, to: Zayn al-Dīn ibn Nujaym, *Al-Baḥr al-Rā'iq*, 2nd ed. (Beirut: Dār al-Maʿrifah, no date), vol. 3, p.117, Ali al-Mirghiyānī, *Al-Hidāyah Sharḥ Bidāyah al-Mubtadi'* (Al-Maktabah al Islāmiyyah, no date), vol. 1, p.196, Mohammad Amin ibn Abidin, Ḥāshiyah Radd al-Muḥtār (Beirut: Dār al-Fikr, 2000), vol.3, p.55.
28. I extracted the above migration patterns from ibn Khaldūn's second half of volume 2 of his history '*al-Mubtada' wa al-Khabar*,' in which he mentioned the companions' conflicts after the Prophet's death. Ibn Khaldūn's account of these controversial events is, in my view, the most balanced.
29. Abu Zahrah, *Tārīkh al-Mathāhib al-Islāmiyyah*, p.458.
30. Ibid.
31. Ibid., p 33.
32. For example, Nasr Hamed Abu-Zaid, *Al-Imām al-Shāfiʿī wa Ta'sīs al-Āīdyūlūjiyyah al-Waṣaṭiyyah*, 3rd ed. (Cairo: Madbūlī, 2003), p.98.
33. According to the Shia school, the Twelve Imams start with ʿAlī ibn Abī-Ṭālib and include his two sons, al-Ḥasan and al-Ḥusayn, and nine other consequent Imams from al-Husayn's offspring: ʿAlī Zayn al-ʿĀbidīn ibn al-Ḥusayn, Moḥammad al-Bāqir, Jaʿfar al-Ṣādiq, Mūsā al-Kāẓim, ʿAlī al-Riḍā, Moḥammad al-Jawād, ʿAlī al-Hādī, al-Ḥasan al-ʿAskarī, and Moḥammad ibn al-Ḥasan al-ʿAskarī.
34. Refer to: ʿAbd al-Raḥmān Abū al- Faraj, *Ṣifah Al-Ṣafwah*, ed. Mahmoud Fakhouri and M. R. Qalaji, 2nd ed. (Beirut: Dār al-Maʿrifah, 1979), Abū Nuʿaym al-Aṣbahānī, *Ḥilyah al-Awliyā' wa Ṭabaqah Al-Aṣfiyā'*, 4th ed. (Beirut: Dār al-Nashr al-ʿArabī, 1985), Aḥmad ibn Khalkān, *Wafiyyāt al-*

*A*ᶜ*yān wa 'Anbā' al-Zamān*, ed. Ihsan Abbas (Beirut: Dār al-Thaqāfah, no date).

35. Moḥammad ibn Idrīs al-Shāfiᶜī, *Al-Risālah*, ed. Ahmad Shakir, (Cairo: al-Madanī, 1939).
36. Abu Zahrah, *Tārīkh Al-Mathāhib al-Islāmiyyah*, p.378.
37. Ibid.
38. Ibid.
39. Ibid.
40. Abū Yūsuf, *Al-Kharāj*.
41. Abu Zahrah, *Tārīkh al-Mathāhib al-Islāmiyyah*, p.420.
42. Ibid.
43. Moḥammad ibn Aḥmad al-Sarkhasī, *'Uṣūl al-Sarkhasī* (Beiut: Dār Al-Maᶜrifah, no date). ᶜAlī ibn Moḥammad al-Bazdawī, *'Uṣūl Al-Bazdawī- Kanz Al-Wuṣūl Ilā Ma*ᶜ*rifah al-'Uṣūl* (Karachi: Jāwīd Press, no date).
44. Al-Sarkhasī, *'Uṣūl al-Sarkhasī*, vol. 1, p.10.
45. Mālik, *Muwaṭṭa' al-Imām Mālik*, ed. M. Fouad Abdul Baqi (Cairo: Dār Iḥyā' al-Turāth al-ᶜArabī, no date).
46. Abu Zahrah, *Tārīkh al-Mathāhib al-Islāmiyyah,* p.420.
47. Ibid.
48. Al-Qarafī, *Al-Dhakhīrah*.
49. Abu Zahrah, *Tārīkh al-Mathāhib al-Islāmiyyah,* p.524.
50. Aḥmad ibn Taymiyah, *Kutub wa Rasā'il wa Fatwā*, ed. Abdul-Rahman al-Najdi, 2nd ed. (Riyadh: Maktabah ibn Taymiyah, no date). Aḥmad ibn Taymiyah, *Al-Musawadah*, ed. M. Mohieldin Abdulhameed (Cairo: al-Madanī, no date). Ibn al-Qayyim, *I*ᶜ*lām Al-Muwaqqi*ᶜ*īn.*
51. Abu Zahrah, *'Uṣūl Al-Fiqh,* p.495.
52. Moḥammad Abu Zahrah, *Al-Imām Zayd* (Cairo: Dār al-Fikr al-ᶜArabī, 1965), p.267.
53. Ibid., p.270.
54. Amr K. al-Nami, "Studies in Ibadhism," (www.Islamfact.com, 2006), Ch.1.
55. Ibid., Ch.2.
56. Ibid.
57. Abu Zahrah, *Tārīkh al-Mathāhib al-Islāmiyyah,* p.700.
58. Ibid.
59. Adnan Farhan, *Ḥarakah al-Ijtihād* ᶜ*Ind al-Shī*ᶜ*ah al-Imāmiyyah*, 1st. ed. (Beirut: Dār al-Hādī, 2004), p.11, Abu Zahrah, *'Uṣūl Al-Fiqh,* p.15.
60. Farhan, *Ḥarakah al-Ijtihād* ᶜ*Ind al-Shī*ᶜ*ah,* p.11.
61. Abu Zahrah, *'Uṣūl Al-Fiqh* p.10.
62. Mahmoud Mohammad Ali, *Al-*ᶜ*Alāqah Bayn al-Manṭiq wa al-Fiqh* ᶜ*Ind Mufakkirī al-Islām* (Cairo: Ein for Human and Social Studies, 2000).

63. Rafiq al-Ajam, *Al-Manṭiq ᶜInd al-Ghazālī fī Abᶜādih al-Arisṭawiyyah wa Khuṣūṣīyātihi al-Islāmiyyah* (Beirut: Dār al-Mashriq, 1989), Abdul-Azim al-Deeb, "Imam Al-Haramain," in *Ghiāth al-'Umam fī Iltiyāth al-Ẓulam* (Doha: al-Shu'ūn al-Dīniyyah, 1400 AH).
64. Refer, for a comprehensive source, to: Keil, ed., *The MIT Encyclopedia of the Cognitive Sciences*.
65. Abū al-Farag, *Ṣifah al-Ṣafwah*, Ḥamad al-Dimashqī, *Al-Kāshif fī Maᶜrifah Man Lahu Rīwāyah fī al-Kutub al-Sittah*, ed. Mohammad Awama, 1st ed. (Jeddah: Dār al-Qiblah li al-Thaqafah al-Islāmiyyah, 1992). Aḥmad ibn Ḥajar, *Taqrīb al-Tahthīb*, ed. Mohammad Awama (Damascus: Dār al-Rashīd, 1986). Aḥmad ibn Ḥajar, *Lisān al-Mīzān*, ed. Dā'irah al-Maᶜārif al-Niẓāmiyyah, 3rd ed. (Beirut: Mu'asasah al-Aᶜlāmī li al-Maṭbūᶜāt, 1986), Mohammad al-Thahabi, *Siyar Aᶜlām al-Nubalā'*, ed. Shoaib and al-Arqusi al-Aarna'ut, *Moḥammad*, 9th ed. (Beirut: *Risālah* Foundation, 1993), Moḥammad al-Bukhārī, *Al-Tārīkh al-Kabīr*, ed. Mohammad Hashim al-Nadawi (Dār al-Fikr, no date), Al-Aṣbahānī, *Ḥīlyah al-Awlīyā'*, Abu Zahrah, *Tārīkh al-Mathāhib al-Islāmiyyah*.
66. Omar Sulaiman al-Ashqar, *Tārīkh al-Fiqh al-Islāmī*, 1st. ed. (Kuwait: Maktabah al-Falāḥ, 1982), p.119.
67. Al-Majalah, *Majallah al-Aḥkām al-ᶜAdliyyah* (Journal of Justice Rulings), p.100.
68. Wael B. Hallaq, "Was the Gate of Ijtihad Closed," *Int. Journal Middle Eastern Studies* 16, no. 1 (1984).
69. I visited some of these mosques where four places of prayer had been assigned to the four Sunni schools – Shāfiᶜī, Mālikīs, Ḥanafīs, and Ḥanbalīs, such as al-Sulṭān Ḥasan Mosque in Cairo. Ninteenth and early twentieth century pictures of the grand mosque of Mecca show a similar arrangement. On the other hand, Shia mosques were always and still remain separate from Sunni mosques.
70. Section 2.2 accounted for some of the hanafi/shāfiᶜī disputes over courts.

CHAPTER FOUR

1. Refer to: Moḥammad ibn Moḥammad ibn al-Jazrī, *Al-Nashr fī al-Qirā'āt al-ᶜAshr* (Cairo: Maktabah al-Qāhirah, no date).
2. Mohamed El-Awa, Al-ᶜAlāqah Bayn al-Sunnah wa al-Shīᶜah, 1st ed. (Cairo: Safīr International Press, 2006).
3. Ibn al-Jazrı, *Al-Nashr fı al-Qirā'āt Al-ᶜAshr*.
4. Mohammad al-Zurqani, *Manāhil al-ᶜIrfān fī ᶜUlūm al-Qur'ān*, 1st ed. (Beirut: Dār al-Fikr, 1996), p.182, Ali Hasaballah, *'Uṣūl Al-Tashrīᶜ al-Islāmī* (Cairo: Dār al-Maᶜārif, no date), p.22.

5. For example: Hasaballah, *'Uṣūl Al-Tashrī*ᶜ, p.23.
6. Abdul-Jabbar, *Al-Mughnī*, vol. 4, p.174, Abdul-Jabbar, *Faḍl al-I*ᶜ*tizāl*, p.139.
7. Moḥammad ibn ᶜAlī al-Shawkānī, *Irshād al-Fuḥūl Ilā Taḥqīq* ᶜ*Ilm al-'Uṣūl*, ed. Mohammed Said al-Badri, 1st ed. (Beirut: Dār al-Fikr, 1992) vol. 1, p.426.
8. ᶜAlī ibn Ḥazm, *Al-Iḥkām fī 'Uṣūl Al-Aḥkām*, 1st ed. (Cairo: Dār al-Ḥadīth, 1983), vol. 5, p.124.
9. Al-Ghazālī, *Al-Mustaṣfā*, vol. 1, p.346. The Authentic Collection of Bukhārī, Hadith No. 2.
10. "He does not speak from some whim; it is merely inspiration that is revealed to him" (Qur'an Surah *al-Najm*, 53:3–4), "Say: It is not up to me to change it of my own accord" (Qur'an Surah *Yūnus*, 10:15), and "If he had mouthed some false statements about Us, We would have seized him by the right hand" (Quran Surah *al-Ḥāqqah*, 69:44). (Irving's translations).
11. Abdul-Khaliq, *Ḥujjiyyah al-Sunnah*, p.166, Dār al-Wafā', Cairo, 1981; Conference of Islamic Jurisprudence held by Imam Mohammad bin Saud Islamic University in Riyadh, "*Al-Ijtihād fī al-Sharī*ᶜ*ah al-Islāmiyyah wa Buḥūth Ukhrā*" – Ijtihad in the Islamic law and other subjects, p.34, Department of Culture and Publications, Riyadh, 1984.
12. For example, Qur'an verses: Surah *al-Anfāl*, 8:67, Surah *al-Tawbah*, 9:43, and Surah ᶜ*Abasa*, 80:1–3.
13. Al-Āmidī, ᶜAlī. *Al-Iḥkām fī Uṣūl Al-Aḥkām*. Edited by Sayid al-Jumaili. 1st ed. (Beirut: Dār al-Kitāb al-ᶜArabī, 1404 AH), vol. 4, p.99.
14. *Ḥujjiyyah al-Sunnah*, p.231; *Al-Ijtihād fī al-Sharī*ᶜ*ah al-Islāmiyyah wa Buhūth Ukhrā* – Ijtihad in the Islamic law and other subjects, p.44.
15. Several narrations. Refer to Abdul-Jalil Issa, *Ijtihād al-Rasūl*, p.132, Dār Al-Bayān, Kuwait, 1948.
16. *Ghīlah* is intercourse during the period of nursing a child. Arabs, before Islam, used to think that it was harmful for the nursing baby if his mother were to be pregnant.
17. Mālik, *Al-Muwaṭṭa'*, p.418, and Muslim, *Ṣaḥīḥ Muslim*, p.542.
18. Abū ᶜAmr ibn al-Ṣalāḥ, *Al-Muqaddimah fī* ᶜ*Ulūm al-Ḥadīth* (Beirut: Dār al-Fikr, 1977).
19. Al-Khoshoui A. M. al-Khoshoui, *Ghāyah al-*ᶜ*Iddah fī* ᶜ*Ulūm al-Iṣṭilāḥ* (Cairo: al-Azhar University, 1992), p.74.
20. I had previously carried out a survey on related opinions in: Auda, *Fiqh al-Maqāṣid*, pp.64–67.
21. El-Awa, *Al-*ᶜ*Alāqah Bayn al-Sunnah wa al-Shī*ᶜ*ah*, pp.34–48.
22. Moḥammad al-Baṣrī, *Al-Mu*ᶜ*tamad fī 'Uṣūl Al-Fiqh*, ed. Khalil al-Mees, 1st ed. (Beirut: Dār al-Kutub al-ᶜIlmiyyah, 1983), vol. 2, p.153.

23. Al-Ghazālī, *Al-Mustaṣfā*, vol. 1, p.142.
24. Abu Zahrah, *'Uṣūl al-Fiqh*, p.109.
25. Ibid., p.112. More analysis of abrogation is provided later.
26. Ibid., p.114.
27. Ibid., p.110.
28. Hasaballah, *'Uṣūl al-Tashrīʿ*, p.112.
29. Abu Zahrah, *'Uṣūl al-Fiqh*, pp.115–17.
30. Ibid., p.116.
31. Ibid., p.119.
32. Ibid., pp.121–25.
33. Ibid.
34. Ibid.
35. Hasaballah, *'Uṣūl al-Tashrīʿ*, p.275.
36. Qur'an, Surah *al-Mā'idah*, 5:3 (trans. Irving).
37. Hasaballah, *'Uṣūl al-Tashrīʿ*, p.279.
38. Ibid., p.283.
39. Mohammad Baqir al-Sadir, *Durūs fī ʿIlm al-'Uṣūl*, 2nd ed. (Beirut: Dār al-Kitāb al-Lubnanī, 1986), p.88.
40. Abu Zahrah, *Al-Imām Zayd*, p.363.
41. Qur'an, Surah *al-Nisā'*, 4:93 – Trans. Mohammad Asad.
42. Abu Zahrah, *'Uṣūl al-Fiqh*, p.135.
43. Qur'an, Surah *al-Nisā'*, 4:92 – Trans. Mohammad Asad.
44. Abu Zahrah, *'Uṣūl al-Fiqh*, p.136.
45. Ibid., p.139.
46. Al-Qaradawi, *Fiqh al-Zakah*, vol. 1, p.240.
47. Abu Zahrah, *'Uṣūl al-Fiqh*, p.141.
48. Qur'an, Surah *al-Ṭalāq*, 65:6 – Trans. Mohammad Asad.
49. Abu Zahrah, *'Uṣūl al-Fiqh*, p.143.
50. Qur'an, Surah *al-Baqarah*, 2:187 – Trans. Mohammad Asad.
51. Abu Zahrah, *'Uṣūl al-Fiqh*, p.144.
52. Ibid., p.140.
53. Which means, for two events A and B, either A or B is true, but not 'A and B,' and not 'neither A nor B.'
54. Al-Qaradawi, *Fiqh al-Zakāh*, vol. 1, p.182.
55. Al-Bukhārī, *Al-Ṣaḥīḥ*.
56. Moḥammad ibn Jarīr al-Ṭabarī, *Jāmiʿ al-Bayān ʿan Ta'wīl Āyī al-Qur'ān* (Beirut: Dār al-Fikr, 1985), vol. 5, p.401.
57. Al-Qaradawi, *Fiqh al-Zakāh*, vol. 1, p.184.
58. Abu Zahrah, *'Uṣūl al-Fiqh*, p.146.
59. Ibid., p.148.

60. Hasaballah, *'Uṣūl al-Tashrī*ᶜ, p.227.
61. Qur'an, Surah *al-Mā'idah*, 5:89, *al-Mujādalah*, 58:4 – Trans. Mohammad Asad.
62. Ali, *Al-Manṭiq wa al-Fiqh*, p.174.
63. Abū ᶜAlī ibn Sīnā, *Remarks and Admonitions*, trans. Shams Inati, vol. 1 (Toronto: Pontifical Institute of Mediaeval Studies, 1984), p.49.
64. Refer to: Aristotle, *The Works of Aristotle, Categories*.
65. Ali, *Al-Manṭiq wa al-Fiqh*, p.179.
66. Al-Ghazālī, *Al-Mustaṣfā*, vol. 1, p.173.
67. Opinion mentioned and criticised in: Ibn Ḥazm, *Al-Muḥllā*, vol. 5, p.88.
68. Ibid.
69. Al-Shawkānī, *Irshād al-Fuḥūl*, p.83, Abū Ḥāmid al-Ghazālī, *Al-Mustaṣfā*, vol. 1, p.187, ᶜAlā' al-Dīn al-Bukhārī, *Kashf al-Asrār* ᶜ*an 'Uṣūl Fakhr al-Islām al-Bazdawī*, ed. Abdullah Mahmoud M. Omar (Beirut: Dār al-kutub al-ᶜIlmiyyah, 1997), vol. 2, p.184.
70. Soltan, "Ḥujiyyah", p.121.
71. Mohammad al-Killini, *'Uṣūl al-Kāfī*, ed. Ali Akbar al-Ghiffari (Tehran: Dār al-Manshūrāt al-Islāmiyyah, no date), vol. 1, pp.178–79, Irshad Abdul-Haqq, "Islamic Law: An Overview of Its Origin and Elements," *Journal of Islamic Law and Culture* 27 (spring/summer) (2002): p. 83.
72. Soltan, "Ḥujiyyah", p.100.
73. Al-Juwaynī, *Al-Burhān*, p. 641.
74. Al-Sarkhasī, *'Uṣūl Al-Sarkhasī*, vol. 1, p.305, al-Rāzī, *Al-Maḥsūl fī* ᶜ*Ilm al-'Uṣūl*, vol. 4, pp. 25–26.
75. Soltan, "Ḥujiyyah", p. 32.
76. Abu Zahrah, *'Uṣūl al-Fiqh*, p197.
77. Ibid., p. 198.
78. Ibn Ḥazm, *Al-Iḥkām*, vol. 8, p.103.
79. Refer to: Abū Bakr al-Baghdādī, *Al-Faqīh wa al-Mutafaqih*, ed. Adil ibn Yusuf al-Gharazi (Saudi Arabia: Dār ibn al-Jawzī, 1421 AH), vol. 1, p.154, al-Juwaynī, *Al-Burhān*, paragraph 627, al-Ghazālī, *Al-Mustaṣfā*, vol. 1, pp. 76, 176, ᶜAbd Allāh ibn Qudāmah, *Al-Mughnī fī Fiqh al-Imām Aḥmad ibn Ḥanbal al-Shaybānī*, 1st ed. (Beirut: Dār al-Fikr, 1985), p.273, al-Baṣrī, *Al-Mu*ᶜ*tamad*, vol.2, p.21, Ibrāhīm al-Fayrūzabādī, *Sharḥ al-Lam*ᶜ, ed. Abd al-Majeed Turki (Beirut: Dār al-Gharb al-Islāmī, 1988), vol. 2, p.666, al-Bukhārī, *Kashf al-Asrār*, p.vol. 2, p.289, Ibn Niẓām al-Dīn al-Anṣārī, *Fawātiḥ al-Raḥamūt Sharḥ Musallam al-Thubūt*, ed. Abdullah Mahmoud M. Omar, 1st ed. (Beirut: Dār al-Kutub Al-ᶜIlmiyyah, 2002), vol. 2, p.213, Ibn Taymiyah, *Al-Musawadah*, p. 316, Mohammad Al-Khudari, *'Uṣūl Al-Fiqh* (Beirut: al-Maktabah al-ᶜAaṣriyyah, 2002), p.280, al-Rāzī, *Al-Maḥsūl fī* ᶜ*Ilm*

al-'*Uṣūl*, vol. 4, p.214, al-Āmidī, *Al-Iḥkām*, vol. 1, p.404.

80. Ayatollah Medhi Sham al-Din, *Al-Ijtihād wa al-Tajdīd fī al-Fiqh al-Islāmī* (Beirut: al-Mu'assassah al-Dawliyyah, 1999), p.23.
81. Hasaballah, *'Uṣūl al-Tashrīᶜ*, p.124, Abu Zahrah, *'Uṣūl al-Fiqh*, p.104, Aḥmad Abū Moḥammad al-Shāshī, *'Uṣūl al-Shāshī* (Beirut: Dār al-Kitāb al-ᶜArabī, 1402 AH), p.325, Bayḍawī, *Tafsīr al-Bayḍawī* (Beirut: Dār al-Fikr, no date), vol. 3, p.5, Jamāl al-Dīn al-Isnawī, *Nihāyah al-Sūl Sharḥ Minhāj al-Wusūl*, ed. Abdul Qadir Mohammad Ali (Beirut: Dār al-Kutub al-ᶜIlmiyyah, 1999), vol. 3, p.4, Abd Allah ibn Aḥmad al-Nasafī, *Kashf al-Asrār Sharḥ al-Muṣannaf ᶜAlā al-Manār*, 1st ed. (Beirut: Dār al-Kutub al-ᶜIlmiyyah, 1998), vol, p.196, al-Baṣrī, *Al-Muᶜtamad*, vol. 2, p.195, al-Shawkānī, *Irshād al-Fuḥūl*, p.198.
82. Ibn Ḥazm, *Al-Iḥkām*, vol. 1, p.121,29,70, al-Rāzī, *Al-Maḥsūl fī ᶜIlm al-'Uṣūl*, vol. 5, p.144, al-Subkī, *Al-'Ibhāj fī Sharḥ al-Minhāj*, vol.3, p.18, al-Āmidī, *Al-Iḥkām*, vol. 4, p.62, al-Baṣrī, *Al-Muᶜtamad*, vol.2, p.299, al-Ghazālī, *Al-Mustaṣfā*, vol. 2, p.557.
83. Ibn Ḥazm, *Al-Iḥkām*, vol. 8, p.103.
84. Soltan, "Ḥujiyyah", p.284.
85. Ibn Ḥazm, *Al-Muḥllā*.
86. A. K. al-Nami, "Studies in Ibadhism (Al-Ibāḍiyyah)" (Ph.D. diss, University of Cambridge, 1971), p36.
87. Al-Āmidī, *Al-Iḥkām*, vol. 4, pp. 9, 10.
88. Ibid., vol. 4, pp. 9–10.
89. Abu Zahrah, *'Uṣūl al-Fiqh*, p.218.
90. Ibid.
91. Al-Ghazālī, *Al-Mustaṣfā*, vol. 2, p.345., Abu Zahrah, *'Uṣūl al-Fiqh*, p.223.
92. Ibid.
93. Abdullah bin Bayah, *ᶜAlāqah Maqāṣid al-Sharīᶜah bi 'Uṣūl al-Fiqh*, 1st ed. (Cairo: al-Furqān Islamic Heritage Foundation, al-Maqāṣid Research Centre, 2006), p.25.
94. Al-Ṭūfī, *Al-Taᶜyīn*, p.239.
95. Abdul-Hakim al-Saadi, *Mabāḥith al-ᶜIllah fī al-Qiyās ᶜInd al-'Uṣūliyyīn* (Beirut: Dār al-Bashā'ir, 1986), p.110.
96. Hasaballah, *'Uṣūl Al-Tashrīᶜ*, p. 155.
97. Ibid.
98. Abu Zahrah, *'Uṣūl al-Fiqh*, p.240.
99. Ibid., p. 241.
100. Ibid.
101. Al-Āmidī, *Al-Iḥkām*, vol. 4, p.216.
102. Al-Nami, "Studies in Ibadhism."

103. Abū Isḥāq al-Shāṭibī, *Al-Iʿtiṣām* (Egypt: Almaktabah al-Tijāriyyah Alkubrā, no date), vol. 2, pp. 129–33.
104. Ibn al-Qayyim, *Iʿlām al-Muwaqqiʿīn*, vol. 3, pp. 3–150.
105. Husein Hamid Hasan, *Naẓariyyah Al-Maṣlaḥah fī al-Fiqh al-Islāmī* (Cairo: Maktabah al-Mutanabbī, 1981), pp. 8–12.
106. Al-Ṭūfī, *Al-Taʿyīn*, p.2, p.239.
107. Mahmoud Abū al-Manaqib al-Zanjani, *Takhrīj al-Furūʿ*, ed. Mohammed Adeeb Salih, 2nd ed. (Beirut: al-Risālah Foundation, 1398 AH), p.320.
108. ʿAlā' al-Dīn al-Kassānī, *Badā'iʿ al-Ṣanā'iʿ fī Tartīb al-Sharā'iʿ*, 2nd ed. (Beirut: Dār al-Kitāb al-ʿArabī, 1982), vol. 1, p.65.
109. Al-Killīnī, *'Uṣūl al-Kāfī*, vol. 1, pp. 192–279.
110. Abu Zahrah, *Tārīkh al-Mathāhib al-Islāmiyyah*, p.700.
111. Abu Zahrah, *'Uṣūl al-Fiqh*, p.205, Al-Shawkānī, *Irshād Al-Fuḥūl*, p.241.
112. Moḥammad ibn Idrīs al-Shāfiʿī, *Al-Umm*, 2nd ed. (Beirut: Dār al-Maʿrifah, 1393 AH), vol. 7, p.301, Ibn Ḥazm, *Al-Iḥkām*, vol. 5, pp. 195–97.
113. Abu Zahrah, *'Uṣūl al-Fiqh*, p.244.
114. Soltan, "Ḥujiyyah", p.460.
115. Al-Shāṭibī, *Al-Muwāfaqāt*, vol. 4, p.207.
116. Al-Sarkhasī, *'Uṣūl al-Sarkhasī*, vol. 2, p.203, Al-Nasafī, *Kashf al-Asrār*, vol. 2, p.292, Hasan, *Naẓariyyah al-Maṣlaḥah fī al-Fiqh al-Islāmī*, p. 590, Abu Zahrah, *Tārīkh al-Mathāhib al-Islāmiyyah*, p. 447.
117. Mohammad Amin ibn Abdan, *Nashr al-ʿArf fī ma Buniya Min al-Aḥkām ʿAla al-ʿUrf* (Cairo: no date), vol. 2, p.119.
118. Abu Zahrah, *'Uṣūl al-Fiqh*, p.268.
119. Soltan, "Ḥujiyyah", p. 522.
120. Al-Shawkānī, *Irshād Al-Fuḥūl*, p. 246.
121. Abu Zahrah, *'Uṣūl Al-Fiqh*, p.271.
122. Al-Shāṭibī, *Al-Muwāfaqāt*, vol. 2, p.249.
123. Abu Zahrah, *'Uṣūl Al-Fiqh*, p.273.
124. Ibid., p.273.
125. Wolfe, *About Philosophy*, p. 90.
126. Qur'an, Surah *al-Anʿām*, 6:90, Surah *al-Shūrā*, 42:13, Surah *al-Mā'idah*, 5:44, Surah *al-Naḥl*, 16:123.
127. Al-Shawkānī, *Irshād al-Fuḥūl*, p.240.
128. Ibid.
129. Al-Anṣārī, *Fawātiḥ al-Raḥamūt*, vol. 2, p.186.
130. Al-Shāfiʿī, *Al-Risālah*, p.1810, Ibn al-Qayyim, *Iʿlām al-Muwaqqiʿīn*, vol. 1, pp. 24, 25.
131. Ibid.
132. Soltan, "Ḥujiyyah", p. 537.

133. Al-Āmidī, *Al-Iḥkām*, vol. 4, p.205.
134. Ibid., vol. 2, p.201, Al-Subkī, *Al-'Ibhāj fī Sharḥ al-Minhāj*, vol. 3, p.205, ʿAbdullāh ibn Qudāmah al-Maqdisī, *Rawḍah al-Nāẓir wa Janah al-Manāẓir*, ed. Abdul Aziz Abdul Rahman Alsaeed, 2nd ed. (Riyadh: Mohammed ibn Saud University, 1399 AH), p.84, Al-Sarkhasī, *'Uṣūl Al-Sarkhasī*, vol. 2, p.206, Al-Anṣārī, *Fawātiḥ al-Raḥamūt Sharḥ Musallam al-Thubūt*, vol. 2, p.186, Ibn Taymiyah, *Al-Musawwadah*, p. 128, Al-Shawkānī, I*rshād al-Fuḥūl*, p.243.
135. Ibn Ḥazm, *Al-Iḥkām*, p.539.
136. Farhan, *Ḥarakah al-Ijtihād ʿInd al-Shīʿah*, p.65.
137. Ibn Taymiyah, *Kutub wa Rasā'il wa Fatwah*, vol. 20, pp. 311, 12, 13, 16, 20, 28.
138. Al-Shāfiʿī, *Al-Risālah*, p.1558.
139. Ibn Ḥazm, *Al-Muḥallā*, vol. 3, pp. 149–61, 331.
140. Al-Sarkhasī, *'Uṣūl Al-Sarkhasī*, vol. 9, p.4, Jalāl al-Dīn al-Suyūṭī, *Al-Ashbāh wa al-Naẓā'ir* (Beirut: Dār al-Kutub al-ʿIlmiyyah, 1403 AH) vol. 1, p.99.
141. Soltan, "Ḥujiyyah", p.628, Abu Zahrah, *'Uṣūl Al-Fiqh*, p.255.
142. Abu Zahrah, *'Uṣūl Al-Fiqh*, p.256.
143. Auda, *Fiqh Al-Maqāṣid*, p.65.
144. Shams al-Dīn ibn al-Qayyim, *Al-Ṭuruq al-Ḥukmiyyah fī al-Siyāsah al-Sharʿiyyah*, ed. M. Jamil Ghazi (Cairo: al-Madanī, no date), vol. 1, p.5.
145. Al-Baṣrī, *Al-Muʿtamad*, vol. 2, p.236.
146. Al-Sadir, *Durūs fī ʿIlm al-'Uṣūl*, p. 380.
147. Abu Zahrah, *'Uṣūl Al-Fiqh*, p.278.
148. Abdul-Jabbar, *Al-Mughniī*, vol.4, p.174, Abdul-Jabbar, *Faḍl Al-Iʿtizāl* p.139.
149. Haitham Sarhan, *Istrātījiyyah al-Ta'wīl al-Dilālī ʿInd al-Muʿtazilah* (Lādhiqiyyah, Syria: Dār al-Ḥiwār, 2003), p.28.
150. Abu Zahrah, *'Uṣūl Al-Fiqh*, p.32.
151. Ibid., p.34.
152. Hasaballah, *'Uṣūl Al-Tashrīʿ*, p. 395.
153. Ibid.
154. Qur'an Surah *Moḥammad* and Surah *al-Baqarah* (trans. Mohammad Asad). Refer to: Abdul-Jabbar, *Al-Mughnī*, vol. 8, p.89, Moḥammed ibn ʿAbdullāh al-Zarkashī, *Al-Baḥr al-Muhīṭ fī 'Uṣūl al-Fiqh*, ed. M. M. Tamir, 1st ed. (Beirut: 2000), vol. 2, p.539.
155. Moḥammad ibn Abū Bakr al-Zarʿī, *Tuḥfah Al-Mawdud bi 'Aḥkām al-Mawlūd*, ed. Abdul Qadir al-Arnaout, 1st ed. (Damascus: Dār al-Bayān, 1971), vol. 1, p.291, Abū Bakr al-Hussaynī, *Kifāyah al-Akhyār fī Ḥal Ghāyah al-Ikhtiṣār*, ed. A. A. Baltaji and M. Wahbi Sulaiman, 1st ed.

(Damascus: Dār al-Khayr, 1994), vol. 1, p.447, Yaḥya Abū-Zakariyyah al-Nawawī, *Al-Majmūʿ* (Beirut: Dār al-Fikr, 1997), vol. 9, p.342, ʿAbdullāh ibn Moḥammed al-Baṭlayawsī, *Al-Inṣāf fī al-Tanbīh ʿAlā al-Maʿānī wa al-Asbāb 'Allatī Awjabat al-Ikhtilāf*, ed. Mohammed Ridwan al-Dayah, 2nd ed. (Beirut: Dār al-Fikr, 1403 AH), vol. 9, p.430.

156. Abu Zahrah, *'Uṣūl Al-Fiqh*, p.311.
157. Al-Zarʿī, *Tuḥfah al-Mawdūd*, vol. 1, p.291, al-Hussaynī, *Kifāyah al-Akhyār*, vol. 1, p.447, al-Nawawī, *Al-Majmūʿ*, vol. 9, p.342, al-Baṭlayawsī, *Al-Inṣāf*, vol. 9, p.430.
158. Hasaballah, *'Uṣūl Al-Tashrīʿ*, p. 395.
159. Al-Baṭlayawsī, *Al-Inṣāf*, vol. 2, p.514, Moḥammed ibn ʿAbdullāh al-Zarkashī, *Sharḥ al-Zarkashī ʿAlā Mukhtaṣar al-Kharqī*, ed. Abdul Moneim Khalil Ibrahim, 1st ed. (Beirut: Dār al-Kutub al-ʿIlmiyyah, 2002), vol. 1, p.317, Al-Shāfiʿī, *Al-Umm*, vol. 4, p.261.
160. For example: Al-Shāfiʿī, *Al-Umm*, vol. 4, p.261.
161. Hasaballah, *'Uṣūl Al-Tashrīʿ*, p.395.
162. Al-Baṭlayawsī, *Al-Inṣāf*, vol. 2, p.467, Ibn Nujaym, *Al-Baḥr al-Rā'iq*, vol. 8, p.196, Al-Ḥasfakī, *Al-Durr al-Mukhtār* (Beirut: Dār al-Fikr, 1386), vol. 6, p.309.

CHAPTER FIVE

1. John L. Esposito, ed., *The Oxford History of Islam* (Oxford: University Press, 1999), p.690.
2. I am using this term after Tariq Ramadan even though my definition is slightly different. Refer to: Tariq Ramadan, *Western Muslims and the Future of Islam* (New York: Oxford University Press, 2004), p.24.
3. Leonard Binder, *Ideological Revolution in the Middle East*, ed. John Wiley (New York: 1964), p.31–40, H. Mintjes, "Mawlana Mawdudi's Last Years and the Resurgence of Fundamentalist Islam," *Al-Mushīr* 22, no. 2 (1980): vol. 22, No.2, pp. 46–73.
4. John Esposito, *Islam and Politics* (Syracuse: Syracuse University Press, 1984), p.216.
5. Yvonne Haddad, "The Islamic Alternative," *The Link* 15, no. 4 (1982): vol. 15, no. 4, pp. 1–14.
6. William Shepard, "Islam and Ideology: Towards a Typology," *Int. Journal Middle Eastern Studies*, no. 19 (1987): No. 19, p.308.
7. John Voll, *Islam: Continuity and Change in the Modern World* (Bolder, Colorado: Westview press, 1982).
8. Fazlur Rahman, *Islam*, 2nd ed. (Chicago: University of Chicago Press, 1979). and Fazlur Rahman, "Islamic Modernism: Its Scope, Method, and

Alternatives," *IJMES* 1, no. 4 (1979): vol. 1, No. 4, pp. 311–17.

9. Akbar S. Ahmed, *Postmodernism and Islam: Predicament and Promise*, 7 ed. (London and New York: Routledge, 2004), p.160.
10. Ramadan, *Western Muslims and the Future of Islam*, pp. 24ff.
11. For example, Bernard, RAND 2004 Report.
12. Al-Qaradawi, *Madkhal*, p.200.
13. Nawal El-Saadawi, *God Dies by the Nile*, 6th ed. (London: Zed Books Ltd, 2002).
14. Refer to: Khalid Abou El-Fadl, *Speaking in God's Name* (Oxford: Oneworld Publications, 2003), Mohammed Shahrour, *Naḥwa 'Uṣūl Jadīdah*.
15. Refer, for example to: Ali Izzet Begoviç, *Al-Iᶜlān al-Islāmī*, trans. Mohamed Yusif Ads, 1st ed. (Cairo: Dār al-Shorūq, no date), p.49, Yusuf al-Qaradawi, *Al-Ijtihād al-Muᶜāṣir Bayna al-Inḍibāṭ wa al-Infirāṭ* (Cairo: Dār al-Tawzīᶜ, 1994), Mohammad Emara, *Tajdīd al-Fikr al-Islāmī* (Cairo: Kitāb Dār al-Hilāl, 1981), Abu al-Ala Mawdudi, *Al-Ḥijāb* (Jeddah: al-Dār al-Saᶜūdiyyah li al-Nashr wa al-Tawzīᶜ, 1986), Mohammad Khatami, *Islam, Liberty, and Development* (Johannesburg: Global Books, 2001), p.24.
16. For example, Emara, *Tajdīd al-Fikr al-Islāmī*, p.5.
17. Abdul-Rahman al-Shaykh, *Fatḥ l-Majīd Sharḥ Kitāb al-Tawḥīd* (Cairo: Mu'ssassah Qurṭubah, no date), pp .13–14.
18. Emara, *Tajdīd al-Fikr al-Islāmī*, p. 5.
19. El-Awa, ed., *Maqāṣid al-Sharīᶜah*.
20. Al-Qaradawi, *Al-Ijtihād al-Muᶜāṣir*, Begoviç, *Al-Iᶜlān al-Islāmī*, Emara, *Tajdīd al-Fikr al-Islāmī*.
21. Khatami, *Islam, Liberty, and Development*, p. 25.
22. Mohammad Abu Al-Farag ibn al-Nadeem, *Al-Fihrist* (Beirut: Dār al-Maᶜrifah, 1978), vol. 1, pp. 296, 300, 306, Ibn Taymiyah, *Kutub wa Rasā'il wa Fatwah*, vol. 1, p.21.
23. For example, al-Juwaynī, *Al-Burhān*, vol.2, p.832, Al-Subkī, *Al-Ibhāj fī Sharḥ al-Minhāj*, vol. 2, p.285, Ahmad al-Shaykh al-Zarqa, *Sharḥ al-Qawāᶜid al-Fiqhiyyah*, ed. Mustafa Ahmad al-Zarqa, 2nd ed. (Damascus: Dār al-Qalam, 1989), vol. 1, p.112, ᶜAlā' al-Dīn al-Mirdāwī, *Al-Taḥbīr Sharḥ al-Taḥrīr fī 'Uṣūl Al-Fiqh*, ed. Awad al-Qarni Abdurahman Jubrain, Ahmad al-Sarrah, 1st ed. (Riyadh: Maktabah al-rushd, 2000), vol. 4, p.1766, al-Qarāfī, *Al-Furūq* (Maᶜa Hawāmishih), vol. 3, p.346.
24. Abū Isḥāq al-Shirāzī, *Al-Lamᶜ fī 'Uṣūl Al-Fiqh* (Beirut: Dār al-Kutub al-ᶜIlmiyyah, 1985), vol.1, p.75.
25. Abū Qudāmah Ashraf al-Kinānī, *Al-Adillah al-Isti'nāsiyyah ᶜInd al-'Uṣūliyyīn*, 1st ed. (Amman: Dār al-Nafā'is, 2005), p.22.
26. Al-Merdāwī, *Al-Taḥbīr Sharḥ al-Taḥrīr fī 'Uṣūl Al-Fiqh*, vol.3, pp. 53, 336,

422, 31, Al-Subkī, *Al-'Ibhāj fī Sharḥ al-Minhāj*, vol. 1, p.216, Abū Ḥāmid al-Ghazālī, *Al-Mankhūl fī Taʿlīqāt al-'Uṣūl*, ed. Mohamed Hasan Hito, 2nd ed. (Damascus: Dār al-Fikr, 1400 AH), p.286, Al-Sarkhasī, *'Uṣūl Al-Sarkhasī*, vol. 1, p.369, Al-Zarkashī, *Al-Baḥr Al-Muḥīṭ*, vol. 4, p.473, Saʿad al-Dīn al-Taftazānī al-Shāfiʿī, *Sharḥ al-Talwīḥ ʿAlā al-Tawḍīḥ li matn al-Tanqīḥ fī 'Uṣūl Al-Fiqh*, ed. Zakariya Umairat (Beirut: Dār al-Kutub Al-ʿIlmiyyah, 1996), vol. 1, p.126, Amir Badshah, *Taysīr al-Taḥrīr* (Beirut: Dār al-Fikr, no date), vol. 1, p.233, Al-Bukhārī, *Kashf al-Asrār*, vol. 4, p.469.

27. Al-Zarkashī, *Al-Baḥr al-Muḥīṭ*, vol. 3, p.32.
28. A-Shāshī, *'Uṣūl Al-Shāshī*, vol. 1, p.76.
29. Al-Zarkashī, *Al-Baḥr al-Muḥīṭ*, vol. 4, p.582.
30. Mohammad Abdul-Hayy al-Laknawi, *Al-Ajwibah al-Fāḍilah li al-As'ilah al-ʿAsharah al-Kāmilah*, ed. Abdul-Fattah Abu Ghuddah (Halab: Maktab al-Maṭbūʿāt al-Islāmiyyah, 1384 AH), p.183.
31. Muslehuddin, *Philosophy of the Islamic Law and the Orientalists*, 1st ed. (Delhi: Markazi Maktaba Islami, 1985), p. 217.
32. Mentioned in: Bernard, RAND 2004 Report.
33. Shahrour, *Naḥwa 'Uṣūl Jadīdah*, p.278.
34. El-Affendi, ed, *Rethinking Islam and Modernity: Essays in Honour of Fathi Osman* (London: Islamic Foundation, 2001), p.45.
35. Shahrour, *Naḥwa 'Uṣūl Jadīdah*, p.323.
36. For a comprehensive and up-to-date online resource on 'Islamic websites,' refer to: Gary Bunt. Virtually Islamic: Research and News About Islam in the Digital Age, 2000 [last visited Mar. 15th, 2007], http://www.virtuallyislamic.com/
37. I am using this term after Tariq Ramadan even though my definition is slightly different. I restrict scholastic traditionalism to one classic school only, but he does not. His 'scholastic traditionalism' is similar to my 'scholastic neo-traditionalism.' Refer to: Ramadan, *Western Muslims and the Future of Islam*, p.24.
38. For example, Ahmad al-Zarqa, *Sharḥ al-Qawāʿid al-Fiqhiyyah*, 2nd ed. (Damascus: Dār al-Qalam, 1998), p.150, Shaykh al-Zarqa is from the Ḥanafī school. For an example of the same approach in the Shia schools, refer to literature on *taqlīd* (immitation), for example: L. Clarke, "The Shiʿi Construction of Taqlid," *Journal of Islamic Studies* 12, no. 1 (2001).
39. Refer to examples from various schools in: Mohammed ibn Ismail al-Sanaani, *Irshād al-Nuqad 'Ilā Taysīr al-Ijtihād*, ed. Salah al-Din Maqbool Ahmad, 1st ed. (Kuwait: Al-Dār al-Salafiyyah, 1405 AH), vol. 1, p.17.
40. Hafiz Anwar, "Wilāyah Al-Mar'ah fī al-Fiqh al-Islāmī" (Masters, Imam Saud Islamic University, Published by Dār Balansiyah, 1999), p. 107.
41. Al-Bukhārī, *Al-Ṣaḥīḥ*, No.7099.

42. Refer to Mohammad al-Ghazaly, who interpreted the Hadith in the context of the Prophet talking about a specific woman, who was at war with Muslims at that time (the daughter of Kisra who ruled Persia after her father's death): Mohammad Al-Ghazaly (Al-Saqqa), *Al-Sunnah al-Nabawiyyah Bayna Ahl al-Fiqh wa Ahl al-Ḥadīth*, 11th ed. (Cairo: Dār al-Shurūq, 1996). Fatima Mernissi presented a more detailed analysis of the political context of the narration of this Hadith and the relevance of its narrator (Abū Bakrah): Fatima Mernissi, *The Veil and the Male Elite: A Feminist Interpretation of Women's Rights in Islam*, trans. Mary Jo Lakeland (Cambridge, Mass.: Perseus Books, 1991). Al-Ghazaly's and Mernissi's views represent typical 'modern' and 'postmodern' approaches, respectively.
43. The term 'neo-traditionalism' is used in: Ebrahim Moosa, "The Poetics and Politics of Law after Empire: Reading Women's Rights in the Contestations of Law," *UCLA Journal of Islamic and Near Eastern Law*, no. 1 (Fall/Winter) (2002), and elsewhere, without specific differentiation between traditionalism and neo-traditionalism. Muslih argued that 'when the traditionalist starts to understand more of the Western challenge then he becomes a "neo-traditionalist."' Refer to: Muslih, *A Project of Islamic Revivalism* (Leiden: University of Leiden, 2006).
44. For example: M. B. Arifin, "The Principles of *Umum* and *Takhsis* in Islamic Jurisprudence" (Ph. D. diss, University of Edinburgh, 1988), Mir Mohammad Sadeghi, "Islamic Criminal Law and the Challenge of Change: A Comparative Study" (Ph. D. diss, London, School of Oriental and African Studies, 1986).
45. A. K. al-Nami, "Studies in Ibadhism (Al-Ibāḍiyyah)" (Ph.D. diss, University of Cambridge, 1971), R. A. A. Rahim, "Certain Aspects of Ijtihad in Islamic Jurisprudence, with Special Reference to the Comparative Study between Sunni and Shiʿi Principles" (M. Phil. diss, University of St. Andrews, 1991), Sham al-Din, *Al-Ijtihād wa al-Tajdīd fī al-Fiqh al-Islāmī*, p.137.
46. Mohammad Nasir al-Din al-Albani, *Wujūb al-Akhdh bi Ḥadīth al-Āḥād fī al-ʿAqīdah wa al Rad ʿalā Shubah al-Mukhālifīn* (Banhā and Kuwait: Dār al-ʿIlm and al-Dār al-Salafiyyah, no date).
47. For example, Usama Khayyat, *Mukhtalaf al-Ḥadīth*, pp. 271–73, Anwar, Wilāyah, *Al-Mar'ah*, pp. 50–120.
48. For example, al-Qaradawi, *Al-Ijtihād al-Muʿāṣir*, p. 24.
49. Al-Qaradawi, *Madkhal*, p.277.
50. Abu Zahrah, *'Uṣūl al-Fiqh*, p. 377, Al-Qaradawi, *Fiqh al-Zakāh*, vol. 1, p.30, Al-Qaradawi, *Madkhal*, p.277, Abdul-Karim Zaidan, *Al-Wajīz fī 'Uṣūl al-Fiqh*, 7th ed. (Beirut: Al-Risālah, 1998), p.411.
51. Wahba al-Zuhaili, *Tajdīd al-Fiqh al-Islāmī, Ḥiwārāt li Qur'ān Jadīd*

(Damascus: Dār al-Fikr, 2000), p.165, Ali Jumah, *Al-Muṣṭalaḥ al-Uṣūlī wa Mushkilah al-Mafāhīm* (Cairo: Al-Maᶜhad al-ᶜĀlamī li al-Fikr al-Islāmī, 1996), p.64.

52. For some examples, refer to: A. A. M. al-Marzouqi, "Human Rights in Islamic Law" (Ph.D. diss, University of Exeter, 1990).
53. ECFR, vol. 1, p.10, June 2002.
54. Ali al-Mawardi, *Al-Aḥkām al-Sulṭāniyyah* (Cairo: al-Maktabah al-Tawfīqiyyah, no date), p.5, Sham al-Dīn ibn al-Qayyim, *Aḥkām Ahl al-Dhimmah*, ed. Abu Bara' and Abu Hamid (Riyadh: Ramadī, 1997), vol. 2, p.728. Recently, some researchers recalled from the *Fiqhī* literature the concept of '*Dār al-ᶜAhd*' (the land of truce) as an additional third category. However, even a three-category classification does not account for the contemporary complexity in international relations. Refer to: N. A. A. al-Yahya, "Ibn Qudamah's Methodology and His Approach to Certain Aspects of the Islamic Law of International Relations in the Hanbali Juristic Tradition" (Ph.D. diss, University of Manchester, 1992), A. M. Asmal, "Muslims under Non-Muslim Rule: The Fight (Legal) Views of Ibn Nujaym and Al-Wansharisi" (Ph.D. diss, University of Manchester, 1998).
55. European Council for Fatwa and Research, Scientific Review of the European Council for Fatwa and Research, vol. 2, Jan. 2003 issue.
56. Ismail Fatani, *Ikhtilāf Al-Dārayn*, 2nd ed. (Cairo: Dār al-Salām, 1998).
57. See for example, Abū Bakr al-Jaṣṣaṣ, *Aḥkām Al-Qur'ān*, ed. Mohammad al-Sadiq Qamhawi (Beirut: Dār Ihyā' al-Turāth, 1984), vol. 2, p.101, Zayn al-Dīn ibn Nujaym, *Al-Baḥr al-Rā'iq*, 2nd ed. (Beirut: Dār al-Maᶜrifah, no date), vol. 3, p.117.
58. Al-Mirghiyānī, *Al-Hidāyah Sharḥ Bidāyah al-Mubtadi'*, vol. 1, p.196, Ibn ᶜĀbidīn, *Ḥāshiyah Radd al-Muḥtār*, vol. 3, p.55, Al-Sīwāsī, *Sharḥ Fatḥ al-Qadīr*, vol. 3, p.258.
59. Abū Dawūd, Tirmidhī, and Ibn Mājah collections, the chapters on marriage.
60. See for example, Mohammad Amin ibn Abidin, *Al-Ḥāshiyah* (Beirut: Dār Al-Fikr, 2000), vol. 3, p.55.
61. For example, Qur'an (2:234): 'There is no blame on you (men) for what they (women) wish to do with themselves in a lawful manner (in marriage).' – Trans. T. B. Irving.
62. For example, Usama Khayyat, "Mukhtalaf al-Ḥadīth " (Masters, 'Umm al-Qurā, Published by Dār al-Faḍīlah, 2001), pp. 271–73.
63. This term was coined by Shaykh Yusuf al-Qaradawi (Oral Discussion, London, UK, March 2nd, 2005, during the Foundational Seminar of al-Maqāṣid Research Centre).
64. Ibn Ḥazm, *Al-Iḥkām*, vol. 2, p.229.

65. Robert Gleave, "Introduction," in *Islamic Law: Theory and Practice*, ed. R. Gleave and E. Kermeli (London: I.B. Tauris, 1997).
66. Shams al-Din, *Al-Ijtihād wa al-Tajdīd fī al-Fiqh al-Islāmī*, p.32. Also refer to: Mohammad Al-Killini, *'Uṣūl al-Kāfī*, ed. Ali Akbar Al-Ghiffari (Tehran: Dār al-Manshūrāt al-Islāmiyyah, no date), vol. 1, pp. 59–62.
67. Ibn Ḥazm, *al-Muḥallā*.
68. Ahmad Idris al-Taan, *Al-Maqāṣid wa al-Munāwarah al-ʿIlmāniyyah*, Muntadā al-Tawḥīd, 2005 [cited Mar. 10th, 2007]. Available from: http://www.eltwhed.com/vb/showthread.php?t=2456, Mohammad Ali Mufti, *Naqd al-Judhūr al-Fikriyyah li al-Dimoqraṭiyyah al-Gharbiyyah* (Riyadh: al-Muntadā al-Islāmī and Majallah al-Bayān, 2002), pp.167–190.
69. Mohamed Arkoun, *Rethinking Islam: Common Questions, Uncommon Answers*, ed. Robert D. Lee, trans. Robert D. Lee (Boulder: Westview Press, 1994), p.221.
70. Wajanat Abdurahim Maymani, *Qāʿidah al-Dhara'iʿ*, 1st ed. (Jeddah: Dār al-Mujtamaʿ, 2000), pp. 608, 22, 32, 50.
71. Copied from: Abou El-Fadl, *Speaking in God's Name*, p.275.
72. Ahmed, *Postmodernism*, p.160.
73. Al-Sharif, *Haqīqah al-Dimuqrāṭiyyah*, p.20.
74. Ibid. pp. 28–48.
75. Ahmed, *Postmodernism*, p.160.
76. Abdullahi al-Naim, "Islam and Human Rights," *Tikkun* 18, no. 1 (2003): p.48.
77. Charles Kurzman, ed., *Modernist Islam, 1840–1940: A Sourcebook* (Oxford: Oxford University Press, 2002), p.4.
78. Ebrahim Moosa, "The Debts and Burdens of Critical Islam," in *Progressive Muslims*, ed. Omid Safi (Oxford: Oneworld, 2003), p.118.
79. Sohail Inayatullah and Gail Boxwell, *Islam, Postmodernism and Other Futures: A Ziauddin Sardar Reader* (London: Pluto Press, 2003), pp. 27, 70, 82.
80. Neal Robinson, *Islam, a Concise Introduction* (Richmond: Curzon Press, 1999), p.161.
81. Mohammad Iqbal, *The Reconstruction of Religious Thought in Islam*, ed. M. Saeed Shaykh (Lahore: 1986), lecture 2.
82. Malcolm H. Kerr, Islamic Reform: *The Political and Legal Theories of Mohammad Abduh and Rashid Rida* (London: Cambridge University Press, 1966), p.108.
83. Mohammad Abduh, *Al-Aʿmāl al-Kāmilah*, ed. Mohammad Emara (Cairo: Dār al-Shurūq, 1993).
84. Francois Geny, *Methode D'interpretation Et Sources En Droit Prive Positif*,

trans. Louisiana State Law Institute, 2nd ed, vol. 1 (1954), vol. 2, p.190.

85. Mohammad Abduh, *Al-Aʿmāl al-Kāmilah*, ed. Mohammad Emara (Cairo: Dār al-Shurūq, 1996).
86. Kerr, *Islamic Reform*, p.188.
87. Ashur, al-Tahir, *Al-Taḥrīr wa al-Tanwīr* (Tunis: Dār Saḥnūn, 1997).
88. Nafi, Basheer, "Tahir ibn Ashur: The Career and Thought of a Modern Reformist Alim, with Special Reference to His Work of Tafsir." *Journal of Qur'anic Studies* 7, no. 1 (2005).
89. Abduh, *Al-Aʿmāl al-Kāmilah*, vol. 4, p.143.
90. Ibid., vol. 1,p. 187.
91. Ibid., vol. 4, p.145.
92. Ibid., vol. 4,p. 143.
93. Ibid., vol. 5, p.546.
94. Ibid., vol.2, p.445.
95. Abū Ḥāmid al-Ghazālī, *Al-Qisṭās al-Mustaqīm* (Beirut: Catholic Publishing House, 1959).
96. For example: Shakti Gawain, *Return to the Garden: A Journey to Discovery* (California: New World Library, 1989), p.155.
97. Fazlur Rahman. "Islamic Modernism: Its Scope, Method, and Alternatives." *International Journal of Middle East Studies* 1, no. 4 (1970), p.229.
98. Published under several titles. See: Ayatollah Mohammad Baqir al-Sadir, "Al-Sunan al-Tārīkhiyyah fī al-Qur'an," in *Imam Al-Sadir: Al-Aʿmāl al-Kāmilah* (Beirut: Dār al-Taʿāruf, 1990), vol. 13, p.38.
99. M. al-Tahir Mesawi, "Al-Shaykh ibn ʿĀshūr wa al-Mashrūʿ Alladhī Lam Yaktamil," in *Maqāṣid al-Sharīʿah al-Islāmiyyah* (Kuala Lumpur: al-Fajr, 1999), p.73.
100. Al-Alwani, Taha Jabir, "Madkhal Ilā Fiqh al-Aqalliyyāt." Paper presented at the European Council for Fatwa and Research, ECFR, Dublin, Jan. 2004, p.45.
101. Abdul-Karim Soroush, "The Evolution and Devolution of Religious Knowledge," in *Liberal Islam: A Sourcebook*, ed. Charles Kurzman (Oxford: Oxford University Press, 1998), p.248.
102. Ibid., p.250.
103. Fazlur Rahman, *Islam*, p.257.
104. Ebrahim Moosa, "Introduction," in *Revival and Reform in Islam: A Study of Islamic Fundamentalism by Fazlur Rahman*, ed. Ebrahim Moosa (Oxford: OneWorld, 2000), p.61.
105. Ibid., p.186.
106. Salwa al-Awa, *Al-Wujūh wa al-Naẓā'ir fī al-Qur'ān al-Karīm*, 1st ed. (Cairo: Dār al-Shurūq, 1998), p.69.

107. Salwa M. S. El-Awa, *Textual Relations in the Quran: Relevance, Coherence and Structure*, 1st ed. (London and New York: Routledge, 2006).
108. An opinion still maintained by some contemporary scholars. See for example, Manna al-Qattan, *Mabāḥith fī ʿUlūm al-Qur'ān*, 11th ed. (Cairo: Wahba, 2000), p.322.
109. Ali Abd al-Raziq, "Message Not Government, Religion Not State," in *Liberal Islam: A Sourcebook*, ed. Charles Kurzman (Oxford: Oxford University Press, 1998), p.32.
110. Al-Māwardī, *Al-Aḥkām*, p.5.
111. James P. Piscatori, *Islamic Countries: Politics and Government* (Princeton: Princeton University Press, 1996), pp. 53–54.
112. Mahmoud Mohamed Taha, "The Second Message of Islam," in *Liberal Islam: A Sourcebook*, ed. Charles Kurzman (Oxford: Oxford University Press, 1998), p.262. 'Islam is both democratic and socialist' is a title of a book that Mahmoud Mohamed Taha promised to write but never got to. In 1985, he was executed for protesting the application of certain 'Islamic laws' in Sudan.
113. Sadiq Sulaiman, "Democracy and Shura," in *Liberal Islam: A Sourcebook*, ed. Charles Kurzman (Oxford: Oxford University Press, 1998), p.98.
114. Mohammad Khalaf-Allah, "Legislative Authority," in *Liberal Islam: A Sourcebook*, ed. Charles Kurzman (Oxford: Oxford University Press, 1998), p.45.
115. Abdulaziz Sachedina, *Islamic Roots of Democratic Pluralism* (Oxford: Oxford University Press, 2001), pp. 38, 83, 132.
116. Rachid Ghannouchi, "Participation in Non-Islamic Government," in *Liberal Islam: A Sourcebook*, ed. Charles Kurzman (Oxford: Oxford University Press, 1998), p.95.
117. Seyyed Mohammed Khatami, *Islam, Liberty and Development* (New York: Institute of Global Cultural Studies, Binghamton University, 1998), p.5.
118. Larry Johnston, *Politics: An Introduction to the Modern Democratic State* (Broadview: Peterborough, Ontario, 1998), p.370.
119. H. Normi, *Comparing Voting Systems* (Reidel Publishing Company, 1987).
120. Saad Eddin Ibrahim, ed, *Egypt, Islam and Democracy: Twelve Critical Essays*, vol. 19, Monograph 3, Cairo Papers in Social Science (Cairo: The American University in Cairo Press, 1996).
121. For example: Leila Ahmed, *Women and Gender in Islam* (New Haven, CT: Yale University Press, 1992), S. S. Ali, "Equal before Allah, Unequal before Man? Negotiating Gender Hierarchies in Islam and International Law" (Ph.D. diss, University of Hull, 1998), Benazir Bhutto, "Politics and the Muslim Woman," in *Liberal Islam: A Sourcebook*, ed. Charles Kurzman

(Oxford: Oxford University Press, 1998), Heba Ra'uf Ezzat, "Al-Mar'ah wa al-Dīn wa al-Akhlāq," in *Hiwārāt li Qarn Jadīd* (Dār al-Fikr: Damascus, 2000), Fatima Mernissi, "A Feminist Interpretation of Women's Rights," in *Liberal Islam: A Sourcebook*. Oxford, ed. Charles Kurzman (Oxford: University Press, 1998), A. B. Mukhtar, "Human Rights and Islamic Law: The Development of the Rights of Slaves, Women and Aliens in Two Cultures" (Ph.D. diss, University of Manchester, 1996), S. Saad, "The Legal and Social Status of Women in the Hadith Literature" (Ph.D. diss, University of Leeds, 1990), S. F. Saifi, "A Study of the Status of Women in Islamic Law and Society, with Special Reference to Pakistan" (Ph.D. diss, University of Durham, 1980), F. A. A. Sulaimani, "The Changing Position of Women in Arabia under Islam During the Early Seventh Century" (M. Phil. diss, University of Salford, 1986), Amina Wadud-Muhsin, "Qur'an and Woman," in *Liberal Islam: A Sourcebook*, ed. Charles Kurzman (Oxford: Oxford University Press, 1998).

122. For a non-apologetic opinion, refer to: Seyyed Hossein Nasr, *Ideals and Realities of Islam* (Boston, Mass.: George Allen and Unwin, 2000), pp. 112–13. However, the view that men and women, '[e]ach has certain duties and functions in accordance with his or her nature and constitution,' poses the complex question on the difference between 'nature' and 'culture.'
123. Al-Māwardī, *Al-Aḥkām*, p.108.
124. Ibid., p.10.
125. Ibid., p.229.
126. Ibid., p.25.
127. Mohammad Shakir al-Sharif, *Ḥaqīqah al-Dīmuqrāṭiyyah*, p.3, Mohammad Ali Mufti, *Naqd al-Judhūr al-Fikriyyah li al-Dīmuqrāṭiyyah*, p.91.
128. Mesawi, M. al-Tahir, "Al-Shaykh ibn Ashur wa al-Mashrūᶜ Alladhī Lam Yaktamil" in *Maqāṣid al-Sharīᶜah al-Islāmiyyah* (Kuala Lumpur: al-Fajr, 1999), p.72.
129. Ibn Ashur, *Al-Taḥrīr*, p.115.
130. Ibn Ashur, al-Tahir. *Alaysa al-Ṣubḥ bi Qarīb*? (Tunis: al-Sharikah al-Tūnisiyyah li-Funūn al-Rasm, 1988), p.204.
131. Ibn Ashur, *Maqāṣid al-Sharīᶜah*, p.115.
132. Ayatollah Mohammad Baqir al-Sadir, *Al-'Usus al-Manṭiqiyyah li al-Istiqrā'*, 4th ed. (Beirut: Dār al-Taᶜāruf, 1982).
133. Ibid.
134. Ibid., p. 486.
135. Mesawi, "Al-Shaykh ibn ᶜĀshūr," p.15.
136. For example, al-Zuhaili, *Tajdīd al-Fiqh al-Islāmī*, p. 165, Jumah, *Al-Muṣṭalaḥ al-'Uṣūlī*, p.64.

137. For example, the execution of Mahmoud Taha and the banishment of Fazlur Rahman for their non-mainstream ideas. More examples in: Piscatori, *Islamic Countries: Politics and Government*, p. 53–54.

138. Sano, *Qirā'āt Maᶜrifiyyah fī al-Fikr al-'Uṣūlī*, p.180.

139. Abduh, *Al-Aᶜmāl al-Kāmilah*, vol. 1, p.187 and vol.3, p.215.

140. Ibid., vol. 3, p.301.

141. Ibid., vol. 3, p.301.

142. Ibid., vol. 4, p.9.

143. Ibid., vol. 2, pp. 199, 329, 663–69.

144. Al-Sadir, *Durūs fī ᶜIlm al-'Uṣūl*, p.243.

145. Ibid., p. 244.

146. Ibid., p. 427.

147. Abdul-Moneim al-Nimr, *Al-Ijtihād* (Cairo: Dār al-Shurūq, 1986) p. 60, Masudul Alam Choudhry, "Syllogistic Deductionism in Islamic Social Choice Theory," *International Journal of Social Economics* 17, no. 11 (1990), Shams al-Din, *Al-Ijtihād wa al-Tajdīd fī al-Fiqh al-Islāmī, p.*159, Soltan, "Ḥujiyyah", pp. 86–198.

148. Jamal al-Banna, *Tajdīd al-Fiqh al-Islāmī, Ḥiwārāt li-Qarn Jadīd* (Damascus: Dār al-Fikr, 2000), vol. 2, 251, Mohammad Al-Ghazaly, *Naẓarāt fī al-Qur'ān* (Cairo: Nahḍah Miṣr, 2002), p.194, Mohammad Nada, *Al-Nāskh fī al-Qur'ān* (Cairo: al-Dār al-ᶜArabiyyah li al-Kutub, 1996), p.9.

149. For example: Luay Safi, *IᶜMāl al-ᶜAql* (Pittsburgh: Dār al-Fikr, 1998), p.130, al-Ghazaly, *Al-Sunnah al-Nabawiyyah*, p.36, al-Alwani, "Madkhal" p.36, al-Nimr, *Al-Ijtihād*, p.147, Ayatollah Shams al-Din, p.21, al-Turabi, *Qaḍāyā*, p.157, al-Ghazaly, *Naẓarāt*, p.19, 125, 161.

150. Ali al-Khafeef, "Al-Sunnah al-Tashrīᶜiyyah," in *Al-Sunnah al-Tashrīᶜiyyah wa Ghair al-Tashrīᶜiyyah*, ed. Mohammad Emara (Cairo: Nahḍah Miṣr, 2001), Hasan al-Turabi, *Qaḍāyā al-Tajdīd: Naḥwa Manhaj 'Uṣūlī* (Beirut: Dār al-Hādī, 2000), p.168, al-Zuhaili, *Tajdīd al-Fiqh al-Islāmī*, vol. 2, p.255, Al-Tahir Ashur, *Al-Taḥrīr wa al-Tanwīr* (Tunis: Dār Saḥnūn, 1997), Mohammad Emara, "Al-Sunnah al-Tashrīᶜiyyah wa Ghair al-Tashrīᶜiyyah," in *Al-Sunnah al-Tashrīᶜiyyah wa Ghair al-Tashrīᶜiyyah*, ed. Mohammad Emara (Cairo: Nahḍah Miṣr, 2001), Safi, *Iᶜmāl al-ᶜAql*, p.153, Shams al-Din, *Al-Ijtihād wa al-Tajdīd fī al-Fiqh al-Islāmī*, p.137.

151. Ibn Ashur, al-Tahir, *Alaysa al-Ṣubḥ bi-Qarīb?* (Tunis: al-Sharikah al-Tūnisiyyah li-Funūn al-Rasm, 1988), p.237.

152. Al-Khafeef, "Al-Sunnah al-Tashrīᶜiyyah,", p.70, Abdul-Majid al-Najjar, *Khilāfah al-Insān Bayna al-Waḥy wa al-ᶜAql* (Virginia: International Institute of Islamic Thought (IIIT), 1993), p.103, al-Nimr, *Al-Ijtihād*, pp.147, 367, al-Turabi, *Qaḍāyā al-Tajdīd*, p.158, Hasan Bin Saleh, "The

Application of Al-Qawāʿid al-Fiqhiyyah of Majallah al-Aḥkām al-ʿAdliyyah: An Analytical Juristic Study with Particular Reference to Jordanian Civil Code and United Arab Emirates Law of Civil Transactions" (Ph.D. diss., University of Lampeter, 2003), M. El-Awa, "The Theory of Punishment in Islamic Law: A Comparative Study" (Ph.D. diss., London, School of Oriental and African Studies, 1972), M. El-Awa, *Fī al-Nidhām al-Siyāsī li al-Dawlah al-Islāmiyyah* (Cairo: Dār al-Shurūq, 1998), p.57.

153. Tabatabaei Lotfi, "Ijtihad in Twelver Shiʿism: The Interpretation and Application of Islamic Law in the Context of Changing Muslim Society" (Ph.D. diss, University of Leeds, 1999).

154. Al-Alwani, "Madkhal," p.36, Al-Ghazaly, *Al-Sunnah al-Nabawiyyah Bayna Ahl al-Fiqh wa Ahl al-Ḥadīth*, p.36, Al-Turabi, *Qaḍāyā al-Tajdīd*, p.159, Attia, *Naḥwa Tafʿīl Maqāṣid Al-Sharīʿah*, p.33, M. A. Baderin, "Modern Muslim States between Islamic Law and International Human Rights Law" (Ph.D. diss, University of Nottingham, 2001), Safi, *Iʿmāl al-ʿAql*, p.154, Bernard G. Weiss, *The Spirit of Islamic Law* (Athens: University of Georgia Press, 1998).

155. Carl Sharif El-Tobgui, "The Epistemology of *Qiyās* and *Taʿlīl* between the Muʿtazilite Abū al-Ḥusayn al-Baṣrī and ibn Ḥazm al-Zāhirī," *UCLA Journal of Islamic and Near Eastern Law*, no. 2 (spring/summer) (2003), Wael Hallaq, *A History of Islamic Legal Theories: An Introduction to Sunnī 'Uṣūl al-Fiqh* (Cambridge: Cambridge University Press, 1997).

156. Al-Nimr, *Al-Ijtihād*, p.346, al-Turabi, *Qaḍāyā al-Tajdīd*, p.166, Attia, *Naḥwa Tafʿīl Maqāṣid al-Sharīʿah*, p.35, Moosa, "Introduction," p.186, Safi, *Iʿmāl al-ʿAql*, p.195.

157. Hasan, *Naẓariyyah al-Maṣlaḥah fī al-Fiqh al-Islāmī*, p.14, al-Turabi, *Qaḍāyā al-Tajdīd*, p.166, Hasan Mohamed Jabir, *Al-Maqāṣid Alkuliyyah wa al-Ijtihād Almuʿāṣir-Ta'sīs Manhaji wa Qur'ānī li Āliyyah al-Istinbāṭ*, 1st ed. (Beirut: Dār al-Ḥiwār, 2001), Ch. 1.

158. For example, refer to: Zaghloul al-Najjar, *Wonderful Scientific Signs in the Qur'an* (London: Al-Firdaws, 2005).

159. V. Taylor and C. Winquist, ed, *Encyclopedia of Postmodernism* (New York: Routledge, 2001), p.xiii.

160. Jim Powell, *Postmodernism for Beginners*. (New York: Writers and Readers Publishing, 1998), p.10.

161. Taylor, ed, *Encyclopedia of Postmodernism*, p.85, Christopher Norris, *Derrida* (London: 1987).

162. Powell, *Postmodernism*, p.104.

163. Ibid., p.232.

164. Jacques Derrida, *Of Grammatology*, trans. Gayatri Chakravorty Spivak (Baltimore: John Hopkins University Press, 1976), p.3.

165. Powell, *Postmodernism*, pp. 101–03.
166. Ibid., p.105.
167. Derrida, according to: John Ellis, *Against Deconstruction* (Princeton, New Jersey: Princeton University Press, 1989), p.51.
168. Ibid.
169. Ibid., p .97.
170. Steven Best and Douglas Kellner, *Postmodern Theory: Critical Interrogations*, ed. Paul Walton (London: Macmillan Press ltd, 1991), p.256.
171. Some researchers described their approaches as 'postmodern,' such as Nasr Abu Zaid, Ziauddin Sardar, Ebrahim Moosa and Haideh Moghissi. I classified the other researchers under the same category based on my understanding of their approaches.
172. Taylor, ed, *Encyclopedia of Postmodernism*, p.85.
173. Powell, *Postmodernism for Beginners*, p.93.
174. Nasr Hamed Abu Zaid, *Mafhūm al-Naṣṣ: Dirāsah fī ʿUlūm al-Qur'ān* (Cairo: Al-Hay'ah al-Miṣriyyah li al-Kitāb, 1990), p.31.
175. Ibid., p.46.
176. For example: Nasr Hamed Abu Zaid, *Al-Imām al-Shāfiʿī wa Ta'sīs al-Āidīūlūjiyyah al-Wasaṭiyyah*, 3rd ed. (Cairo: Madbūlī, 2003), p.15, Arkoun, "Rethinking Islam Today," p.211, El-Tobgui, "Epistemology of Qiyās", Hasan Ḥanafī, *Al-Turāth wa al-Tajdīd* (Beirut: Dār al-Tanwīr, 1980), p.45, Moosa, "Debts and Burdens," p.123.
177. A common deconstructionists' theme. Refer to: Ellis, *Against Deconstruction*, pp. 8–13. Also endorsed by Abu Zaid in Nasr Hamed Abu Zaid, "Divine Attributes in the Qur'an," in *Islam and Modernity: Muslim Intellectuals Respond*, ed. John Cooper, Ronald L. Nettler and Mohamed Mahmoud (London: I.B.Tauris, 1998), p.194.
178. For example: Derrida, *Of Grammatology*, p.3.
179. Hanafi, *Al-Turāth wa al-Tajdīd*, p.108.
180. Ibid., p. 103.
181. Talal Asad, *The Idea of an Anthropology of Islam* (Washington, DC: Georgetown University Center for Contemporary Arab Studies, 1986), p.14.
182. Ibid.
183. Taylor, ed, *Encyclopedia of Postmodernism*, p.178, Friedrich Meinecke, *Historicism: The Rise of a New Historical Outlook*, trans. J. E. Anderson (London: 1972).
184. Abu Zaid, "Divine Attributes in the Quran," p.199, Arkoun, "Rethinking Islam Today," p.211.
185. Abu Zaid, *Al-Imām al-Shāfiʿī*, p.209, Moosa, "Debts and Burdens," p.114.
186. Moghissi, *Feminism and Islamic Fundamentalism: The Limits of Postmodern Analysis*, p.141.

187. Ibn Warraq, "Apostasy and Human Rights," *Free Inquiry*, Feb/March 2006 no date, p.53.
188. Moosa, "Introduction," p.42.
189. Christopher Berry Gray, ed, *The Philosophy of Law Encyclopedia* (New York and London: Garland Publishing, 1999), p.371.
190. Moosa, "Introduction," p.42.
191. Ibid., p.37.
192. Moghissi, *Feminism and Islamic Fundamentalism: The Limits of Postmodern Analysis*, p.140.
193. Arkoun, "Rethinking Islam Today," p.221.
194. Shams al-Dīn ibn al-Qayyim, *Iᶜlām al-Muwaqqiᶜīn*, ed. Taha Abdul Rauf Saad (Beirut: Dār al-Jīl, 1973), vol. 1, p.333.
195. Quotes are his. Shams al-Din, *Al-Ijtihād wa al-Tajdīd fī al-Fiqh al-Islāmī*, p.128.
196. Ibid., p.129.
197. El-Affendi, ed., *Rethinking Islam*, p.45.
198. Hasan al-Turabi, *Emancipation of Women: An Islamic Perspective*, 2nd ed. (London: Muslim Information Centre, 2000), p.29. Also, oral discussion, Khartoum, Sudan, August 2006.
199. Roger Garaudy, *Al-Islām wa al-Qarn al-Wāḥid wa al-ᶜUshrūn: Shurūṭ Nahḍah al-Muslimīn*, trans. Kamal Jadallah (Cairo: Al-Dār al-ᶜĀlamiyyah li al Kutub wa al-Nashr, 1999), pp. 70, 119.
200. Soroush, "The Evolution and Devolution of Religious Knowledge," p.250.
201. Shahrour, *Naḥwa 'Uṣūl Jadīdah*, p.125.
202. Al-Ghazaly, *Al-Sunnah al-Nabawiyyah*, p.161.
203. Oral Discussion, Sarajevo, Bosnia, May 2007, 18th regular session for the European Council for Fatwa and Research.
204. Refer to Qaradawi's article in: Mohamed Saleem El-Awa, ed., *Maqāṣid al-Sharīᶜah al-Islāmiyyah: Dirāsāt fī Qaḍāyā al-Manhaj wa Qaḍāyā al-Taṭbīq* (Cairo: al-Furqan Islamic Heritage Foundation, al-Maqāṣid Research Centre, 2006) p. 117–121.
205. Taha Jabir al-Alwani, *Issues in Contemporary Islamic Thought* (London-Washington: International Institute of Islamic Thought (IIIT), 2005), pp.164–166.
206. For example: Abu Zaid, *Al-Imām al-Shāfiᶜī*, p.15, Arkoun, "Rethinking Islam Today," p.211, Ḥanafī, *Al-Turāth wa al-Tajdīd*, p.45, Moosa, "Debts and Burdens," p.123.
207. Abdul-Jabbar, *Al-Mughnī*, vol. 4, p.174, Abdul-Jabbar, *Faḍl al-Iᶜtizāl*, p.139.
208. Sarhan, *Istrātījiyyah al-Ta'wīl al-Dilālī ᶜInd al-Muᶜtazilah*, p.30.

209. Abdul-Jabbar, *Al-Mughnī*, vol. 4, p.174.
210. Abu Zaid, *Al-Imām al-Shāfiʿī*, p.15, Hanafi, *Al-Turāth wa al-Tajdīd*, p.45.
211. Powell, *Postmodernism*, p.101. Same view held by Moosa in "Poetics."
212. Taylor, ed, *Encyclopedia of Postmodernism*, p.67.
213. Ibid.
214. For example, Mernissi, *The Veil and the Male Elite*, p.53, Moghissi, *Feminism and Islamic Fundamentalism: The Limits of Postmodern Analysis*, p.53.
215. Taylor, ed, *Encyclopedia of Postmodernism*, pp. 148–49.
216. Shahrour, *Naḥwa 'Uṣūl Jadīdah*, p.359, Keven A. Reinhart, "When Women Went to Mosques: Al-Aydini on the Duration of Assessments," in *Islamic Legal Interpretation: Muftis and Their Fatwas*, ed. Brinkley Messick, Mohammad Khalid Masud, and David S. Power (Cambridge, Mass.: Harvard University Press, 1996).
217. For example, Mernissi, *The Veil and the Male Elite*, pp. 46–49, 53, Moghissi, *Feminism and Islamic Fundamentalism: The Limits of Postmodern Analysis*, pp. 21–22.
218. Fatima Mernissi, *Mā Warā' al-Ḥijāb*, 1st ed.(Damascus: Dār Ḥawrān, 1997), p.170.
219. Ibid., p.147, 63, 76, 81. However, Mernissi's work in '*The Veil and the Male Elite*' falls under what I could call 'modernist re-interpretion' rather than 'postmodern deconstruction.'
220. Omid Safi, ed., *Progressive Muslims: On Justice, Gender and Pluralism* (Oxford: One World, 2003), pp.197–203.
221. Ibid., p.217.
222. Abu Zaid, *Al-Imām al-Shāfiʿī*, p.44. Alternative (neo-traditional) views in: A. K. Ali, "Al-Shāfiʿī's Contribution to Hadith with an Annotated Translation of His Work Jimāʿ Al-ʿIlm" (Ph.D. diss, University of Edinburgh, 1996), A. H. Othman, "Shāfiʿī and the Interpretation of the Role of the Qur'an and the Hadith" (Ph.D. diss, St. Andrews, 1997), A. S. M. Shukri, "The Relationship between ʿIlm and Khabar in the Work of Al-Shāfiʿī" (Ph.D. diss, St. Andrews, 1999).
223. Patricia Crone, *Roman, Provincial and Islamic Law: The Origins of the Islamic Patronate*, Cambridge Studies in Islamic Civilization (Cambridge: Cambridge University Press, 2002).
224. Wael Hallaq, "The Quest for Origins or Doctrine? Islamic Legal Studies as Colonialist Dscourse," *UCLA Journal of Islamic and Near Eastern Law*, no. 2 (Fall/Winter) (2003).
225. Abdul-Majeed Al-Sagheer, *Al-Fikr al-'Uṣūlī wa Ishkāliyyah al-Ṣulṭah al-ʿIlmiyyah fī al-Islām*, 1st ed., Dirāsāt Islāmiyyah (Islamic Studies) (Beirut: Dār

al-Muntakhab al-ʿArabī, 1994), pp. 21–28.

226. Taylor, ed., *Encyclopedia of Postmodernism*, p.299.
227. Ibid., p.67. Also see: Edward Said, *Orientalism* (New York: Vintage Books, 1979).
228. For example, Moosa, Robinson, Stewart, Piscatori, Sardar, Hasan, Mughissi, and Hallaq, as referred below.
229. Moosa, "Introduction," p24.
230. Robinson, *Islam*, p.230. See also: P. J. Stewart, *Unfolding Islam* (Reading, U.K: Garnet Publishing, 1994), p.95.
231. Hasan Hanafi, "Maqāṣid al-Sharīʿah wa Ahdāf al-'Ummah," *Al-Muslim al-Muʿāṣir*, no. 103 (2002): p. 100.
232. Tariq al-Bishri, *Māhiyyah al-Muʿāṣarah* (Cairo: Dār al-Shurūq, 1996), p.13.
233. Piscatori, *Islamic Countries: Politics and Government*, p.56.
234. Ataullah Bagdan Kopanski, "Orientalism Revisited: Bernard Lewis' School of Political Islamography," *Intellectual Discourse* 8, no. 2 (2000): vol. 8, p.133.
235. Inayatullah, *Islam, Postmodernism and Other Futures: A Ziauddin Sardar Reader*, p.123, Moghissi, *Feminism and Islamic Fundamentalism: The Limits of Postmodern Analysis*, p.52, Moosa, "Introduction," p.24.
236. Hussein Hasan, "Book Review: Islamic Law and Culture 1600–1840 by Haim Gerber," *Journal of Islamic Studies* 12, no. 2 (2001): p. 203.
237. Hallaq, "The Quest for Origins." Also refer to: Mohammad al-Azami, *On Schacht's Origins of Mohammadan Jurisprudence* (Riyadh: King Saud University and John Wiley, 1985).
238. H. A. R. Gibb, *Islam: A Historical Survey*, 2nd ed. (Oxford: Oxford University Press, no date), pp. 25–27, Ignaz Goldziher, *Introduction to Islamic Theology and Law*, trans. Andras and Ruth Hamori (Princeton: Princeton University Press, 1981), pp. 7–13, Joseph Schacht, "Foreign Elements in Ancient Islamic Law," *Comparative Legislation and International Law* 32 (1950), Joseph Schacht, *An Introduction to Islamic Law*, 2nd ed. (Oxford: Clarendon Press, 1982), p.22.

CHAPTER SIX

1. Ibn Taymiyah, *Kutub wa Rasā'il wa Fatwa* (Books, Letters and Legal Opinions), vol. 13, p.113.
2. Al-Subkī, *Al-Ibhāj fī Sharḥ al-Minhāj*, vol. 1, p.39.
3. Al-Haj, *Al-Taqrīr*, vol. 1, p.26.
4. For example, refer to: El-Fadl, *Speaking in God's Name*.
5. Refer to, for example: al-Haj, *Al-Taqrīr*, vol. 3, p.158, Jalāl al-Dīn al-Suyūtī, *Al-Dur Al-Manthūr* (Beirut: Dār al-Fikr, 1993) vol. 3, p.86.

6. Ahmad ibn Taymiyah, *Naqd Marātib al-Ijmāᶜ*, 1st ed. (Beirut: Dār al-Fikr 1998).
7. Soltan, "Ḥujiyyah", p100.
8. Mawil Izzi Dien, *Islamic Law: From Historical Foundations to Contemporary Practice*, ed., Carole Hillenbrand (Edinburgh: Edinburgh University Press ltd, 2004), p.47.
9. Shahrour, *Naḥwa 'Uṣūl Jadīdah*, p.207.
10. For example: al-Haj, *Al-Taqrīr*, vol. 3, p.158.
11. El-Fadl, *Speaking in God's Name*, p.275.
12. Garaudy, *Al-Islam*, p.103.
13. Al-Haj, *Al-Taqrīr*, vol. 3, p.412, Al-Shawkānī, *Irshād Al-Fuḥūl*, vol. 1, p.140.
14. Refer, for examples, to: Aḥmad ibn Ḥajar, *Fatḥ al-Bārī Sharḥ Ṣaḥīḥ al-Bukhārī* (no date), vol. 13, p.320, al-Haj, *Al-Taqrīr*, vol. 1, p.28, Al-Subkī, *Al-Ibhāj fī Sharḥ al-Minhāj*, vol. 3, p.259, Abdul-Malik al-Juwanī, *Al-Burhān fī ᶜUlūm al-Qur'ān*, 4th ed. (Al-Manṣūrah, Egypt: al-Wafā', 1997), vol. 2, p.868.
15. Al-Bukhārī, *Kashf al-Asrār*, vol. 4, p.27.
16. Refer to: Nicholas Rescher, "Arabic Logic", ed. Paul Edwards, *The Encyclopedia of Philosophy* (New York: Macmillan, 1967), vol. 4, p.526, Al-Walīd ibn Rushd (Averröes), *Faṣl al-Maqāl fī Taqrīr Mā Bayn al-Sharīᶜah wa al-Ḥikmah Min Ittiṣāl* (Decisive Argument on the Connection between the Islamic Law and Philosophy. Translated As: On the Harmony of Religions and Philosophy, in Averröes, the Philosophy and Theology of Averröes, Trans. Mohammed Jamil-al-Rahman) (A.G.Widgery, 1921 [cited January 18th 2005]); available from http://www.muslimphilosophy.com.
17. Al-Ghazālī, *Al-Mustaṣfā*, vol. 1, p.252.
18. Ibid.
19. Auda, Ph.D. thesis, p. 70.
20. Moḥammad ibn ᶜUmar al-Rāzī, *Al-Maḥṣūl*, ed. Taha Jabir al-Alwani (Riyadh: Imam Mohammad University Press, 1400 AH), vol. 1, pp. 547–73.
21. Hasan al-Shafie, *Al-Āmidī*, p.150.
22. Al-Juwaynī, *Al-Burhān*, vol. 2, p.590.
23. Al-Shāṭibī, *Al-Muwāfaqāt*, vol. 1, p.29.
24. Ibid., vol. 2, p.61.
25. For example: Hasan al-Turabi, *Al-Tafsīr al-Tawḥīdī*, 1st ed., vol. 1 (London: Dār al-Sāqī, 2004), p.25.
26. Ibn Ashur, *Maqāṣid al-Sharīᶜah al-Islāmiyyah*, p.50, Al-Alwani, *Maqāṣid Al-Sharīᶜah*, Al-Qaradawi, *Kayf Nataᶜāmal Maᶜa al-Qur'ān al-ᶜAẓīm?*
27. Al-Turabi, *Al-Tafsīr al-Tawḥīdī*.
28. Ibid., p.20.

29. Smuts, *Holism and Evolution*, p.v.
30. Korzybski, *An Introduction to Non-Aristotelian Systems and General Semantics*, p.217.
31. Smuts, *Holism and Evolution*, pp. 270–72.
32. Gerard Jahami, *Mafhūm al-Sababiyyah Bayn al-Mutakallimīn wa al Falāsifah: Bayn al-Ghazālī wa Ibn Rushd*, 2nd ed. (Beirut: Dār al-Mashriq, 1992), pp. 78–79.
33. Refer, for example, to: Al-Āmidī, *Al-Iḥkām*, vol. 3, p.249. Ibn Rushd (Averröes), al-Walīd, *Tahāfut al-Tahāfut*. Edited by Sulaiman Donya. 1st ed. (Cairo: Dār al-Maʿārif, 1964), p.785, Ibn al-Qayyim, *Iʿlām al-Muwaqqiʿīn*, vol. 3, p.3, al-Tayyib, "Naẓariyyah al-Maqāṣid," al-Shāṭibī, *Al-Muwāfaqāt*, vol. 2, p.6.
34. Abduh, *Risālah al-Tawḥīd*, p.26.
35. Korzybski, *An Introduction to Non-Aristotelian Systems and General Semantics*, Book I, p.5.
36. David K. Naugle, *Worldview: The History of a Concept* (Grand Rapids: Eerdmans, 2002), p.2.
37. Sire, James W., *Naming the Elephant* (Downers Grove, IL: Inter Varsity Press, 2004), pp. 19–20.
38. O. B. Jenkins, *What Is Worldview?* (1999 [cited Jan. 2006]); available from http://orvillejenkins.com /worldview/worldvwhat.html.
39. Richard DeWitt, *Worldviews: An Introduction to the History and Philosophy of Science* (Malden, MA: Blackwell, 2004), p. 3.
40. Sire Naming, *Worldviews: Crosscultural Explorations of Human Beliefs*, 3rd ed. (Prentice Hall, 1999), pp.19–20.
41. Ibid., p.iv.
42. Jenkins, *What Is Worldview?*
43. DeWitt, *Worldviews: An Introduction to the History and Philosophy of Science*, p.5.
44. Abdul-Fattah, Saif. "On Imam Mohamed Abdu's Worldview" Paper presented at the Centennial of Shaykh Mohamed Abdu (Bibliotheca Alexandrina, Alexandria, Egypt Dec. 2005), p.7.
45. Sire, *Naming*, p.28, Naugle, *Worldview: The History of a Concept*, p. 29.
46. For example: Al-Majala, *Majallah al-Aḥkām al-ʿAdliyyah* (Journal of Justice Rulings) item 43, 45. Also: Ibn ʿĀbdīn, *Al-Ḥashiyah* (Side Notes), vol. 4, p.556.
47. Soltan, "Ḥujiyyah", p.620.
48. Masoud ibn Musa Flousi, *Madrasah al-Mutakalimīn* (Riyadh: Maktabah al-Rushd, 2004), p.354.
49. Such as '*walad*' and '*laḥm*,' could mean 'children' or 'boys' and 'beef' or 'beef

and birds,' respectively, depending on one's region and dialect.

50. The hadith also mentioned '*aqiṭ*,' which is a kind of food that is unknown in nowaday's Arabic cuisine. According to al-Zubaydī (sixteenth century CE): *Aqiṭ* is goat or camel milk that is cooked and left to dry in order to use in cooking – Moḥammad al-Zubaydī, *Tāj al-ʿArūs fī Jawāhir al-Qāmūs* (Beirut: Dār al-Nashr, no date). Many 'modernist' scholars, usually citing the Ḥanafī school, allow paying an equivalent amount of money instead. However, the literal application of this charity is still dominant in countries like nowadays Saudi Arabia.
51. Ibn al-Qayyim, *Aḥkām Ahl al-Dhimmah*, vol. 2, p.728.
52. Sabiq, *Fiqh al-Sunnah*, vol. 3, p.29.
53. Peters, Rudolph. "Murder in Khaybar: Some Thoughts on the Origins of the Qasama Procedure in Islamic Law," *Islamic Law and Society* 9, no. 2 (2002), p.133.
54. Aḥmad ibn Taymiyah, *Iqtiḍā' al-Ṣirāṭ al-Mustaqīm Mukhālafah Aṣḥāb al-Jaḥīm*, ed. Mohammad Hamid, 2nd ed. (Cairo: Maṭbaʿah al-Sunnah, 1369 AH), pp.148–50.
55. Ibid., pp. 158, 59, 60, 37, respectively.
56. This is also the opinion of the majority of schools of law. For a comparative survey, refer to Ibn Rushd: Ibn Rushd (Averröes), *Bidāyah al-Mujtahid wa Nihāyah al-Muqtaṣid* (the Starting Point of the Deliberator and the Ending Point of the Conservative), vol. 2, p.12.
57. Ibn al-Qayyim, *Al-Ṭuruq al-Ḥukmiyyah*, vol. 1, p.5.
58. Ibn Ḥajar, *Fatḥ al-Bārī Sharḥ Ṣaḥīḥ al-Bukhārī*, p.375.
59. Jordan is an example, according to personal experiences of some Jordanian friends.
60. This is the case in most of the mosques that I have been to in the UK, to my surprise.
61. DeWitt, *Worldviews: An Introduction to the History and Philosophy of Science*, p.5.
62. Such as the philosophers' claim of the enternity of the universe (*qidam al-ʿĀlam*). In the famous Ghazālī-Averroes *tahāfut* (Incoherence) debate, Averroes argued that saying that the universe is eternal in the sense that it has no end (Arabic: *abadī*), as al-Ghazālī believes, is not different from saying that the universe is eternal in the sense that it has no beginning (Arabic: *azalī*, *qadīm*), as the Greeks and other philosophers had said.
63. Aḥmad ibn Taymiyah, *Dār' Taʿarruḍ al-ʿAql wa al-Naql* (Beirut: Dār al-Kutub al-ʿIlmiyyah, 1997), vol. 3, p.218.
64. Al-Suyūṭī, *Al-Dur al-Manthūr*, vol. 3, p.86, Abū ʿAmr ibn al-Ṣalāḥ, *Fatāwa ibn al-Ṣalāḥ*, 2005.

65. Ibid.
66. Hasan Bashir Salih, *ʿAlāqah al-Manṭiq bi al-Lughah ʿInd Falāsifah al-Muslimīn* (Alexandria: Al-Wafā', 2003), p.86.
67. Al-Deeb, "Imam al-Ḥaramayn," p.39.
68. Essmat Nassar, *Al-Khiṭāb al-Falsafī ʿInd ibn Rushd wa Atharuhu fī Kitābāt Moḥammad ʿAbduh wa Zakī Najīb Maḥmūd* (Cairo: Dār al-Hidāyah, 2003), pp. 16–21.
69. Wadie Mustafa, "Ibn Ḥazm wa Mauqifuhu Min al-Falsafah wa al-Manṭiq wa al-Akhlāq" (M.A. Thesis, Alexandria University, Published by al-Majmaʿ al-Thaqāfī, 2000).
70. Ibn Taymiyah, *Dār' Taʿaruḍ al-ʿAql wa al-Naql.*
71. Mustafa, "Ibn Ḥazm," p.203.
72. Al-Ghazālī, *Al-Mustaṣfā fī 'Uṣūl al-Fiqh.*
73. Refer to: ʿAlī ibn Ḥazm, *Taqrīb al-Manṭiq*, ed. Ihsan Abbas, 1st ed. (Beirut: no date).
74. Refer to: G.H. Von Wright, "Deontic Logic," *Mind*, New Series 60, no. 237 (1951).
75. Anwar al-Zaabi, *Ẓāhiriyyah ibn Ḥazm al-Andalusī: Naẓariyyah al-Maʿrifah wa Manāhij al-Baḥth* (Amman: International Institute of Islamic Thought, 1996), p.49.
76. Ibid., pp.100–03.
77. John F. Sowa, *Knowledge Representation: Logical, Philosophical, and Computational Foundations* (Pacific Grove: Brooks, 2000), p.359.
78. W. Hallaq, *Ibn Taymiyya against the Greek Logicians* (Oxford: Clarendon Press, 1993).
79. Ibid.
80. Quoted in: Abu-Yarub al-Marzuqi, "Iṣlāḥ al-ʿAql fī al-Falsafah al-ʿArabiyyah" (Ph.D. diss, Published by The Centre of Arabic Unity Studies, 1994), p.176.
81. Ibn Taymiyah, *Dār Taʿaruḍ al-ʿAql wa al-Naql*, vol.1, p.203.
82. Al-Marzuqi, "Iṣlāḥ al-ʿAql fī al-Falsafah al-ʿArabiyyah", p.177, Al-Ajam, *Al-Manṭiq ʿInda al-Ghazālī.*
83. Ibn Taymiyah, *Dār Taʿaruḍ al-ʿAql wa al-Naql*, vol. 3, p.218.
84. Abū Ḥāmid al-Ghazālī, *Tahāfut al-Falāsifah (Incoherence of the Philosophers).* Translated by M. S. Kamali (Pakistan Philosophical Gongress, 1963 [cited January 18th 2005]); available from http://www.muslimphilosophy.com.
85. Al-Ghazālī, *Al-Mustaṣfā fī 'Uṣūl al-Fiqh*, p.3.
86. Rosalind Ward Gwynne, *Logic, Rhetoric, and Legal Reasoning in the Qur'an* (London and New York: Routledge, 2004), p.156. Also, al-Ajam, *Al-Manṭiq*

ʿ*Inda al-Ghazālī*, pp. 163–65. The two inferences mentioned here could be formally explained as follows: Modus Ponens: If it is true that "if P is true, then Q is true," then if P is true, then Q will be true. Modus Tollens: If it is true that "if P then Q is true," then if Q is not true, then it means that P is not true.

87. Qur'an, Surah *al-Anbiyā'*, 21:21.
88. Abū Ḥāmid al-Ghazālī, *Al-Qisṭās al-Mustaqīm* (Beirut: Catholic Publishing House, 1959), p.62.
89. Al-Ajam, *Al-Manṭiq* ʿ*Inda al-Ghazālī*, p.65.
90. Ibid.
91. Disjunctive syllogism: Either one side or the other is true (or maybe both). They are not both false. So if you know that one side is false, then it must be the case that the other side is the true side. Formally, if p v q and ~p. Therefore, q (is true).
92. Abū Ḥāmid al-Ghazālī, *Maḥakk al-Naẓar* (Cairo: al-Maṭbaʿah al-Adabiyyah, no date), p.43.
93. Hypothetical Syllogism: If we have two implication statements, where the first side of one is the same as the second side of the other. Then we can eliminate this common component and connect the remaining sides together with another. For example, if p ==> q (p implies q) and q ==> r. Therefore, p ==> r. Al-Ghazālī used q for the ʿ*illah* (cause) in this example.
94. Al-Ghazālī, *Maḥakk al-Naẓar*, p.31.
95. For example, Ibn Taymiyah and Ibn Ḥazm. Refer to: Al-Ajam, *Al-Manṭiq* ʿ*Inda al-Ghazālī*.
96. ʿAlī al-Subkī, *Legal Opinions* (Lebanon: Dār al-Maʿrifah), vol. 2, p.644.
97. Von Wright, "Deontic Logic."
98. Ibid.
99. For a few examples of the application of this ruling, refer to: Al-Subkī, *Al-Ibhāj fī Sharḥ al-Minhāj*, vol. 1, p.118., Al-Rāzī, *Al-Maḥṣūl*, vol. 2, p.322, Al-Ghazālī, *Al-Mustaṣfā fī 'Uṣūl al-Fiqh* (the Purified Source on the Fundamentals of Law), vol. 1, p.57, Aḥmad ibn Taymiyah, *Al-Musawwadah fī 'Uṣūl al-Fiqh*, 2nd ed. (Cairo: Maktabah al-Madanī, no date), p.58, Al-Shāṭibī, *Al-Muwāfaqāt*, vol. 1, p.125.
100. C. W. DeMarco, "Deontic Legal Logic," in *The Philosophy of Law: An Encyclopedia*, ed. Christopher Gray (New York and London: Garland Publishing, 1999).
101. Ibid.
102. Rescher, *Arabic Logic*, vol. 4, p.526.
103. Ibid., vol. 4, p.527.
104. Majid Fakhry, *A History of Islamic Philosophy*, 2nd ed. (London, New York: Longman, Colombia University Press, 1983), p.353.

105. Ibn Rushd, *Faṣl al-Maqāl*.
106. Ibid.
107. Nassar, *Al-Khiṭāb al-Falsafī*, Al-Turabi, *Qaḍāyā al-Tajdīd*, p.193.
108. Atif al-Iraqi, *Al-Naz*ʿ*ah al-*ʿ*Aqliyyah fī Falsafah ibn Rushd*, 5th ed. (Cairo: Dār al-Maʿārif, 1993), p.369.
109. Gray, ed, *The Philosophy of Law Encyclopedia*, p.439.
110. Al-Iraqi, *Al-Naz*ʿ*ah al-*ʿ*Aqliyyah fī Falsafah ibn Rushd*, p.70.
111. Flousi, *Madrasah al-Mutakallimīn*, p.332.
112. Ali, *Al-Manṭiq wa al-Fiqh*, p.150.
113. Ibn Taymiyah, *Dār Ta*ʿ*aruḍ al-*ʿ*Aql wa al-Naql*, vol. 1, p.14.
114. Ibid., vol. 1, pp. 15–23.
115. Abdallah Rabi, *Al-Qaṭ*ʿ*iyyah wa al-Ẓanniyah fī 'Uṣūl al-Fiqh al-Islāmī* (Cairo: Dār al-Nahar, no date), pp. 24–27.
116. Abū Ḥāmid al-Ghazālī, *Maqāṣid Al-Falāsifah* (Cairo: Dār al-Maʿārif, 1961), p.3.
117. Ali Jumah, ʿ*Ilm 'Uṣūl al-Fiqh wa* ʿ*Alaqatuhu bi al-Falsafah al-Islāmiyyah* (Cairo: Al-Maʿhad al-ʿĀlamī li al-Fikr al-Islāmī, 1996), p.29.
118. Sulaymān Abū Dāwūd, *Al-Sunan* (Damascus: Dār al-Fikr), vol. 3, p.257.
119. Al-Ḥākim al-Nīsābūrī, *Al-Mustadrak* ʿ*Alā al-Ṣaḥīḥayn* (Beirut: Dār al-Kutub al-ʿIlmiyyah, 1990), vol. 2, p.255.
120. Al-Bukhārī, *Al-Ṣaḥīḥ*, vol. 5, p.2216.
121. Al-Nīsābūrī, *Al-Mustadrak* ʿ*Alā al-Ṣaḥīḥayn*, vol. 1, p.553.
122. Al-Bukhārī, *Al-Ṣaḥīḥ*, vol. 2, p.532.
123. Ibn Rushd, *Bidāyah Al-Mujtahid*, vol. 2, p.43.
124. Al-Swāsī, *Sharḥ Fatḥ al-Qādir*, vol. 2, p.192, Ibn Abdul-Barr, *Al-Tamhīd*, vol. 4, p.216.
125. Ibn Ḥajar, *Fatḥ al-Bārī Sharḥ Ṣaḥīḥ al-Bukhārī*, vol. 10, p.375.
126. For example: ʿAlī al-Āmidī, *Al-Iḥkām fī 'Uṣūl al-Aḥkām* (Beirut: Dār al-Kitāb al-ʿArabī, 1404 AH), vol. 4, p.249.
127. Mentioned and not supported by: Abū Bakr al-Bayhaqī, *Al-Sunan* (Madinah: Al-Dār, 1989), vol. 6, p.124.
128. Mentioned and not supported in: Moḥammad al-Ṣanʿānī, *Subul Al-Salām* (Beirut: Dār Ihyā' al-Turāth al-ʿArabī, 1379 AH), vol. 3, p.227.
129. Biltaji, *Manhaj* ʿ*Umar*, p.190.
130. Ibid., p.190.
131. Jalāl al-Dīn al-Suyuṭī, *Tadrīb al-Rāwī* (Riyadh: Maktabah al-Riyadh al-Ḥadīthah, no date), vol. 2, p.180.
132. For example, Ibn al-Jazrī (d. 1429 CE), in his book on the narrations of the Qur'an, counted 80 parallel 'chains of narrators' for the Qur'an and elaborated on their variations. Refer to: Ibn al-Jazrī, *Al-Nashr fī al-Qirā'āt al-*ʿ*Ashr*, pp. 117–280.

133. Ibn al-Ṣalāḥ, *Al-Muqaddimah fī ᶜUlūm al-Ḥadīth*, p.28.
134. Ibn Taymiyah, *Al-Musawwadah fī 'Uṣūl al-Fiqh*, p.223.
135. Ibn Taymiyah, *Kutub wa Rasā'il wa Fatwā*, pp. 78–83.
136. El-Fadl, *Speaking in God's Name*, p.238.
137. For example: Al-Suyūṭī, *Al-Dur al-Manthūr*, vol. 3, p.86.
138. Their reason is the 'uncertainty' in these methods. Refer to: Soltan, "Ḥujiyyah", Ch.3.
139. Al-Ghazālī, *Al-Mustaṣfā*, p.304.
140. This is according to al-Ghazālī's Ashᶜarite school, which believes that God 'does not have to have' causes/purposes behind His actions, as explained in Section 1.3.
141. Al-Ghazālī, *Al-Mustaṣfā fī 'Uṣūl al-Fiqh*, p.279, Al-Shāṭibī, *Al-Muwāfaqāt*, vol. 4, p.129, Ibn Taymiyah, *Kutub wa Rasā'il wa Fatwā*, vol. 19, p.131.
142. Al-Ghazālī, *Maqāṣid Al-Falāsifah*, p.62.
143. Ibn Taymiyah, *Kutub wa Rasā'il wa Fatwā*, vol. 19, p.131.
144. Abdul-Aziz al-Bukhari, *Kashf Al-Asrār* (Beirut: Dār al-Kutub al-ᶜIlmiyyah, 1997), vol. 3, p.77.
145. For examples, refer to: Auda, *Fiqh Al-Maqāṣid*, pp. 65–68.
146. Al-Subkī, *Al-Ibhāj fī Sharḥ al-Minhāj*, vol. 3, p.218.
147. Al-Bukhārī, *Al-Ṣaḥīḥ*, p. 69.
148. Ibid.
149. Auda, *Fiqh Al-Maqāṣid*, p.106.
150. Abū Bakr al-Mālikī ibn al-ᶜArabī, *ᶜĀriḍah al-Aḥwadhī* (Cairo: Dār al-Waḥy al-Moḥammadī, no date), vol. 10, p.264.
151. For example, refer to: Badran Badran, *Adillah al-Tarjīḥ al-Mutaᶜāriḍah wa Wujuh al-Tarjīḥ Baynahā* (Alexandria: Mu'assasah Shabāb al-Jāmiᶜah, 1974).
152. Auda, *Fiqh Al-Maqāṣid*, p.64.
153. Al-Suyūṭī, *Al-Ashbāh wa al-Naẓa'ir*, vol. 1, p.192.
154. Ayatollah Mohammad Baqir al-Sadir, *Durūs fī ᶜIlm Al-'Uṣūl*, 2nd ed. (Beirut: Dār al-Kitāb al-Lubnānī, 1986), vol. 2, p.222.
155. For example, refer to: Al-Rāzī, *Al-Tafsīr Al-Kabīr*, vol. 3, p.204, al-Faḍl ibn al-Ḥussain al-Tubrūsī, *Majmaᶜ Al-Bayān fī Tafsīr al-Qur'ān* (Beirut: Dār al-ᶜUlūm, 2005), vol. 1, p.406, Nada, Al-Naskh Fi Al-Qur'an p. 25.
156. Badran, *Adillah Al-Tarjīḥ*, ch. 4.
157. Al-Haj, *Al-Taqrīr*, vol. 3, p.4.
158. Auda, *Fiqh al-Maqāṣid*, pp. 105–10.
159. Abdul Majeed al-Sousarah, *Manhaj Al-Tawfīq wa al Tarjīḥ Bayn Mukhtalaf al-Ḥadīth wa Atharuhu fī al-Fiqh al-Islāmī*, 1st ed. (Amman: Dār al-Nafā'is, 1997), p.395.

160. Trans. M. Asad.
161. Verses 2:256, 6:13, 23:96, 30:60, 41:46, 109:6, respectively. (trans. M. Asad).
162. Burhan Zuraiq, *Al-Ṣaḥīfah: Mīthāq al-Rasūl*, 1st ed. (Damascus: Dār al-Numayr and Dār Maᶜad, 1996), p.353.
163. Ibid., p.216.
164. Based on the same survey of the books of hadith that I carried out, as mentioned above.
165. Al-Alwani, "Maqāṣid al-Sharīᶜah," p.89.
166. As suggested by a number of jurists. For example: al-Shāfᶜī, *Al-Risālah*, pp. 272–75, Mohammad al-Zurqani, *Sharḥ al-Zurqānī ᶜAlā Muwaṭṭa' al-Imām Mālik*. 1st ed. (Beirut: Dār al-Kutub al-ᶜIlmiyyah, no date), vol. 1, p.229.
167. Al-Siwāsī, *Sharḥ Fatḥ al-Qādir*, vol. 1, p.311, al-Sarkhasī, *'Uṣūl al-Sarkhasī*, vol. 1, p.12, Al-Kasānī, *Badā'iᶜ al-Ṣanā'iᶜ*, vol. 1, p.207.
168. Al-Shāfᶜī, *Al-Risālah*, pp. 272–75.
169. Moḥammad ibn ᶜĪssā al-Tirmidhī, *Al-Jāmiᶜ al-Ṣaḥīḥ Sunan al-Tirmidhī*, ed. Ahmad M. Shakir (Beirut: Dār Iḥyā' al-Turāth al-ᶜArabī, no date), vol. 2, p.275.
170. Al-Nawawī, Al-Majmūᶜ, vol. 4, p.145.
171. Al-Ghazālī, *Al-Mustaṣfā*, vol. 1, pp.172–74.
172. Ibn Ashur, *Maqāṣid al-Sharīᶜah al-Islāmiyyah*, p. 236.
173. Ibn Nujaym, *Al-Baḥr al-Rā'iq*, vol. 3, p.117, al-Mirghiyānī, *Al-Hidāyah Sharḥ Bidāyah al-Mubtadi'*, vol. 1, p.197.
174. Al-Siwāsī, *Sharḥ Fatḥ al-Qādir*, vol. 3, p.258.
175. Ibn ᶜAbidīn, *Hāshiyat Radd al-Muḥtār*, vol. 3, p.55.
176. Mohammad al-Ghazaly, *Naẓarāt fī Al-Qur'ān* (Cairo: Nahḍah Miṣr, 2002), p.194.
177. Al-Nīsābūrī, *Al-Mustadrak ᶜAlā al-Ṣaḥīḥayn*, vol. 2, p.255.
178. Ibn Rushd, *Bidāyah al-Mujtahid*, vol. 2, p.43.
179. Moḥammad ibn Ismāᶜīl al-Ṣanᶜānī, *Subul al-Salām Sharḥ Bulūgh al-Marām Min Adilah al-Aḥkām*, ed. Mohammad Abdul Aziz Al-Khouli (Beirut: Dār Ihyā' al-Turāth al-ᶜArabī, 1379 AH), vol. 3, p.227.
180. Ibid.
181. Ibid.
182. Ibn Ashur, *Maqāṣid al-Sharīᶜah al-Islāmiyyah*, p.234.
183. Von Jhering, *Law as a Means to an End (Der Zwick Im Recht)*, p.xxii.
184. Ibid., p. lvii.
185. Geny, *Methode D'interpretation Et Sources En Droit Prive Positif*, vol. 2, p.142.
186. Von Jhering, *Law as a Means to an End*, p.lix, Geny, *Methode D'interpretation*, vol. 2, p.142.

187. Italics are his. Von Jhering, *Law as a Means to an End*, pp. 7–9.
188. Geny, *Methode D'interpretation*, vol. 2, p.190.
189. Von Jhering, *Law as a Means to an End*, "Introduction", p.xxii.
190. For example, Abdullah bin Bayah, *Āmālī al-Dilālāt wa Majāli al-Ikhtilāfāt*, 1st ed. (Jeddah: Dār al-Minhāj, 2007), p.361, and Al-Turabi, *Qaḍāyā al-Tajdīd*, p.157.
191. Al-Shāṭibī, *Al-Muwāfaqāt*, vol. 2, p.25.
192. Ibn Ashur, *Maqāṣid al-Sharīʿah al-Islāmiyyah*, p.225.
193. Moghissi, *Feminism and Islamic Fundamentalism: The Limits of Postmodern Analysis*, p.140.
194. Arkoun, "Rethinking Islam Today," p.221.
195. Al-Marzuqi, "Iṣlāḥ al-ʿAql fī al-Falsafah al-ʿArabiyyah," p.12.
196. Moosa, "Poetics."
197. Abu Zahrah, *'Uṣūl al-Fiqh*, p.139.
198. Al-Turabi, *Al-Tafsīr al-Tawḥīdī*, p.20, Jabir, *Al-Maqāṣid Alkuliyyah*, p.35.
199. For example: Al-Alwani, "Madkhal Ilā Fiqh al-Aqalliyyāt", p.36, Al-Ghazaly, *Al-Sunnah al-Nabawiyyah*, pp. 19, 125, 61, Al-Ghazaly, *Naẓarāt fī al-Qur'ān*, p. 36, al-Nimr, *Al-Ijtihād*, p.147, al-Turabi, *Qaḍāyā al-Tajdīd*, p.157, Yassin Dutton, *The Origins of Islamic Law: The Qur'an, the Muwaṭṭa' and Madinan ʿAmal* (Surrey: Curzon, 1999) p.1, John Makdisi, "A Reality Check on Istihsan as a Method of Islamic Legal Reasoning," *UCLA Journal of Islamic and Near Eastern Law*, no. 99 (fall/winter) (2003), A. Omotosho, "The Problem of al-Amr in Usul al-Fiqh" (Ph.D. diss, University of Edinburgh, 1984), Safi, *Iʿmāl al-ʿAql*, p.130, Shams al-Din, *Al-Ijtihād wa al-Tajdīd fī al-Fiqh al-Islāmī*, p.21.
200. Ibn Ashur, *Maqāṣid al-Sharīʿah al-Islāmiyyah*, Chapter 6.
201. I referred here to Mohamed al-Tahir Mesawi's translation of Ibn Ashur's book on *Maqāṣid*: Mohammad al-Tahir ibn Ashur, *Ibn Ashur Treatise on Maqāṣid al-Sharīʿah*, trans. Mohamed El-Tahir El-Mesawi (London-Washington: International Institute of Islamic Thought (IIIT), 2006).
202. Al-Āmidī, *Al-Iḥkām*, vol. 5, p.391.
203. Ibn Qudāmah, *Al-Mughnī*, vol. 3, p.42.
204. Ibid.
205. Aristotle, *The Works of Aristotle*.
206. For example: Al-Ghazālī, *Al-Mustaṣfā*, al-Rāzī, *Al-Tafsīr al-Kabīr*, vol. 3, p.133, al-Suyūṭī, Jalāl al-Dīn, *Tadrīb al-Rāwī fī Sharḥ Taqrīb al-Nawawī*. Ed. by Abdul Wahab Abdul Latif (Riyadh: Maktabah al-Riyādh al-Ḥadīthah, no date), vol. 1, p.277, al-Haj, *Al-Taqrīr*, vol. 1, p.86, al-Shāfʿī, al-Āmidī, p.149.
207. Hassaan, *Naẓariyyat al-Maṣlaḥah fī al-Fiqh al-Islāmī*.
208. Gray, ed, *The Philosophy of Law Encyclopedia*, p.428.

209. Al-Juwaynī, *Al-Ghayyāthī*, p.253, al-Ghazālī, *Al-Mustaṣfā*, vol. 1, p.172, al-Rāzī, *Al-Maḥṣūl fī ʿIlm al-'Uṣūl*, vol. 5, p.222, al-Āmidī, *Al-Iḥkām* vol. 4, p.286, al-Ṭūfī, *Al-Taʿyīn*, p.239.
210. Ibn Qudāmah, *Al-Mughnī*, vol. 5, p.148.
211. Al-Sarkhasī, *'Uṣūl al-Sarkhasī*, vol. 9, p.205.
212. Ibid., vol. 5, p.117.
213. Ibid.
214. Ibid., vol. 16, p.25.
215. Ibid., vol. 5, p.62.
216. Ibid., vol. 5, p.181.
217. Ibid., vol. 1, p.50.
218. Ibid., vol. 3, p.53.
219. Al-Qarāfī, *Al-Dhakhīrah*, vol. 1, p.153. Al-Qarāfī, *Al-Furūq (Maʿa Hawāmishih)*, vol. 2, p.60, Burhān al-Dīn ibn Farḥūn, *Tabṣirah al-Hukkām fī 'Uṣūl al-Aqḍiyah wa Manāhij al-Aḥkām*, ed. Jamal Marashli (Beirut: Dār al-Kutub al-ʿIlmiyyah, 1995), vol. 2, p.270.
220. Al-Qarāfī, *Al-Dhakhīrah*, vol. 1, p.153. Al-Qarāfī, *Al-Furūq (Maʿa Hawāmishih)*, vol. 2, p.60.
221. Ibn Farḥūn, *Tabṣirah al-Hukkām*, vol. 2, p.270ff.
222. Ibn Ashur, *Maqāṣid al-Sharīʿah al-Islāmiyyah*, p.234.
223. Ibn Ashur mentioned, for example: 'Now [as for you, O Mohammad,] We have not sent you otherwise than to mankind at large' (34:28), 'Say [O Mohammad]: "O mankind! Verily, I am an Apostle to all of you"' (7:158), and the hadith: 'An apostle used to be sent specifically to his own people, while I have been sent to all of mankind' (Muslim).
224. Ibn Ashur, *Maqāṣid al-Sharīʿah al-Islāmiyyah*, p. 236.
225. Al-Qarāfī, *Al-Furūq (Maʿa Hawāmishih)*, vol. 4, p.49. Abu Zahrah, *'Uṣūl al-Fiqh*, p.278.
226. Al-Qarāfī, *Al-Dhakhīrah*, vol. 1, p.151, Ibn Abdul-Salām, *Qawāʿid al-Aḥkām fī Maṣliḥ al-Ānām*, vol. 1 p. 23.
227. Ibn Taymiyah, *Kutub wa Rasā'il aa Fatwā*, vol. 2, p.214.
228. Ibid., vol. 1, p.56.
229. Al-Turabi, *Qaḍāyā al-Tajdīd*, p.167.
230. For example, refer to Mohammad Mehdi Shamsuddin, "Maqāṣid al-Sharīʿah," Mohammad Hussain Fadlullah, "Maqāṣid al-Sharīʿah," al-Alwani, "Maqāṣid al-Sharīʿah", and Abdulhadi al-Fadli, "Maqāṣid al-Sharīʿah," in *Maqāṣid al-Sharīʿah*, ed. Abduljabar al-Rufaʿi (Damascus: Dār al-Fikr, 2001). Also refer to Qaradawi's *Madkhal*.
231. Shamsuddin, "Maqāṣid al-Sharīʿah," p.26.

BIBLIOGRAPHY

Abū al- Faraj, ʿAbd al-Raḥmān, *Ṣifah al-Ṣafwah*, ed. Mahmoud Fakhouri and M. R. Qalaji, 2nd ed. (Beirut: Dār al-Maʿrifah, 1979).

Abd al-Raziq, Ali, "Message Not Government, Religion Not State," in *Liberal Islam: A Sourcebook*, ed. Charles Kurzman (Oxford: Oxford University Press, 1998).

Abduh, Mohammad, *Risālah al-Tawḥīd*. Edited by Mohammad Rashid Rida. 15th ed. (Cairo: Dār al-Manār, 1953).

———, *Al-Aʿmāl al-Kāmilah*, ed. Mohammad Emara (Cairo: Dār al-Shurūq, 1993).

Abdul-Fattah, Saif, "On Imam Mohamed Abdu's Worldview" Paper presented at the Centennial of Shaykh Mohamed Abdu (Bibliotheca Alexandrina, Alexandria, Egypt Dec. 2005).

Abdul-Haqq, Irshad, "Islamic Law: An Overview of Its Origin and Elements," Journal of Islamic Law and Culture 27 (spring/summer) (2002).

Abd al-Jabbār, Abū al-Ḥasan al-Qāḍī, *Al-Mughnī fī Abwāb al-Tawḥīd wa al-ʿAdl*. Edited by Taha Hussein and Ibrahim Madkoor (Cairo: Egyptian Ministry of Culture, 1965).

———, *Faḍl al-Iʿtizāl wa Ṭabaqāt al-Muʿtazilah*. Edited by Fouad Sayed. (Tunis: al-Dār al-Tunisiyyah li al-Nashr, 1974).

Abu-Zaid, Nasr Hamed, *Al-Imām al-Shāfiʿī wa Ta'sīs al-Āīdyūlūjiyyah al-Wasaṭiyyah*, 3rd ed. (Cairo: Madbūlī, 2003).

Abū Dāwūd, Sulaymān, *Al-Sunan* (Damascus: Dār al-Fikr).

Abū Yūsuf, Yaʿqub, *al-Kharāj* (Cairo: al-Maṭbaṭʿah al-Amīriyyah, 1303 AH)).

Abu Zahrah, Mohammad, *'Uṣūl Al-Fiqh* (Cairo: Dār al-Fikr al-ʿArabī, 1958).

———, *Al-Imām Zayd* (Cairo: Dār al-Fikr al-ʿArabī, 1965).

———, *Tārīkh al-Mathāhib al-Islāmiyyah* (Cairo: Dār al-Fikr al-ʿArabī, no date).

Abu Zaid, Nasr Hamed, *Al-Imām al-Shāfiʿī wa Ta'sīs al-Āīdyūlūjiyyah al-Waṣaṭiyyah*, 3rd ed. (Cairo: Madbūlī, 2003).

———, "Divine Attributes in the Qur'an," in *Islam and Modernity: Muslim Intellectuals Respond*, ed. John Cooper, Ronald L. Nettler and Mohamed Mahmoud (London: I.B.Tauris, 1998).

———, *Mafhūm al-Naṣṣ: Dirāsah fī ᶜUlūm al-Qur'ān* (Cairo: Al-Hay'ah al-Miṣriyyah li al-Kitāb, 1990).

Ackoff, R, *Creating the Corporate Future* (New York: John Wiley, 1981).

———, "Towards a System of Systems Concepts," Management Science 17, no. 11 (1971).

Ahmed, Akbar, *Postmodernism and Islam: Predicament and Promise*, 7 ed. (London and New York: Routledge, 2004).

Ahmed, Leila, *Women and Gender in Islam* (New Haven, CT: Yale University Press, 1992).

al-Ajam, Rafiq, *Al-Manṭiq ᶜInd al-Ghazālī fī Abᶜādih al-Arisṭawiyyah wa Khuṣūṣīyātih al-Islāmiyyah* (Beirut: Dār al-Mashriq, 1989).

al-Albani, Mohammad Nasir al-Din, *Wujūb al-Akhdh bi Ḥadīth al-Āḥād fī al-ᶜAqīdah wa al Rad ᶜAlā Shubah al-Mukhālifīn* (Banhā and Kuwait: Dār al-ᶜIlm and al-Dār al-Salafiyyah, no date).

al-Shaykh, Abdul-Rahman, *Fatḥ al-Majīd Sharḥ Kitāb al-Tawḥīd* (Cairo: Mu'ssassah Qurṭubah, no date).

al-Ālūsī, Shihāb al-Dīn, *Rūḥ al-Maᶜānī fī Tafsīr al-Qur'ān al-ᶜAẓīm* (Beirut: Dār Iḥyā' al-Turāth al-ᶜArabī, no date).

al-Alwani, Taha Jabir. "Madkhal Ilā Fiqh al-Aqalliyyāt." Paper presented at the European Council for Fatwa and Research, ECFR, Dublin, Jan. 2004.

———, "Maqāṣid al-Sharīᶜah," in *Maqāṣid al-Sharīᶜah*, ed. Abdul-Jabbar al-Rifaie (Damascus: Dār al-Fikr, 2001).

———, *Maqāṣid al-Sharīᶜah*, 1st ed. (Beirut: IIIT and Dār al-Hādī, 2001).

———, *Issues in Contemporary Islamic Thought* (London–Washington: International Institute of Islamic Thought (IIIT), 2005).

al-Āmidī, ᶜAlī Abū al-Ḥasan, *Al-Iḥkām fī 'Uṣūl al-Aḥkām*. (Beirut: Dār al-Kitāb al-ᶜArabī, 1404 AH).

al-ᶜĀmirī, Abū al-Ḥasan al-Faylasūf, *al-Iᶜlām bi-Manāqib al-Islām*, ed. Ahmad Ghurab (Cairo: Dār al-Kitāb al-ᶜArabī, 1967).

al-Anṣārī, Ibn Niẓām al-Dīn, *Fawātiḥ al-Raḥamūt Sharḥ Musallam Al-Thubūt*, ed. Abdullah Mahmoud M. Omar, 1st ed. (Beirut: Dār al-Kutub Al-ᶜIlmiyyah, 2002).

al-Aṣbahānī, Abū Nuᶜaym, *Ḥīlyah al-Awliyā' wa Ṭabaqah al-Aṣfiyā'*, 4th ed. (Beirut: Dār al-Nashr al-ᶜArabī, 1985).

al-Ashqar, Omar Sulaiman, *Tārīkh al-Fiqh al-Islāmī*, 1st. ed. (Kuwait: Maktabah al-Falāḥ, 1982), p.119.

al-Azami, Mohammad, *On Schacht's Origins of Mohammadan Jurisprudence*. (Riyadh: King Saud University and John Wiley, 1985).

al-Baghdādī, Abū Bakr, *Al-Faqīh wa al-Mutafaqih*, ed. Adil ibn Yusuf al-Gharazi (Saudi Arabia: Dār ibn al-Jawzī, 1421 AH).

al-Banna, Jamal, *Tajdīd al-Fiqh al-Islāmī, Ḥiwārāt li-Qarn Jadīd* (Damascus: Dār al-Fikr, 2000).

al-Baṣrī, Moḥammad al-Ṭayyib, *Al-Muʿtamad fī ʿUṣūl al-Fiqh*, ed. Khalil al-Mees, 1st ed. (Beirut: Dār al-Kutub al-ʿIlmiyyah, 1983 CE/1403 AH).

al-Baṭlayawsī, ʿAbdullāh ibn Moḥammad, *Al-Inṣāf fī al-Tanbīh ʿAlā al-Maʿānī wa al-Asbāb ʿAllatī Awjabat al-Ikhtilāf*, ed. Mohammed Ridwan al-Dayah, 2nd ed. (Beirut: Dār al-Fikr, 1403 AH).

al-Bayhaqī, Abū Bakr, *Al-Sunan* (Madinah: al-Dār, 1989).

al-Bazdawī, ʿAlī ibn Moḥammad, *ʿUṣūl Al-Bazdawī- Kanz Al-Wuṣūl Ilā Maʿrifah al-ʿUṣūl* (Karachi: Jāwīd Press, no date).

al-Bishri, Tariq, *Māhiyyah al-Muʿāṣarah* (Cairo: Dār al-Shurūq, 1996).

al-Bouti, M. Said Ramadan, *Ḍawābiṭ al-Maṣlaḥah fī al-Sharīʿah al-Islāmiyyah*, 6th ed. (Damascus: al-Risālah Foundation, 2001).

al-Bukhārī ʿAlāʾ al-Dīn, *Kashf al-Asrār ʿan ʿUṣūl Fakhr al-Islām al-Bazdawī*, ed. Abdullah Mahmoud M. Omar (Beirut: Dār al-Kutub al-ʿIlmiyyah, 1997)

al-Bukhari, Abdul-Aziz, *Kashf al-Asrār* (Beirut: Dār al-Kutub al-ʿIlmiyyah, 1997).

al-Bukhārī, Moḥammad, *Al-Tārīkh al-Kabīr*, ed. Mohammad Hashim al-Nadawi (Dār al-Fikr, no date)

———, *al-Ṣaḥīḥ*, ed. Mustafa al-Bagha, 3rd ed. (Beirut: Dār ibn Kathīr, 1986)

al-Deeb, Abdul-Azim, "Imam Al-Haramain," in *Ghiāth al-ʿUmam fī Iltiyāth al-Ẓulam* (Doha: al-Shu'ūn al-Dīniyyah, 1400 AH).

al-Dimashqī, Ḥamad, *Al-Kāshif fī Maʿrifah Man Lahu Rīwāyah fī al-Kutub al-Sittah*, ed. Mohammad Awama, 1st ed. (Jeddah: Dār al-Qiblah li al-Thaqāfah al-Islāmiyyah, 1992).

al-Eini, Bar al-Din, *ʿUmdah al-Qārī Sharḥ Ṣaḥīḥ al-Bukhārī* (Beirut: Dār Iḥyāʾ al-Turāth al-ʿArabī, no date).

al-Fadli, Abdulhadi, "Maqāṣid al-Sharīʿah," in *Maqāṣid al-Sharīʿah*, ed. Abdul-Jabbar al-Rifaie (Damascus: Dār al-Fikr, 2001),

al-Fayrūzabādī, Ibrāhīm, *Sharḥ al-Lamʿ*, ed. Abd al-Mageed Turki (Beirut: Dār al-Gharb al-Islāmī, 1988)

al-Ghazālī, Abū Ḥāmid, *Al-Mankhūl fī Taʿlīqāt al-ʿUṣūl*, ed. Mohamed Hasan Hito, 2nd ed. (Damascus: Dār al-Fikr, 1400 AH).

———, *Al-Mustaṣfā fī ʿIlm Al-ʿUṣūl*, ed. Mohammed Abdul-Salam Abdul Shafi, 1st ed. (Beirut: Dār al-Kutub al-ʿIlmiyyah, 1413 AH).

———, *Al-Qisṭās al-Mustaqīm* (Beirut: Catholic Publishing House, 1959).

———, *Maḥakk al-Naẓar* (Cairo: al-Maṭbaʿah al-Adabiyyah, no date).

———, *Maqāṣid Al-Falāsifah* (Cairo: Dār al-Maʿārif, 1961).

———, *Tahāfut al-Falāsifah* (Incoherence of the Philosophers). Translated by M. S. Kamali (Pakistan Philosophical Congress, 1963 [cited January 18th 2005]); available from http://www.muslimphilosophy.com.

al-Ghazaly, Mohammad, *Naẓarāt fī al-Qur'ān* (Cairo: Nahḍah Miṣr, 2002).

———, *Al-Sunnah al-Nabawiyyah Bayna Ahl al-Fiqh wa Ahl al-Ḥadīth*, 11th ed. (Cairo: Dār al-Shurūq, 1996).

al-Haj, Ibn Amir, *Al-Taqrīr wa al-Taḥbīr fī ᶜIlm Uṣūl al-Fiqh* (Beirut: Dār al-Fikr, 1996).

al-Ḥasfakī, *Al-Durr al-Mukhtār* (Beirut: Dār al-Fikr, 1386).

al-Hussaini, Abū Bakr *Kifāyah al-Akhyār fī Ḥal Ghāyah al-Ikhtiṣār*, ed. A. A. Baltaji and M. Wahbi Sulaiman, 1st ed. (Damascus: Dār al-Khayr, 1994).

al-Iraqi, Atif, *Al-Nazᶜah al-ᶜAqliyyah fī Falsafah ibn Rushd*, 5th ed. (Cairo: Dār al-Maᶜārif, 1993).

al-Isnawī, Jamāl al-Dīn, *Nihāyat al-Sūl Sharḥ Minhāj al-Wusūl*, ed. Abdul Qadir Mohammad Ali (Beirut: Dār al-Kutub al-ᶜIlmiyyah, 1999).

al-Jaṣṣaṣ, Abū Bakr, *Aḥkām Al-Qur'ān*, ed. Mohammad al-Sadiq Qamhawi (Beirut: Dār Ihyā' al-Turāth, 1984)

al-Jazri, Al-Mubarak, *Al-Nihāyah fī Gharīb al-Ḥadīth wa al-Athar* (Beirut: Al-Maktabah al-ᶜIlmiyyah, 1979).

al-Juwaynī, Abdul-Malik, *Al-Burhān fī 'Uṣūl al-Fiqh*, ed. Abdul-Azim al-Deeb, 4th ed. (Manṣūrah: al-Wafā', 1418 AH/1998 CE).

———, *Ghīath al-Umam fī Iltiyath al-Ẓulam*, ed. Abdul-Azim al-Deeb (Qatar: Wazārah al-Shu'ūn al-Dīniyyah, 1400 AH).

al-Juwaynī, Abdul-Malik, *Al-Burhān fī ᶜUlūm al-Qur'ān*, 4th ed. (Al-Manṣūrah, Egypt: al-Wafā', 1997).

al-Kassānī, ᶜAlā' al-Dīn, *Badā'iᶜ al-Ṣanā'iᶜ fī Tartīb al-Sharā'iᶜ*, 2nd ed. (Beirut: Dār al-Kitāb al-ᶜArabī, 1982).

al-Khafeef, Ali, "Al-Sunnah al-Tashrīᶜiyyah," in *Al-Sunnah al-Tashrīᶜiyyah wa Ghayr al-Tashrīᶜiyyah*, ed. Mohammad Emara (Cairo: Nahḍah Miṣr, 2001)

al-Khoshoui, Al-Khoshoui A. M., *Ghāyah al-ᶜIddah fī ᶜUlūm al-Iṣṭilāḥ* (Cairo: al-Azhar University, 1992).

Al-Khudari, Mohammad, *'Uṣūl Al-Fiqh* (Beirut: al-Maktabah al-ᶜAaṣriyyah, 2002).

Al-Killini, Mohammad, *'Uṣūl al-Kāfī*, ed. Ali Akbar Al-Ghiffari (Tehran: Dār al-Manshūrāt al-Islāmiyyah, no date)

al-Kinānī, Ashraf Abū Qudāmah, *Al-Adillah al-Isti'nāsiyyah ᶜInd al-'Uṣūliyyīn*, 1st ed. (Amman: Dār al-Nafā'is, 2005).

al-Laknawi, Mohammad Abdul-Hayy, *Al-Ajwibah al-Fāḍilah li al-As'ilah al-ᶜAsharah al-Kāmilah*, ed. Abdul-Fattah Abu Ghuddah (Halab: Maktab al-Maṭbūᶜāt al-Islāmiyyah, 1384 AH).

al-Majalah, Jamᶜiyyah, *Majallat al-Aḥkām al-ᶜAdliyyah*, ed. Najib Hawawini (Karkhaneh Tijārah Kutub, no date).

al-Mirdāwī, ᶜAlā' al-Dīn, *Al-Taḥbīr Sharḥ al-Taḥrīr fī 'Uṣūl Al-Fiqh*, ed. Awad al-

Qarni Abdurahman Jubrain, Ahmad al-Sarrah, 1st ed. (Riyadh: Maktabah al-Rushd, 2000).

al-Marzouqi, A. A. M., "Human Rights in Islamic Law." (Ph.D. diss, University of Exeter, 1990).

al-Marzuqi, Abu-Yarub, "Iṣlāḥ al-ʿAql fī al-Falsafah al-ʿArabiyyah" (Ph.D. diss, Published by The Centre of Arabic Unity Studies, 1994).

al-Māwardī, ʿAlī, *Al-Aḥkām al-Sulṭāniyyah* (Cairo: al-Maktabah al-Tawfīqiyyah, no date).

Al-Mirghiyānī, ʿAli, *Al-Hidāyah Sharḥ Bidāyah Al-Mubtadi'* (Al-Maktabah al Islāmiyyah, no date).

al-Nīsābūrī, Al-Ḥākim, *Al-Mustadrak ʿAlā al-Ṣaḥīḥayn* (Beirut: Dār al-Kutub al-ʿIlmiyyah, 1990).

al-Najjar, Abdul-Majid, *Khilāfat al-Insān Bayna al-Waḥy wa al-ʿAql* (Virginia: International Institute of Islamic Thought (IIIT), 1993).

al-Najjar, Zaghloul, *Wonderful Scientific Signs in the Qur'an* (London: Al-Firdaws, 2005).

al-Nami, Amr K., "Studies in Ibadhism," (www.Islamfact.com, 2006).

al-Nasafī, Abd Allah ibn Aḥmad, *Kashf al-Asrār Sharḥ al-Muṣannaf ʿAlā al-Manār*, 1st ed. (Beirut: Dār al-Kutub al-ʿIlmiyyah, 1998).

al-Nawawī, Yaḥya Abū-Zakariyah, *Al-Majmūʿ* (Beirut: Dār al-Fikr, 1997).

al-Nimr, Abdul-Moneim, *Al-Ijtihād* (Cairo: Dār al-Shurūq, 1986).

al-Qaradawi, Yusuf, *Al-Ijtihād al-Muʿāṣir Bayna al-Inḍibāṭ wa al-Infirāṭ* (Cairo: Dār al-Tawzīʿ, 1994).

———, *Fi Fiqh Al-Aqalliyat Al-Muslimah*. 1st ed. Cairo: Wahba, 2001.

———, "Fiqh al-Zakah" (Ph.D. diss, al-Azhar University, Egypt, Published by al-Risālah, 15th ed, 1985).

———, *Kayf Nataʿāmal Maʿa al-Qur'ān al-ʿAẓīm?*, 1st ed. (Cairo: Dār al-Shorūq, 1999).

———, *Madkhal li-Dirāsah al-Sharīʿah al-Islāmiyyah* (Cairo: Wahba, 1997).

al-Qarāfī, Shihāb al-Dīn, *al-Dhakhīrah* (Beirut: Dār al-ʿArab, 1994).

———, *al-Furūq* (Maʿa Hawāmishihi), ed. Khalil Mansour (Beirut: Dār al-Kutub al-ʿIlmiyyah, 1998).

al-Qattan, Mannaʿ, *Mabāḥith fī ʿUlūm al-Qur'ān*, 11th ed. (Cairo: Wahba, 2000).

al-Qummī, Ibn Bābawayh al-Ṣadūq, *ʿIlal Al-Sharā'iʿ*, ed. Mohammad Sadiq Bahr al-Ulum (Najaf: Dār al-Balāghah, 1966).

al-Rāzī, Moḥammad ibn ʿUmar, *Al-Maḥṣūl*, ed. Taha Jabir al-Alwani (Riyadh: Imam Mohammad University Press, 1400 AH).

———, *Al-Tafsīr Al-Kabīr* (Beirut: Dār al-Kutub al-ʿIlmiyyah, 2000).

al-Saadi, Abdul-Hakim, *Mabāḥith al-ʿIllah fī al-Qiyās ʿInd al-'Uṣūliyyīn* (Beirut: Dār al-Bashā'ir, 1986).

al-Sadir, Ayatollah Mohammad Baqir, *Al-'Usus al-Manṭiqiyyah li al-Istiqrā'*, 4th ed. (Beirut: Dār al-Taᶜāruf, 1982).

———, *Durūs fī ᶜIlm al-'Uṣūl*, 2nd ed. (Beirut: Dār al-Kitāb al-Lubnanī, 1986).

———, "Al-Sunan al-Tārīkhiyyah fī al-Qur'an," in *Imām Al-Ṣadir: Al-Aᶜmāl al-Kāmilah* (Beirut: Dār al-Taᶜāruf, 1990).

al-Sagheer, Abdul-Majeed, *Al-Fikr al-'Uṣūlī wa Ishkāliyyah al-Ṣulṭah al-ᶜIlmiyyah fī al-Islām*, 1st ed., Dirāsāt Islāmiyyah (Islamic Studies) (Beirut: Dār al-Muntakhab al-ᶜArabī, 1994).

al-Samaᶜani, Abu Muzafar, *Qawāṭiᶜ al-'Adillah fī al-'Uṣūl*, ed. Ismail al-Shafie (Beirut: Dār al-Kutub al-ᶜIilmiyyah, 1997).

al-Ṣanᶜānī, Moḥammad ibn Ismāᶜīl, *Subul al-Salām Sharḥ Bulūgh al-Marām Min Adilat al-Aḥkām*, ed. Mohammad Abdul Aziz Al-Khouli (Beirut: Dār Ihyā' al-Turāth al-ᶜArabī, 1379 AH).

———, *Irshād al-Nuqad 'Ilā Taysīr al-Ijtihād*, ed. Salah al-Din Maqbool Ahmad, 1st ed. (Kuwait: Al-Dār al-Salafiyyah, 1405 AH).

al-Sarkhasī, Moḥammad ibn Aḥmad, *'Uṣūl al-Sarkhasī* (Beiut: Dār al- Maᶜrifah, no date).

al-Shafie, Hasan, *Al-Āmidī wa Ārā'uhu al-Kalāmiyyah*, 1st ed. (Cairo: Dār al-Salām, 1998)

al-Shāfiᶜī, Moḥammad ibn Idrīs, *Al-Umm*, 2nd ed. (Beirut: Dār al-Maᶜrifah, 1393 AH).

———, *Al-Risālah*, ed. Ahmad Shakir, (Cairo: al-Madanī, 1939).

al-Sharif, Mohammad Shakir, *Ḥaqīqah al-Dīmuqrāṭiyyah* (Riyadh: Dār al-Waṭan, 1992).

al-Shāshī, Abū Moḥammad, *'Uṣūl al-Shāshī* (Beirut: Dār al-Kitāb al-ᶜArabī, 1402 AH).

al-Shāshī, Al-Qaffāl, "Maḥāsin al-Sharā'iᶜ," in *Fiqh Shāfiᶜī*, Manuscript No. 263 (Cairo, Dār al-Kutub: 358 AH/ 969 CE).

al-Shāṭibī, Abū Isḥāq, *Al-Iᶜtiṣām* (Egypt: Almaktabah al-Tijāriyyah Alkubrā, no date).

———, Ibrāhīm al-Ghirnāṭī Diraz (Beirut: Dār al-Maᶜrifah, no date).

al-Shawkānī, Moḥammad ibn ᶜAlī, *Irshād al-Fuḥūl Ilā Taḥqīq ᶜIlm Al-'Uṣūl*, ed. Mohammed Said al-Badri, 1st ed. (Beirut: Dār al-Fikr, 1992).

al-Shaybani, Ali, *Al-Kāmil fī al-Tārīkh*, 2nd ed. (Beirut: Dār al-Nashr, 1994).

al-Shirāzī, Abū Isḥāq, *Al-Lamᶜ fī 'Uṣūl Al-Fiqh* (Beirut: Dār al-Kutub al-ᶜIlmiyyah, 1985).

al-Siwāsī, Kamāl al-Dīn, *Sharḥ Fatḥ al-Qādir*, 2nd ed. (Beirut: Dar al-Fikr, no date).

al-Sousarah, Abdul Majeed, *Manhaj Al-Tawfīq wa al Tarjīḥ Bayn Mukhtalaf al-*

Ḥadīth wa Atharuhu fī al-Fiqh al-Islāmī, 1st ed. (Amman: Dār al-Nafā'is, 1997).

al-Subki, ᶜAlī, *Al-'Ibhāj fī Sharḥ al-Minhāj* (Beirut: Dār al-Nashr, 1983).

———, *al-Fatāwā*. (Lebanon: Dār al-Maᶜrifah, no date).

al-Suyūṭī, Jalāl al-Dīn, *Al-Ashbāh wa al-Naẓā'ir* (Beirut: Dār al-Kutub al-ᶜIlmiyyah, 1403 AH).

———, *Al-Dur Al-Manthūr* (Beirut: Dār al-Fikr, 1993).

———,*Tadrīb al-Rāwī fī Sharḥ Taqrīb al-Nawawī*. Ed. by Abdul Wahab Abdul Latif (Riyadh: Maktabah al-Riyādh al-Ḥadīthah, no date).

al-Taan, Ahmad Idris, *Al-Maqāṣid wa al-Munāwarah al-ᶜIlmāniyyah*, Muntadā al-Tawḥīd, 2005 [cited Mar. 10th, 2007]. Available from: http://www.eltwhed.com/vb/showthread.php?t=2456

al-Ṭabarī, Moḥammad ibn Jarīr, *Jāmiᶜ al-Bayān ᶜan Ta'wīl Āyī al-Qur'an* (Beirut: Dār al-Fikr, 1985).

al-Taftazānī al-Shāfiᶜī, Saᶜad al-Dīn, *Sharḥ al-Talwīḥ ᶜAlā al-Tawḍīḥ li matn al-Tanqīḥ fī 'Uṣūl Al-Fiqh*, ed. Zakariya Umairat (Beirut: Dār al-Kutub Al-ᶜIlmiyyah, 1996).

al-Tayyib, Ahmad, "Naẓariyyah al-Maqāṣid ᶜInd al-Shāṭibī wa Madā Irtibāṭihā bi al-'Uṣūl al-Kalāmiyyah," *al-Muslim al-Muᶜāṣir*, no. 103 (2002).

al-Dhahabi, Mohammad, *Siyar Aᶜlām al-Nubalā'*, ed. Shoaib Aaaran'ut and Mohammad al-'Arqusied, 9th ed. (Beirut: Risālah Foundation, 1993).

al-Tirmidhī, Moḥammad ibn ᶜĪssā, *Al-Jāmiᶜ al-Ṣaḥīḥ Sunan al-Tirmidhī*, ed. Ahmad M. Shakir (Beirut: Dār Iḥyā' al-Turāth al-ᶜArabī, no date).

al-Tubrūsī, al-Faḍl ibn al-Ḥussain, *Majmaᶜ Al-Bayān fī Tafsīr al-Qur'ān* (Beirut: Dār al-ᶜUlūm, 2005).

al-Ṭūfī, Najm al-Dīn, *al-Taᶜyīn fī Sharḥ al-Arbaᶜīn* (Beirut: al-Rayyān, 1419 AH).

al-Turabi, Hasan, *Al-Tafsīr al-Tawḥīdī*, 1st ed., vol. 1 (London: Dār al-Sāqī, 2004).

———, *Emancipation of Women: An Islamic Perspective*, 2nd ed. (London: Muslim Information Centre, 2000).

———, *Qaḍāyā al-Tajdīd: Naḥwa Manhaj 'Uṣūlī* (Beirut: Dār al-Hādī, 2000).

al-Yahya, N. A. A., "Ibn Qudamah's Methodology and His Approach to Certain Aspects of the Islamic Law of International Relations in the Hanbali Juristic Tradition" (Ph.D. diss, University of Manchester, 1992).

al-Zaabi, Anwar, *Ẓāhiriyyah ibn Ḥazm al-Andalusī: Naẓariyyah al-Maᶜrifah wa Manāhij al-Baḥth* (Ibn Hazm's Literalism: Epistomology and Methodology), (Amman: International Institute of Islamic Thought, 1996).

al-Zanjani, Mahmoud Abu al-Manaqib, *Takhrīj al-Furūᶜ*, ed. Mohammed Adeeb Salih, 2nd ed. (Beirut: al-Risālah Foundation, 1398 AH).

al-Zarᶜī, Moḥammad ibn Abū Bakr, *Tuḥfat Al-Mawdūd bi 'Aḥkām al-Mawlūd*,

ed. Abdul Qadir al-Arnaout, 1st ed. (Damascus: Dār al-Bayān, 1971).
al-Zarkashī, Badr al-Dīn, *Al-Ijābah Li'īrād mā Istadrakathu ʿĀ'isha ʿAlā al-Ṣaḥabah*, ed. Said Al-Afghani, 2nd ed. (Beirut: Al-Maktab al-Islāmī, 1970).
———, *Al-Baḥr Al-Muhīṭ fī 'Uṣūl Al-Fiqh*, ed. M. M. Tamir, 1st ed. (Beirut: 2000).
———, *Sharḥ al-Zarkashī ʿAlā Mukhtaṣar al-Kharqī*, ed. Abdul Moneim Khalil Ibrahim, 1st ed. (Beirut: Dār al-Kutub al-ʿIlmiyyah, 2002).
al-Zarqa, Ahmad al-Shaykh, *Sharḥ al-Qawāʿid al-Fiqhiyyah*, ed. Mustafa Ahmad al-Zarqa, 2nd ed. (Damascus: Dār Al-Qalam, 1989).
al-Zubaydī, Moḥammad, *Tāj al-ʿArūs fī Jawāhir al-Qāmūs* (Beirut: Dār al-Nashr, no date).
al-Zuhaili, Wahba, *Tajdīd al-Fiqh al-Islāmī, Ḥiwārāt li Qur'ān Jadīd* (Damascus: Dār al-Fikr, 2000).
al-Zurqani, Mohammad, *Sharḥ al-Zurqānī ʿAlā Muwaṭṭa' al-Imām Mālik*. 1st ed. (Beirut: Dār al-Kutub al-ʿIlmiyyah, no date).
Ali, A. K., "Al-Shāfiʿī's Contribution to Hadith with an Annotated Translation of His Work Jimāʿ Al-ʿIlm" (Ph.D. diss, University of Edinburgh, 1996).
Ali, Mahmoud Mohammad, *Al-ʿAlāqah Bayn Al-Manṭiq wa al-Fiqh ʿInd Mufakkirī al-Islām* (Cairo: Ein for Human and Social Studies, 2000).
Ali, S. S., "Equal before Allah, Unequal before Man? Negotiating Gender Hierarchies in Islam and International Law" (Ph.D. diss, University of Hull, 1998).
Al-Naim, Abdullahi, "Islam and Human Rights," *Tikkun* 18, no. 1 (2003).
Anwar, Hafiz, "Wilāyah Al-Mar'ah fī al-Fiqh al-Islāmī" (Masters, Imam Saud Islamic University, Published by Dār Balansiyah, 1999).
Arifin, M. B., "The Principles of ʿ*Umūm* and *Takhṣīṣ* in Islamic Jurisprudence" (Ph.D. diss, University of Edinburgh, 1988).
Aristotle, *Ethics*. Translated by W.D. Ross. Edited by J.L. Ackrill. (London: Faber & Faber, 1973).
———, *The Works of Aristotle*, vol. 1, Great Books of the Western World (London: Encyclopaedia Britannica INC, 1990).
Arkoun, Mohamed, "Rethinking Islam Today," in *Liberal Islam: A Sourcebook*, edited by Charles Kurzman. (Oxford: Oxford University Press, 1998).
———, *Rethinking Islam: Common Questions, Uncommon Answers*, ed. Robert D. Lee, trans. Robert D. Lee (Boulder: Westview Press, 1994).
Asad, Talal, *The Idea of an Anthropology of Islam* (Washington, D.C: Georgetown University Center for Contemporary Arab Studies, 1986).
Asmal, A. M., "Muslims under Non-Muslim Rule: The Fight (Legal) Views of Ibn Nujaym and Al-Wansharisi" (Ph.D. diss, University of Manchester, 1998).

Attia, Gamal, *Naḥwa Tafʿīl Maqāṣid al-Sharīʿah* (Amman: al-Maʿhad al-ʿĀlamī li al-Fikr al-Islāmī, 2001).

———, *Tajdīd al-Fiqh al-Islāmī* (Beirut: Dar al-Fikr, 2000).

Auda, Jasser, *Fiqh al-Maqāṣid: Ināṭah al-Aḥkām al-Sharʿiyyah bi-Maqāṣidihā* (Virginia, IIIT: al-Maʿhad al-ʿĀlamī li al-Fikr al-Islāmī, 2006).

———, "Dawarān al-Aḥkām al-Sharʿiyyah Maʿa Maqāṣidihā Wujūdan wa ʿAdaman: Dirāsah 'Uṣūliyyah Nāqdiah Taṭbṭīqiyyah (Change of Statutes According to Their Purposes: A Methodological, Critical and Applied Study)" (Master of Jurisprudence diss., Islamic American University, 2004).

———, "Cooperative Modular Neural Network Classifiers," Ph. D. Thesis (University of Waterloo, 1996).

——— and M. Kamel, "A Modular Neural Network for Vague Classification." Lecture notes in *Computer Science* Vol. 2005: *Lecture notes in Artificial Intelligence* (2000).

———, "From the 'Preservation of Necessities' to the 'Development of the Nation': The Effect of Worldview on the Cognition of Purposes of the Islamic Law." Conference: Purposes of Islamic Law and Means of Achieving them in Muslim Societies. International Islamic University of Malaysia, Malaysia.

———, "Purposes and Causes of Islamic Rulings." In *Studies in the Philosophy of Islamic Law: Theory and Applications*, Research Centre in the Philosophy of Islamic Law, London, U.K.

———, "Renewal of Islamic Thought is Necessary for Facing Islamic Global Challenges." *Al-Madinah Daily* (Medina, Saudi Arabia: Year 72, No. 15657).

———, "Basing Islamic Rulings on their Purposes." *At-Tajdīd Journal*, (International Islamic University of Malaysia, Issue 19/1, Malaysia).

———, "Islam" in *Encyclopedia of the Developing World* (New York: Routlege).

———, "On Imam Mohamed Abdu's Worldview" Paper presented at the Centennial of Shaykh Mohamed Abdu (Bibliotheca Alexandrina, Alexandria, Egypt Dec. 2005)

———, "Purposes versus Causes for the Islamic Rulings." Islamic Heritage Foundation Symposium on the Purposes of Islamic Law, London, U.K., March, 2005.

———, "A Framework for Applying Systems Theory in Islamic Judicial Reasoning." *Journal of the International Institute of Advanced Systems Research* (IIAS), Special Edn.: Systems Theory in Theology, (Baden-Baden, Germany, July, 2004).

———, "Abrogation of Rulings Methodology: A Critique." *Intellectual Discourse Journal*, Islamic University of Malaysia, Vol. 12, No. 2, Malaysia, 2004.

Audi, Robert, *The Cambridge Dictionary of Philosophy*, 2nd ed., vol. 1 (Cambridge: Cambridge University Press, 1999).

Baderin, M. A., "Modern Muslim States between Islamic Law and International Human Rights Law." (Ph.D. diss, University of Nottingham, 2001).

Badran, Badran, *Adillah al-Tarjīḥ al-Mutaʿāriḍah wa Wujūh al-Tarjīḥ Baynahā* (Alexandria: Mu'assasah Shabāb al-Jāmiʿah, 1974).

Badshah, Amir, *Taysīr al-Taḥrīr* (Beirut: Dār al-Fikr, no date).

Bayḍawī, *Tafsīr al-Bayḍawī* (Beirut: Dār al-Fikr, no date).

Bayah, Abdallah bin, *ʿAlāqah Maqāṣid al-Sharīʿah bi 'Uṣūl al-Fiqh*, 1st ed. (Cairo: al-Furqān Islamic Heritage Foundation, al-Maqāṣid Research Centre, 2006)

———, *Āmālī al-Dilālāt wa Majāli al-Ikhtilāfat*, 1st ed. (Jeddah: Dār al-Minhāj, 2007).

Beany, Michael, "Analysis", *Stanford Encyclopedia of Philosophy* (2003 [cited Jan. 5th, 2007]); available from http://plato.stanford.edu/entries/analysis/.

Beer, S., *Brain of the Firm* (London: Penguin Press, 1972)

Begoviç, Ali Izzet, *Al-Iʿlān al-Islāmī*, trans. Mohamed Yusif Ads, 1st ed. (Cairo: Dār al-Shorūq, no date).

Bentham, Jeremy, *An Introduction to the Principles of Morals and Legislation* http://utilitarianism.com, 1781 CE [cited Jan. 10th, 2007].

Bernard, Cheryl, *Civil Democratic Islam, Partners, Resources, and Strategies.* (Santa Monica: RAND, 2004).

Bertalanffy, L. Von, "General Systems Theory." *Main Currents in Modern Thought*. Vol. 71, 1955.

Bhutto, Benazir, "Politics and the Muslim Woman," in *Liberal Islam: A Sourcebook,* ed. Charles Kurzman (Oxford: Oxford University Press, 1998).

Biltaji, *Manhaj ʿUmar Ibn al-Khaṭṭāb fī al-Tashrīʿ*, 1st ed. (Cairo: Dār al-Salām, 2002).

Bin Saleh, Hasan, "The Application of Al-Qawāʿid al-*Fiqhiyyah* of Majallat al-Aḥkām al-ʿAdliyyah: An Analytical Juristic Study with Particular Reference to Jordanian Civil Code and United Arab Emirates Law of Civil Transactions" (Ph.D. diss, University of Lampeter, 2003).

Binder, Leonard, *Ideological Revolution in the Middle East*, ed. John Wiley (New York: 1964).

Blackburn, Simon, *The Oxford Dictionary of Philosophy* (Oxford: Oxford University Press, 1996).

Bora Laskin Law Library, University of Toronto. *International Protection of Human Rights* (2004 [cited Jan. 15th, 2005]); available from http://www.law-lib.utoronto.ca/resguide/humrtsgu.htm.

Boulding, K., *Ecodynamics* (London: Sage Publications, 1978).

———, "General Systems as a Point of View," in *Views on General Systems Theory*, ed. A. Mesarovic (New York: John Wiley, 1964).

Bowler, D., *General Systems Thinking* (New York: North Holland, 1981).

Bunt, Gary, Virtually Islamic: Research and News About Islam in the Digital Age, 2000 [last visited Mar. 15th, 2007], http://www.virtuallyislamic.com/

Carson, Robert and Ewart Flood, *Dealing with Complexity: An Introduction to the Theory and Application of Systems Science*, vol. 2 (New York and London: Plenum Press, 1993).

Checkland, Peter, *Systems Thinking, Systems Practice* (New York: Wiley, 1999).

Choudhry, Masudul Alam, "Syllogistic Deductionism in Islamic Social Choice Theory," International Journal of Social Economics 17, no. 11 (1990): 4–21.

Churchman, W., *The Design of Inquiring Systems: Basic Concepts of Systems and Organizations* (New York: Basic Books, 1979).

Clarke, L., "The Shiʿi Construction of Taqlid," *Journal of Islamic Studies* 12, no. 1 (2001): 40–64.

Cook, N., *Stability and Flexibility: An Analysis of Natural Systems.* (New York: Pergamon Press, 1980).

Corning, Peter A., "Synergy: Another Idea Whose Time Has Come?" *Journal of Social and Evolutionary Systems*, vol. 1, no. 21 (1998).

Craig, Edward, ed. *The Routledge Encyclopedia of Philosophy*, (London: Routledge, 1998).

Crone, Patricia, *Roman, Provincial and Islamic Law: The Origins of the Islamic Patronate*, Cambridge Studies in Islamic Civilization (Cambridge: Cambridge University Press, 2002).

De Chardin, T., *The Phenomenon of Man*, no date.

DeMarco, C. W., "Deontic Legal Logic," in *The Philosophy of Law: An Encyclopedia*, ed. Christopher Gray (New York and London: Garland Publishing, 1999).

Derrida, Jacques, *Of Grammatology*, trans. Gayatri Chakravorty Spivak (Baltimore: John Hopkins University Press, 1976).

Descartes, René, *Rules for the Direction of the Mind: The Philosophical Writings of Descartes*, ed. J. Cottingham et al. (Cambridge: Cambridge University Press, 1684).

DeWitt, Richard, *Worldviews: An Introduction to the History and Philosophy of Science* (Malden, MA: Blackwell, 2004).

Dutton, Yassin, *The Origins of Islamic Law: The Qur'an, the Muwaṭṭa' and Madinan ʿAmal* (Surrey: Curzon, 1999).

Dworkin, Gerald, "Introduction" in *Morality, Harm, and the Law*, edited by Gerald Dworkin. (Oxford: Westview Press, 1994).

El-Affendi, Abdelwahab, ed. *Rethinking Islam and Modernity: Essays in Honour of Fathi Osman* (London: Islamic Foundation, 2001).

El-Awa, Mohamed S, "The Theory of Punishment in Islamic Law: A Comparative Study" (Ph.D. diss, London, School of Oriental and African Studies, 1972).

———, *Al-ʿAlāqah Bayn al-Sunnah wa al-Shiʿah*, 1st ed. (Cairo: Safīr International Press, 2006).

———, *al-Fiqh al-Islāmī fī Ṭarīq al-Tajdīd* (Cairo: al-Maktab al-Islāmī, 1998).

———, Fī al-Nidhām al-Siyāsī li al-Dawlah al-Islāmiyyah (Cairo: Dār al-Shurūq, 1998).

———, ed. *Maqāṣid al-Sharīʿah Al-Islāmiyyah: Dirāsāt fī Qaḍāyā Al-Manhaj wa Qaḍāyā al-Taṭbīq* (Cairo: al-Furqān Islamic Heritage Foundation, al-Maqāṣid Research Centre, 2006).

El-Awa, Salwa M. S., Textual Relations in the Quran: Relevance, Coherence and Structure, 1st ed. (London and New York: Routledge, 2006).

———, *Al-Wujūh wa al-Naẓā'ir fī al-Qur'ān al-Karīm*, 1st ed. (Cairo: Dār al-Shurūq, 1998).

El-Fadl, Khalid Abou, *Speaking in God's Name* (Oxford: Oneworld Publications, 2003).

El-Raysuni, Ahmad, *Naẓariyyat al-Maqāṣid ʿind al-Imam al-Shāṭibī*, 1st ed. (Herndon, VA: IIIT, 1992).

——— , Mohammad al-Zuhaili, and Mohammad O. Shabeer. "Ḥuqūq al-Insān Miḥwar Maqāṣid al-Sharīʿah," Kitāb al-Ummah, no. 87 (2002).

El-Saadawi, Nawal, *God Dies by the Nile*, 6th ed. (London: Zed Books Ltd, 2002).

El-Tobgui, Carl Sharif, "The Epistemology of *Qiyās* and *Taʿlīl* between the Muʿtazilite Abū al-Ḥusayn al-Baṣrī and ibn Ḥazm al-Zāhirī," *UCLA Journal of Islamic and Near Eastern Law*, no. 2 (spring/summer) (2003).

Ellis, John, *Against Deconstruction* (Princeton, New Jersey: Princeton University Press, 1989).

Emara, Mohammad, *Tajdīd al-Fikr al-Islāmī* (Cairo: Kitāb Dār al-Hilāl, 1981).

———, "Al-Sunnah al-Tashrīʿiyyah," in Al-Sunnah al-Tashrīʿiyyah wa Ghair al-Tashrīʿiyyah, ed. Mohammad Emara (Cairo: Nahḍah Miṣr, 2001).

Esposito, John, *Islam and Politics* (Syracuse: Syracuse University Press, 1984).

———, ed., *The Oxford History of Islam* (Oxford: University Press, 1999).

European Council for Fatwa and Research, ECFR, *Scientific Review of the European Council for Fatwa and Research*. Edited by Abdul-Majid al-Najjar. Vol. 1–11. Dublin, since June 2002.

Ezzat, Heba Ra'uf, "Al-Mar'ah wa al-Dīn wa al-Akhlāq," in *Hiwārāt li Qarn Jadīd* (Dār al-Fikr: Damascus, 2000).

Fadlullah, Mohammad Hussain, "Maqāṣid al-Sharīᶜah," in *Maqāṣid al-Sharīᶜah*, ed. Abduljabar al-Rufai (Damascus: Dār al-Fikr, 2001).

Fakhry, Majid, *A History of Islamic Philosophy*, 2nd ed. (London, New York: Longman, Colombia University Press, 1983).

Farhan, Adnan, *Ḥarakah al-Ijtihād ᶜInd al-Shīᶜah al-Imāmiyyah*, 1st. ed. (Beirut: Dār al-Hādī, 2004).

Fatani, Ismail, *Ikhtilāf Al-Dārayn*, 2nd ed. (Cairo: Dār al-Salām, 1998).

Fivaz, R., *L'ordre Et La Volupte* (Lausanne: Presses Politechniques Romandes, 1989).

Flousi, Masoud Ibn Musa, *Madrasah al-Mutakallimīn* (Riyadh: Maktabat al-Rushd, 2004).

Garaudy, Roger, *Al-Islām wa al-Qarn al-Wāḥid wa al-ᶜUshrūn: Shurūṭ Nahḍah al-Muslimīn*, trans. Kamal Jadallah (Cairo: Al-Dār al-ᶜĀlamiyyah li al-Kutub wa al-Nashr, 1999).

Gawain, Shakti, *Return to the Garden: A Journey to Discovery* (California: New World Library, 1989).

Geny, Francois, *Methode D'interpretation Et Sources En Droit Prive Positif*, trans. Louisiana State Law Institute, 2nd ed, vol. 1 (1954).

Ghannouchi, Rachid, "Participation in Non-Islamic Government," in *Liberal Islam: A Sourcebook*, ed. Charles Kurzman (Oxford: Oxford University Press, 1998).

Gharajedaghi, Jamshid, "Systems Methodology: A Holistic Language of Interaction and Design. Seeing through Chaos and Understanding Complexities," in systemsthinkingpress.com (2004).

———, *Systems Thinking: Managing Chaos and Complexity*. A Platform for Designing Business Architecture (Boston: Butterworth-Heinemann, 1999).

Gibb, H. A. R., *Islam: A Historical Survey*, 2nd ed. (Oxford: Oxford University Press, no date).

Gleave, Robert, "Introduction," in *Islamic Law: Theory and Practice*, ed. R. Gleave and E. Kermeli (London: I.B. Tauris, 1997).

Goldziher, Ignaz, *Introduction to Islamic Theology and Law*, trans. Andras and Ruth Hamori (Princeton: Princeton University Press, 1981).

Gray, Christopher Berry, ed. *The Philosophy of Law: An Encyclopedia* (New York and London: Garland Publishing, 1999).

Gwynne, Rosalind Ward, *Logic, Rhetoric, and Legal Reasoning in the Qur'an* (London and New York: Routledge, 2004)

Haddad, Yvonne, "The Islamic Alternative," *The Link* 15, no. 4 (1982).

Hallaq, Wael, *Ibn Taymiyya against the Greek Logicians* (Oxford: Clarendon Press, 1993).

———, *A History of Islamic Legal Theories: An Introduction to Sunnī 'Uṣūl al-Fiqh* (Cambridge: Cambridge University Press, 1997).

———, "The Quest for Origins or Doctrine? Islamic Legal Studies as Colonialist Dscourse," UCLA Journal of Islamic and Near Eastern Law, no. 2 (Fall/Winter) (2003).

———, "Was the Gate of Ijtihad Closed," *Int. Journal Middle Eastern Studies* 16, no. 1 (1984).

Hanafi, Hasan, *Al-Turāth wa al-Tajdīd* (Beirut: Dār al-Tanwīr, 1980).

———, "Maqāṣid al-Sharīᶜah wa Ahdāf al-'Ummah," *al-Muslim al-Muᶜāṣir*, no. 103 (2002).

Hasaballah, Ali, *'Uṣūl Al-Tashrīᶜ al-Islāmī* (Cairo: Dār al-Maᶜārif, no date).

Hassaan, Hussein Hamid, *Naẓariyyah Al-Maṣlaḥah fī al-Fiqh al-Islāmī* (Cairo: Maktabah al-Mutanabbī, 1981).

Hasan, Hussein, "Book Review: Islamic Law and Culture 1600–1840 by Haim Gerber," *Journal of Islamic Studies* 12, no. 2 (2001).

Hintikka, Jaakko and Remes, *The Method of Analysis*, ed. D. Reidel (Dordrecht: 1974).

Hitchins, D., *Putting Systems to Work* (New York: John Wiley, 1992).

———, *Advanced Systems, Thinking and Management* (Norwood, MA: Artech House, 2003).

Hoffman, Murad, *al-Islām ᶜĀm Alfayn* (Islam in the Year Two Thousand), 1st ed. (Cairo: Maktabah al-Shurūq, 1995).

Ibn Abidin, Mohammad Amin, *Ḥāshiyah Radd al-Muḥtār* (Beirut: Dār al-Fikr, 2000).

———, *Nashr al-ᶜArf fī ma Buniya Min al-Aḥkām ᶜAla al-ᶜurf* (Cairo: no date).

Ibn Abd al-Barr, Abū ᶜUmar, *al-Tamhīd*, ed. Mohammad al-Alawi and Mohammad al-Bakri (Morrocco: Wazārah ᶜUmūm al-Awqāf, 1387 AH).

Ibn ᶜAbd al-Salām, al-ᶜIzz, *Qawāᶜid al-Aḥkām fī Maṣāliḥ al-Anām* (Beirut: Dār al-Nashr, no date).

———, Maqāṣid al-Ṣalāh. Edited by Iyad al-Tabba. 2nd ed. Beirut: Dār al-Fikr, 1995.

———, *Maqāṣid al-Ṣawm*, ed. Iyad al-Tabbaᶜ, 2nd ed. (Beirut: Dār al-Fikr, 1995).

Ibn Abidin, Mohammad Amin, *Ḥāshiyah Radd al-Muḥtār* (Beirut: Dār al-Fikr, 2000).

Ibn Ādam, Yaḥyā, *al-Kharāj* (Lahore, Pakistan: al-Maktabah al-ʿIlmiyyah, 1974).

Ibn al-ʿArabī, Abū Bakr al-Mālikī, *Al-Maḥsūl fī Uṣūl al-Fiqh*, ed. Hussain Ali Alyadri and Saeed Foda, 1st ed. (Amman: Dār al-Bayāriq, 1999).

———, *ʿĀriḍah al-Aḥwadhī* (Cairo: Dār al-Waḥy al-Moḥammadī, no date).

Ibn al-Jazrī, Moḥammad ibn Moḥammad, *Al-Nashr fī al-Qirā'āt al-ʿAshr* (Cairo: Maktabah al-Qāhirah, no date).

Ibn al-Nadeem, Mohammad Abu Al-Farag, *Al-Fihrist* (Beirut: Dār al-Maʿrifah, 1978)

Ibn al-Qayyim, Shams al-Dīn, *Aḥkām Ahl al-Dhimmah*, ed. Abu Bara' and Abu Hamid (Riyadh: Ramadī, 1997).

———, *Al-Ṭuruq al-Ḥukmiyyah fī al-Siyāsah al-Sharʿiyyah*. Edited by M. Jamil Ghazi. Cairo: al-Madani, no date.

———, *Iʿlām Al-Muwaqqiʿīn*, ed. Taha Abdul Rauf Saad (Beirut: Dār al-Jīl, 1973)

Ibn al-Ṣalāḥ, Abū ʿAmr, *Al-Muqaddimah fī ʿUlūm al-Ḥadīth* (Beirut: Dār al-Fikr, 1977).

———, *Fatāwa ibn al-Ṣalāḥ*, 2005.

Ibn Ashur, al-Tahir, *Alaysa al-Ṣubḥ bi Qarīb*? (Tunis: al-Sharikah al-Tūnisiyyah li-Funūn al-Rasm, 1988).

———, *Al-Taḥrīr wa al-Tanwīr* (Tunis: Dār Saḥnūn, 1997).

———, *Maqāṣid al-Sharīʿah al-Islāmiyyah*, ed. el-Tahir el-Mesawi (Kuala Lumpur: al-Fajr, 1999).

———, *Uṣūl Al-Niẓām Al-Ijtimāʿī fī al-Islām*, ed. Mohammad el-Tahir el-Mesawi (Amman: Dār al-Nafā'is, 2001).

———, *Ibn Ashur, Treatise on Maqāṣid al-Shariʿah*, trans. Muhammad el-Tahir el-Mesawi, (London,Washington: International Institute of Islamic Thought (IIIT), 2006).

Ibn Farḥūn, Burhān al-Dīn, *Tabṣirah al-Hukkām fī 'Uṣūl al-Aqḍiyah wa Manāhij al-Aḥkām*, ed. Jamal Marashli (Beirut: Dār al-Kutub al-ʿIlmiyyah, 1995).

Ibn Ḥajar, Aḥmad, *Fatḥ al-Bārī Sharḥ Ṣaḥīḥ al-Bukhārī*, (Opened by the Creator: Explaining the Authentic Collection of Bukhārī), no date.

———, *Lisān al-Mīzān*, ed. Dā'irah al-Maʿārif al-Niẓāmiyyah, 3rd ed. (Beirut: Mu'asasah al-Aʿlām li al-Maṭbūʿāt, 1986).

———, *Taqrīb al-Tahthīb*, ed. Mohammad Awama (Damascus: Dār al-Rashīd, 1986).

Ibn Ḥazm, ʿAlī, *Al-Iḥkām fī 'Uṣūl Al-Aḥkām*, 1st ed. (Cairo: Dār al-Ḥadīth, 1983).

———, *al-Muḥallā*, ed. Lajnah Iḥyā' al-Turāth al-ʿArabī, 1st ed. (Beirut: Dār al-Āfāq, no date).

———, *Taqrīb al-Manṭiq*, (Facilitating Logic), ed. Ihsan Abbas, 1st ed. (Beirut: no date).

Ibn Kathīr, Ismāʿīl, *Al-Bidāyah wa al-Nihāyah,* (no date).

Ibn Khaldūn, ʿAbd al-Raḥmān, *Muqaddimah ibn Khaldūn*, 5th ed. (Dār al-Qalam, 1984).

Ibn Khalkān, Aḥmad, *Wafiyyāt al-Aʿyān wa 'Anbā' al-Zamān*, ed. Ihsan Abbas (Beirut: Dār al-Thaqāfah, no date).

Ibn Manẓūr, Moḥammad, *Lisān al-ʿArab* (Beirut: Dār Ṣādir, no date).

Ibn Nujaym, Zayn al-Dīn, *Al-Baḥr al-Rā'iq*, 2nd ed. (Beirut: Dār al-Maʿrifah, no date).

Ibn Qudāmah al-Maqdisī, ʿAbdullāh, *Rawḍah al-Nāẓir wa Janah al-Manāẓir*, ed. Abdul Aziz Abdul Rahman Alsaeed, 2nd ed. (Riyadh: Mohammed ibn Saud University, 1399 AH).

———, *Al-Mughnī fī Fiqh al-Imām Aḥmad ibn Ḥanbal al-Shaybānī*, 1st ed. (Beirut: Dār al-Fikr, 1985).

Ibn Rushd, Al-Walīd, (Averröes), *Bidāyah al-Mujtahid wa Nihāyah al-Muqtaṣid* (Beirut: Dār al-Fikr, no date).

———, *Faṣl al-Maqāl fī Taqrīr Mā Bayn al-Sharīʿah wa al-Ḥikmah Min Ittiṣāl* (Decisive Argument on the Connection between the Islamic Law and Philosophy. Translated As: On the Harmony of Religions and Philosophy, in Averröes, the Philosophy and Theology of Averröes, Trans. Mohammed Jamil-al-Rahman) (A.G.Widgery, 1921 [cited January 18th 2005]); available from http://www.muslimphilosophy.com.

———, *Mukhtaṣar Manṭiq Arisṭo*, ed. Jirar Jahami (Beirut: Dār al-Fikr al-Lubnānī, 1992).

———, *Tahāfut al-Tahāfut*. Edited by Sulaiman Donya. 1st ed. (Cairo: Dār al-Maʿārif, 1964).

Ibn Sīnā, Abū ʿAlī, *Remarks and Admonitions*, trans. Shams Inati, vol. 1 (Toronto: Pontifical Institute of Mediaeval Studies, 1984).

Ibn Taymiyah, Aḥmad, *Al-Musawadah*, ed. M. Mohieldin Abdulhameed (Cairo: al-Madanī, no date).

———, *Daqā'iq al-Tafsīr*, ed. Mohammad al-Julainid (Damascus: Mu'asasah ʿUlūm al-Qur'an, 1404 AH).

———, *Dār' Taʿarruḍ al-ʿAql wa al-Naql* (Beirut: Dār al-Kutub al-ʿIlmiyyah, 1997).

———, *Iqtiḍā' al-Ṣirāṭ al-Mustaqīm Mukhālafah Aṣḥāb al-Jaḥīm*, ed. Mohammad Hamid, 2nd ed. (Cairo: Maṭbaʿah al-Sunnah, 1369 AH).

———, *Kutub wa Rasā'il wa Fatwā*, ed. Abdul-Rahman al-Najdi, 2nd ed. (Riyadh: Maktabah ibn Taymiyah, no date).

———, *Naqd Marātib al-Ijmāʿ*, 1st ed. (Beirut: Dār al-Fikr 1998).

Ibrahim, Saad Eddin, ed, *Egypt, Islam and Democracy: Twelve Critical Essays*, vol. 19, Monograph 3, Cairo Papers in Social Science (Cairo: The American University in Cairo Press, 1996).

Imam, Mohammad Kamal, *al-Dalīl al-Irshādī Ilā Maqāṣid al-Sharīʿah al-Islāmiyyah* (London: al-Maqāṣid Research Centre, 2007).

Inayatullah, Sohail and Gail Boxwell, *Islam, Postmodernism and Other Futures: A Ziauddin Sardar Reader* (London: Pluto Press, 2003).

Iqbal, Mohammad, *The Reconstruction of Religious Thought in Islam*, ed. M. Saeed Shaykh (Lahore: 1986).

Izzi Dien, Mawil, *Islamic Law: From Historical Foundations to Contemporary Practice*, ed., Carole Hillenbrand (Edinburgh: Edinburgh University Press ltd, 2004).

Jabir, Hasan Mohamed, *Al-Maqāṣid Alkuliyyah wa al-Ijtihād Almuʿāṣir-Ta'sīs Manhaji wa Qur'ānī li Āliyyah al-Istinbāṭ*, 1st ed. (Beirut: Dār al-Ḥiwār, 2001).

———, "al-Maqāṣid fī al-Madrasah al-Shīʿiyyah", in: El-Awa, Mohamed Saleem, ed. *Maqāṣid al-Sharīʿah al-Islāmiyyah: Dirāsāt fī Qaḍāyā al-Manhaj wa Qaḍāyā al-Taṭbīq* (Studies in the Philosophy of Islamic Law: Theory and Applications). 1st ed. (Cairo: al-Furqan Islamic Heritage Foundation, Al-Maqāṣid Research Centre, 2006) p.325. Also: Oral Discussion over the issue in Alexandria, Egypt, August, 2006.

Jahami, Gerard, *Mafhūm al-Sababiyyah Bayn al-Mutakallimīn wa al Falāsifah: Bayn Al-Ghazālī wa Ibn Rushd*, 2nd ed. (Beirut: Dār al-Mashriq, 1992).

Jenkins, O. B., *What Is Worldview?* (1999 [cited Jan. 2006]); available from http://orvillejenkins.com /worldview/worldvwhat.html.

Johnston, Larry, *Politics: An Introduction to the Modern Democratic State* (Broadview: Peterborough, Ontario, 1998).

Jordan, J., *Themes in Speculative Psychology* (London: Tavistock Publications, 1968).

Jughaim, Numan, *Ṭuruq al-Kashf ʿan Maqāṣid al-Shāriʿ* (International Islamic University, Malaysia. Published by Dār al-Nafā'is, 2002).

Jumah, Ali, *Al-Muṣṭalaḥ al-Uṣūlī wa Mushkilah al-Mafāhīm* (Cairo: Al-Maʿhad al-ʿĀlamī li al-Fikr al-Islāmī, 1996).

———, *ʿIlm 'Uṣūl al-Fiqh wa ʿAlaqatuhu bi al-Falsafah al-Islāmiyyah* (Cairo: Al-Maʿhad al-ʿĀlī li al-Fikr al-Islāmī, 1996).

Kant, Immanuel, *Fundamental Principles (Groundwork) of the Metaphysics of Morals* (Buffalo, NY: Promatheus, 1987).

Katz, D. and Kahn, L., *The Social Psychology of Organizations* (London: John Wiley, 1966).

Keil, Robert, A. Wilson, and C. Frank, ed., *The MIT Encyclopedia of the Cognitive Sciences* (London: The MIT Press, 1999).

Kellner, Steven and Douglas Best, *Postmodern Theory: Critical Interrogations*, ed. Paul Walton (London: Macmillan Press Ltd, 1991).

Kendall, Kenneth, E. Kendall & Julie E., *Systems Analysis and Design*, 4th ed. (New Jersey: Prentice-Hall, 1999).

Kerr, Malcolm H., *The Political and Legal Theories of Mohammad Abduh and Rashid Rida* (London: Cambridge University Press, 1966).

Khalaf-Allah, Mohammad, "Legislative Authority," in *Liberal Islam: A Sourcebook*, ed. Charles Kurzman (Oxford: Oxford University Press, 1998).

Khatami, Mohammad Seyyed, *Islam, Liberty, and Development* (Johannesburg: Global Books, 2001).

———, *Islam, Liberty and Development* (New York: Institute of Global Cultural Studies, Binghamton University, 1998).

Khayyat, Usama, "Mukhtalaf al-Ḥadīth" (Masters, 'Umm al-Qurā, Published by Dār al-Faḍīlah, 2001).

King, Hugh R., "A. N. Whitehead and the Concept of Metaphysics," *Philosophy of Science* (1947).

Kirchner, J. W., "The Gaia Hypothesis: Are They Testable? Are They Useful?" in *Scientists on Gaia*, ed. S. Schneider (Cambridge, New York: MIT Press, 1991).

Klir, G., *Architecture of Systems Problem Solving* (New York: Plenum Publishing Corp, 1985).

Koestler, A., *The Ghost in the Machine* (London: Arkana, 1967).

Kopanski, Ataullah Bagdan, "Orientalism Revisited: Bernard Lewis' School of Political Islamography," *Intellectual Discourse* 8, no. 2 (2000).

Korzybski, Alfred, *An Introduction to Non-Aristotelian Systems and General Semantics*, Fourth ed. (Lakeville, Connecticut: The International Non-Aristotelian Library Publishing Company, 1958).

Kurzman, Charles, ed., *Modernist Islam, 1840–1940: A Sourcebook* (Oxford: Oxford University Press, 2002).

Laszlo, Ervin, *The World System* (New York: George Braziller Inc, 1972).

———, *Introduction to Systems Philosophy – Towards a New Paradigm of Contemporary Thought* (New York: Gordon and Breach, Science Publishers, 1972).

———, *The Systems View of the World: A Holistic Vision for Our Time* (Hampton Press, 1996).

Law.Dictionary.Com http://dictionary.law.com/, [cited Jan. 2007].

Layish, Aharon, "Interplay between Tribal and Shari Law: A Case of Tibbawi Blood Money in the Sharia Court of Kufra," *Islamic Law and Society* 13, no. 1 (2006).

Litterer, J., *Organizations: Systems, Control and Adaptation* (New York: John Wiley, 1969).

LOC, Library of Congress, Romanization Tables 1997 [cited January 20th 2005]. Available from http://www.loc.gov/catdir/cpso/romanization/arabic.pdf.

Locke, John, *An Essay Concerning Human Understanding*, ed. P. H. Nidditch, 4 ed. (Oxford: Oxford University Press, 1975), 4th ed.

Lorenz, Konrad Z., "The Fashionable Fallacy of Dispensing with Description" (paper presented at the 25th International Congress of Physiological Sciences, Munich, July 25–31, 1971).

Lotfi, Tabatabaei, "Ijtihad in Twelver Shiᶜism: The Interpretation and Application of Islamic Law in the Context of Changing Muslim Society" (Ph.D. diss, University of Leeds, 1999).

Lovelock, J., *The Ages of Gaia* (New York: Norton and Co, 1988).

Luhmann, Niklas, *Law as a Social System*, trans. Klaus Ziegert. Introduction by Richard Nobles and David Schiff (Oxford: Oxford University Press, 2004).

Makdisi, John, "A Reality Check on Istihsan as a Method of Islamic Legal Reasoning," *UCLA Journal of Islamic and Near Eastern Law*, no. 99 (Fall/Winter) (2003).

Mālik, *Muwaṭṭa' al-Imām Mālik*, ed. M. Fouad Abdul Baqi (Cairo: Dār Iḥyā' al-Turāth al-ᶜArabī, no date).

Maslow, A. H., *Motivation and Personality*, 2nd ed. (New York: Harper and Row, 1970).

———, "A Theory of Human Motivation," *Psychological Review*, no. 50 (1943).

Maturana, H. & V. Varela, *The Tree of Knowledge* (London: Shambala, 1992).

Mawdudi, Abu al-Ala, *Al-Ḥijāb* [The Veil] (Jeddah: al-Dār al-Saᶜūdiyyah li al-Nashr wa al-Tawzīᶜ, 1986).

Maymani, Wajanat Abdurahim, *Qāᶜidah al-Dharā'iᶜ*, 1st ed. (Jeddah: Dār al-Mujtamaᶜ, 2000).

Meinecke, Friedrich, *Historicism: The Rise of a New Historical Outlook*, trans. J. E. Anderson (London: 1972).

Mernissi, Fatima, "A Feminist Interpretation of Women's Rights," in *Liberal Islam: A Sourcebook*. Oxford, ed. Charles Kurzman (Oxford: University Press, 1998).

———, *Mā Warā' al-Ḥijāb*, 1st ed.(Damascus: Dār Ḥawrān, 1997).

———, *The Veil and the Male Elite: A Feminist Interpretation of Women's Rights in Islam*, trans. Mary Jo Lakeland (Cambridge, Mass.: Perseus Books, 1991).

Mesawi, M. al-Tahir, "Al-Shaykh ibn Ashur wa al-Mashrūᶜ Alladhī Lam

Yaktamil" in *Maqāṣid al-Sharīʿah al-Islāmiyyah* (Kuala Lumpur: al-Fajr, 1999).

Messick, Brinkley, "When Women Went to Mosques: Al-Aydini on the Duration of Assessments," in *Islamic Legal Interpretation: Muftis and Their Fatwas*, ed. Mohammad Khalid Masud, and David S. Power (Cambridge, Mass.: Harvard University Press, 1996).

Miller, J., *Living Systems* (New York: McGraw-Hill, 1978).

Mintjes, H., "Mawlana Mawdudi's Last Years and the Resurgence of Fundamentalist Islam," *al-Mushīr* 22, no. 2 (1980).

Moghissi, Haideh, *Feminism and Islamic Fundamentalism: The Limits of Postmodern Analysis* (New York: Zed Books, 1999).

Moosa, Ebrahim, "The Debts and Burdens of Critical Islam," in *Progressive Muslims*, ed. Omid Safi (Oxford: Oneworld, 2003).

———, "Introduction," in *Revival and Reform in Islam: A Study of Islamic Fundamentalism by Fazlur Rahman*, ed. Ebrahim Moosa (Oxford: OneWorld, 2000)

———, "The Poetics and Politics of Law after Empire: Reading Women's Rights in the Contestations of Law," *UCLA Journal of Islamic and Near Eastern Law*, no. 1 (Fall/Winter) (2002).

Mufti, Mohammad Ali, *Naqd al-Judhūr al-Fikriyyah li al-Dīmuqrāṭiyyah al-Gharbiyyah* (Riyadh: al-Muntadā al-Islāmī and Majallah al-Bayān, 2002).

Mukhtar, A. B., "Human Rights and Islamic Law: The Development of the Rights of Slaves, Women and Aliens in Two Cultures" (Ph.D. diss, University of Manchester, 1996).

Muslehuddin, Mohammad, *Philosophy of the Islamic Law and the Orientalists*, 1st ed. (Delhi: Markazi Maktaba Islami, 1985).

Muslih, *A Project of Islamic Revivalism* (Leiden: University of Leiden, 2006).

Muslim, Abū al-Ḥussain, *Ṣaḥīh Muslim*, ed. Mohammad Fouad Abdul-Baqi (Beirut: Dār Iḥyā' al-Turāth al-ʿArabī, no date).

Mustafa, Wadie, "Ibn Ḥazm wa Mauqifuhu Min al-Falsafah wa al-Manṭiq wa al-Akhlāq" (M.A. Thesis, Alexandria University, Published by al-Majmaʿ al-Thaqāfī, 2000).

Nada, Mohammad, *Al-Nāskh fī al-Qur'ān* (Cairo: al-Dār al-ʿArabiyyah li al-Kutub, 1996).

al-Nami, A. K., "Studies in Ibadhism (Al-Ibaḍiyyah)" (Ph.D. diss, University of Cambridge, 1971).

Naming, Sire, *Worldviews: Crosscultural Explorations of Human Beliefs*, 3rd ed. (Prentice Hall, 1999).

Nasr, Seyyed Hossein, *Ideals and Realities of Islam* (Boston, Mass.: George Allen and Unwin, 2000).

Nassar, Essmat, *Al-Khiṭāb al-Falsafī ʿInd ibn Rushd wa Atharuhu fī Kitābāt Moḥammad ʿAbduh wa Zakī Najīb Maḥmūd* (Cairo: Dār al-Hidāyah, 2003).

Naugle, David K., *Worldview: The History of a Concept* (Grand Rapids: Eerdmans, 2002).

Normi, H., *Comparing Voting Systems* (Reidel Publishing Company, 1987).

Norris, Christopher, *Derrida* (London: Sage, 1987).

Omar, Mohammad Abdul-Khaliq, *Reasoning in Islamic Law*, 3rd ed. (Cairo: M. Omar, 1999).

Omotosho, A., "The Problem of al-Amr in Usul al-Fiqh" (Ph.D. diss, University of Edinburgh, 1984).

Ongley, John, "What Is Analysis? Review of Michael Beany's 'Analysis'," *Bertrand Russell Society Quarterly*, no. 127 (2005).

Othman, A. H., "Shafieʿi and the Interpretation of the Role of the Qur'an and the Hadith" (Ph.D. diss, St. Andrews, 1997).

Peters, Rudolph, "Murder in Khaybar: Some Thoughts on the Origins of the Qasama Procedure in Islamic Law," *Islamic Law and Society* 9, no. 2 (2002).

Piscatori, James P., *Islamic Countries: Politics and Government* (Princeton: Princeton University Press, 1996).

Powell, Jim, *Postmodernism for Beginners* (New York: Writers and Readers Publishing, 1998).

Powers, W.T., *Behaviour: The Control of Perception* (New York: Aldine de Gruyter, 1973).

Rabie, Abdallah, *Al-Qaṭʿiyyah wa al-Ẓanniyyah fī 'Uṣūl al-Fiqh Al-Islāmī* (Cairo: Dār al-Nahar, no date).

Rahim, R. A. A., "Certain Aspects of Ijtihad in Islamic Jurisprudence, with Special Reference to the Comparative Study between Sunni and Shiʿi Principles" (M. Phil. diss, University of St. Andrews, 1991).

Rahman, Fazlur, "Islamic Modernism: Its Scope, Method, and Alternatives." International Journal of Middle East Studies 1, no. 4 (1970).

———, *Islam*, 2nd ed. (Chicago: University of Chicago Press, 1979).

Ramadan, Tariq, "Stop in the Name of Humanity," *Globe and Mail* (London) Wednesday, March 30, 2005.

———, *To Be a European Muslim* (Leicester: Islamic Foundation, 1999).

———, *Western Muslims and the Future of Islam* (New York: Oxford University Press, 2004).

Rand, Ayn, "The Objectivist Ethics: The Virtue of Selfishness" (1964).

Rawls, John, *A Theory of Justice* (The Belknap Press of Harvard University Press, 1971).

Reed, Stephen, *Cognition: Theory and Applications*, 4th ed. (USA: Brooks/Cole, 1996).

Rescher, Nicholas, "Arabic Logic", ed. Paul Edwards, *The Encyclopedia of Philosophy* (New York: Macmillan, 1967).

Rida, Mohammad Rasheed, *al-Waḥī al-Moḥammadī: Thubūt al-Nubuwwah bi al-Qur'ān* (Cairo: Mu'asasah ʿIzz al-Dīn, no date).

———, "Mujmal al-Aḥwāl al-Siyāsiyyah," Al-ʿUrwah al-Wuthqā, Feb. 29th, 1898 CE.

Robinson, Neal, *Islam, a Concise Introduction* (Richmond: Curzon Press, 1999).

Roolvink, R. et al., *Historical Atlas of the Muslim Peoples* (Amsterdam, 1957). Available in soft form on: http://www.princeton.edu/thumcomp/dimensions.html (visited: April 13, 2006).

Saad, S., "The Legal and Social Status of Women in the Hadith Literature" (Ph.D. diss, University of Leeds, 1990).

Sabiq, al-Sayed, *Fiqh Al-Sunnah* (Cairo: Dār al-Fatḥ li al-Iʿlām al-ʿArabī, 1994).

Sachedina, Abdulaziz, *Islamic Roots of Democratic Pluralism* (Oxford: Oxford University Press, 2001).

Sadeghi, Mir Mohammad, "Islamic Criminal Law and the Challenge of Change: A Comparative Study" (Ph. D. diss, London, School of Oriental and African Studies, 1986).

Safi, Luay, *IʿMāl al-ʿAql* (Pittsburgh: Dār al-Fikr, 1998).

Safi, Omid, ed., *Progressive Muslims: On Justice, Gender and Pluralism* (Oxford: One World, 2003).

Said, Edward, *Orientalism* (New York: Vintage Books, 1979).

Saifi, S. F., "A Study of the Status of Women in Islamic Law and Society, with Special Reference to Pakistan" (Ph.D. diss, University of Durham, 1980).

Salih, Hasan Bashir, *ʿAlāqah al-Manṭiq bi al-Lughah ʿInd Falāsifah al-Muslimīn* (Alexandria: Al-Wafā', 2003).

Salih, Mohammed Osman, "al-Islām Huwa Niẓām Shāmil Liḥimāyah wa Taʿzīz Ḥuqūq al-Insān" (paper presented at the International Conference on Islam and Human Rights, Khartoum, 2006).

Salk, J.E., *Anatomy of Reality* (Westport, Connecticut: Greenwood Publishing Group Inc, 1983).

Sano, Quttub, *Qirā'ah Maʿrifiyyah fī al-Fikr al-'Uṣūlī*, 1st ed. (Kuala Lumpur: Dār al-Tajdīd, 2005).

Sarhan, Haitham, *Istrātījiyyah al-Ta'wīl al-Dilālī ʿInd al-Muʿtazilah* (Lādhiqiyyah, Syria: Dār al-Ḥiwār, 2003).

Schacht, Joseph, "Foreign Elements in Ancient Islamic Law," Comparative Legislation and International Law 32 (1950).

———, *An Introduction to Islamic Law*, 2nd ed. (Oxford: Clarendon Press, 1982).

Shahrour, Mohammed, *Naḥwa 'Uṣūl Jadīdah li al-Fikr al-Islāmī*, Dirāsāt Islāmiyyah Muʿāṣirah. (Damascus: al-Ahalī Press, 2000).

Shaikhi-Zadah, Abdel-Rahman, *Majmaʿ al-Anhur* (Beirut: Dār al-Kutub al-ʿIlmiyyah, 1998).

Shams al-Din, Ayatollah Medhi, *Al-Ijtihād wa al-Tajdīd fī al-Fiqh al-Islāmī* (Beirut: al-Mu'assassah al-Dawliyyah, 1999).

———, "Maqāṣid al-Sharīʿah," in *Maqāṣid al-Sharīʿah*, ed. Abduljabar al-Rufai (Damascus: Dār al-Fikr, 2001).

Shepard, William, "Islam and Ideology: Towards a Typology," *Int. Journal Middle Eastern Studies*, no. 19 (1987).

Shukri, A. S. M, "The Relationship between ʿIlm and Khabar in the Work of Al-Shafieʿi." (Ph.D. diss, St. Andrews, 1999).

Simon, H, *The Sciences of the Artificial* (London: MIT Press, 1969).

Sire, James W, *Naming the Elephant* (Downers Grove, IL: Inter Varsity Press, 2004).

Skyttner, Lars, *General Systems Theory: Ideas and Applications* (Singapore: World Scientific, 2002).

Smuts, J., *Holism and Evolution*, reprint ed. (Westport, Connecticut: Greenwood Press, 1973).

Soltan, Salahuddin, "Ḥujiyyah al-Adillah al-Mukhtalaf ʿAlayhā fī al-Sharīʿah al-Islāmiyyah." Ph.D. diss., Cairo University, 1992.

Soroush, Abdul-Karim, "The Evolution and Devolution of Religious Knowledge," in *Liberal Islam: A Sourcebook*, ed. Charles Kurzman (Oxford: Oxford University Press, 1998).

Sowa, John F., *Knowledge Representation: Logical, Philosophical, and Computational Foundations* (Pacific Grove: Brooks, 2000).

Stewart, P. J., *Unfolding Islam* (Reading, U.K: Garnet Publishing, 1994).

Sulayman, Sadiq, "Democracy and Shura," in *Liberal Islam: A Sourcebook*, ed. Charles Kurzman (Oxford: Oxford University Press, 1998).

Sulaimani, F. A. A., "The Changing Position of Women in Arabia under Islam During the Early Seventh Century" (M. Phil. diss, University of Salford, 1986).

Sweeney, Eileen C., "Three Notions of Resolution and the Structure of Reasoning in Aquinas," The Thomist 58 (1994).

Taha, Mahmoud Mohamed, "The Second Message of Islam," in *Liberal Islam: A Sourcebook*, ed. Charles Kurzman (Oxford: Oxford University Press, 1998).

Taylor, V. and Winquist, C., ed, *Encyclopedia of Postmodernism* (New York: Routledge, 2001).

UNDP, United Nation Development Programme UNDP, *Annual Report 2004* (2004 [cited Feb. 5th, 2005]); available from http://www.undp.org/annualreports/2004/english.

UNHCHR, United Nations High Commission for Human Rights UNHCHR, *Specific Human Rights Issues* (July, 2003 [cited Feb. 1st, 2005]); available from http://www.unhchr.cah/Huridocda/Huridoca.nsf/(Symbol)/ E.CN.4. Sub.2.2003.NGO.15.En.

Voll, John, *Islam: Continuity and Change in the Modern World* (Bolder, Colorado: Westview press, 1982).

Von Bertalanffy, Ludwig, "General Systems Theory: Foundations, Development, Applications" (New York: George Braziller, 1969).

———, "General Systems Theory," *Main Currents in Modern Thought* 71, no. 75 (1955).

———, "The History and Status of General Systems Theory," in *Trends in General Systems Theory*, edited by George J. Klir, 407–26. (New York: Wiley-Interscience, 1972).

Von Glaserfeld, E., *The Construction of Knowledge: Contributions to Conceptual Semantics* (California: Intersystems Seaside, 1987).

Von Jhering, Rudolf, *Law as a Means to an End* (Der Zweck im Recht), trans. Isaac Husik, 2nd reprint ed. (New Jersey: The Lawbook Exchange (Originally published 1913 by Boston Book Co.), 2001).

Von Wright, G.H., "Deontic Logic," *Mind, New Series* 60, no. 237 (1951).

Wadud-Muhsin, Amina, "Qur'an and Woman," in *Liberal Islam: A Sourcebook*, ed. Charles Kurzman (Oxford: Oxford University Press, 1998).

Warraq, Ibn, "Apostasy and Human Rights," *Free Inquiry*, Feb/March 2006.

Weaver, W., "Science and Complexity," *American Scientist* 36, no. 194 (1948).

Weiss, Bernard G., The Spirit of Islamic Law (Athens: University of Georgia Press, 1998).

WLUML, Women Living under Muslim Laws [cited Jan 5th, 2006]; available from http://www.wluml.org/english

Wolfe, Robert Paul, *About Philosophy*, 8th ed. (New Jersey: Prentice-Hall, 2000).

Zaidan, Abdul-Karim, *Al-Wajīz fī 'Uṣūl al-Fiqh*, 7th ed. (Beirut: Al-Risālah, 1998).

Zuraiq, Burhan, *Al-Ṣaḥīfah: Mīthāq al-Rasūl*, 1st ed. (Damascus: Dār al-Numayr and Dār Maᶜad, 1996).

GLOSSARY OF ISLAMIC TERMS

ʿadl, justice/fairness
ʿamal, tradition (usually, of the People of Madinah)
ʿamd, intentionally
ʿaql, reason
ʿaraḍ, accident
ʿibādāt, acts/rituals of worship
ʿibārah, clear expression
ʿiddah, waiting period (for women, after divorce)
ʿillah, cause/reason/ratio legis
ʿilm, knowledge
ʿilm ḥadīth, science of narration
ʿilm kalām, Islamic philosophy of religion
ʿirḍ, honor
ʿitrah, Prophet's next of kin
ʿumūm, general expressions / generality
ʿurf, custom/tradition
āḥād, single-chained narration
ahl al-athar, supporters of narrations
ahl al-ra'ī, supporters of opinions
ahliyyah, legal capacity
ahliyyah adā', active legal capacity
ahliyyah wujūb, receptive legal capacity
akhlāq makrumāt, virtues
amr, order
aṣl, primary situation
bidʿah, innovation
bulūgh, puberty
ḍaʿīf, weak (narration)
dalīl, evidences
dalīl ʿaqlī, rational evidence
dalīl ikhtirāʿ, evidence of creation
dalīl kullī, holistic evidence
dalīl riʿāyah, evidence of sustainance
dalīl wujūd, evidence of existence
darūrah, necessity
ḍarūrāt, necessities
dhāt, essence
dhātī intrinsic
dilālah, implication
dilālah ʿaqlīyah, rational implication
dilālah ʿadad, implication of numbers
dilālah lafẓ, the implication of a term/ expression
dilālah siyāq, implication of the context
fahm, understanding
farʿ, secondary situation
fāsid, void/incorrect
fatḥ al-dharā'iʿ, opening the means
fatāwā, legal opinions/edicts
fiʿl khalqī, creation-related actions
fiʿl tashrīʿī, law-related actions
fiqh wāqiʿ, understanding of the status quo
fiṭrah, natural disposition
ghayr wāḍiḥ, unclear term
ḥadd, definition

ḥadd riddah, punishment for apostasy
ḥājiyāt, needs
ḥarām, sin/forbidden/ prohibited/unlawful/sanctuary
ḥarfiyyah, literalism
ḥassan, embellished/beautiful
ḥikmah, wisdom (behind a ruling)
ḥujjiyyah, juridical authority
ḥukm, ruling/rule
ḥukm taklīfī, accountability ruling
ḥukm waḍʿī, declaratory ruling
ḥurriyyah, freedom
iʿtibār, validity
idrāk, cognition
ijmāʿ, consensus
ijtihad, new/diligent reasoning/ reflection/judgement/ independent judgement
iltzām, association/correlation
īmā', implicit implication
inḍibāt, consistency/exactness
iqtiḍā', implying omittance
ishārah, indirect implication
iṣlāḥ, reform
ʿiṣmah, infallibility
isti'nās, supporting evidence
istiḥsān, juridical preference
istiṣḥāb, presumption of continuity
istiṣnāʿ, purchase with order
jamʿ bayn al-adillah, conciliation between evidences
juz'īyāt, partials
kalāmiyyūn, theologians/philosophers of religion
khafī, implicit/hidden
kulliyyāt, universals
madhāhib, traditional schools of Islamic law
mafhūm, understood by implication
mafhūm ghāyah, limit implication
mafhūm laqab, title implication
mafhūm mukhālafah, contrary implication
mafhūm muwāfaqah, coherence implication
mafhūm sharṭ, condition implication
mafhūm waṣf, attribute implication
mafsadah, mischief
majāz, allegorical
makrūh, detested/discouraged
mandūb, recommended/encouraged
māniʿ, hindrance
manṭiq, logic
maqāṣid, purpose/objective/principle/ intent/goal/end
marjiʿ taqlīd, imitation (Shia) Reference
marjūḥ, outweighed
mas'alah, juridical case/issue
maṣāliḥ mursalah, unrestricted interests
mashhūr, famous (narration)
maṣlaḥah, interest/benefit/welfare
matn, content/body
muʿāmalāt, worldly transactions
mu'awwal, (re-)interpreted
mubāḥ, lawful
mufassar, explained
muḥkam, firmly constructed (expression)
mujmal, general
mukallaf, subject
mulā'im, reconciled attribute
munāsabah qiyās, appropriate attribute for analogy
munāsib, appropriate attribute
mursal, disconnected-end of chain of narrators
muṣawwibah, validators

mushkal, ambiguous
muṭābaqah, complete accord
mutashābih, resembling
mutawātir, most famous
muttaṣil, connected chain of narrators
nahī, negative order
naskh, abrogation
naṣṣ, script/text
qabīḥ, repugnant/ugly
qaṭʿī, certain
qawāʿid, basic rules
qiyās, analogical reasoning
qiyās awlā, obvious analogy
qiyās jalī, obvious analogy
qirā'āt ʿashr, popular ten readings of the Qur'an
ribā nasī'ah, deferred usury
rukhaṣ, provisions
sabab, reason
sababiyyah, principle of causation
sadd al-dharā'iʿ, blocking the means
sanad, chain of narrators
ṣarīḥ, clearly started
shadā'id, strictnesses
sharʿu man qablanā, previous jurisprudence
shariʿah, revealed law/way of life
sharṭ, condition
shumūl, scope
shūra, consultation
ṣiḥḥah, correctness/authenticity
taʿāruḍ, opposition
ta'wīl, interpretation
taʿaddī, extension
taʿāruḍ al-adillah, disagreement/opposition between evidences
taḍammun, partial accord
tafsīr, exegesis
tafsīr mawḍūʿī, contextual exegesis
taghrīb, westernization
taḥqīq manāṭ, asserting the realization of ratio legis
taḥsīn wa taqbīḥ, embellishment and repugnance
taḥsīniyyāt, luxuries
tajdīd, renewal
takhrīj manāṭ, extraction of the grounds
takhṣīṣ, Specification
tamyīz, age of differentiation
tanqīḥ manāṭ, eliminating the alternatives /ratio decidendi
tawḥīd wa ʿadl, oneness of God and justice
ummah, nation
uṣūl dīn, fundamentals of religion
uṣūl fiqh, fundamentals of Islamic law
waḍʿ ḥadīth, forging of narrations
wājib, obligation/required
waṣaṭiyyah, centrism/moderation
wuḍūḥ, clarity
ẓāhir, apparent meaning
ẓāhiriyyah, literalists
zakah, obligatory charity
ẓannī, probable/speculated
ẓuhūr, visibility/clarity

GENERAL INDEX

Abdel-Raziq, Ali, 173
Abdu, Mohammad
  influences of, 169–70
  Islamic modernism, 27, 144
  maṣlaḥah-based interpretations, 176–77
  science based exegesis, 170–71
  uṣūl revisionism, 177
ʿAbdullah ibn ʿAbbas, 61, 74
ʿAbdullah ibn ʿUmar, 61, 74–75
ʿAbdullah ibn Ahmad, 67
ʿAbdullah ibn Masʿud, 79
Abou El-Fadl, Khaled, 148, 150, 215
abrogation (*naskh*), 89, 155, 219–24
Abū ʿAlī, 194
Abū Dharr, 234
Abū Ḥanīfa, 65–66
Abū Hāshim, 194
Abū Ḥāzim, 110
Abū al-Huzaīl, 194
Abū Thawr, 65
Abū Yūsuf, 66
Abū Zaid, Nasr, 182, 190
Ackoff, R., 36, 51
acts of worship, 11
advice, intent of, 235
age of differentiation, 141
ahl al-athar, 61, 64
ahl al-ra'ī, 61, 63
ahlīyah (legal capacity), 140–42
Ahmad ibn ʿĪsā ibn Zayd, 67
Aḥmad ibn Hanbal, 65
Ahmad, Akbar, 148
ʿĀ'ishah, 62, 74, 86, 219, 225
al-Albānī, 164
ʿAlī ibn Abī-Ṭālib, 62, 74, 78, 86
Ali, Yusuf, 57
al-Alwani, Taha
  on gender equality, 187–88
  maqāṣid identified by, 8
  new reading of the scripts, 173
ʿamal ahl al-madīnah. *See* Madinah's tradition
ambiguity in contracts, 239
ambiguous terms, 92
al-Āmidī, 2, 54
Al-ʿĀmirī al-Faylasūf, 16, 22
analogy, 112–20
  basing juridical preference on, 125
  contradictions with texts, 119–20
  multiple *qiyās*, 120
  multiple step process for, 116–8
  obvious, 94–95
  priority over indirect implication, 97
  Qiyās al-awlā, 97
  via purposes, 236–38
analysis, systems approach to, 31–33
ʿAntarah, 23
anthropocentrism, 26
anti-eurocentrism, 161
apologetic interpretation of the Qur'an, 155, 174–76
apostasy, 24
apparent evidences (*ẓāhir*), 89, 91

appropriateness (in analogy), 117
approval, levels of, 136
Arab world,
  development, xxii
  injustice in, xxii
  culture, 242
Aristotle, 32, 49, 207–8
Arkoun, Mohamed, 182
Asad, Talal, 184
al-Ashʿarī, Abū al-Hasan, 194
Ashʿarites, 53–54
al-Athram, Abū Bakr, 67
atomic systems, 43
atomism, 197
attribute (*al-waṣf*) in contrary implication, 98, 228
authority, levels of, 153–56
autopoiesis, as necessary for living system, 37
Averroes, 210
al-Awazāʿī, 65
al-Azdī, Jābir ibn Zayd, 68

Bahbahānī, 166
al-Balkhī, Abū Zayd, 13–14, 247
Banū Qurayẓah, 9
al-Bāqir, Imam, 68
basis of stability principle, 41
al-Bayḍawī, 46
al-Bazdawī, 66
Beer, S., 40
belief, freedom of, 24
Bertalanffy, Ludwig Von, 34
Bin Bayyah, Abdallah, 16
blocking the means, 125–27, 167, 241
books, wide distribution of, 157
Boulding, K., 37, 42
Bowler, D., 37
brain drain, 22
business management, 38

camel, battle of, 86
cancellation, as method of resolving uncertainty, 221
categorisation
  concept-based compared with feature-based, 48–49
  in development of schools of thought, 70
  of disciplines, xxv, 249
causality, 26–27
causation, limitation of, 198–200, 250
centrism, 151
certainty
  spectrum of, 211–8
  in *maqāṣid*, 21
Checkland, Peter, 43
child custody, 226
Churchman, W., 36
clarity in source texts, 89–93
classificatory trees, 32
closed systems, 35
co-evolutionary Gaia, 42
cognition, separating the revealed from, 194–96
cognitive culture, xxvi, 201–6
cognitive nature of Islamic law, 45–46
cognitive science, xxvi
colonial period, 144
Companions
  conflicts between, 61
  consensus of, 109
  legal debates among, 60
  maqāṣid in ijtihad of, 9–13
  opinions of, juridical validity of, 128–29
comparative fiqh, 144

compensation for unintentional killing, 205
complexity in systems, 38
complexity, proof of, 30
concept-based categorisation, 48–49, 70
conception and assent scheme, 105
conceptions in medieval logic, 88
conciliation, as method of resolving uncertainty, 219
conditions (*al-sharṭ*) in contrary implication, 98, 228
consensus, 109–12
  as mechanism of consultation, 193–94
  basing juridical preference on, 124
  groundless claims of, 193
conservative traditionalism, 147–48
consultation (*al-shūrā*), 94, 193–94
contemporarisation of *maqāṣid* terminology, 21–22
content incoherence, 232–33
continuity, presumption of, 70, 131–32, 243
contracts, ambiguity in, 239
contradiction, 218
contrary implication, 98–100
control theory, 43
Cook, N., 43
correlation between systems and the outside world, 31, 45
counselling, intent of, 235
Critical Legal Studies, 189–90, 255
Crone, Patricia, 190
custody of children, 226
custom (*ʿurf*)
  basing juridical preference on, 125
  and cognitive culture, xxvi
  as an evidence, 130–31
  implicit conditions, 202
  intersection with fiqh, 196
  purpose of universality, 241–43
  qānūn and, 57–59
cybernetic control principles, 41

Damdam, Sons of, 23
darkness principle, 40
darūrat. *See* necessity
Draz, Abdullah, 172
De Chardin, T., 42
declaratory rulings, 139–40
declination, era of, 75
decompositional analysis, 26, 31–33, 38
deconstruction, 180–84
deductive logic, 237
definitions, 211
democracy, 174–75
deontic logic, 209
Derrida, Jacques, 180
development, 24–25
DeWitt, Richard, 205
differentiation in complex systems, 35
dignity, preservation of, 23
dilālah al-lafẓ , 12
dilālah al-maqṣid, 12
dimensionality, 50–51
disciplines, scope of, xxv-xxvi
Doi, Abdur-Rahman, 148

economic growth, 24
Egyptian law, 58
al-Eini, 46
El-Awa, 173
elimination, as method of resolving uncertainty, 220
embellished actions, 52–53

ends (*al-ghāyah*) in contrary implication, 98
entropy, 35
epistemological systems hierarchy, 43
equifinality, 35
Esposito, John, 145
essence-based definitions, 211
European Fiqh Council for Fatwa and Research, 165, 164
evidence
  linguistic, 105–7, 197, 252
  rational, 252–53
  spectrum of certainty, 211–8
  uncertainty of, 197–98
  prioritisation of, 132–35
evolutionary paradigms, 42
exactness in using analogy, 115
exegesis
  abrogation of verses, 222
  apologetic interpretation, 155, 174–76
  purposeful interpretation, 232–33
  science based exegesis, 170–71
  thematic interpretation, 171–74, 199
experimental logic, 171
explained evidences (*mufassar*), 89–90
extension in analogy, 115

fallacies, 200
family, preservation of offspring as *maqṣid*, 22
famous narrations, 83
al-Fārābī, 210
fatwas, xxiii, 234
feature-based categorisation, 49, 70
feedback principles, 41
feminism, 150, 175, 189
fiqh
  cognitive nature of, 45–46
  comparative fiqh, 144
  custom (*ʿurf*), intersection with, 196
  defined, xxiii, 56
  differentiation from shariʿah, 59–60
  prominent books on, 158
  See also schools of Islamic law
firmly constructed evidences (*muḥkam*), 89–90
Fivaz, R., 42
freedom, 6, 247
Friday sermon, 205
fundamentalism
  categorisation of, 145–46
  postmodernist fundamentalism, 168
  RAND typology, 147

Gaia system, 42
Garoudi, Rouget, 186
gender equality, 187–88
general *maqāṣid*, 5
generality in terms, 101–2
Gény, 229
Ghannouchi, Rachid, 175
Gharajedaghi, Jamshid, 38, 51
al-Ghazālī, Abū Ḥāmid
  consensus (ijmāʿ), definition of, 109
  contributions to *maqāṣid* theory, 248
  development of al-Juwaynī's work, 18
  Greek logic, use of, 208–9
  Ibn Taymiyah's criticism of, 211–12
  on ijtihad of the Prophet, 82

influence of Greek philosophy, 69
preservation, theory of, 22
probability in an effective cause (ʿ*ilal*), 216–18
religion, preservation of, 24
Shafiʿi school, 59
terminology used by, 2
on theory of mean, 53
validating all ijtihad, 194
al-Ghazaly, Mohammad
differentiation between means and ends, 187
inclusion of justice and freedom in *maqāṣid*, 6
thematic interpretations of the Qur'an, 172
goal-based classification of systems, 39
goal-seeking, 35, 51–52
goals, compared with purposes, 51
God, proofs of existence of through a systems approach, 29–30
Greek philosophy
impact of, 105–7
influence of on Shāfiʿī school, 68–69
traditional warnings against, 206–7
guidance, intent of, 234

al-Hadad, al-Tahir, 182
Haddad, Yvonne, 145
hadith. *See* narrations
Hadramawt, 234
Hallaq, Wael, 190
Hamed, al-Tijani, 172
Ḥammād , 62
Ḥanafī school
abrogation, precedence of over conciliation, 155
analogy, avoidance of in ʿ*ibādāt*, 115
contrary implication, rejection of, 98–99
development of *uṣūl*, 65–66
evidences, prioritisation of, 132–35
Ibn Masʿūd's version of the Qur'an, 79
implications, classification of, 94–95
implicit conditions from custom, 202
influence of ʿĀ'ishah on, 62
juridical preference, use of, 122
killing, definition of, 92
levels of obligation, 138–39
mursal hadiths, use of, 87
opinions of Companions, juridical validity of, 128
prominent jurists, 158
resolving contradictory narrations, 221
on sunnah as specifying Qur'anic expressions, 80
al-ẓāhir evidences, 91
Hanafi, Hasan, 182–83
Ḥanbalī school
consensus, definition of, 110–11
development of, 67
evidences, prioritisation of, 132–35
juridical preference, use of, 122
maṣlaḥah al-mursalah, 122
mursal hadiths, avoidance of, 87
opinions of Companions, juridical validity of, 128
prominent jurists, 158
Ḥarb, 67
Hassan, 181

Hegel, 32
Heidegger, 180
hierarchies of Islamic law, 48–49
hierarchies within systems, 35
hierarchy principle, 40
historicity of means, 184–88
Hitchins, D. K., 35, 38
Hizb-ut-Tahrir, 147
Holism, 34, 38
holistic evidence in Islamic law, 46–47, 199
holistic philosophical analysis, 32–33
holistic theology, 200–201
holon feature, 38
homeostasis principle, 41
homeostatic Gaia, 42
honor killings, 58
honor, preservation of, 22–23
human development, 24–25, 249
human dignity, preservation of, 23
human rights, 23, 159

Ibāḍī school
  evidences, prioritisation of, 132–35
  juridical preference, use of, 122
  history, 68
  on Prophetic acts of worship, 81
  prominent jurists, 158
  trusted narrators, 86
Ibn ʿĀbidīn, 90
Ibn Abū Laylā, 66
Ibn al-ʿArabī, Abū Bakr, 67
Ibn al-Jazrī, 78
Ibn al-Musayyab, 154
Ibn al-Qayyim, Shams al-Dīn
  contributions to *maqāṣid* theory, 20
  on Islamic law as based on justice and mercy, xxi-xxii
  on wisdom and welfare, 185–86
  position on embellishment and repugnance doctrine, 54
Ibn al-Ṣalāḥ, 59, 206, 215
Ibn Ashur, al-Tahir
  on care of family as a *maqṣid*, 22
  exegesis of, 170
  faiths, freedom of, 24
  maqāṣid identified by, 6
  maṣlaḥah-based interpretations, 176–77
  prioritisation of *maqāṣid* with broader scope, 5
  on the Prophetic sunnah, 81
  prophetic intents, 233–34
  rough set, 195
Ibn Bābawayh, 244, 247
Ibn Farḥūn, 241
Ibn Ḥazm al-Ẓāhirī
  alternatives to Greek logic, 207
  analogy, critique of, 114
  Companions, prohibition of imitating, 129
  consensus, critique of, 112
  literalist approach, 9, 11
  position on Madinah's tradition, 129–30
  groundless claims of consensus, 193
Ibn Ibāḍ, ʿAbdullāh, 68
Ibn Qudāmah, 237
Ibn Rushd
  multiple truths theory, 194
  persecution of, 207
  position on embellishment and repugnance doctrine, 54
Ibn Sīnā, 210
Ibn Taymiyah
  position on embellishment and repugnance doctrine, 54

cognitive faculty, 46
contention of the superiority of Arabs, 203
critique of Aristotelian logic, 207–8
critique of essence-based definitions, 211–12
establishing matters of belief with *āḥād* narrations, 215
on Ibn Ḥazm's claims of consensus, 193
Madinah's tradition, 129
as *uṣūli* scholar in the Ḥanbalī school, 67

Ibn Wahb, 67
Ibn Warraq, 185
Ibrāhīm al-Nakhᶜī, 62
ideologies, Islamic
ideology-oriented theories, 168
introduction to, 145–46
RAND classification of, 147–50
script-based classifications of, 150–53

ijmaᶜ. *See* consensus
ijtihad
necessity of, in all times, 47–48
of Companions, *maqāṣid* in, 9–13
of the Prophet, 82
purpose-oriented, 11–12, 244–45
revealed, 193–94

imams, 65–69
implications
contrary, 98–100
defined, 93
Ḥanafī classification of, 94–95
Shāfiᶜī classification of, 95–96

incoherence in narrations, resolving, 232–33
inductive logic, 210, 237
influential Gaia, 42
information processing systems, hierarchy of, 42
injustice, xxii
intents, prophetic, 233–36
interpretation (*ta'wīl*), 89
interrelated hierarchies of Islamic law, 48–49
interrelationships in a system, 35
Iqbal, Mohammad, 144, 169–70
iqtiḍā', 95
Iranian revolutionaries, 147, 149
Iraq, 62
irrationality, 26–27
Irving, T. B., 57
ishārah, 94
Islam
and politics, 173–74
demographics of, xxii

Islamic law
cognitive nature of, 45–46
consensus (*See* consensus)
contemporary theories, 253
current applications of, xxvii
current sources of, 159
current tendencies in, 160–62
defined, 56–57, 250–51
emergence of philosophy of, 16–17
fiqh and shariᶜah, differentiating between, 59–60
imams, 65–69
interrelated hierarchies of, 48–49
modern changes to theories in, 144
multi-dimensionality of system of, 49–51
openness of system of, 47–48
proposed classification for theories of, 253–55
purposefulness of system of, 51–55

Qur'an as source of law, 77–79
sunnah as source of law, 79–88
terrorism in the name of, xxi-xxii
three meanings of, xxiii-xxiv
universality of, 241–43
wholeness of system of, 46–47
See also schools of Islamic law; *uṣūl al-fiqh*
Islamic modernism
as reinterpreting Islam to fit conclusions of science, 27
defined, 168–69
literalist trends in, 230
Islamic postmodernism. *See* postmodernism, Islamic
Islamic systems philosophy, 29
isti'nās (supporting evidence), 154
istiḥsān. *See* juridical preference
istiṣḥāb (presumption of continuity), 70, 131–32, 243

Jaʿfar al-Ṣādiq, 65, 68, 74
Jaʿfarī school
analogy, rejection of, 112
consensus, definition of, 110
evidences, prioritisation of, 132–35
on *istiṣḥāb* (presumption of continuity), 132
juridical preference, rejection of, 122
maṣlaḥah, rejection of, 122
muḥkam (firmly constructed) terms, classification of, 94–96
previous jurisprudence, rejection of, 128
prominent jurists, 158
Jābir ibn Zayd, 62
Jhering, 229
Jordan, J., 39
judgeship, intent of, 234
Juma, Ali, 212
juridical preference, 122–25, 239–41
juridical tricks, 20
justice, as basis of Islamic law, xxi–xxii
al-Juwaynī, Abd al-Malik
on consensus, 111
contributions to *maqāṣid* theory, 248
holistic analogy, 199
influence of Greek philosophy, 69
levels of necessity theory, 17
reconstruction of Islamic law, 17–18
terminology used by, 2

Kahn, L., 36
al-Karkhı, Abū al-Ḥasan, 224
Katz, D., 36
Khalaf-Allah, Mohammad, 174
al-Khallāl, Abū Bakr, 67
Khatami, Mohammad, 149, 175
Khaybar, 234
killer, definition of, 92
killing, unintentional, compensation for, 205
Kirchner, J. W., 42
Klir, G., 43
Koestler, A., 38
Korzybski, 200
Kurzman, Charles, 168

al-Laknawī, 155
land of Islam/land of war classification, 165
Laszlo, 42
law, philosophy of, xxvi, 16, 47, 116, 135, 210, 229, 238
leadership, intent of, 234

legal capacity, 140–42
legislation, intent, 234
limits (*al-ghāyah*) in contrary implication, 98–99, 228
linguistic evidence, 105–7, 197–98, 252
literalism, 151, 204, 230
literature, wide distribution of, 157
logcentrism, 180
logic
 deductive, 237
 deontic, 209
 experimental, 171
 Greek, use of, 208–9
 inductive, 210, 237
 medieval, conceptions in, 88
 modern, xxvi
 'Other logic', 181
logocentrism, 180–81
London, xxi
Lovelock, J., 42
Luhmann, Niklas, 37
luxuries, 3–4

madhhab. *See* schools of Islamic law
Madinah's tradition, 80
 Companions, imitating, 129
 in Maliki school, 129–30
 opinions of Companions, juridical validity of, 128–29
mainstream secularism, 148
Mālik
 juridical preference, use of, 123–4
 maṣlaḥah mursalah, 121
 on multiple *qiyās*, 120
 al-Muwaṭṭa', 61
Mālikī school
 analogy in, 115
 blocking the means (*sadd al-dharā'i*ᶜ), 125–27
 consensus, definition of, 109
 development of, 67
 evidences, prioritisation of, 132–35
 juridical preference, use of, 122
 killing, definition of, 92
 Madinah's tradition, 129–30
 mursal hadiths, use of, 87
 prominent jurists, 158
 on specifying Qur'anic expressions, 80
manāṭ (in analogy), 116
*maqāṣid al-sharī*ᶜ*ah*
 classical conceptions of, 246–48
 close link with *maṣlaḥah*, 2
 compared with rituals, 204
 contemporary conceptions of, 248–49
 definitions, 1–3
 developments between 5th and 8th centuries AH, 13–16
 early theories of, 13–16
 human development as, 24–25
 implications on the law, 227–246
 in ijtihad of the Companions, 9–13
 levels of necessity, 3
 modern criticisms of traditional classifications of, 4–5
 as multi-dimensional structure, 8
 relation to *uṣūl al-fiqh*, xxv
Maqsood, Ruqaiyyah, 148
Mardin, Serif, 148
marriage and consent, 225
al-Marwazī, Abū Bakr, 67
maṣlaḥah, 120–22
 basing juridical preference on, 125
 close link with *maqāṣid*, 2
 maṣlaḥah-based interpretations, 176–77

precedence over *naṣṣ*, 90
purposes, coherence with, 238
reason behind development of, 16–17
maṣlaḥah mursalah, 121–22
Maslow, Abraham, 4, 246
Maturana, H., 37
Maturidis, 53–54
al-Māwardī, 176
maximum power principle, 42
al-Maymūnī, ʿAbdullāh, 67
mean, theory of, 53
meanings (*maʿānī*), 105
means and ends, differentiating between, 187
means, blocking (*sadd al-dharā'iʿ*), 125–27, 167, 241
means, opening, 241
mercy, as basis of Islamic law, xxi–xxii
Mernissi, Fatima, 189
Mill, J.S., 210
Miller, J., 42
mind, preservation of, 22
modern logic, xxvi
modernism, 145–46, 148
modernist philosophy, 26
Moghissi, 184
molecular systems, 43
Moosa, Ebrahim, 169, 182
most famous narrations, 83
Muʿawiyah, 86
al-mufassar, 91
mujtahids, 109
multi-dimensionality
in Islamic law, 49–51, 211
and postmodernism, 226–7
resolving opposition through, 218–26
spectrum of certainty, 211–8
multi-disciplinary research, 249
multifinality, 35
multigoal-seeking systems, 39
multiple *qiyās*, 120
mursal hadiths, 87
Mūsā al-Kāzim, 68
al-Muṣawwibah, 194
Muslims
honor of, sanctity of, 23
impact of colonial period, 144
prevalence of under-development among, xxii
Muʿtazilī school
conflict with Ashʿarī school, 59
consensus in, 111
differentiation between acts of worship and worldly acts, 81–82, 81
embellished and repugnant acts, 52
evidences, prioritisation of, 132–35
on analogy, 114
prominent jurists, 158
reason, as source of law, 79
al-Muwaṭṭa', 61, 67

Nāfiʿ, 62
an-Naim, Abdullah, 168
narrations
basing juridical preference on, 124
famous and most famous, 83–84
forging of, 61
opposition, resolution of, 218–26
popular hadith collections, 158
purposeful interpretation, 232–33
resolving contradictions with analogy, 119–20
resolving opposing, 155

science-oriented reinterpretation, 179–180
single-chained, 80, 84–85
specific and general, 101–2
spectrum of, 211–8
uṣūl revisionism, 177–78
verification procedures, 84
narrations in schools of law, 71–75
al-Naẓẓām, 114
necessity (*darūrah*)
basing juridical preference on, 124
in relation to partial rulings, 21
levels of, 3 (chart), 17
needs, 3–4. *See also* necessity
negative feedback principle, 41
negentropy, 35
neo-literalism, 151, 166–68
neo-rationalism, 188–89
neo-traditionalism, 164–66
non-living systems, 43
number (*al-ʿadad*) in contrary implication, 98–99, 228

obvious analogy, 94–95
offspring, preservation of as *maqṣid*, 22
omittance, 95
one-dimensional thought, 50–51
open systems, 35
openness, 38, 47–48
openness, philosophical, 206–11
opposition, resolution of, 218–26
optimising Gaia, 42
order, proof of, 30
orderliness in systems, 37
organised complexity, 38
organismic analogy, proof of, 30
Osman, Fathi, 172, 186
'Other logic', 181

Pappus, 31
parallel levels, 42
partial *maqāṣid*, 5
partial orientation of philosophical analysis, 32–33
partial rulings, 21
philosophy, traditional warnings against, 206
philosophy for Islamic law, 16–17
philosophy of law, xxvi
Pickthall, Marmaduke, 57
Plato, 32
political theory, neutrality and Islam, 173–75
positive feedback principle, 41
post-colonialism, 190–91
postmodernism
and multidimensionality, 227–28
approaches to Islamic law, 180–82
Critical Legal Studies, 189–90
historicity of means, 184–88
neo-rationalism, 188–89
post-colonialism, 190–91
postmodernist fundamentalism, 168
post-structuralist deconstruction, 182–84
use of deconstructionist concepts, 27
post-structuralism, 182–84
Powers, W. T., 43
Preservation, al-Ghazālī's theory of, 22
presumption of continuity, 70, 131–32, 243
previous jurisprudence, 127–28
primary situation in analogy, 113, 115
primary sources, 107

processing levels, 42
prophetic ijtihad, 82
prophetic purposes, 233–36
punishment, al-ʿĀmirī's theory of, 22
purposefulness, 227–28
  analogy via purpose, 236–38
  behavior, proof of, 30
  as common grounds for schools of law, 243–44
  concept of, 29
  as criteria for ijtihad, 244–45
  implications of the purpose, 228–32
  interests coherent with, 238
  interpretations of primary sources, 232–33
  of Islamic law, 51–55
  juridical preference based on, 239–41
purpose-oriented ijtihad, 11–12
purposes, compared with goals, 51
purpose-seeking systems, 52

al-Qaffāl al-Shāshī al-Kabīr, 14–15, 69, 247
qānūn, 57–59
al-Qaradawi, Yusuf
  inclusion of human dignity in *maqāṣid*, 5
  on *jilbāb* as means of achieving modesty, 187
  maqāṣid identified by, 6–8
  as a reformist, 148, 150
  on zakah, adapting rulings of, 11
al-Qarāfī, Shihāb al-Dīn
  contributions to theory of *maqāṣid*, 19
  development of Malik's methodology, 67
  opening and blocking the means, 241
  on prophetic intents, 233
  on prophetic sunnah, 81
  terminology used by, 2
al-Qasṭalānī, Quṭb al-Dīn, 19
qiyās. *See* analogy
qualified expressions, 102–5
al-Qummī, Ibn Bābawayh, 16
Qur'an
  Abduh's exegesis of, 170
  apologetic and radical interpretations, 155, 174–76
  exegesis, books on, 157 (*See also* exegesis)
  historicist approach, 184
  post-structuralist deconstruction, 182–84
  qualified expressions, 102–5
  as primary source of law, 77–79
  specific and general verses, 101
  sunnah in relation to, 80
  ta'wīl, 154
  thematic interpretation, 171–74
Quraysh, 190
Qutb, Sayyid, 172

radical fundamentalism, 147
radical secularism, 148
Rahman, Fazlur, 146, 168, 173
Ramadan, Tariq, 146
RAND, 147–50, 253
rational evidence, 252–53
al-Rāzī, Fakhr al-Dīn
  on uncertainty of linguistic evidence, 197–98
  terminology used by, 2
reason, as source of law, 79, 188–89
receptive legal capacity, 141
redundancy of resources principle, 41
reformist reinterpretation, 171–74
reformist traditionalism, 147–48

regulation in systems, 35
regulation, proof of, 30
relaxation time principle, 41
religion, preservation of, 24
renaissance, 26
renewal, 44
repugnant actions, 52–53
resembling terms (*mutashābih*), 93
revealed ijtihad, claims of, 193–94
Rida, Rashid
  exegesis of the Qur'an, 170
  inclusion of women's rights in *maqāṣid*, 5
  maqāṣid identified by, 6
rituals, 204
Robinson, Neil, 169
rulings
  change of, with cognitive culture, 201–6
  classification of (chart), 136
  levels of approval, 136
  obligations and prohibitions, 136–37
  optional levels, 137–38
Russell, Bertrand, 33, 49

Saadawi, Nawal, 148, 150
Sachedina, Abdulaziz, 174
*sadd al-dharā'i*ᶜ (blocking the means), 125–27, 167
al-Sadir, Ayatollah, 172, 177–78
al-Sagheer, Abdul Majeed, 190
Said, Edward, 190
Saᶜīd ibn al-Musayyab, 62
Salafi movement, 147, 149, 151
Ṣāliḥ ibn Aḥmad, 67
Sālim, 62
Salk, J. E., 42
al-Ṣanaᶜānī, 226
Sardar, Ziauddin, 169
al-Sarkhasī , 66
Saudi High Council of Fatwa,167
scholars, credibility of, 109
scholastic neo-traditionalism, 164–66
scholastic traditionalism, 162–63
schools of Islamic law
  ahl al-ra'ī and ahl *ahl al-athar*, 61, 63–64
  declination, era of, 75
  disputes between, 59
  history, 60–64, 251
  imams, 65–69
  interconnectedness between, 74
  madhāhib categorisation, critique of, 69–71
  purposefulness as common ground between, 243–44
  scholastic neo-traditionalism, 164–66
  scholastic traditionalism, 162–63
  sources of legislation 69 (chart)
  studentship and narration, 71–75
science, 26–27, 170–71
science-oriented reinterpretation, 179–180
scope of terms, 100–101, 103–4
scriptural fundamentalism, 147
secondary situation in analogy, 113
secondary sources, 107
sectarian divisions, 243–44
secularism, 145–46, 151
self-organising systems principle, 41
self-renewal, 44, 206–11
sermons in Arabic, 205
Shāfiᶜī school
  acceptance of some *mursal* hadith, 87, 154
  analogy, priority over indirect implication, 97
  contrary implication, 98–99

development of, 68–69
evidences, prioritisation of, 132–35
implications, classification of, 95–96
juridical preference, rejection of, 122
position on Madinah's tradition, 129
on sunnah as specifying Qur'anic expressions, 80
Shahrur, Mohammad, 148, 150, 186
Shamsuddin, Ayatollah Mahdi, 186, 244
Sharᶜiah. *See* Islamic law
sharᶜu man qablanā (previous jurisprudence), 127–28
al-Shāṭibī, Abū Isḥāq
contributions to *maqaṣid* theory, 20–21
on embellishment and repugnance doctrine, 54
holistic features of Islamic law, 199
on levels of necessity, 4
on when purpose-oriented ijtihad is appropriate, 11
al-Shaybānī, Moḥammad ibn al-Ḥasan, 66, 239
Shepard, William, 145
Shia jurists, use of *maqāṣid* among, 16
Shia schools
embellished and repugnant acts, 52
jurisprudential differences with Sunni schools, 86
literalist tradition in, 166
mursal hadiths, use of, 87
similarity with Sunni schools, 244
trusted narrators, 86
See also Jaᶜfarī school; Zaydī school
shūrā (consultation), 94, 174
silent consensus, 111
single-chained narrations, 80, 84–85
Skyttner, Lars, 40
socialism, 174
Soroush, Abdul-Karim, 149, 173, 186
specific *maqāṣid*, 5
specification (*takhṣīṣ*), 89, 103–4
stagnation, 151
steady-state principle, 41
studentship in schools of law, 71–75
subatomic systems, 43
Suboptimalisation principle, 40
Sufism, 13
Sulaiman, Sadek, 174
Sulaymān ibn Yasār, 62
Sunnah, 79–88
Sunni schools
jurisprudential differences with Shia schools, 86
similarity with Shia, 244
trusted narrators, 86
supporting evidence (*isti'nās*), 154
Sword, verse of, 222
synthesism, 38
systematic incoherence, resolving, 232–33
systematic interpretation, 171
systems, defined, 33
systems theory, xxvi
systems-based analysis
cognitive nature of Islamic law, 45–46
complexity in, 38
defined, 26
features of, 34–35

hierarchies and levels, 37
hierarchies, theories of, 42–45
interrelated hierarchies of Islamic law, 48–49
introduced, 33–34
Islamic law, wholeness of system of, 46–47
Islamic, 29
multi-dimensionality of Islamic law, 49–51
openness of Islamic law, 47–48
proofs of existence of God, 29–30
purposefulness of Islamic law, 51–55
systems as real or mental creations, 30–31
of theories of Islamic law, 255–58

al-Tabari, 100
al-Tabtabai, 171
Taha, Mahmoud Mohamed, 174
al-Tahtawi, Rifaa, 144
ta'wīl, 154
teleological Gaia, 42
teleology, 26–27
terrorism, in the name of 'Islamic law', xxi–xxii
textual evidences (*naṣṣ*), 89–90
theft, halting punishment for based on *maqāṣid*, 12
thematic interpretation of the Qur'an, 171–74, 199, 232
thieves, definition of, 92
Tibi, Bassam, 148
title (*al-laqab*) in contrary implication, 98, 228
al-Tirmidhī, al-Ḥakīm, 13
traditionalism
categorisation of, 147–48
scholastic neo-traditionalism, 164–66
scholastic, 162–63
transformation in systems, 35
truth, multiplicity of, 194
al-Ṭūfī, Najm al-Dīn
maṣlaḥah al-mursalah, 122
on *maṣlaḥah* overriding a specific/case-based *naṣṣ*, 90
terminology used by, 2
al-Turabi, Hasan, 172, 186, 199, 243

ʿUmar ibn al-Khaṭṭāb
application of principles of *maqāṣid*, 9–11
influence of on schools of law, 74
Umm Salamah, 226
uncertainty, 197–98, 237
unclear rulings, 89
United Nations Development Programme, xxii
United States Supreme Court, 238
Universal Islamic Declaration of Human Rights, 23, 159, 248
universality of Islamic law, 241–43
unorganised complexity, 38
ʿurf. *See* custom
ʿUrwah ibn al-Zubair, 75
uṣūl al-fiqh
analogy, 112–20
blocking the means, 125–27
clarity in source texts, 89–93
Companions, juridical validity of opinions of, 128–29
consensus, 109–12
continuity, presumption of, 131–32
current sources of law, 159
custom (*See* custom)
development of in the Ḥanafī school, 65–66
evidences, prioritisation of, 132–35

fundamental sources, 76–77, 251–52
juridical preference, 122–25
Madinah's tradition, 129–30
maṣlaḥah (*See maṣlaḥah*)
Qur'an as source of law, 77–79
reason as source of law, 79, 188–89
relation to *maqāṣid al-sharʿiah*, xxv
summary chart, 69
sunnah as source of law, 79–88
as a system, 45
See also Islamic law
uṣūl revisionism, 177–79
ʿUthmān ibn ʿAffān, 61, 77

Validators, the, 194
validity, in analogy, 115
Varela, V., 37
verification of narrations, 84
viability principle, 41
viable system model, 40
visibility in analogy, 115
Voll, John, 145
von Wright, 209

Wahhabi movement, 147, 149, 151
waiting (*al-tawaqquf*), as method of resolving uncertainty, 220
wealth, preservation of, 24
Weaver, W., 38
Whitehead, A. N., 33
whole terms (*mujmal*), 92
wholeness of Islamic law, 46–47
women, testimony of, 186
worldview, 201–6

al-ẓāhir, 91
Ẓāhirī school, 65
analogy, rejection of, 112–4
definition of consensus, 109
evidences, prioritisation of, 132–35
juridical preference, rejection of, 122
maṣlaḥah, rejection of, 122
neo-literalism, 166
on single-chained narrations, 84
on sunnah as specifying Qur'anic expressions, 80
previous jurisprudence, rejection of, 128
prominent jurists, 158
reconstruction of Aristotle's syllogism, 207
zakah
adapting rules of based on *maqāṣid*, 10–11
inconsistencies in number, 99–100
al-Zarkashī , 154
Zayd ibn ʿAlī, 65, 67
Zaydī school, 67
analogy, rejection of, 112
Companions, on imitating, 129
consensus, definition of, 110
juridical preference, rejection of, 122
maṣlaḥah, rejection of, 122
muḥkam (firmly constructed) terms, classification of, 94–96
prominent jurists, 158
on sunnah as specifying Qur'anic expressions, 80

- References used in this work were primarily in Arabic and English.
- The translation of the quotes I used from Arabic sources are all mine, except otherwise indicated.
- As for the Qur'anic verses, the translation I deemed most suitable to represent the meaning of the verse(s) is quoted and the translator is mentioned. Otherwise, I translated verse(s) based on my experience with both languages, and explained the difference between my translation and other popular translations.
- The translation of hadith quoted throughout the book is mine. All the hadiths mentioned in the book are at least at the degree of 'good' (*ḥassan*), from a classic 'science of narration' point of view. However, the general procedure of 'authentication' in traditional science of narrations is critically analysed within the systematic analysis of the fundamental (*uṣūl*) concepts.
- It is also important to note that Arabic words and expressions usually bear more than one meaning, and thus, could be translated in more than one way. In the text, I used the translation that I deemed most suitable to the context, and included a glossary of the most frequently used Arabic terms in the end of this book, which shows multiple possible meanings for some terms.
- I often followed (between brackets) the English-translated juridical terms with their original Arabic terms, as they appear in literature written in the Arabic language. This is meant to enable readers familiar with the Arabic language to capture all additional 'shades of meanings' that the Arabic terms might imply.
- Popular Arabic terms in this discipline, such as *uṣūl*, fiqh, and fatwa, are sometimes used interchangeably with their translations after the first time they are mentioned (and translated).
- Dates are shown according to both the Islamic calendar (hijrā, labelled AH) and the Gregorian calendar (*mīlādī*, labelled CE). Date conversion, when needed, was carried out using Tarek's Universal Calendar Converter (version 8).*
- I also used a number of charts to illustrate the analysis presented throughout. The charts are mine, unless otherwise indicated.

Finally, the nature of this book is 'analytic.' There is no process of gathering empirical data from 'participants' in order to form some statistics-based conclusions, in a Social Sciences sense. However, I directly asked a number of scholars/researchers in various countries about their opinions and positions regarding a number of issues. Thus, I mentioned those opinions in the body of this work, attributed them to their holders, and added endnotes that indicate the country and date in which these oral discussions took place.

*Universal Converter, Tarek's Hijri/Gregorian/Julian/Hebrew/Chinese Universal Calendar Converter (version 8). Available from http://bennyhills.fortunecity.com/elfman/454/calindex